D1712863

MILTON
AND THE SONS OF GOD
The Divine Image in
Milton's Epic Poetry

God the Father, God the Son, Christ as Son Incarnate, Adam as man and thus the Son of God – these complex filial relationships are a distinctive recurring theme in the poetry of John Milton. Comparing the views of Milton with those of Calvin, the Socinians, and the Cambridge Platonists, Hugh MacCallum presents in this study a new and clearly defined interpretation of Milton's emphasis on filial freedom and filial growth.

After a short review of figures of mediation in the minor poems and *Samson Agonistes*, MacCallum turns to the pre-existent Son as he is defined in Milton's theology and characterized in *Paradise Lost*. He shows how subtly and effectively the poet dramatizes the growth of the Son to an earned Godhead. Turning to Adam's sonship, MacCallum traces the relationship from the innocence in which Adam progressively actualizes the image of God, through the Fall, to the ultimate restoration of sonship. The final chapters deal with the Incarnate Christ, the mediator who is at once God and man.

Throughout, MacCallum places Milton's views in the context of Reformed thought and thereby illustrates the originality and uniqueness of the poet's vision.

HUGH MAC CALLUM is a member of the Department of English, University of Toronto.

1.13.24
2.16.5
2.4.17,25

MILTON
AND THE
SONS OF GOD

The Divine Image
in Milton's Epic Poetry

Hugh MacCallum

UNIVERSITY OF TORONTO PRESS
Toronto Buffalo London

© University of Toronto Press 1986
Toronto Buffalo London
Printed in Canada

ISBN 0-8020-5679-2

Printed on acid-free paper

Canadian Cataloguing in Publication Data

MacCallum, Hugh, 1928–
Milton and the sons of God

Includes bibliographical references and index.
ISBN 0-8020-5679-2
1. Milton, John, 1608–1674 –
Criticism and interpretation.
2. God in literature.
I. Title.
PR3588.M22 1986   821'.4   C86-093186-2

For Barbara

Contents

Preface

This study grew out of the conviction that Milton's art is intimately connected to his thought and his experience. Sonship offers a nexus which draws together these varied but related strands. No doubt its position as a centre of significance in Milton's writing is in part due to its importance in the Bible, an importance seized upon and elaborated by the religious thinkers of the Reformation. But the state of being a son appears to have a special meaning – personal, spiritual, and even aesthetic – for Milton. He has perceptive and telling things to say about other family roles and relationships, but sonship retains a seminal place in his thought about religious experience, and it shapes his presentation of man as image of God. My effort has been to show that his views on this subject, while indebted to the age, were original and distinctive, and that they informed the dramatization of God and man in his two epic poems.

Some of the ideas in this study have been with me for many years. The treatment in chapter 5 of the history of the world in the last books of *Paradise Lost* contains a much revised version of passages from an article entitled 'Milton and Sacred History,' published in *Essays in English Literature from the Renaissance to the Victorian Age*, ed Millar MacLure and F.W. Watt (Toronto: University of Toronto Press 1964), pp 149-68. The discussion of Milton, the Cambridge Platonists, and the Socinians in chapter 2 is taken with little revision from a section of an article entitled ' "The Most Perfect Hero": The Role of the Son in Milton's Theodicy,' published in *'Paradise Lost': A Tercentenary Tribute*, ed Balachandra Rajan (Toronto: University of Toronto Press 1969), pp 79-105. I am grateful to the University of Toronto Press for permission to draw from these articles. Some of the ideas in chapter 5 concerning the return of Adam's memory after the Fall were first presented in a lecture to the Modern Language Association of America in 1979.

My greatest debts are to those Dioscuri of Milton studies in Canada, A.S.P. Woodhouse and Arthur E. Barker. They first taught me how to read Milton, and made me aware of his development, his thought, and his art. Whatever virtue the present study may have derives in the end from their learning and insight; its limitations are my own.

I have been assisted by a host of scholars and critics, many of whom are mentioned in the text and the notes. To certain figures, however, it has not been possible to record my debts adequately. In particular I wish to mention my dependence on Maurice Kelley, whose work on *De Doctrina Christiana* I encountered at almost every turn in my argument concerning Milton's ideas. My efforts to understand Milton's thought have also been repeatedly assisted by the work of W.K. Hunter, Barbara Lewalski, and C.A. Patrides, while my interpretation of his poetry (as indeed of all poetry) owes much to the criticism of Northrop Frye and Balachandra Rajan. To my students, too, I owe much, and I am particularly conscious of the way my interest in Milton's poetry has been revitalized and my understanding of it clarified by the members of my graduate seminars over the years.

The research for this study was conducted primarily at the British Library in London, and at the Thomas Fisher Rare Book Library and the John P. Robarts Research Library at the University of Toronto. I was assisted in the summer of 1978 by a Canada Council Research Scholarship. I am grateful to the readers appointed by the University of Toronto Press for their helpful suggestions, and to Judy Williams who acted as copy-editor at the Press for her assistance in preparing the manuscript for publication. This book has been published with the help of a grant from the Canadian Federation for the Humanities, using funds provided by the Social Sciences and Humanities Research Council of Canada.

Douglas Scott generously made available the word processing and printing facilities used to prepare the final draft, which was typed by my wife. That her support, understanding, and encouragement were essential to the completion of this book is commemorated – along with much else – by the dedication.

Milton and the Sons of God

CHAPTER ONE

Introduction

This study is concerned principally with the epic poetry of John Milton, and seeks to explore that poetry in terms of Milton's theological and moral conception of sonship. The poet's lifelong preoccupation with the relation between God and man centres on the figure of the mediator who expresses God's nature through filial acts. First and foremost, mediation is provided by God's divine Son, a being who in his pre-existent form sits at the right hand of the Father in heaven, but who also by his Incarnation unites God and man in a unique way. But other beings, both angelic and human, may also lay claim to the title 'son of God,' and through service may mediate God's will. Thus the image of God the creator is made manifest by filial acts through which the creature realizes freedom, expresses reason and love, and in these ways accommodates the divine nature to the creation.

These were also preoccupations of the age. Protestants stressed the sonship of believers, and interpreted the restoration of the divine image in terms of the filial relation. They frequently cited St Paul's remark (Romans 8:14), 'as many as are led by the Spirit of God, they are sons of God.' The language of sonship is pervasive in Protestantism, and while it takes on a particular colouring when used by the more radical groups, such as the Quakers, the Socinians, or the Family of Love, it is also seminal in the conservative thought of the Reformation, and holds an important place in the writing of John Calvin.

Scripture suggests three relations comprehended by the notion of divine sonship. The first is restricted to divine beings. The express image of God the Father is God the Son (Hebrews 1:3). Next is the relation that extends from the Father to all believers through the Son.

Believers who seek to perfect their sonship and renew the image of God in their natures by faith in Christ are 'conformed to the image of his Son' (Romans 8:29). The third relation is founded on the Old Testament rather than the New. There man is said to be created in the image or likeness of God (Genesis 1:26), and thus a relation is suggested between God and *all* men. The Fall has of course marred this relation, either destroying or disfiguring man's likeness to God. But theologians generally assume that a connection can be made between the creation of man in the image of God and his recreation as a son by adoption. So viewed, the terms embrace past, present, and future: the image is a gift in the purpose of God from the beginning, it is now actually given to believers with the gift of faith, and it is a promise of future fulfilment that will be revealed at the end of our era.[1]

All three relations are explored in Milton's writing and are of special importance to the epics. In *Paradise Lost* the word *son* is used with reference to a variety of characters and in a variety of contexts. There is a divine being who is the only begotten Son of God, who holds that position by merit more than birthright, and who will become the Son of Man as well as God; there is also God's youngest son, man, who is created in true filial freedom but loses it through disobedience and must undergo a process of repentance and regeneration before his relation with God is restored through adoption; there are the other sons of light and darkness, the good and evil angels, who participate in the process of man's trial; and there is, finally, the grotesque perversion of the filial relationship exemplified by Death's response to Satan. *Paradise Regained* directs intense concentration on what it means to be a Son of God, a phrase which exasperates Satan ('The Son of God I also am, or was, / And if I was, I am; relation stands,' 4.518-19), and which is defined through the merit demonstrated by Jesus. Sonship, then, is an idea of great potency in Milton's writing. In examining the epics, I will concentrate both on the Son of God (pre-existent and incarnate) and on Adam as examples of the filial relationship, but some attention will also be paid to Eve – whose position parallels with variation that of Adam – and to the angels.

Sonship is normally explained in terms of conformity to the *imago dei*, and *image* is thus another important term in this study. Milton uses the word in the traditional way by which it applies to rational offspring. The sons of God are his images. Whether throned in heaven or incarnate in the flesh on earth, Christ is the true image of the Father; man is God's 'latest Image' (*Paradise Lost*, 4.567), Adam directly and Eve through

Adam, but with the Fall, the divine image forsakes them and can be restored only through suffering, repentance and renewal. Satan, the 'Idol of Majestie Divine' (ibid, 6.101), provides along with his infernal companions, Sin and Death, a parody of the proper function of the image of God. A study of the images of God in the epic poems will lead to an examination of the relation of the creature to the creator, that Father who is the source of all being. As Ira Clark has observed, the image of God became an emblem for Milton, for 'it contains the potential and impact of Christian history — of man's original glory and perfection, his vast and degrading descent, and his magnificent opportunity for regeneration.'[2] Milton's conception of sonship, of being a true image of God (both terms are necessary, although they overlap), lies at the heart of his ethical thought:

> Christian liberty is that whereby we are loosed as it were by enfranchisement, through Christ our deliverer, from the bondage of sin, and consequently from the rule of the law and of man; to the intent that being made sons instead of servants, and perfect men instead of children, we may serve God in love through the guidance of the Spirit of truth.   (Works, XVI, 153-5)

This passage from *De Doctrina Christiana* expresses a radical yet organizing impulse which was at work in Milton's thought at least as early as his revolutionary pamphlets on episcopacy. For Milton, as A.S.P. Woodhouse remarks, perfect freedom is synonymous with perfect virtue, and Christian liberty 'may be not inadequately defined as *order self-imposed from within.*'[3] The whole law, moral as well as judicial and ceremonial, is abrogated by Christ, and, as Milton put the matter in 1644, dissolved into charity (*Works*, IV, 76). Although such a condition of liberty was known to some before the Gospel, it was not clearly expressed until the time of Christ and his disciples.

A rich and far-reaching passage from *Tetrachordon* explains how the image of Christ is restored in man as he achieves a state of filial freedom:

> It is enough determin'd, that this Image of God wherin man was created, is meant Wisdom, Purity, Justice, and rule over all creatures. All which being lost in *Adam*, was recover'd with gain by the merits of Christ. For albeit our first parent had lordship over sea, and land, and aire, yet there was a law without him, as a guard set over him. But Christ having cancell'd the handwriting of ordi-

nances which was against us, *Coloss.* 2.14. and interpreted the fulfilling of all through charity, hath in that respect set us over law, in the free custody of his love, and left us victorious under the guidance of his living Spirit, not under the dead letter; to follow that which most edifies, most aides and furders a religious life, makes us holiest and likest to his immortall Image, not that which makes us most conformable and captive to civill and subordinate precepts ... (*Works*, IV, 74-5)

Here are many of the elements of the pattern at the centre of this study — the cycle by which the image of God was given to man, lost, and recovered; the definition of that image as a state of freedom and love above the law; the identification of the Son of God as the highest exemplar of this state and the agent by whom man may regain it. These preoccupations shape much of Milton's thought and writing, and play a crucial part in the epics.

The importance of trial in Milton's ethic is evident in his treatment of sonship. The epics show that a true sense of identity is achieved only by those who are able to realize that the self exists through relationships both with God and with other created beings. The only begotten Son of God grows from affirmation to affirmation, proving himself in heaven and on earth to be by merit more than birthright Son of God. His progress repeatedly demonstrates the nature of the filial relationship to the Father, providing a touchstone for true responses and a model for imitation. His acts of creation, destruction, and recreation express the different aspects of that virtue which is at last seen to be 'Above Heroic' (*Paradise Regained*, 1.15). Unfallen man increases in understanding of himself and his relation to God, and moves towards a full and living awareness of the nature of free obedience. After the Fall trial becomes a painful process for him, but if successfully endured it leads to a rediscovery of the image of the Son of God.

Trial is necessary to full understanding. In both epics Milton's presentation of the process of learning is remarkably subtle and revealing. It is characterized by an emphasis on learning as the free response of the individual within a context that is both challenging and full of promise. A failure of response leads to bondage to the ego, 'Thy self not free, but to thy self enthrall'd' (*Paradise Lost*, 6.181). Learning draws upon memory and imagination, as well as reason and choice. Partial understandings, even misunderstandings, lead through trial to more adequate comprehension. The final end of the educational process brings together freedom and obedience, mercy and justice, and enables love to interpret the law.

The terms *image* and *son* both point to Milton's preoccupation with the idea of mediation. His theology is orthodox in stressing the importance of that act of atonement by which Christ functions as a mediator for the salvation of mankind. But mediation has a further significance in Milton's view of action, for all heroes, divine and human, serve to unify God and his creation. The Son of God in *Paradise Lost* acts as the image of the Father through acts of creation and retribution, as well as atonement, and without his Word the Father would not be manifest. Other characters in the poem also perform acts of mediation. Eve apprehends God partly through Adam; unfallen man is the link between heaven and the lower creatures; Raphael and Michael communicate God's instructions to man, accommodating heavenly truth to human powers. In Milton's universe the separation of the rational creation into discrete individuals appears to be for the purpose of trial, the end of this beneficent process being the return of all creatures to unity in God. The figures who act as mediators further the process by which the creation becomes 'more spritous, and pure' (*Paradise Lost*, 5.475) as earth is joined to heaven. Milton's concern with such heroes extends throughout his career, being evident in the early poetry as well as in *Samson Agonistes* and the two epics.

In examining the idea of sonship in the poetry, I shall draw upon Milton's theological views as these are expressed in prose, and particularly in *De Doctrina Christiana*. This is always a delicate operation, for poetry and prose communicate in radically different modes. Close readings, it is true, give evidence of a remarkable coherence of the poetry and the prose in treatments of such complex or subtle subjects as the state of innocence, the exaltation of the pre-existent Son, and the growth of the incarnate Son. The poetry, however, develops further the human implications of doctrinal issues, while setting aside divisive formulations. In particular, it sets out to recreate from scripture the kind of experience of deity which precedes dogmatic theological formulations. In his treatment of God in the poetry Milton is attempting to push behind theoretical doctrines and to present in imaginative and sensuous terms the subject matter of which they are but formal interpretations. He seeks to provide a renewed vision of God and his sons at the level not of abstract theory but of literary experience. The theological treatise directs us towards a right reading of the poetry, but cannot be substituted for the poetry's significance.

Having recognized such limits, however, it is worth stressing the importance of Milton's prose to the student of his poetry. The connection needs to be reasserted at a time when there is a tendency to reduce Milton's thought to commonplaces of the period interrupted by private eccentricities, to view his theological tractate as an obstacle to the understanding of his poetry, and to revive once again the misleading notion that there existed in Milton a deep split between intellect and artistic imagination. Like W.B. Yeats, but with different and more traditional means, Milton sought to hammer his thoughts into unity. Theology was clearly for him a unifying discipline, bringing experience into relation with revealed truth through reason, providing a context for the ethical intelligence. For Milton, theology and poetry should come together in a common effort to accommodate God's revelation to the mind of man; both are capable of enabling man to think of God what is worthy of him.

In exploring Milton's ideas of sonship in poetry and prose, I have made substantial use of the work of Calvin, and I have also employed such other writers of Reformed dogmatics as William Ames, his teacher Henry Perkins, John Wollebius, and John Owen. In the first half of the seventeenth century these writers were considered exponents of the established doctrines of the Reformed Church, doctrines that were maintained on an international front. But the theology of the Church of England, firmly Calvinist at the beginning of the century, was to be subject to repeated revision and criticism as Calvinism lost its hold on men's loyalties, and in its decline gave way in large measure to the Arminianism that flourished in the later years of the century. By placing Milton's views in the context of Reformed dogmatics, we can isolate with some accuracy the unorthodox and radical elements which they contain, and see how these elements are assimilated to more conventional beliefs. This process is made easier by the seemingly traditional organization of doctrines and argument in his theological work, *De Doctrina Christiana*. Milton seems by this to be inviting comparison with the bodies and marrows of divinity produced by Calvin and his successors, for he aims, like them, at a synthesis of ideas and beliefs revealed primarily through scripture. The result is a tractate that invokes tradition but also departs from it, combining intellectual continuity with radical dislocation. (The process has some similarity to Milton's originality in his treatments of poetic genre.) History has given the process a special point, since Milton was putting his new wine in old bottles at exactly the time at which Calvinist orthodoxy was weakening in vitality.

It is worth asking why Milton set about his reform of theology, and especially of Christology, by invoking the systems of divinity written by Calvinists. We can begin our answer by acknowledging that the task Milton had set himself was immensely difficult – no less than a fresh analysis of scripture for its primary revelation – and some framework within which to develop his position seems an important desideratum. So much, a little grudgingly, is implied by Milton's own account of the growth of his work. But it is also important to recognize that his fierce rejection of tradition and custom does not entail a total repudiation of the past. He recognized that the community of believers forms a continuity in time, and that each genuine effort of the intellect makes a contribution to the restoration of the shattered body of truth. Past theologians bear witness to the truth, even though they do not thereby become authorities.

The question of why Milton employs a conservative form for what is often a radical content is linked to another: why does he not make more explicit use of the radical thinkers of his own time and place?[4] Christopher Hill has argued that Milton was deeply influenced in important ways by the 'third culture,' the radical culture that had its roots in the lower class. The third culture had given rise to Lollard, Anabaptist, and Familist trends in popular thought, and in the seventeenth century found expression in the Ranters, Quakers, Muggletonians, Levellers, Diggers, and other more or less extreme groups. Hill urges that Milton did not work in isolation, that it is a mistake to hunt for his intellectual sources only in the classical philosophers and early Christian theologians, and that we should remind ourselves of what ideas were current in London taverns at the time. A number of current ideas are of obvious relevance to Milton: biblicism, anti-trinitarianism, anti-clericalism, materialism, mortalism, antinomianism. Milton's heresies were 'the common currency of radical circles,' yet Hill is quick to acknowledge that Milton himself was not an extreme radical. The poet is thus uncertainly poised, his allegiance divided between the secondary culture of Protestant ethic (itself a reaction to the establishment – the traditional culture of courts and bishops) and the lower-class third culture. His radicalism, Hill thinks, was cut short by social considerations of which he was only partly aware.[5]

Much about this argument is suggestive. Yet it is easier to illustrate in the sphere of political controversy than in the more subtle and rarefied realm of theology. Anti-clericalism is more obviously a popular and accessible topic than anti-Trinitarianism. Moreover, as Hill is the first to admit, popular culture seldom takes the form of written records. The popularity of some of Milton's ideas can only be attested in a general way by reference to church courts prosecuting heretics and orthodox spokesmen damning them, to anecdotes about radicals, and to short tracts issued surreptitiously by imprisoned thinkers. But it is seldom that the idea is matched by a literary statement of the sort that might appeal to Milton and might thus be viewed as possible source or close analogue to his treatment of the idea. A humanist of wide-ranging literary training, Milton valued coherence of thought and decorum of expression. Hill's 'third culture' helps us to understand the way Milton's ideas connect with his age, but does not generally enable us to comprehend the significance of his formulation of his ideas. No doubt there are exceptions. Milton would have respected Paul Best's courage, but not his style; John Biddle, on the other hand, he would have acknowledged as a writer of genuine and serious learning.

As we move away from the tavern and the conventicle, we find many international works of a radical bent which would have appealed to Milton by their qualities of method and exegesis as well as their ideas. The *Racovian Catechism*, for example, contains much that is paralleled in Milton's work. It is probable, I think, that an impulse from Hill's 'third culture' would not much affect Milton unless he could follow it into such higher realms of Reformed argument. The writing of its representatives must all too often have seemed to him little more than a cry from the heart. Thus in *The Doctrine and Discipline of Divorce* he refers to the 'fanatic dreams' of the sectaries and then qualifies his criticism by remarking, in parenthesis, 'if we understand them not amisse' (Works, III, ii, 426). In his more optimistic moments, it is true, Milton hoped that all God's Englishmen might soon be prophets. But he did not assume that all prophets would immediately speak the same tongue. The perfection of the temple in this world is made up of many moderate varieties and brotherly dissimilitudes. Not all contributions to the progress of truth will be of the same kind, and while all will be reconciled in the Christian community, Milton felt himself to be responsible for a particular kind of contribution, one that drew on the resources of scholarship, wide learning, and rational method. Thus, years later, he was able to assure society that if an expensive university education in the Fathers and councils were no longer to be required for ministers 'yet we may be confident, ... let the state but erect in public good store of libraries, and there will not want men in the church, who of their own inclinations will become able in this kind against papist or any other adversary' (*Works*, VI, 95).

Hill argues that Milton attached less significance to the Reformation than to the 'Waldenses and in England Wycliff and his Lollard successors, the humble Marian martyrs and the persecuted sectaries.'[6] That is perhaps true in matters of inspiration and national exhortation. But when Milton sought to give intellectual expression to the ongoing revelation of man's relation to God, he did so in a manner which shows him acutely aware of the theological systems of the Reformed church and inviting comparison with them. It must also be acknowledged that Reformed thought, especially as embodied in Calvin's *Institutes*, still had much radical potential. While by the mid-seventeenth century its political and social implications had been explored, it retained its intellectual potency as a body of ideas which could be applied by individuals in a changing world. The 'learned Mr. Calvin,' in both his *Institutes* and his biblical commentary, combined admirable scholarship with a challenging and vigorous treatment of theology. At least some of the radical tradition finds expression in Calvin's writings, although usually with a degree of qualification that restrains its ramifications; even when Calvin is opposing extreme positions his sensitivity to them brings the controversy to life. This latter point is especially true of Calvin's treatment of the Son of God; and where Calvin draws back, Milton presses on.

Milton, then, developed his theology not only out of scripture, but also out of a kind of dialogue with the systems of dogmatics. Thus he achieves the effect of a personal credo set against one of the most powerful intellectual systems of religious thought in his age. The radical direction of his thought has been well defined by Mary Ann Radzinowicz: 'Milton's heresies remain the clearest available index by which to measure his theological independence, his own continuing answers to the challenge he put before every man, the challenge to internalize one's own concept of divinity in order to make it the sole authority for faith.'[7] To internalize, however, requires the presence of something external which provides the subject matter for the operation. Even Milton's God appears to externalize through creation in order that all may gradually return to him and be made one with him again. Progressive understanding of the godlike potentiality of man involves a movement from the more outward apprehension of truth to a more inward and spiritual one. Milton is in any case not the kind of original thinker who tries to blaze an entirely new trail to the truth. His interpretations imply, even when they do not formally state, the presence of earlier and less adequate formulations. He repeatedly turns the language and concepts of Reformed theology in a direction which humanizes religion and employs man's standards of right and wrong, but he needs the challenge provided by the tradition in order to shape his response.

This is true, I believe, both of the prose and the poetry. We will see the process in Milton's treatment of such themes as the trial of the pre-existent Son, the unity of the incarnate Son, and the freedom of unfallen and fallen man. Sometimes the position to be challenged is explicitly stated, but more frequently it is only invoked by implication. But the rhythm so released seems to have been crucial to Milton's processes of thought and feeling. It establishes a creative relation between old truth and new, and between the ideas of the Christian community and the discoveries of the individual who pursues his investigations with scripture and the spirit as his only guides. Sometimes the challenge comes from a doctrine which is clearly not only old but also, in the writer's view, false. Such is the case in his discussion of the Trinity. But frequently, as in the case of the career of the Divine Son, we shall find that the ideas of Reformed theology are revised and reoriented, rather than simply dismissed. Perhaps the most basic illustration of the pattern is in the relation of scripture and the spirit, since the former provides the subject for the internalizations of the latter, and neither can operate without the other. The radical thrust of Milton's thought is certainly one of the elements crucial to his enduring appeal, but it can be adequately understood only if we observe how he directed it to his age.

A full treatment of sonship in the thought and writing of Milton is beyond the scope of the present study. Such a treatment would take into account both the gradual evolution implied by Milton's practice in the early poems, and the more theoretical and often radical developments of the prose written in the forties and early fifties.

The motif of the human figure who mediates between heaven and earth is a recurrent preoccupation of the poetry published in the volume of 1645. Such a figure is found even in the early elegy *On the Death of a Fair Infant dying of a Cough*, a poem which anticipates *On the Morning of Christ's Nativity* in certain striking ways. As the elegy builds to a climax, the dead child is viewed as a guardian figure, rather like the Attendant Spirit in *Comus*, disguised in human likeness only in order to lead men to scorn the world. When the climax is reached, however, this Platonic messenger gives way to an image of mediation in which the stress falls on sacrifice as the poet asks why the child did not stay 'here below' in order 'To slake this wrath whom sin hath made our foe' and 'stand 'twixt us and our deserved smart.' Hugh MacLean is clearly right in judging that the treatment of mediation in the passage reaches towards the idea of a redeemer.[8] The lines recall the doctrine of Christ's satisfaction for sin. Here is an idea of great importance to Milton, and the problem of bringing it into relation with active ethical heroism, and its attendant imaginative themes, will prove a preoccupation of the later poetry. In this early work the idea is treated suggestively but briefly. The curt conclusion which the speaker addresses to the infant – 'But thou canst best perform that office where thou art' – suggests his acknowledgment of the secondary nature of the child's role and her difference from the divine mediator who alone can heal the world. Rather than turning her into a surrogate for Christ, the conclusion suggests that she has a real but limited significance within the larger movement of divine providence.

On the *Morning of Christ's Nativity* is a poem written to celebrate 'the Son of Heav'ns eternal King.' The Son stands firmly at the centre of the poem's meaning, and the reader is continually aware of him both as child and as God. Initially we are conscious primarily of his divine aspect. The opening stanzas stress his descent from the courts of everlasting day to our dark world. The Incarnation is viewed in a manner which anticipates its treatment in *Paradise Lost*, a decision by the pre-existent Son in the council of heaven leading to his adoption of human nature in order to act as man's ransom. The emphasis on choice and on the collaboration of Father and Son in the plan to redeem man will remain characteristic of Milton's thought, even though 'Trinal Unity' is not a phrase that would have recommended itself to the poet of *Paradise Lost*. Theology is being transmuted into dramatic narrative. The Incarnation is viewed as an unusual royal progress, the Son first resolving to divest himself of glory and to submit to humiliation, then giving up the form of God (*De Doctrina Christiana* and the later poetry will stress the account of this process of kenosis found in Philippians 2:6-8), and finally descending to earth and becoming manifest as a child who is welcomed and celebrated by angels and men with light, music, poetry, and sweet perfumes.

From this point on we are repeatedly made aware of the Son's human as well as divine nature. It is worth emphasizing that the *Nativity* is much less forgetful of the child in the manger than some readings suggest. While Milton does not treat the flesh in sensuous language, or in a language of concrete immediacy, he does convey emphatically a view of the Son as both babe and God, as an epiphany of the eternal in time. The continuing importance of the infant in the scene of his Nativity – smiling, dreaded, or asleep – provides the human centre that draws into itself the other manifestations of the Son as 'Creator great,' redeemer, and 'dreadful Judge.' The abstract principles of Truth and Mercy, Justice and Peace, do not lead the poem 'away from the incarnate towards the ideate,'[9] but rather clarify the moral quality of the acts of the Son on earth as in heaven. This moral world of reason and choice is essential to the human nature which the Son has come to renew. There is a progressive quality to the revelation of the child's nature which should not be overlooked, and which is dialectical in tendency. Characteristic of this process is the threefold rhythm which amplifies the significance of the Son by each return to the manger. The detail reinforces this process by its alternation of cosmic and particular, historical and immediate, supernatural and natural. It is incorrect to say that the Christ of Milton's poem is a symbol of unity and truth rather than a babe and a person.[10] Moving back and forth between the child in the manger and the logos, as the patterns of the poem encourage him to do, the reader is led to feel that there has been a union of the shepherd's wonder at the human child and the wise men's wonder at the renewal of history. The characteristic balance of the poem is displayed in its statement of the relations of the human and the divine.

The opening stanzas of *The Passion*, like those of the *Nativity*, introduce the divine hero who is the subject of the poem, emphasizing the love which led him to enter the 'fleshly Tabernacle' in order to sacrifice himself for mankind. The mediator figure is clearly identified at the outset of both poems, although in *The Passion* a mood of sorrow is rather self-consciously introduced to replace the joy of the earlier piece. *The Passion* also reveals that interest in the Son's voluntary acceptance of redemptive suffering which will later find expression in the heavenly council of book 3 of *Paradise Lost*.

The early stanzas of *The Passion* comprise the most successful part of the fragment, arousing a sense of the mystery of the Incarnation and Crucifixion. Soon, however, the poet tries to confine his 'roving' verse to the suffering Christ, although there appears to be some reluctance in his decision to ignore the active figure celebrated by other poets. More important, in concentrating on sorrow, aesthetically conceived as the sounds of soft lute and still viols, he is in danger of losing sight of the significance of the Crucifixion, its place in the process of redemption. *The Passion*, unlike the *Nativity*, fails to integrate mood and theme, perhaps because Milton is unable to find the language to write about the passive heroism of the suffering Christ. The mood he seeks is related to that developed in *Il Penseroso*, where melancholy proves conducive to an ecstasy which brings 'all Heav'n before mine eyes.' But the sweet melancholy that verges on the contemplative state is not really appropriate to the sorrow of the Crucifixion, a subject which cannot be handled by a speaker who lacks an urgent awareness of sin. Milton's speaker enters on his subject determined to arouse grief, but without a sense of the source of grief in human weakness and failure or of the pressing need for an antidote. In his major poems Milton will make many references to sorrow and woe, but always in connection with sin and the experience of repentance. In *The Passion*, however, the emotion is isolated and treated as an end in itself, and it is not surprising that he cannot proceed from the prelude to the hymn proper.

Milton clearly saw the fragment as a significant failure, for he published it both in 1645 and 1673. Its flaw is recognized, if indirectly, in what is probably the next poem he wrote on the life of Christ. *Upon the Circumcision* recalls *Nativity* in its opening lines, but soon makes it clear that joy is now to be replaced by mourning. This changing of notes to tragic is very like the opening of *The Passion*; sorrow is no longer an end in itself, however, and we soon discover that this poem differs from the earlier one in significant ways. Here the Crucifixion is an event that lies in the future. It is brought to mind by foreshadowing, the circumcision acting as a type or emblem of Christ's suffering and death. In thus locating the Crucifixion as an event to come in the future, this little poem adopts a viewpoint also found in the two epics. *Upon the Circumcision* also differs from its predecessor in the firm sense of point of view which it establishes. A hymn or public prayer, it is spoken throughout in the first person plural, so that it becomes the utterance of a poet who acts as representative Christian and speaks for mankind.

The two stanzas of the poem show two aspects of the Son. First he is the infant of the Gospel story, worshipped by shepherds and angels. The pity of his suffering in this world is established in lines of unusual beauty addressed to the angels. The second stanza presents the pre-existent Son who accepts humiliation in order to make satisfaction for the sins of mankind. (In describing this act, Milton again echoes the passage from Philippians 2:7 which is important in his later doctrine of kenosis as developed in prose and poetry.) As in the *Nativity* and the *Passion*, we see the pre-existent Son give up divine power in order to humble himself by becoming man. Indeed the entire stanza is a lucid statement of certain ideas central to Milton's mature thought. They appear here for the first time, and his adherence to them and to the language in which they are expressed will remain remarkably consistent over the years. Man is unable to fulfil the covenant of works, and so is justly condemned to death. But the Son of God 'Intirely satisfi'd' the law on behalf of man, bore the wrath due to man's sin, and thus resolved the conflict of justice and mercy through 'exceeding love.' In being obedient to the law at the circumcision, the Son illustrates both how he has given up his divine glory and how he will suffer to release man from the law at his Crucifixion. This Pauline view of the atonement will reappear in the Father's remarks during the council in heaven in book 3 of *Paradise Lost* and at the climax of Michael's narrative in book 12. It is the view affirmed in *De Doctrina Christiana*.

Placed beside *The Passion*, *Upon the Circumcision* has the effect of a retraction. The poet no longer seeks to indulge in a melancholy ecstasy. Rather he points at once to the origin, nature, and effect of Christ's suffering. Aesthetic concerns become secondary to moral and doctrinal ones. While touching on ideas of great importance to Milton, however, the poem offers only a limited view of them. The Son is conceived in terms of the heroic act of love by which he releases man from death, but he is not treated as the guide and examplar who will enable his followers to achieve liberty under the Gospel. The poem does not directly consider the moral issues suggested by St Paul's reference in Romans 2:29 to 'circumcision ... of the heart, in the spirit, and not in the letter,' issues shortly to become of momentous importance to Milton. The absence of this subject might tempt one to the view that the poem is unfinished,[11] except that the sombre and epigrammatic close is so very successful.

At a Solemn Music comes closer to recreating the rich vision of the *Nativity* than does *Upon the Circumcision*, but it achieves this effect without direct reference to the history of the Son of God. Once again, the speaker emphasizes that harmony cannot be restored until the disproportions of sin have been banished, but here the Son of God does not appear in explicit form to resolve the problem. The divine figure on the throne is mysteriously vague, as in Revelation, our attention being directed to the spectacle around the throne. Moreover Milton does not follow Revelation in distinguishing between God and his Lamb.[12] The 'great Lord' whose love controls the music of the creation might remind us of the Son, who is associated with the creation in the *Nativity*, but no specific identification is made and the deity remains simply 'God.' At the close the notion that the saints live in God as his musicians might again bring the Son to mind through the doctrine of the mystical body of Christ, and it is just possible that Milton intended the word 'consort' to have as a secondary meaning 'spouse' or 'sharer' and thus to refer to Christ. But while the divine acts of creation and restoration recall the Son, the poem avoids making n explicit distinction among the persons of the Godhead.

The preoccupations of the lyrics that deal with the Son of God continue to find expression in the poetry which centres on human heroes, although here a new range of reference – classical, Platonic, allegorical – is introduced. Heroic virtue that mediates between heaven and earth, uniting divine and human elements, is a theme in many of the early poems as later in some of the sonnets and in *Samson Agonistes*. Concern with the divine and human aspects of the hero certainly provides one of the more important elements in the 1645 collection of poems.

In *A Mask presented at Ludlow Castle*, or *Comus*, the most interesting mediator figure is the Lady herself. Standing between two worlds and receiving the attentions of good and evil beings, she is the embodiment of innocent beauty and of virtue with its layers of restrictive and affirmative meaning. Above all else, the Lady is free. She represents the power of reason to choose temperately among the goods of the earth, and to rise with the assistance of grace to pure visions of sacred yet heartfelt delight. Chastity in the masque is essentially freedom, and in exercising choice the Lady refuses to surrender to the inferior forms of pleasure that rob the soul of self-conscious autonomy. Her integrative function, by which she unites nature and grace and mediates between higher and lower elements, is brought out not only in her speeches, but even more in the action of the masque as a whole, with its music, dancing, and rich symbolism.

So like Satan in some respects, Comus nonetheless remains a mere sign of evil rather than a dramatic and psychologically convincing expression of it. In spite of his mimicry of human moods, evil in the masque remains an inhuman abstraction. Nor does the masque treat very clearly of the sacrifices that must be made by those seeking through trial to be virtuous. The general impression given by the work as a whole is that the Lady is constant to the virtues instilled in her by nature and upbringing, and that it is not necessary for her to come to terms with internal sin and inadequacy. While the need for Sabrina's aid points to limitations in the Lady's ability to act, it does not seem to indicate error or feebleness in her moral sense.

Yet there are moments when the trial of the Lady comes to life in terms of psychological response. The most interesting is at the climax of the temptation in Comus' palace. In this scene there is no fear or hesitation in the Lady's repudiation of Comus, and she is sustained from the start by her anger at him as well as her faith in heaven. Her trial seems to lie rather in her frustration at being physically subject to an opponent who is beneath reason. Her final speech of repudiation opens with a firm defence of temperance, then rises, in lines Milton presumably added after the completion of the first drafts of the masque (778-805), in an impassioned appeal to the doctrines of chastity and virginity. The turning point is marked by a rhetorical pause – 'Shall I go on? / Or have I said anow?' – and the words that follow are of a higher mood and suggest that the Lady has found inspiration outside herself. It is about inspiration, indeed, that she speaks, claiming that she could respond to falsehood with such 'sacred vehemence' that 'all thy magick structures rear'd so high, / Were shatter'd into heaps o're thy false head' (797-8). If she has such powers, why doesn't she use them? We might think of the Christ-child in the *Nativity* driving out the pagan gods, or the Son of *Paradise Lost* casting out the rebels. Such heroic achievement is apparently beyond the Lady. Her physical paralysis is matched by a spiritual frustration which inexplicably prevents her from using the powers she possesses. The final image of ruin, which might remind one of the fate of Samson, suggests that the Lady does not employ such sacred vehemence because the overthrow of her enemy would inevitably bring with it the loss of her own life.

The Lady's rapture, anger, and anguish at this point draw attention to the way her trial involves suffering and takes the form of a kind of passion. Here we draw closer to the reality of evil, seeing its effects not only on brutalized souls but on the virtuous. The moment is a little like that in *Fair Infant* at which the virgin soul is no longer disguised as a star or an angel but is seen in relation to 'Swift-rushing black perdition.' But the masque turns away from this kind of confrontation with evil. The Lady says nothing further, and instead of acting as a dramatic protagonist she becomes a centre for symbolic statement in the remainder of the masque. The masque celebrates the progress in illumination of the virtuous initiate, but does not reach beyond its mythology to the Christian understanding of the cost of such progress. Only a few moments in the experience of the heroine suggest that there may be another dimension to the achievement of virtue.

The elegy is another genre which provided Milton with an opportunity to explore the mediator figure. The characteristic movement of the Christian funeral elegy is one that leads from despair and sorrow, often presented in pagan terms, to a religious consolation. Normally that consolation takes the form of a vision of the dead person in heaven, now restored to full and harmonious life. A third element of the pattern which is frequently present is the recognition that the dead person will continue to assist the living either through memory or perhaps as some kind of guardian spirit. This draws attention to a final point, namely that the speaker is at the centre of the drama, his passion and restoration providing a psychological imitation of the death and resurrection of the person being commemorated by the elegy. The dead person thus stands as a mediator between two worlds or levels of experience, the life of time with its testing and tragedy, and the heavenly life in which human nature realizes its full potential. He acts upon the poet to raise him from despair to a renewed acceptance of life. Milton can be seen experimenting with these patterns in such poems as *Elegy III, In Obitum Praesulis Wintoniensis, In Obitum Praesulis Eliensis, An Epitaph on the Marchioness of Winchester*, and the *Epitaphium Damonis*. It is *Lycidas*, however, which provides the most interesting illustration of the way in which the elegiac process may draw imaginative force from the figure of the Son.

Lycidas undergoes the humiliation of death and is then exalted to heaven, emerging by the close as a type of Christ. The singer first reviews the unfulfilled life of Lycidas as poet and prophet, then turns in the third and final movement of the poem to the vision of the translation of Lycidas at the hand of Christ. Christ is present through the poem by implication – as the true shepherd, as the prophet, priest, and king imitated by his followers, as the true God who dies and rises again to renew the world. Milton's use of the pastoral elegy form, however, enables him to approach the figure of Christ through types and shadows. Images from nature and classical myth point to a reality beyond themselves, a reality which they only figure in a partial and imperfect way. As Northrop Frye remarks, 'Christ does not enter the poem as a character, but he pervades every line of it so completely that the poem, so to speak, enters him.'[13] Even the mitred speaker who denounces the hireling shepherds, whose identity has recently proved controversial, appears to be only a representative of Christ rather than Christ himself.[14] Everything in *Lycidas* points to Christ, but he appears only once in the oblique but climactic reference to 'him that walk'd the waves' (173).

The mourner speaks in the first person, and so we are surprised to find another voice in the epilogue which identifies the mourner as the 'uncouth Swain' (186). The monody has dramatized the swain's attempt to express and master his grief. His questioning of the tragedy leads to three moments of clarification concerning the justice and mercy of God. The first two are given respectively in the words of Apollo and of St Peter, and concern the reward God provides for creative virtue and his punishment of evil. But these manifestations of divine providence do not remedy the loss, and in the third movement the swain is brought to the verge of despair by the pity and terror of his young friend's death. Yet just as all hope seems to have given place to visions of desolation, there is a sudden turn. The singer passes from partial or false consolations to true comfort: 'Weep no more, woful Shepherds weep no more, / For *Lycidas* your sorrow is not dead ... ' (165-6). This change is both surprising and yet expected, coming with a sense of inevitability. It has been prepared for by the process of the singer's thought as he laments, questions, and analyses, yet it represents an abrupt release from the paralysis that appeared to be dominating him. He has found new resources within that enable him to sing and celebrate the translation of Lycidas to heaven, and the dramatic way in which this change occurs is clearly intended to suggest that his efforts have been rewarded by grace.[15] Thus the singer also sinks low and then mounts high in response to the living strength of the Son of God; he, too, imitates Christ by suffering, and is released from that trial by Christ.

Lycidas, then, goes much further than *Comus* in representing the subtleties and refluxes of the mind in the process of responding to evil. The inwardness of the dramatic process is marked. The problems raised by the justice and mercy of God, stated doctrinally in *Upon the Circumcision*, are here felt on the pulses. The importance of mercy and love is demonstrated by a process that reveals the inadequacy of justice alone and the inevitability of human weakness and tragic loss. Unlike the *Nativity* or *At a Solemn Music*, however, the elegy does not immediately and directly place its subject within the larger patterns of providential history and revealed doctrine. The singer expresses himself through the pastoral conventions of elegy, and seeks to make them expressive of greater things; the Christian reality is present in much of his song largely through allusion, typology, and glancing reference. Christ, around whom the whole poem turns and who makes the resolution possible, is present only in one line. But while the swain is in himself not capable of speaking with prophetic voice, he can record and indeed recreate those strains of a higher mood which come in response to his questioning and shrink the pastoral stream. Starting from a position that offers a restricted view of the tragic event, the speaker strives to see beyond the circumscribed mode in which he operates and finally earns the inspiration to do so.

Samson Agonistes treats the mediator figure in a manner that recalls *Lycidas*. The play opens with a soliloquy, and this is symptomatic of the fact that in this drama the real action is interior. The hero's gaze is turned inward, and his speeches are full of self-analysis. He explores his experience closely, reliving the past again and again and seeking for a way to escape from the anguish of being self-enclosed. While the speaker of *Lycidas* reflects on the hints and approximations of truth provided by pagan mythology, Samson approaches the service of God through the law and Jewish history. Even at the outset of the play, however, he has seen beyond certain interpretations of the law, recognizing that his sin lies not in his breaking of a ceremonial taboo or in his failure to fulfil national aspirations, but in his personal relation to God. He will not be made a scapegoat for the guilt of others, but studies his sin and the nature of God's justice until he realizes that he has reached a point at which service may once again be possible. As in *Lycidas* the change occurs suddenly, almost instantaneously, and this suggests that the central figure is reacting to an invisible presence. Samson's initial refusal to go to the games is based on the law, but he reverses his position in response to 'rouzing motions' (1382) which intimate that he is about to be given the long-awaited opportunity for action. Meditation on God's providence and his own responses has led Samson to the point at which he can see the mercy as well as the justice of God, and as he puts his will in God's hands he unknowingly anticipates the fulfilment of the law by the Gospel. For a Christian audience his experience provides a type or foreshadowing of renovation, that process which leads from the near despair of the fallen condition to the renewed faith and liberty of the regenerate.[16] But the play remains a tragedy, for in Samson's world there is no adequate consolation for his suffering, and no promise of personal salvation. While Samson's story is a significant episode in the history of God's providence, as the Epistle to the Hebrews recognizes in placing him among the saints (11:32), the participants in the episode have only an uncertain and fragmentary sense of its providential significance and no conception of the nature and role of the Son of God. Manoa and the Chorus experience tragic catharsis, but they do not look towards an epilogue in heaven.

The date of the composition of *Samson Agonistes* is the subject of much controversy and remains unsettled. One thing appears certain, however: the drama was composed a significant period of years after *Lycidas*, probably not earlier than 1645. Quite likely written during the period when the epics were composed, it may even be the last of Milton's poetic works.[17] In the years separating *Lycidas* and *Samson Agonistes*, Milton changed in certain important ways. The concern with liberty and the law that plays such an important role in *Samson Agonistes* is present only rarely in the poetry up to and including *Lycidas*, and is never given full articulation in those years. Scholars have studied the growth of Milton's conception of Christian liberty through the pamphlets of the forties and fifties, and it is clear that his thinking on this subject helped to shape his major poetry, the two epics and the drama.

The history of the development of his view of Christ in the period of the polemical prose must some day be thoroughly examined. Such a study would be an important adjunct to studies of his conception of Christian liberty. In the forties certain radical impulses began to express themselves in his handling of the figure of the Son. In battling against the bishops, he took up the faith of 1 Corinthians 1:27, characteristic of so much Puritan polemic, and repeated it again and again: 'But God hath chosen the foolish things of the world to confound the wise; and God hath chosen the weak things of the world to confound the things which are mighty.' In the pamphlets of the forties Christ is the source of this mysterious power, and the historical process is viewed as leading to the union of believers in Christ and the revelation of his kingdom. While the Son is seen as the exemplar of acts of creation and destruction, his central function is that of freeing his followers from bondage by fulfilling and abrogating the law, thus dissolving the whole law into charity. The growth of this radical aspect of Milton's view of Christ separates the treatment of the Son in the early poetry from that in the epics. While in the early poetry the Son of God is seen as freeing man from the brutalizing effects of the pagan gods, or even from the penalties of the law, these are limited anticipations of what is to come and there is little that prepares the student of Milton's thought for the intense concern with liberty that characterizes his treatment of the Son in the epics. Eventually this emphasis on the liberating role of the Son, first seen in the anti-episcopal tracts of the early forties, was complemented by an unorthodox emphasis on the Son's subordinate role in relation to the Father. In the anti-episcopal tracts Milton could mock those who held Arian or subordinationist views,[18] yet by 1660 he maintained that the nature of the Son is indeed divine, but distinct from and clearly inferior to the nature of the Father (*Works*, XIV, 337). This view, too, was to affect the poetry, and distinguish the treatment of the Son in the epics from that in the early poems.

Nonetheless our study of the Son in the epics will find many of the preoccupations of the early poetry. The mediator who unites divine and human natures and resolves the conflict of justice and mercy will continue to be of central importance. The history of God's providence will again be expressed in terms of the acts of creation, destruction, and recreation performed by the Son. The doctrine that the Son's act of self-sacrifice makes satisfaction for the sins of mankind will also remain important, but will be brought into closer relation to the interest in inner growth to sonship already evident in the response of the narrator in such poems as the *Nativity* and *Lycidas*.

In the epics, however, these issues will be treated more fully and with a new sense of their significance which is both imaginative and intellectual. The exploration of the three modes of sonship in the poetry is enriched by the coherence and originality of thought achieved in the theology of *De Doctrina Christiana*, and that theology in turn draws some of its force and relevance from its determination to respond to intellectual currents of the age.

I will begin by examining Milton's treatment of the pre-existent Son. Chapter 2 discusses the positions adopted in *De Doctrina Christiana* concerning the divine being called the Son, and his relations with Father and Spirit. Chapter 3 takes up these issues as they are presented in *Paradise Lost*. Chapters 4 and 5, while making some use of Milton's prose, concentrate on the treatment of man as divine image and son in *Paradise Lost*, looking first at his creation in God's likeness, then at the renewal of the divine image in preparation for the adoption of the individual believer, and finally at the image of God in history. The final two chapters, 6 and 7, seek first to establish Milton's theology of the incarnate nature of the Son, and then to explore the growth of Jesus in *Paradise Regained* and to examine the manner in which his temptation serves to educate those who seek to be sons of God.

CHAPTER TWO

Milton's Doctrine of
Son and Spirit

The ideas about God which Milton developed in *De Doctrina Christiana* were of real and central importance to his thought and to his view of Christian experience. They contributed to the argument and design of his major poems. The significance of these ideas is best understood within the context provided by Reformed thought concerning the Godhead. It is true that the early Fathers of the church offer some interesting parallels, but there is no convincing evidence that Milton's theology of the Son was shaped primarily by ancient writers. Too frequently the exploration of his possible debts to the early Fathers has led to the conclusion that his beliefs lack coherence and originality. When we change our point of view, however, and examine Milton's argument in terms of the theology of his age, its implications become clear and its solutions prove more consistent, pointed, and resourceful. The Protestant orthodoxy of his time, carefully and continuously elaborated in Reformed dogmatics, is perhaps best expressed in its chief source – Calvin's *Institutes of the Christian Religion*. Departures from that orthodoxy were not uncommon, and at least some of Milton's more unconventional ideas show an affinity with the theology of the more radical thinkers of the age. My aim in this chapter, then, is to examine Milton's views on the relations of Father, Son, and Spirit with reference to the arguments of Calvin and some of his successors and opponents. I hope that this approach will make clear Milton's effort to develop a coherent and original position in such a way as to avoid the labyrinths of controversy while yet remaining responsive to the thought of his contemporaries.

Milton makes it abundantly clear, of course, that he is indebted to no other theologians for his conclusions. He rejects human authority in the determination of matters of faith. Each believer must work out his own position for himself, having no other divine rule or authority without but scripture, and no other within but the illumination of the Holy Spirit. Milton's theology is important precisely because it was founded on this intellectual freedom, and thus shared a common source and was continuous with his other moral and poetic ideas.

But we can only fully appreciate Milton's originality, his use of his freedom, by viewing his thought within the intellectual history of his age. So viewed, his 'orthodox' as well as his 'heterodox' ideas prove distinctive and interesting. Moreover we must bear in mind that Milton's fierce intellectual independence did not exclude respect for and interest in the thought of others, a concern for lights both new and old. While he came to recognize that his hope for a nation of prophets was premature, he continued to think that the regenerate form an intellectual as well as a spiritual community, a company of free prophets, adding truth to truth in order to raise the temple, to make whole again the dismembered body of truth. That is why he kept on writing.[1]

Calvin and the Second Person of the Trinity

The Reformation produced a revaluation of the nature and office of Christ. Neither Luther nor Calvin, however, was initially predisposed to use the abstract and philosophical language traditionally employed in discussions of the Person of Christ and his place in the Trinity. Luther, seeking freedom from metaphysical prepossessions and language, once averred that 'if my Soul loathes this word *homoousios* and I do not wish to use it, I shall not on that account be a heretic. For who will compel me to use it provided I hold to the reality which was defended in the councils from scripture.'[2] Yet in spite of this distrust of the language of councils, Luther found it necessary to use non-biblical terms when defending the doctrine of the essential unity of Father and Son against heresy, and he often cites the ecumenical creeds as worthy bearers of truth about Christ. The emergence of anti-Trinitarian opinion in the radical wing of the Reformation increased the need for such language, leading him to elaborate on the divinity of Christ in order to protect the confession of faith. He affirmed three hypostases in one *ousia* even though he doubted the adequacy of such language.[3] He maintained that the Son as divine image not only provides a resemblance, but fully contains the whole substance and nature of God. Luther gives due weight to the Gospel theme of the Son who is 'sent' to us,[4] but he is not in danger of slipping into a subordinationist manner of speech. He underscores Christ's claim to be God, the assertion of Christ's divinity in the Gospel of St John, and the presence of the Trinity in the Old Testament. In controversy with figures such as Casper Schwenckfeld, Luther elaborated his version of the so-called *communicatio idiomatum*, the doctrine of the communication of properties between the two natures of Christ, and using this doctrine he described how the two distinct natures of God and man are untied in the undivided person of Christ.[5] Struggling with heresies against the true understanding of the Incarnation and the Trinity, Luther came to see his experience with the radicals partly in terms of a parallel with the age when Arianism flourished, a period which he considered one of the darkest in history.[6] It appears that the struggle was necessary not because Trinitarian doctrine is in itself a rewarding subject for reflection, but because it secures the function of Christ as the true source of knowledge of and faith in God.

Calvin's concern with Trinitarian doctrine began early and continued late. In 1537, at the beginning of his ministry, he drew criticism from the scholar Pierre Caroli, who accused him of not holding the true doctrines of the Trinity because he avoided the classical terminology and refused Caroli's demand that he sign the Athanasian creed with its anathemas. In that same year the synod of Lausanne was persuaded by Calvin of the truth of his position, and deprived Caroli of his charge.[7] Along with others, Calvin signed a statement of belief in the Trinity against the false accusations of Caroli. His reservations about the use of non-biblical language in discussions of the Godhead yielded to a sense of the importance of such language as a guard against heresies threatening the biblical witness of the triune God.[8] His controversy with Michael Servetus, coming to a climax in the events which led to Servetus' death at the stake in 1553, irrevocably committed Calvin to his position. His conception of the orthodox Trinitarian doctrine was expressed not only in the tracts against the errors of Servetus (of which the most significant is *Defense of the Orthodox Faith*), but in the prominent place given to the rebuttal of Servetus and the assertion of the true belief in the *Institutes*. Milder and more private conferences were held in these years between Calvin and the Italian reformers of unitarian persuasion such as Giorgius Blandrata, and the uncle of Faustus Socinus, Laelius. In 1558 the Italian congregation at Geneva in consultation with Calvin and two magistrates imposed a Trinitarian statement as a test of membership.[9]

Yet despite Calvin's consistency and persistence in defending Trinitarian orthodoxy, he appears to do so not because of the richness of his response to the doctrine in itself, but because it supports other beliefs of great importance to him, such as the doctrine of the union of divine and human natures in the mediator or the analysis of regeneration in terms of Father, Son, and Spirit.[10] The final shape of the *Institutes* is itself evidence of Trinitarian interests, since Calvin abandoned the form suggestive of a catechism in which he had originally cast his treatise and adopted in its place a structure which stresses the three persons of the Trinity.

In the *Institutes* Calvin begins his discussion of the Trinity by observing that God's immensity deters us from measuring him by our sense, and his spiritual nature forbids us to indulge in carnal or earthly speculation concerning him. The Trinity is a mystery. If we cannot understand the substance of the sun, how can we expect to understand the essence of God? The human mind enters a labyrinth when it indulges curiosity and neglects the guidance of the divine oracles, the scriptures.[11]

Yet Calvin argues that in a matter of such importance as the Trinity, Christians must not be held at all times to the very syllables of scripture. The unerring standard of speaking as well as thinking is derived from the Bible, but with respect to those parts of scripture which are dark it is permissible to use other terms: 'what prevents us from explaining in clearer words those matters in Scripture which perplex and hinder our understanding, yet which conscientiously and faithfully serve the truth of Scripture itself, and are made use of sparingly and modestly and on due occasion?'[12] He considers that the appeal to scripture is often abused by the enemies of pure and sound doctrine, and that excessive fastidiousness about the use of non-scriptural terms can be a sign of the heretic who seeks to pervert the text. His brief review of the position of the Fathers and councils concerning the Trinity is designed to show that firmness in meeting misinterpretation should be accompanied by modesty in recognizing the poverty of human language in so high a matter. Calvin seems uncomfortable but resolute as he insists that since all will not concur in the right use of scriptural language, it is necessary to reply to the Arian that the Son is consubstantial with the Father, and to the Sabellian that there is a Trinity of persons in one divine essence.

Seeking to keep the argument as simple as possible, Calvin nonetheless finds that he must follow the councils of the past in using such terms in order to protect the truth. He affirms that the ancient writers were right to place emphasis on the single word *homoousios*, for that word distinguished between Christians and blasphemers. Yet he makes such observations with a restraint bordering on reluctance, and one is left with the impression that the defence of orthodoxy in this area is a task which has been imposed on Calvin by the age.[13]

In his main argument he seeks to prove from scripture the divinity of both the Son and the Holy Spirit. The Son is the Word which from the beginning was God and was with God; the source of all inspiration, and with the Father the maker of all things, the Word becomes incarnate as Christ for man's salvation. The Spirit also exerts sovereign power at the creation and inspires the prophets; man's justification is the work of the Spirit, for from the Spirit alone all good gifts proceed. All the peculiar attributes of the Godhead are ascribed to the Spirit in the same way as to the Son. Calvin proves his arguments in each case by appealing to both Old and New Testament passages, and he makes particular use of the Pauline epistles and the Gospel of St John.[14]

Calvin asserts both the distinction of the Persons and the unity of the Godhead. This distinction involves an order: 'the Father is thought of first, then from him the Son, and finally from both the Spirit. For the mind of each human being is naturally inclined to contemplate God first, then the wisdom coming forth from him, and lastly the power whereby he executes the decrees of his plan.'[15] Because the Persons carry this order with them, whenever mention is made of the Father and Son, or of the Father and Spirit together, the name of God is specially given to the Father. This order does not involve any subordination of divinities, as Calvin affirms by appealing to Augustine's dictum: 'Christ with respect to himself is called God; with respect to the Father, Son.'[16] The one single essence contains all three persons or hypostases, and in each hypostasis the whole nature is understood, so that Father, Son, and Spirit are all from eternity, the essence in each case being unbegotten. Thus the essence of the Son is without beginning, while his Person has its origin in God.[17] The final section of the chapter on the Trinity Calvin directs at modern heresy, and particularly at that form of subordination-ism which assumes a Son and Spirit who do not share in the divine essence. If the difference between Father and Son is placed in essence, then the true deity of the Son is annihilated, for 'without essence, and indeed the whole essence, [it] cannot exist.'[18] It is a 'detestable fiction' to maintain that essence is proper to the Father alone, as if he were the deifier of the Son.

A fruitful faith, Calvin maintained, ought not to fix only on the essence of Christ, but should respond to his power and office.[19] While Calvin's discussion of the Trinity is defensive – an attempt to keep the mystery with a minimum of scholastic language – his treatment of Christ as mediator is expansive and affirmative. Calvin celebrates the drama and the wonder of the office of the mediator, setting out vividly the stages by which it is fulfilled. His strong sense of the shape of the career of the mediator was to affect all subsequent Reformed theology. It was Calvin, rather than Luther, who clearly established the doctrine of the threefold office of Prophet, Priest, and King,[20] and he also gave distinctive emphasis to the process of the Son's humiliation and exaltation.

By implication, if not more formally, Calvin distinguishes between a general sense in which the Son may be called mediator and a more specific sense. In the general sense, the Son was mediator from the beginning of creation. Preserving and ordering the creation, he held primacy over the angels and acted as head of the Church, so that the angels and men were joined to God through the Son. His leadership appeared in the rays of the divine image so conspicuous in unfallen Adam, and man would have continued to need a mediator even if he had remained without sin.[21] In the more specific sense, the Son became a mediator in the flesh to redeem fallen man. Although predetermined before all ages, this divine act is a response to human sin. Calvin forcefully rejects the surmise of Osiander that the Son would inevitably have become man as part of the process by which the creatures grow towards God. On the contrary, the Incarnation was a specific measure of the divine will with regard to sin. Calvin's account of the decrees of God has implicit in it the drama of the council in heaven in book 3 of *Paradise Lost*:

> Since our iniquities, like a cloud cast between us and him, had completely estranged us from the Kingdom of Heaven ... no man, unless he belonged to God, could serve as the intermediary to restore peace. But who might reach to him? Any one of Adam's children? No, like their father, all of them were terrified at the sight of God. ... One of the Angels? They also had need of a head, through whose bond they might cleave firmly and individually to their God. ... The situation would surely have been hopeless had the very majesty of God not descended to us, since it was not in our power to ascend to him. Hence, it was necessary for the Son of God to become for us 'Immanuel, that is, God with us'. ...[22]

In becoming mediator in the flesh, however, the Son does not give up his unqualified position of dominion over all. There is no cessation or diminution of his general mediatorial function during his Incarnation: 'the Son of God descended from heaven in such a way that, without leaving heaven, he willed to be borne in the virgin's womb, to go about the earth, and to hang upon the cross; yet he continuously filled the world even as he had done from the beginning!'[23]

For Calvin the mystery of the Incarnation centres on the fact that Christ the mediator is both Son of Man and Son of God. Christ's true humanity was united with his divinity in such a way that each nature remained entire yet the two natures constituted only one person. Calvin adopts the doctrine of the *communicatio idiomata*, giving it his own special emphasis. Scripture sometimes attributes to Christ qualities which embrace both natures without applying specifically to either. Thus Paul's assertion that he is 'first-born of every creature' (Colossians 1:15) applies to his divinity, his being said to grow in stature, wisdom, and favour with God and Man (Luke 2:52) is appropriate only to his humanity, whereas those things which refer to the office of mediator, such as his power to forgive sins and to bestow righteousness, comprehend both natures.[24] Calvin emphasizes the act of kenosis by which the Son humbled himself by adopting a clothing of flesh and the form of a servant. Christ in his humanity grew, serving the Father obediently and taking on human infirmities and affections, although not sin, so that he suffered grief, fear, and dread, but not despair. Yet the divine nature was not surrendered in the act of kenosis, but remained veiled, only the outward insignia of majesty being abandoned. This means that all his acts were in the fullest sense voluntary, being willed by this divine nature.[25]

In his divine nature, Christ is the eternal Son. Calvin directs a strong attack against Servetus and the Socinians for the error of maintaining that Christ is the Son of God because begotten of God in human nature. The name of the true and only begotten Son belongs to Christ from the beginning, for he is Son not by his human nature but on account of his Godhead and eternal essence. The eternal word was already the Son of God before he was clothed with flesh; indeed, the name *Son* is not applicable to the office of mediator in itself, but applies only because the mediator was God manifest in the flesh.[26]

The office of mediator, with its union of human and divine natures, exists only for a time. Although ordained from eternity, it has a beginning, middle, and end. Calvin viewed nature and history as God's theatre, and his strong sense of the dramatic and epic potential of the career of the mediator is one of his chief legacies to Reformed theology. The structure of the divine drama is shaped by the process through which the Son accepts humiliation and is exalted. The drama unfolds through a series of great but mysterious occasions: the act of kenosis, by which the Son hid himself in the form of a servant (Philippians 2:8); the period of subjection, when the majesty of God is not annihilated but alternately concealed under the low condition of the flesh and manifested through it, as in the miracles; the crowning glory and honour (Hebrews 2:7) when Christ is declared to be the Son of God by his resurrection (Romans 1:4); the ascension to the right hand of the Father (Mark 16:19, Ephesians 1:20-2, Philippians 2:10), where as assessor and vicegerent the Son is given all power that his hand may govern, cherish, and sustain man, gradually bringing us to full communion with God so that we become Sons of God by adoption through the offices of the Son of God by nature; the last judgment, which is regarded as the last act of the Son's reign; the return by the Son of his name and crown and kingdom to the Father, that God may be all in all (1 Corinthians 15:28,24). The drama of the Son is universal in Christian thought and experience, but Calvin gives it a distinctive emphasis, heroic yet mysterious, a recognizable and dialectical shape, and a specific biblical ground.[27]

In Calvin's treatment of the mediator there is an element of subordinationism which was to be repeated in the systems of divinity which were inspired by the *Institutes*. This subordinationist element, however, is carefully restricted to the person and office of the mediator. Calvin holds it as a key of true interpretation that those things in scripture which refer to the office of the mediator are not spoken of the divine or human natures simply. Repeatedly he distinguishes what is said about or by the mediator from what is proper to the eternal Son: 'For even though [the Son] consistently calls all the power he holds "the benefit and gift of the Father," he merely means that he reigns by divine power. Why did he take the person of the mediator? He descended from the bosom of the Father and from imcomprehensible glory that he might draw near to us.'[28] In this way Calvin can speak of the subordination of the person of the mediator and yet insist on the equality in divinity of the Son. The divine nature of the eternal Son is present in the man Christ, veiled yet manifest in the flesh. But during his incarnate life the Son is also simultaneously in heaven, filling the world as from the beginning. After Christ's death on the cross, the human nature is located in heaven (for Calvin rejects the Lutheran doctrine of the omnipresence of the body of Christ), while the universal presence of the divine nature remains unchanged. Ultimately, however, the office of mediator, with its union of divine and human natures, will no longer be necessary, and the saints will enjoy the immediate presence of the Godhead of the Son. At the climax of the grand providential scheme, when the Kingdom is returned to the Father, Christ's own Godhead will no longer be veiled even in part, but will shine forth of itself.[29] Thus while Calvin gives some attention to the way in which the mediator witholds divine powers and voluntarily accepts a subordinate role not only in his humiliation but after his exaltation, he is in no danger of neglecting the true identity of the Son as God, and he repeatedly insists on the connection between the theology of the mediator and that of the Trinity.

Milton, Calvin, and the Son as Mediator

Milton's theological treatise, *De Doctrina Christiana*, appears to have reached the state of a fair copy by the early 1660s, at which time Milton was in the midst of composing *Paradise Lost*. It was thus being finished almost exactly a century after Calvin wrote the first version of the *Institutes*. Like the *Institutes*, Milton's treatise grew over a period of many years. Whatever may be concluded about its doctrinal character, its lineage is clear enough. It belongs with the systems and 'marrows' of divinity produced by Reformed writers of Calvinistic persuasion in the later sixteenth and earlier seventeenth centuries. Scholars have shown that the form and argument of *De Doctrina Christiana* was directly influenced by the *Compendium Theologiae Christianae* (1626) of John Wollebius and the *Medulla Sacrae Theologiae* (1632) of William Ames, two firmly Calvinistic divines.[30] Milton himself refers to other theologians of the tradition, such as H. Zanchius (whose *Religione Christianae* first appeared in 1619), and A. Polanus (whose *Syntagma Theologiae Christianae* appeared in 1625), and the age gave rise to many other comprehensive theological systems of similar persuasion. The international character of Calvinism found expression in the common form of its dogmatics. Thus while *De Doctrina Christiana* uses methods and reaches conclusions which show affinity with the more radical thought of the period, its structure, its topics, and even its language invoke the tradition of European Calvinist divinity, and the fountainhead of that tradition is of course the *Institutes of the Christian Religion*.

That Milton avoids direct and explicit use of Calvin's theological treatise is less surprising than might at first appear. Reformed writers wished to base their arguments on scripture rather than human authority, and tended to assume a consensus of essential doctrine. Thus Wollebius in his *Compendium Theologiae Christianae* makes only passing reference to Calvin. Moreover, Milton's conception of the sufficiency of scripture is more uncompromising and exclusive of other authority than is usual even in the Reformed theology of the age. His aim, as he tells us, is to put as much as possible into the very words of scripture and to avoid human authorities and traditions (*Works*, XIV, 11). Beginning his work by gathering the scripture passages relevant to topics in the manner exemplified by the *Loci Communes* of Philipp Melanchthon, he subsequently made use, as he rather bitterly admits, of the more diffuse volumes of divinity which present conflicting arguments over certain heads of faith (*Works*, XIV, 5). In this way his treatise assumed a shape accommodated to Reformed dogmatics.

Christ is as central to *De Doctrina Christiana* as to the *Institutes*, but the similarities and differences in emphasis in the Christology of the two works are instructive. Like Calvin, Milton stresses the way the mediator is both man and God, but unlike Calvin he asserts that the Son can be divine without being of one essence with the Father. Everything which Calvin argues in his chapter on the Trinity (*Institutes*, I, xiii) is repudiated by Milton. As we shall see, the doctrine of the Trinity is for Milton not established as a mystery by scripture, but is rather a false mystery invented by man. Feeling even greater repugnance than Calvin for the abstract Greek and Latin terminology used in defining Trinitarian dogma, he insists that if such language is to be employed it must not be forced to embrace a meaningless contradiction (e.g. *Works*, XIV, 221-32).

Calvin became suspicious of those who insisted that all doctrine must be expressed in the very language of scripture. For Milton, however, 'we are not obliged to say of Christ what the Scriptures do not say' (*Works*, XIV, 273). While Milton does not attack the language of Nicea directly, he makes a number of sallies mocking the 'barbarous ignorance of the schools' and the use of non-biblical language to maintain an absurd paradox with a maximum of obstinacy and argumentativeness (*Works*, XIV, 209). Later, in *Of True Religion, Haeresie, Schism, Toleration and the growth of Popery*, he approves of the Arians and Socinians for holding that the 'terms of Trinity, Triunity, Coessentiality, Tri-personality, and the like' were 'Scholastic Notions, not to be found in Scripture' (*Works*, VI, 169). The truth need not be dug from out of a mass of ambiguities and obscurities, as with the riddle of an oracle. We may drink our fill from the purest fountains of truth (*Works*, XIV, 269). In practice this means that the classical language of Trinitarianism is used by Milton primarily to deny the traditional formulation of Trinitarian dogma. Even so, his use of such terms as hypostasis and essence is usually grudging, leaving the impression that he wishes to cut through much nonsense in order to reassert a rational use of language. In seeking to determine the significance of key scriptural passages, he appeals frequently to logic and to the ordinary use of words (*Works*, XIV, 309). While he has learned from Erasmian scholarship concerning Trinitarian texts, his method has more affinity with the systematic rationalism of the Socinian attack on Trinitarian doctrine.

Most of chapter 5 of *De Doctrina* is a rigorous examination of the qualities attributed to God throughout scripture. The result is an acceptance of the distinction of the persons of Father, Son, and Spirit, and a denial of their unity of essence. Milton agrees that their relations imply an order, but insists that it is an order based on subordination. He is in the position repudiated by Calvin when he remarked that those who distinguish the Father and the Son in terms of essence make the Father the deifier of the Son.[31]

Adopting the Reformed concept of the subordination of the mediator, Milton alters it by removing the restraints of Trinitarian orthodoxy. Repeatedly in *De Doctrina* he comes back to the point that the mediator is in no sense less than the Son. When in scripture the Son speaks of the Father as greater than himself or when it is said that the Son was sent by the Father, or that he was obedient to the Father, or that the Father gives all things into the hands of the Son, it is according to Milton important to recognize that the name of Father does not signify the three persons or the whole essence of the Trinity. The things said of the mediator are also said of the Son in the fullest sense (*Works*, XIV, 223, 305, 329): 'he never could have become a mediator, nor could he have been sent from God, or have been obedient to him, unless he had been inferior to God and the Father as to his nature' (*Works*, XIV, 263). This is the exact reverse of Calvin's position.[32] The difference between the two is strikingly illustrated at point after point. Calvin, for example, places reliance on John 1:1 as proof of the Son's divinity: 'In the beginning was the Word, and the Word was with God, and the Word was God.'[33] But Milton asserts that 'in the beginning' does not mean from eternity, and 'was God' is not an assertion of identity of essence but means rather that 'he was with God, that is, in the bosom of the Father, as it is expressed in v. 18' (*Works*, XIV, 253). Calvin's favourite passage to describe Christ incarnate is perhaps 1 Timothy 3:16: 'God was manifest in the flesh.' Milton follows Erasmus in considering the text suspect, but concludes that even if correct, it does not prove the divinity of the Son, but means simply that God the Father was made manifest in the Son, his image, for 'in any other way he is invisible' (*Works*, XIV, 265). The comparison of Milton's and Calvin's treatments of the Passion brings their differences into sharp focus. Both consider that Christ's suffering was real and dreadful. For Calvin, the divine power veiled itself for a moment, and in his human nature Christ was troubled: 'he did not will as man what he willed according to his divine nature.'[34] But Milton sees the finitude of the Son in his anguish: 'why then did the Son call upon the Father? Because he felt even his divine nature insufficient to support him under the pains of death' (*Works*, XIV, 331).

Milton thus departs from Calvin and his followers by his uncompromising monotheism and his consequent belief in the subordination of the Son. The monotheism is introduced at the outset of *De Doctrina*, in the second chapter 'Of God', where evidence is gathered to show that there is only one supreme God, the Father of Jesus Christ (*Works*, XIV, 149ff). In chapter 5 he demonstrates the failure of Trinitarian doctrine, and sets out in detail the biblical witness to the subordination of the Son. The basic line of argument here is that all the things said in scripture of the mediator are also said of the Son. All things have been given to the Son, not to the mediator only. Those who use the *communicatio idomatum* to assign attributes sometimes to the human nature, sometimes to the divine, are acting as sophists and are in danger of making a sophist out of Christ. The Son is not self-existent like the supreme God, but was begotten by a decree of the Father (*Works*, XIV, 185). He is thus not coessential with the Father, being begotten within the bounds of time, the first born of all created things (*Works*, XIV, 307-9). This generation has nothing to do with the essence of deity, and occurred by the free will of the Father. Unity and infinity are attributes of the supreme God, and these belong only to the Father, who clearly cannot beget a coequal deity. The nature of the Son is distinct from that of the Father, and inferior to it even though divine: 'to be the one invisible God, and to be the only-begotten and visible, are things so different that they cannot be predicted of one and the same essence'

(*Works*, XIV, 337-9; see also 311-3). As Milton runs through the attributes of the Son, and shows how his qualities are secondary and derivative, the contrast with Calvin's treatment of the Son is evident. For Calvin, the divine attributes are simply veiled in the incarnate Son, occasionally flashing out in miraculous acts. But Milton sees them all as gifts conferred by the Father.

Such gifts are conferred not because the Father begot the Son, but because he loves him (*Works*, XIV, 305). The love of the Father is initiated by the obedience of the Son. In this sense the Son merits the gifts of the Father, showing himself to be worthy of his exaltation: Christ, 'having triumphed over death, and laid aside the form of a Servant, ... was exalted by God the Father to a state of immortality and of the highest glory, partly by his own merits, and partly by the gift of the Father, for the benefit of mankind; wherefore he rose again from the dead, ascended into heaven, and sitteth on the right hand of God' (*Works*, XV, 309-11). Milton places a significant emphasis on the merit of the Son, viewing it as a cause of the exaltation. The passage recalls the poetry, being consistent with, if less dramatic than, the lines in *Paradise Lost* where the Father states that the Son is 'By Merit more than Birthright Son of God,' or those in *Paradise Regained* where the Father speaks of the 'consummate vertue' of 'This perfect Man, by merit call'd my Son.'

Calvin was at pains to prevent a misunderstanding of the merit of the Son. God is the primary cause of the merit of Christ, and the function of that merit is to obtain grace for man. The Son did not acquire some new quality for himself at his exaltation, but revealed his divine nature: 'he who gave away the fruit of his holiness to others testifies that he acquired nothing for himself.'[35] Milton's Son, by contrast, is exalted 'partly by his own merits.' Exaltation is a 'fulness' that Christ receives from God 'in the sense in which we shall receive our fulness from Christ' (*Works*, XIV, 339). Such divine honour, the gift of the Father, is received by the Son on account of his merit.

While Calvin rejected this idea, it would not have seemed novel to many of his successors. Stressing that the Son did not receive new glory according to his divine nature, many argued that there was nonetheless a real communication of honour and glory to his human nature or to his mediatorial office. Some held that in accordance with his developing humanity, Christ can receive in his human nature new gifts and perfections, and perhaps even new power and authority which he did not possess before. Such a process leaves open the possibility that the Son in some sense earns his exaltation. If the humiliation of Christ is properly the cause of his exaltation, he possesses merit for us as mediator, but for himself as man. Rejecting the Lutheran view of the exaltation of the Son's human nature as the result of the communication of divine attributes, some of the Reformed explained it entirely in terms of human merit.[36]

In this context, Milton's statement about the way Christ's exaltation applies to both his natures seems a conventional expression of Reformed opinion: 'both participate in his exaltation; his Godhead, by its restoration and manifestation; his manhood, by an accession of glory' (*Works*, XV, 315). The human nature is exalted by being raised to heaven, the divine nature by being restored to its original glory. But because the Son does not possess his original glory in his own right as equal to the Father, Milton's statement takes on novel implications. Both in prose and poetry Milton makes it clear that the Son does not continue to act apart from his manifestation as mediator. It is the Son, not simply the mediator, who through trial and merit regains the place of glory at the right hand of the Father, raising human nature also.

Calvin, as we saw, provides a compelling statement of the idea that the mediator has a career in which his exaltation is made manifest. Milton, too, stresses this pattern, both in the poetry and the prose treatise. In the treatise he speaks of the three degrees of the Son's exaltation – resurrection, ascension into heaven, and sitting at God's right hand – but it is clear that at some earlier point in time ('in the beginning,' but *not* from eternity) the Son was first exalted to his place in heaven. *Paradise Lost*, as we shall see, also presents a series of exaltations – at the elevation of the Son over the angels, his overthrow of the rebel angels, his creation of the world, his acceptance of the role of mediator, and his resurrection and ascension. As the Father puts it, commenting on the Incarnation, 'thy Humiliation shall exalt / With thee thy Manhood also to this Throne' (3.313-14). For Calvin, the Incarnation does not prevent the Son from continuing to act as preserver and ruler of all being. Milton, however, does not present his Son as exercising divine power in heaven while incarnate on earth. On the contrary, when the Father accepts the Son's proposal to ransom man, he says 'I spare / Thee from my bosom and right hand' (3.278-9), and in *Paradise Regained* we do indeed find the Father alone in heaven while the Son is on earth. *De Doctrina* makes it clear that while Christ is at one in mind and spirit with the Father during the period he is on earth ('as befitted a great prophet,' *Works*, XIV, 315) his divine nature is fully engaged in his manifestation as mediator. Milton apparently agrees with Calvin in distinguishing the Son's general work of mediation by which he acts as creator and sustainer of all things from the special work of mediation by which he redeems man. But for Milton, the Incarnation involves the temporary surrender of the general work of mediation as part of the humiliation of the Son. It is the Son, not simply the mediator, who through trial and merit regains the place of glory at the right hand of the Father, raising human nature also.

The person of the mediator, both God and man, is exalted to heaven and becomes universal king. In the manner of Calvin (and unlike the Lutherans, who generally endorsed the doctrine of the omnipresence of the body of Christ), Milton stresses that after the resurrection the humanity of the Son will be located in heaven, so that he will reign as 'Son both of God and Man' (3.316). *Paradise Lost* explains that all power is given by the Father to the Son so that he can 'reign for ever,' yet as in Calvin's eschatology the time will come after the last judgment when the work of mediation is over and the Son lays his regal sceptre aside so that God, in St Paul's words (1 Corinthians 15:28), 'shall be All in All' (3.341). The seeming contradiction is explained in *De Doctrina*, where we are told that there will be no end to the Son's kingdom 'for all ages' (Hebrews 1:8), that is, 'so long as the ages of the world endure, until "time" itself "shall be no longer," ... until everything which his kingdom was intended to effect shall have been accomplished' (*Works*, XVI, 367). The end of the kingdom is thus one of perfection and consummation, 'like the end of the law.'

The theological treatise is a little more curious and specific about the schedule of the last things than is the poem, although they agree in main outline. According to *De Doctrina*, the 'reign of glory' commences with the second coming of Christ as the Son of man to reign on earth. The period of judgment will be prolonged, a reign rather than a judicial session. It appears to include the thousand years mentioned in the mysterious account in Revelation 20:1-17 in which the saints rule with Christ. After this period is over, Satan and his forces are thrown down and condemned to everlasting punishment, and judgment is pronounced on the whole human race. With the punishment of the wicked and the complete glorification of the righteous, the last end will come, and Christ hands over the Kingdom to God the Father, that God may be all in all. The polluted world will be destroyed in conflagration, and the saints glorified in eternal and happy life consisting chiefly of the sight of

God and the possession of a new heaven and earth (see book 1, chapter xxxiii).

The poem omits reference to the millenial rule of Christ and the final rebellion of Satan, but stresses the second coming of the Son, his reign and judgment, his dissolution of Satan 'with his perverted World,' and the creation of

> New Heav'ns, new Earth, Ages of endless date
> Founded in righteousness and peace and love
> To bring forth fruits Joy and eternal Bliss. (12.549-51)

Of six specific references in *Paradise Lost* to the last things, only the Father's remarks at 3.339-41 and the Son's parallel statement at 6.731-3 describe clearly the ending of the reign of glory, although several passages suggest that the judgments of time will give place to the mysterious fulfilment of eternity – 'beyond is all abyss, / Eternitie, whose end no eye can reach' (12.555-6). But the Father's statement of how finally God shall be all in all comes at the end of a speech of such fervour, majesty, and strength that it establishes the final end of foreseeable history once and for all.

In the poem, Milton does not indicate in what manner or even whether the Son has continuing identity in eternity after all has become God. In the treatise, however, his gloss on 1 Corinthians 15:27 makes his position clear: 'after he shall have laid aside his functions as mediator, whatever may be his greatness, or whatever it may previously have been, he must be subject to God and the Father' (*Works*, XIV, 263). In this, Milton is again quite unlike Calvin, for the latter considers that finally the glory of the second person of the Trinity will shine forth without any veil and the Son will be seen to be of one essence with the Father. Milton's cryptic comparison of the end of the reign of glory with the end of the law opens up the possibility that the new unity within God will be another and perhaps final stage in the process of internalizing which distinguishes the Gospel from the law.

Milton's Originality

Protestants repudiated with disdain the claim of certain Catholic writers that Trinitarian doctrine is to be accepted since it is taught by the church. Yet while they agreed that in this matter as in others the scripture alone provides the faithful with sufficient guidance, most conceded that the defence of true doctrine against misunderstanding and heresy requires the use of a limited number of non-scriptural terms. In this caution they were not unlike some of the bishops at the Council of Nicea. Bullinger is representative in his warm endorsement of the way the early church handled the Arian heretics. He notes with approval that the early defenders of the faith did not at once make use of non-scriptural language, but employed it only when their slippery opponents compelled them to do so.[37]

Calvin, as we have seen, establishes a clear model for the Reformed conception of the Trinity. He provides a firm assertion of the distinction of the persons in the unity of the Godhead; an incisive account of the mediator which insists on the unity of the two natures, human and divine, in one person; a dramatic statement of the career of the mediator expressed through his offices of prophet, priest, and king; and a method of acknowledging the subordination of the mediator while yet securing the equality in divinity of the Son. The major points are repeated by such successors to Calvin as John Wollebius and William Ames. Wollebius, who published his *Compendium Theologiae Christianae* in 1626, begins his discussion of the Persons of the Godhead by noting that words such as 'person', 'Trinity', and '*homoousian*' are not found in scripture and yet are consistent with scripture and wisely employed by the church, and proceeds to emphasize that the three persons are coessential, their unity consisting in identity of essence, equality, and circumincession. At the Incarnation, Wollebius argues, the Son became God-Man, uniting the human nature to the divine nature so that the properties of each are preserved in 'one divinely human person.' While the Son is God, coessential and coequal with the Father, he is as mediator subordinate, and this subordination remains even in the state of glory, for his human nature is exalted in such a way as not to put it on a level with the divine.[38]

In England similar views of the Godhead are to be found in such representative works of Calvinist persuasion as William Perkin's *An Exposition of the Symbole or Creed of the Apostles* (1595), and John Owen's *Vindicae Evangelicae or The Mystery of the Gospell Vindicated, and Socinianism Examined* (1655), or in the confession of faith and the catechisms published by the Westminster Assembly.

By contrast, Milton's doctrine of the Son is clearly subordinationist. He rejects the compromise by which non-scriptural language is used to defend a doctrine supposedly based on scripture. Although influenced by Calvin's conception of the office of the mediator, he departs from

Calvin at certain critical points. Stressing the union of the divine and human natures in the mediator, he nonetheless concludes that the subordinate role of the mediator is indicative of the subordination of the Son, and he denies that the divine Persons are united by a single essence. Like Calvin, he believes firmly that Christ the mediator is both God and man. Unlike Calvin, he concludes that the defence of Trinitarian doctrine is too great a price to pay in order to ensure the divinity of Christ. He appears to have decided that the better course is to follow scripture in classifying the Incarnation as a mystery which cannot be adequately explained in rational terms.

Some aspects of Milton's discussion of the Son do not fit easily into the pattern of his response to Calvinism. One such is his idea of the generation of the Son from the substance of the Father: 'God imparted to the Son as much as he pleased of the divine nature, nay of the divine substance itself, care being taken not to confound the substance with the whole of the essence' (*Works*, XIV, 193). It has been argued that here he is influenced by Tertullian, whose subordinationist view Milton notes in *Of Prelatical Episcopacy* (*Works*, III, i, 97), remarking that Tertullian held the Father to be the 'whole substance' and the Son 'a derivation, and portion of the whole.' But there is no clear evidence that Milton was following Tertullian, a writer whose view of the role of the church in defining doctrine was somewhat different from to his own. Rather his position should be seen as a consequence of his theory of divine creation. When so viewed, it is cleared from the difficulties raised by certain modern interpreters.

W.B. Hunter, with support from the other critics who wrote the essays gathered in *Bright Essence: Studies in Milton's Theology*, urges that Milton's conception of the production of the Son by the Father from his own substance provides the basis for his conception of the Trinity as three essences or three hypostases in one substance. Because of his conception of essence or hypostasis as individuality or individual being, Hunter argues, Milton cannot use the Augustinian definition of the Trinity as 'one essence, three substances,' but his language reverses that definition, making the three essences consubstantial. Thus, according to Hunter, Milton might believe that he was supporting the *homoous-ian* doctrine that is at the heart of the Nicene Creed.[39]

But when Milton claims that his doctrine is consonant with the 'celebrated confession' of the faith of the saints (*Works*, XIV, 353), he is surely referring not to the so-called Nicene Creed, but to the Apostles' Creed,[40] to which he returns in the closing sentence of his ·chapter on the Son: 'Finally, this is the faith proposed to us in the Apostle's Creed, the most ancient and universally received compendium of belief in the possession of the Church' (*Works*, XIV, 357). Barbara Lewalski, in a telling refutation of Hunter's view, notes that the *homoousian* doctrine was developed at Nicea not primarily as a way of defining the substantial unity of the Godhead, but rather to assert that the Son shared the same divine nature as the Father, while Milton's declaration that the Son may share the Father's substance though not his whole essence prepares for precisely the opposite conclusion: it is 'a way of asserting that God's essence, always equated by Milton with the divine nature itself, is radically incommunicable to any other because it can pertain only to one hypostasis or person, the Father, and because its attributes such as Unity and Infinity can in no sense be shared.'[41] Milton does not use the term consubstantial, as Hunter admits, and it is significant that when he wishes to stress the unity of the Son with the Father he does so not in terms of a shared substratum, but rather in terms of a union in love, agreement, spirit, and glory (*Works*, XIV, 213). The Son is God 'only by proximity and love, not in essence' (*Works*, XIV, 255 – and thus, surely, not God as supreme being by substance). Henry Bullinger, stating the orthodox position in language acceptable to the Reformed, provides an illuminating comparison and contrast: 'it is sufficient for the godly simply, according to the scriptures and the apostles creed to believe and confess, that there is one divine nature or essence, wherein are the Father, the Son and the Holy Ghost. Neither is it greatly material whether ye call them substances, or subsistences or persons, so that ye do plainly express the distinctions betwixt them ... confessing ... the unity, that ye confound not the Trinity ... [42] Whatever the language, it is precisely the distinction within unity which Milton wishes to deny.

Milton's concern with the doctrine of shared substance thus pertains more directly to his theories about creation than to his notion of the bond uniting the Son and the Father. Moreover, as Woodhouse, Lewalski, and others have noted, the claim that the Son shares in the substance of the Father takes on a rather different appearance, and moves closer to the Arian view, when placed in the context of Milton's general theory of creation *de Deo*, not *ex nihilo*.[43] While Milton does not, like the Arians, hold that the Son was created out of nothing, he is close to the Arian view in his denial of a completely unique status to the relations of Father and Son. For Milton nothing can come from nothing, everything is made from matter produced from God. Thus although his terms differ from those of the Arians, his emphasis is similar. Both diminish the uniqueness of the Son's generation – the Arians by saying that the Son, like all things, was created out of nothing, Milton by saying that the Son, like all things, was created out of God.

In this connection it should be noted that Milton does not appear to view the creation of the Son as differing in kind from the rest of creation. The special term 'only begotten' he reserves for the anointing of the Son as 'Messiah' by the Father.[44] The Son, then, was created or produced or generated at a point in time by the action of God's will, the Father being under no necessity to create the Son. While the first of the creation, the Son is clearly part of the creation even though his nature is divine. The Son receives all things from the Father – 'not only the name of God and of Jehovah, but all that pertains to his own being, that is to say, his individuality, his existence itself, his attributes, his works, his divine honours' (Works, XIV, 303). As Lewalski remarks, the emphasis falls throughout 'upon the will and the conscious donation of the Father.'[45] Lacking omniscience and omnipotence, the Son performs his works of creation and recreation as the instrument of the Father. His limitations and mutability give moral significance to his freedom to choose and to respond to the Father.

Milton thus appears to depart from the definition of the Son provided by the Nicene Creed: 'the only-begotten Son of God, Begotten of His Father before all worlds, God of God, Light of Light, Very God of Very God, Begotten, not made. ... ' This conclusion accords with the sense of going against tradition which Milton conveys rhetorically throughout chapter 5. The unorthodoxy of his position stands out even more sharply if, as Kelley and Lewalski suggest, we consider the implications of the Nicene Creed in the light of the anathemas which were attached to it as a gloss on its meaning. The anathemas condemn those who deny the Son's eternity or who believe that he was created out of nothing, that he was created or had a beginning, that he is of an essence different from the Father, or that he is subject to change. This interpretation of the creed was strengthened at the Council of Constantinople, and in the Athanasian Creed the position which Milton opposes found comprehensive expression.[46] Milton, as he was very much aware, was systematically repudiating a well-established view of the Son.

Arian seems a term of real if limited use in discussions of Milton's thought. While it does not comprehend his position, it draws attention to certain important elements in his view that the Son, although divine, is a creature and thus not coessential with the Father but subordinate to him. Like the Arians, Milton emphasizes the deliberate gift of divine attributes by the Father to the Son and appears to assume that the Son is mutable, subject to change, and lacking omniscience. Of particular interest is the way the views he shares with the Arians serve to distinguish his position from that of some of the early Fathers. Thus his emphatic rejection of the emanation theory, which he sees as marked by the same kind of empty paradoxes that characterize Trinitarian thought in general, and his insistence upon will and response in his description of the Son's subordinate relation to the Father, run counter to that tradition in early Christology which sees the relation as inevitable.

There is no evidence that Milton would have labelled his position Arian (such classification he repudiated in any case by his insistence on the primacy of scripture), but he would surely have recognized the Arian elements in his doctrine of the Son. A generic sense of the term, in which it is virtually synonymous with 'anti-Trinitarianism,' was established by Milton's day, and appears in his usage of the term in his tract *Of True Religion*. The term serves to remind us of the differences between his subordinationism and, on one hand, that of certain Cambridge Platonists for whom emanationist doctrine is important, or, on the other, that of the Socinians, for whom as a rule the Son has no existence before the Incarnation.[47] Anti-Trinitarianism is another term that is appropriate to Milton's position, as Kelley has abundantly proved, calling it a 'classic instance' in its display of the commonplaces of the movement, especially 'the condemnation of the three-in-one formula as a doctrine unsupported by scripture, contrary to reason, the product of human interpretation, and maintained by such man-made terms as trinity, essence, substance, hypostasis, and person.'[48] Milton's attack on the traditional conception of the Trinity is indeed one of the central issues in his reform of dogma. To the Son, he devotes the longest and most complex chapter in his treatise, a chapter which reiterates in every possible context the belief that Son and Father are one in will but not in essence or individual identity. He is perfectly well aware that he is flying in the face of orthodoxy, that he is espousing a doctrine not found in that creed which has at present 'general acceptation' (*Works*, XIV, 177), that he is reversing the very formulae by which the orthodox of his age maintained the Trinitarian doctrine.[49] It is this very awareness which drives him tirelessly forward in his argument.

Why, one might ask, was the matter of such consuming importance to him? At least part of the answer is found in his belief that the doctrine of the Trinity is an insult to man's reason. The justification of God's ways to man is only possible if man is willing to think of God what is worthy of him. Milton's treatise is full of admonitions to think what is fitting, or suitable, or reasonable, of the deity. In the doctrine of the Trinity he found the central example of perverse speculation, of 'the deceitfulness of vain philosophy' (*Works*, XIV, 193). The advocates of the doctrine call it a mystery, he notes, but it is not so called in scripture. It is, rather, a man-made mystery, a false mystery in which reason is used to establish a position contrary to reason. Rather than forming subtle imaginations about the drama of three personalities in one Godhead, we should hold to the recognizable relationships between Father and Son which God has chosen to reveal to us (*Works*, XIV, 197, 217; XV, 265). We should, that is, be content with the images and analogues, the ordinary forms of speech and thought, by which God has accommodated himself to our imaginations.

In view of the argument of the fifth chapter as a whole, and of its polemical nature, it is surprising that the critics of *Bright Essence* have been so reluctant to accept the extreme nature of Milton's subordinationism in *De Doctrina Christiana*. Even more surprising, however, is the charge that Milton has in the treatise inadvertently stumbled into tritheism. In arguing this view, C.A. Patrides denies Milton the claim to monotheism which is so central to his treatise, and urges that by positing the participation of the Son and the Holy Spirit in the 'substantia' of the supreme Father, Milton unwittingly endorses not one but three gods.[50] But 'participation' is a misleading word here unless qualified. As we saw earlier, the divine substance is something given by the Father to the Son, and Milton does not speak of the special unity of Father and Son in terms of a substratum. All creation may in some sense be said to share the divine substance, but Milton is careful to reinforce the distinction between the Father and the Creation, even in the crucial case of the Son's Incarnation: 'if the Son be of the same essence with the Father, and the same Son after his hypostatical union coalesce in one person with man, I do not see how to evade the inference, that man also is the same person with the Father, an hypothesis which would give birth to not a few paradoxes' (*Works*, XIV, 313). Rather the Son is one with the Father in the same manner that we are one with him: 'that is, not in essence, but in love, in communion, in agreement, in charity, in spirit, in glory' (*Works*, XIV, 213). Active participation is a result of the response of the will, not an ontological given. The repeated comparison between the Son's unity in will with the Father and the unity in will with Son and Father achieved by the saints suggests that this kind of 'participation,' while making the creature more God-like, does not approximate the participation of persons in the Godhead as conceived by Trinitarians: 'Christ has received his fulness from God, in the sense in which we shall receive our fulness from Christ' (*Works*, XIV, 339).[51] If we accept Milton's claim that there is only one self-existent God, his view of the Son – and the Spirit – falls into place as a definite form of subordinationism.

No doubt Milton was aware that many problems remain, but he was not seeking a comprehensive rational formulation in his account of the Godhead. He knew that some things were beyond the scope of reason. Scripture is a sacred given: it is a sign of proper humility to recognize that some matters are beyond our ken. Yet scripture is accommodated to our minds and imaginations. To complain that Milton ignores the traditional language by which 'Father' and 'Son' are metaphors of 'transcendent reality,' as does Patrides,[52] is to overlook Milton's quest to think what is worthy of God, his effort to view scripture in the light of moral intelligence.

After the complexity of Milton's argument concerning the Trinity, his remarks on the doctrine of the Incarnation seem at first sight more traditional and relatively straightforward. There are, in fact, some difficulties even here, but these may be left until we turn to *Paradise Regained*. What is surprising is that Milton accepts the paradoxes of the Incarnation when he has repudiated those of the Trinity. The incarnate Son, he explains, has a twofold nature, being both divine and human: 'one ens, one person, is formed of this mutual hypostatic union of two natures or essences' (*Works*, XV, 271). The statement is in keeping with the orthodoxy established at the Council of Chalcedon. Milton rejects with scorn the notion that there are three persons in one Godhead, but accepts the doctrine that in Christ two natures unite in one being. The explanation for this apparent inconsistency is not far to seek. The Incarnation is a true mystery, an event that surpasses the reach of man's reason, while the Trinity is a false mystery created by human ingenuity. The basis for such a distinction is found in scripture, which speaks frequently of the mystery of the Incarnation, but never of the mystery of the Trinity (*Works*, XV, 263). Thus he does not reduce the union of the two persons in Christ to an ethical and metaphoric union, as he might have done if he had followed Nestorian tradition.[53] The union is an ontological fact, a union of substances and not merely of wills. Since it is a mystery, however, 'it behoves us to cease from devising subtle explanations, and to be contented with remaining wisely ignorant'

(*Works*, XV,273). Here, at the point where nature and the divine meet, Milton finds an event which defines the limits of human reason.

Milton's Doctrine of the Spirit

God also communicates himself through his Spirit. Milton gave much thought over the years to the work of the Spirit in illuminating the minds and liberating the wills of the regenerate. His theology of the nature of the Spirit, however, is curiously restrained and spare. Nonetheless, he says enough to indicate that in this area, also, his view of the Godhead is unorthodox. He would find completely unacceptable Calvin's assertion that all the peculiar attributes of the Godhead are ascribed to the Spirit in the same way as to the Son. He admits the existence of the Holy Spirit as a person, but somewhat grudgingly: 'the Holy Spirit, inasmuch as he is a minister of God, and therefore a creature, was created or produced of the substance of God, not by a natural necessity, but by the free will of the agent, probably before the foundations of the world were laid, but later than the Son, and far inferior to him' (*Works*, XIV, 403). Admitting that this figure is not clearly distinguished from the Son, he finds the chief mark of differentiation in the subordinate position of the Holy Spirit, who does not, like the Son, dislay the brightness of the glory of God and the express image of his person.

As in the case of the Son, *De Doctrina Christiana* reviews the passages used by Trinitarians to support the doctrine that the Holy Spirit is God, and attempts to show that their arguments are false. Milton maintains that throughout much of scripture the term *spirit* refers not to a person, but to the power and virtue of the Father, or of the Father through the Son. This is true of the entire Old Testament and much of the New. Milton's view is based on the idea that the nature and office of the Spirit were not made known until Pentecost. Promised by Jesus (Luke 24:49; 16:7), breathed into the apostles by him after his death and resurrection (John 20:22), the Spirit was poured forth in their hearts as they undertook the work of spreading the Gospel (*Works*, XIV, 373). Indeed, until the ministry of Christ, the Holy Spirit was 'not yet given, nor believed in, even by those who prophesied that it should be poured forth in the latter times' (*Works*, XIV, 363). Thus at the annunciation Joseph and Mary must have associated the Spirit with either the Father himself, or his divine power, 'inasmuch as the personality and divinity of the Holy Spirit are not acknowledged by the Jews even to the present day' (*Works*, XIV, 389).

Through much of scripture, then, the Spirit can be taken to mean the power of the Father, exerted either directly or through an intermediate such as the Son or an angel. Such power operates on occasions when there is some kind of theophany in which the divine nature is made manifest, its most characteristic function being the revelation of God through an inward voice or light that brings wisdom and spiritual gifts. Milton gives this general sense prominence in his interpretation of New Testament, as well as Old Testament, passages, finding that 'under the Gospel, what is called the Holy Spirit, or the Spirit of God, sometimes means the Father himself,' sometimes 'the virtue and power of the Father,' sometimes 'a divine impulse, or light or voice, or word, transmitted from above either through Christ ... or by some other channel.' There is also the more specific signification by which Spirit refers to 'the person itself of the Holy Spirit, or its symbol,' or to 'the donation of the Spirit itself, and of its attendant gifts' (*Works*, XIV, 363-71).

The defence of Trinitarian beliefs usually involves the assumption of a progressive element in revelation. Evidence gradually accumulated through history is gathered into a significant pattern and understood in terms of the Gospel. Milton's argument concerning the Holy Spirit stubbornly refuses to acknowledge such progressive revelation of the third person. The fact that neither David, nor Mary and Joseph, nor 'any other Hebrew, under the old covenant, believed in the personality of that "good" and "Holy Spirit"' (*Works*, XIV, 363) is used as an argument that it is not necessary to assume the operation of such a Spirit in those times. He cites Hebrews 1:1 (*Works*, XIV, 369) to urge that the term *spirit* refers to diverse, if related, phenomena: 'God at sundry times and in divers manners spake in time past unto the fathers by the prophets.' As person, the role of the Spirit is manifest in the founding and continuance of the church of Christ, particularly as this exists in the temple of the regenerate heart. It is only here that Milton finds evidence of the operation of a divine person who is distinct from Father and Son. Even so, this person remains shadowy, 'evidently ... inferior to both Father and Son, inasmuch as he is represented and declared to be subservient and obedient in all things; to have been promised, and sent, and given; to speak nothing of himself; and even to have been given as an earnest.'

Inferior to the Son, the Holy Spirit also lacks omnipresence and omnipotence. It apparently does not possess mediatorial functions, nor is it 'engaged by the obligations of a filial relation to pay obedience to the Father ... '(*Works*, XIV, 377). This latter point is particularly interesting. The Son provides a model of filial obedience, and it is through the Son that man learns the nature of his relation to the Father as it is discovered in Christian liberty. The Spirit does not have such a function. Lacking a filial role, the Spirit seems close to pure process. It is the Comforter which brings hope and the gifts necessary for the regenerate to believe and to bear witness, renewing the law on the heart, illuminating scripture. The emergence of the Holy Spirit appears to be part of the growth into renewal of man.

Emphasis by Reformed theologians on the special role of the Spirit in Gospel times is of course quite common. Even such a relatively conservative figure as John Owen, for example, begins his treatise on communion with the Holy Ghost by remarking that the foundation of such communion consists 'in his *mission*, or sending to be our *Comforter* by Jesus Christ,' and observes that the '*peculiar foundation*' lies in Jesus' words in John 15:26.[54] The difference between Milton and writers like Owen is that for him the operation of the Spirit under the Gospel is not placed within the larger context, elaborated from the whole of the Bible, that identifies the Spirit as a distinct person equal to Father and Son.

Milton's treatment of the Holy Spirit as a person is largely negative. His chapter opens by emphasizing the manifold uses of the term *spirit* in scripture, and closes by systematically denying that the Holy Spirit is God or possesses the divine attributes. By contrast, Calvin's statement of the Reformed position in the *Institutes* is throughout affirmative. Calvin argues that all the peculiar attributes of the Godhead are ascribed to the Spirit in the same way as to the Son. Omnipresent and omnipotent, the Spirit sustains, invigorates, and quickens all things both in heaven and on earth.[55] The Spirit's work of sanctification is seen by Calvin as essential to the mediatorial function of Christ, for the Spirit is the bond by which Christ effectively unites us to himself.[56] With an emphasis quite different from that of Milton, Calvin can assert that the Spirit is the author of man's regeneration, being the seed and root of heavenly life in us.[57]

Milton could hardly have mounted this attack on the orthodox doctrine without the impetus provided by such new tendencies in theology as those found in the writing of the Socinians. The *Racovian Catechism* covers much of the same ground as *De Doctrina Christiana* in its contention that 'the Holy Spirit is a virtue or energy flowing from God to men, and communicated to them: whereby he separates them from others, and consecrates them to his service.'[58] But while Milton could have found support in the *Catechism* for the doctrine that the Spirit is often the power of God,[59] the idea that it is sometimes a person ran counter to the main tendency of Socinian thought. Milton's awareness of this tendency is evident in a revealing passage in which he admonishes those Trinitarians who attribute 'to mere virtues the properties of persons' and thus furnish arguments to 'commentators who interpret the Holy Spirit as nothing more than the virtue and power of the Father' (*Works*, XIV, 399). Rather mischievously, Milton is suggesting that if his circumscribed doctrine of the Holy Spirit is rejected, the alternative most likely to gain credence is a view which denies the distinct existence of a third person altogether. It is a curious fact, however, that Milton's doctrine is very similar to that of the English Socinian, John Biddle, who maintained that it is impossible 'to embrace either the opinion of *Athanasius*, who held the holy Spirit to be a Person of supream Deity, or that of *Socinus*, who believed him to be the divine power or efficacy, but no Person. ... '[60] Exactly in the manner of Milton, Biddle argues that this person is inferior not only to the Father, but to Christ ('as man, since his exaltation'), for 'he that is given and disposed of by another, must be inferior in dignity to him that giveth him.'[61] It is a strange doctrine for Biddle to hold, since it seems out of keeping with his rejection of the pre-existent Son: but it fits quite snugly into Milton's scheme, in which the pre-existent Son holds the place of pre-eminence from the beginning of the creation. Nothing could be clearer than that Milton has departed from the orthodox view of the third person of the Trinity.

Cambridge Platonists, Socinians, and the Office of the Mediator

Efforts to explain the development of Milton's theology of the Son and Spirit in terms of his response to the Ante-Nicene fathers have not proved entirely persuasive. Milton was undoubtedly aware that some of his positions were close to those of Origen or Tertullian, but he was unwilling to appeal to merely human authority. Such an appeal was part of the armoury of the anti-Trinitarian movement, and Milton's refusal to employ this weapon is itself significant. Something, however, must be said about the relation of his thought about God to some of the more innovative or radical tendencies in the speculations of the seventeenth century.

One of the most intellectually distinguished schools of thought to reveal a preoccupation with the Trinity is that of the Cambridge Platonists, and some modern criticism, emphasizing Milton's affinities with the Cambridge school, urges that he must to some degree be included in the group.[62] This is certainly true if we have in mind the ethical emphasis that runs through the writings of the group and finds characteristic expression in the thought of Whichcote or John Smith, but the Trinitarian speculations of men like Henry More and Ralph Cudworth are another matter altogether. Both these philosophers set out to reveal a correlation between the Christian Trinity and the Trinity of the Neo-Platonists. Their aim is to prove that the truths of Christian revelation were accessible, although in a dark and confused manner, to natural theologians who either lived before Christ or were unaware of Christianity. Such a correlation, they felt, would secure the doctrine of the Trinity from the charge of irrationality. There is, of course, an historical aspect to the argument as well. According to Cudworth, the true Christian Trinity had been revealed to Moses, and through him to Plato, but the later Platonists adulterated the doctrine.[63] Both Cudworth and More are impressed by the element of subordinationism in the Trinity of the pagan philosophers, and they agree that the crucial passages concerning the Son in the Athanasian Creed should be interpreted generously in order to permit the Christian Platonist to retain an element of subordinationism.[64]

Superficially, their aim has something in common with Milton's, and it is obviously important that such speculation was in progress at Cambridge during the period. But it is a mistake, I think, to find in the work of these Platonists a very close parallel to Milton's views. In the first place, the Neo-Platonic conception of the necessary and eternal emanation of the second person from the first, and of the third from the second, is quite unlike Milton's creationist view. For Milton, as we have seen, the Son was created at a particular time by an act of volition on the part of the Father. The whole thrust of his interpretation supports the importance of will in the divine economy. Not only is there no trace of the Neo-Platonic One-Soul-Mind terminology in his discussion, but he is even chary of employing the traditional Logos terminology in connection with the Son.

Secondly, Milton would never appeal to the philosophers in a matter of this kind. It is particularly instructive to consider the gap which separates his view of this subject from that of Henry More. The core of their differences can be found in their contrasting attitudes towards mystery. While Milton was bringing his treatise on Christian doctrine to fulfilment, More was writing *An Explanation of the grand Mystery of Godliness*, a work which contains a sustained plea for the reinstatement of the concept of mystery in theology. More takes his stand in opposition to the kind of rationalism and biblicism represented by the Socinians. His theme is that 'perpetual expectation' arouses wonder and respect. What does it matter, he asks, 'if the bottom of the Well be fathomless, if the Water we reach be but pure and useful? ... those that contend for such an *absolute plainess and clearness in all points of Religion*, shew more of clownishness and indiscretion then of wit and judgment taking it very ill that anything in The Mysterie of Godliness should be so *mysterious*, as that their conceited *Reason* should not be able to comprehend it.'[65]

The whole emphasis here is alien to Milton, who accepts in a fairly extreme form the Protestant dictum that the scripture is plain and perspicuous in all things necessary to salvation.[66] In More's view, however, the very lack of definition is stimulating. The Christian philosopher 'conceives a peculiar pleasure' in the 'confused divination or obscure representation of things.'[67] He becomes an initiate, penetrating ever further into an intelligible but inexhaustible mystery, finding spiritual nourishment in the very process of learning. And chief among the great inexhaustible mysteries are the doctrines of '*the Triunity of the Godhead* and *the Divinity of Christ.*'[68] More's approach, then, presents a paradigm of those methods which Milton rejects. His love of mysteries is representative of the kind of gnosticism that Milton resists at every turn, and that he seeks to eliminate by his doctrine that God accommodates his truth to the imagination of man. Mysteries, Milton implies, are never fit subjects for meditation: thus, as we have seen, the Trinity is a false, man-made mystery, while the Incarnation, precisely because it is a true mystery, is forbidden as a subject of speculation. There is little doubt that when More chastised those who seek 'absolute plainess and clearness' in religion he had in mind the Socinians, and it is probable that he was thinking of the most prominent of the English Socinians, John Biddle. Biddle's attitude to mysteries is quite uncompromising, and strongly reminiscent of Milton's. He considers the false mystery of the Trinity an error which endangers the whole structure of Reformed doctrine. Turning the tables on More, he argues that the Trinity is a pagan mystery which was produced by the influence of the Platonic philosophers on the early church. The Council of Nicea, he maintains, was 'beholding to the Platonists' for the notion of the coessentiality of the three persons of the Trinity, and for overlaying the simple meaning of the Gospel with high and witty notions that obscure the true humanity of Christ.[69] Henry More is singled out by Biddle for particular criticism as an example of the kind of Platonist who scorns the plain and certain word of God in favour of mystical interpretations.[70]

Milton, I suggest, is much closer in his views to the Socinianism of Biddle than to the Platonism of More. The whole tenor of Biddle's approach to the mystery of the Trinity, with his unflagging determination to 'assert nothing ... but onely introduce the Scripture faithfully uttering its own assertions,'[71] is reminiscent of Milton. The attempt to associate Milton with Socinianism has been criticized on the ground that the English Socinians were 'relatively unimportant writers who never achieved any real intellectual leadership.'[72] But such a view does not take into account the pervasiveness of Socinian ideas in the period, the influence which such ideas exerted over writers who sympathized but were not converts, and the prestige lent to the movement by the scholarship of its continental exponents. Biddle himself was a school teacher, a humanist, and a man prepared to suffer with patience for his beliefs, and Milton could hardly have failed to sympathize with him. Attempts to show the direct influence of particular Socinian writers on Milton have proved inconclusive,[73] but there can be little doubt, I think, that the movement exercised a profound and lasting influence upon him.

During his Italian journey Milton paused at Sienna, where Faustus Socinus was born a century earlier. It would not be surprising if during those conversations with 'many persons of rank and learning' in Florence, there was mention o the Siennese nobleman whose sect was now flooding Europe with literature. It was on the same journey, it is worth remembering, that he met 'the learned Hugo Grotius,' whose liberal theology caused him to be repeatedly associated with Socinianism.[74] Although the exact point at which Milton became aware of Socinianism is in doubt, definite evidence exists to prove that by 1650 he had come into contact with the seminal work of the movement in England, the *Racovian Catechism*, which was reissued in a Latin edition in 1651, and in a free English translation, almost certainly by Biddle, in 1652.[75] His familiarity with Socinian attitudes is evident throughout his theological treatise,[76] and it appears probable that he included them among those 'heretics, so called,' whose views, he maintains, are frequently closer to the truth of scripture than are the views of those considered orthodox (*Works*, XIV, 15).

There was good reason for Milton's interest in the Socinians. They, too, were constructing a theodicy and justifying God's ways to men. They, too, developed doctrine in response to a double pressure – the demand that it be scriptural, and the demand that it be rational. Passing from Milton's *De Doctrina Christiana* to the *Racovian Catechism* of the Socinians, one experiences a shock of recognition. Not only is their approach to the Bible very similar to Milton's, but they are like him in their frequent admonitions to think of God what is morally worthy of him. It is not surprising, then, that both works give prominence to the same doctrines, and especially to those concerned with the nature of Christ. Yet when we turn to particular issues, the gulf which separates Milton from the Socinians becomes increasingly evident.

The principle which informs Socinian theology in the *Racovian Catechism* is that of combating the Calvinist emphasis on grace, with its corollaries of predestination and saving faith. This revision of doctrine leads into three main areas of controversy. First, the Socinians reject the doctrine of the Trinity. The *Catechism* maintains, as does Milton, that this doctrine is both unscriptural and contrary to reason.[77] Secondly, they reject the doctrine of the pre-existence of the Son. Christ, they argue, was the 'first born of every creature' only in the sense that he was the first man to be made new under the Gospel. He was, indeed, fully human, possessing neither divine power nor divine knowledge in himself, and whatever supernatural qualities he revealed in his acts were received as a gift from the Father.[78] Basically, then, the Socinian treatise urges the heresy known as Ebionism or Photinism: Christ was an unusually good man who received divine favour because of his merit. His chief function is exemplary.

This attack on the idea of Christ's divinity, however, leads on to a third major departure from orthodoxy. Protestant thought concerning the atonement made by Christ had become unusually rigid, inflexible, and uniform. From Luther and Calvin to Ussher and Lancelot Andrewes, Protestant theologians insisted on interpreting the atonement in terms of the doctrine of satisfaction.[79] Man, it was held, is incapable of making expiation for sin, and for this reason the Son of God became his substitute and paid the penalty which he had incurred. In his death, Christ bore the punishment due to man's sin, and consequently satisfied divine justice. The Socinian aims find their fullest realization in the rejection of this satisfaction doctrine. It is, they argued, a doctrine which presents an unworthy picture of God, for it shows him unable to forgive sin freely and it introduces an absurd conflict between his attributes of justice and mercy. Moreover, the doctrine takes away the motive for moral action. If the satisfaction made by Christ is perfect, then man need not contribute anything. Indolence may go hand in hand with virtue. Thus their argument ends by urging that men should imitate Christ, rather than rely on his imputed merit.

Milton's theology, I believe, was shaped to a significant extent by his response to Socinian thought. The movement must have held for him the value of a touchstone for theology which, while not without mystical elements, is oriented towards man, and which places a strong emphasis on moral values. He used it, perhaps, as a counterpoise for Calvinism, with its emphasis on faith and on grace. The humane God of the Socinians acted as a foil to the awesome deity of the Calvinists. Yet Milton was quite deliberately avoiding both extremes, and as he on one hand revised and modified Calvinist doctrine, so, on the other, he distinguished his view at point after point from that of the Socinians.

With the Socinian rejection of the concept of a Trinity he is in general agreement, and much of the detail of his argument finds a close parallel in the *Catechism*. But he has no sympathy with their conception of the Son: 'certain it is' he writes, 'whatever some of the moderns may allege to the contrary, that the Son existed in the beginning, under the name of logos or word, and was the first of the whole creation, by whom afterwards all other things were made' (*Works*, XIV, 181). He is careful to make it clear that the biblical phrase 'the first born of every creature' refers to the first being created by God, and he mocks the subtleties of those who seek to deny the pre-existence of the Son in order to maintain his 'merely human nature' (*Works*, XV, 263). That pre-existent Son, moreover, possesses in Milton's view a share of divine substance, and when he becomes incarnate his nature is twofold, both divine and human. At every stage Milton is deliberately excluding the Socinian position, and embracing the view they characterize as Arian.[80]

It is in his handling of the doctrine of Christ's satisfaction, however, that Milton takes the greatest pains to distinguish himself from the Socinians. He clearly has them in mind when he writes of those who, evading the evidence of scripture,'maintain that Christ died, not in our stead, and for our redemption, but merely for our advantage in the abstract, and as an example to mankind' (*Works*, XV, 317-19). His own position, set forth both in poetry and prose, was perfectly orthodox.[81] As

But this is a notorious doctrine of Pelagius (see Vossius).

(the Father explains during the council in heaven in book 3 of *Paradise Lost*, Adam and his whole posterity must die as a result of the Fall,

> Dye hee or Justice must; unless for him
> Som other able, and as willing, pay
> The rigid satisfaction, death for death. (210-12)

The entire council, indeed, rises to a climax in the revelation of the Son's role as ransom, and one cannot escape the conclusion that this was a doctrine of peculiar importance to the poet.

In his reform of doctrine, Milton's method often recalls the rational biblicism of the Socinians and Erastians. His rejection of emanationist ideas, and his refusal to employ pagan philosophers when he can draw on the light from above expressed through scripture, set him at a distance from the more metaphysically minded Cambridge Platonists. Like the Socinians, he was disinclined to meditate on mysteries, but sought a religion based on scripture and regenerate reason which would provide an image of God in harmony with the highest ethical ideals and practices. Milton reveals one of the deepest strains in his thinking when he remarks in a relatively early tract, *The Doctrine and Discipline of Divorce*, that in the law God appears to man 'as it were in human shape ... gives himself to be understood by men, judges and is judged, measures and is commensurat to right reason ... ' (*Works*, III, iii. 440). Yet Milton was not prepared to follow the Socinians in their depreciation of the supernatural elements in religion and their exclusive insistence on the doctrine of clear ethical import. Against such views he maintained the pre-existence of the Son, the dual nature of the incarnate Christ, and the doctrine of satisfaction. The result is a theological position which offers parallels to the thought of the age, but remains a distinctive and individual statement.[82]

Following the course of Milton's reaction against the Socinian theology, we might be tempted to feel that he has, at least temporarily, abandoned his effort to accommodate the theology of the Son to human values. His legalistic formulation of the satisfaction doctrine seems in particular to be at odds with the spirit of rational interpretation. The necessary sacrifice of the Son draws attention to something in the Father which is difficult to assess in terms of man's principles and rules, and the conflict of justice and mercy cannot be easily placed within a framework of purely human values. The Son's redemptive act is in any case an act which man cannot imitate; whereas it reconciles God to

[Handwritten margin notes:]

(a) Note that mercy comes into M's theodicy because in M's traditional account it is simply revenge (retributive justice) sidetracked. If mercy meant justice forborne or unpursued, then it wd mean injustice. Mercy & justice somehow have to coincide. Another solution wd be to revise the idea of justice --but M isn't up to defying the story-- only to deforming it, even where it's indefensible

(b) Xp is capable of growth but not of sin. Why are A and E given another kind of freedom? Isn't X's good enough?

(c)

man, it also emphasizes man's helplessness, his inability to atone for sin, his dependence on grace.

But satisfaction is for Milton only one function of the Son's work of mediation. The other major function is the renewal of the image of God in man. These two major aspects of the work of the Son are of course central to much Christian theology. In Romans, one of the touchstones for comment on the subject, St Paul first emphasizes the idea of free justification by grace through the redemption that is in Christ (chapters 3-5), and then explores the way in which the Spirit of Christ works in the sons of God (chapters 6-8). As J.I. Packer observes, Calvin follows this Pauline sequence, adding to the thought of Christ *for* us that of Christ *in* us: 'In Christ we are justified (pardoned and accepted), adopted, given access to our heavenly Father, and progressively changed into Christ's image through self-denial and works of love.'[83] It is interesting that Calvin seeks to stress both sides of what he calls the twofold benefit derived through faith in Christ – the reconciliation with the Father and regeneration. Repeatedly he insists that 'Christ is not outside us but dwells within us. Not only does he cleave to us by an indivisible bond of fellowship, but with a wonderful communion, day by day, he grows more and more into one body with us, until he becomes completely one with us.'[84] The very shape of the *Institutes* makes a point about this issue, for the discussion of justification (III, xi) comes after the treatment of regeneration (II, vi, xvi-xvii). The effect of this order (which was followed also by Milton) is to emphasize the integration of the two aspects of the Son's work of mediation.

In the controversies of the earlier seventeenth century, it proved increasingly difficult to preserve in harmony the twofold emphasis. Anthony Tuckney, a Calvinist member of the Westminster Assembly who attempted to uphold the primacy of Faith agains the liberalizing movement inspired by his former pupil at Cambridge, Benjamin Whichcote, complains about the attitude to the atonement taken by Whichcote and his associates. He understood Whichcote to maintain that the reconciliation 'doth not operate on God, but on Us ... Divinity, which my heart riseth against.'[85] But Whichcote responds by arguing that Christ is both an advocate for man, and a principle of grace within him. Those men flatter themselves, he writes, 'who thinke of reconcili-ation with God, by means of a Saviour, acting upon God in their behalfe, and not also working in or upon them, to make them God-like.' Both aspects of the work of Christ are important, but the first, his satisfaction for man's sins, is something that can be known once and for all by a 'thorowe consideration,' while the second, man's transformation into the 'spirit[,] image and nature' of Christ, is a continuing process within each individual.[86]

Milton, too, stresses that the Son is a true mediator who exercises his influence on man as well as God, and he does so with a self-conscious deliberation which suggests that he is fully aware of the kind of difficulty exemplified by the Tuckney-Whichcote debate. Throughout *De Doctrina Christiana* he consistently envisages the Son's mediation as involving two main ojects. The first, as we have seen, is the reconciliation of God to man, and this the Son accomplishes by fulfilling the law and paying the required price. His second object is the renovation of man, 'that we may be conformed to the image of Christ, as well in his state of humiliation as of exaltation' (*Works*, XV, 333). Regeneration is thus a process both external and internal. Externally, it takes the form of justification – because of the satisfaction made by Christ, his merit is imputed to man through faith. Internally, it takes the form of the restoration of the image of God in the believer. The understanding is restored in great part to its primitive clearness, and the will to its primitive liberty, by the new spiritual life in Christ (*Works*, XVI, 5).[87] This distinction, handled with the greatest care by Milton throughout his treatise, enables him to describe the Son both as an outward Saviour and as an inward principle of new life. Preserving the distinction between formal doctrine of satisfaction and the inward realization of Christ, Milton would have agreed with Whichcote that the Son of God is 'A principle of divine life within us, as well as a Saviour without us.'[88]

CHAPTER THREE

The Spirit and the Son
in Epic Poetry

My study of the Spirit and the Son in the epics will make some use of *De Doctrina Christiana* as a gloss on specific passages. The fact that the treatise can be used in this way does not mean that the poetry exists for the purpose of stating Milton's theological beliefs. *Paradise Lost* and *Paradise Regained* are not polemical and do not engage in theological controversy. The treatment of religion in the poetry seems designed to transcend divisive issues as far as possible, and to rise above party lines. Nor was there for Milton as Christian anything hypocritical in this tactic, which is in keeping with the genial mood of his preface to the most controversial chapter of *De Doctrina Christiana*, the chapter on the Son: 'I impose my authority on no one, but merely propose what I think more worthy of belief than the creed in general acceptation' (*Works*, XIV, 177). In that age of doctrinal conflict, intelligent men were frequently grateful that salvation does not hang on the niceties of theological definition, and Milton the theologian was under no obligation to trepan Milton the poet into using *Paradise Lost* as a vehicle for correcting the errors of the age.[1]

The history of the response of readers to *Paradise Lost* suggests that while the poem offers a distinctive and challenging representation of God, it does not strike even the theologically minded reader as being heterodox in an explicit manner. The early critics provide a particularly interesting witness, since they lacked *De Doctrina*. On the whole, they do not seem to have been greatly disturbed by problems respecting the poet's orthodoxy, although there are occasional symptoms of unease. John Toland, in his *Life* (1698), declined to defend Milton's poems against 'those People who brand 'em with Heresy and Impiety; for to

[handwritten margin note: False di-chotomy. PL is non-partisan yet polemical; there is a common enemy]

incur the Displeasure of certain ignorant and supercilious Critics, argues free thinking, accurat writing, and a generous Profession of Truth.'[2] This apology indicates that complaints about Milton's religious views continued to supplement complaints about his politics. The divorce tracts no doubt provided fuel. Toland was notorious as a deist, however ('a poor creature in all respects' according to Bishop Warburton),[3] and his eulogy of Milton as a free thinker was hardly likely to allay suspicions.

Milton's treatment of the Son caused some suspicion. Charles Leslie, a staunch opponent of Socinianism and deism, argued in his 'Preface to *The History of Sin and Heresy*' (1698) that Milton in *Paradise Lost* (5.600ff) tends towards theological aberration through his invention of the story of the day in heaven on which the Son is declared lord and king of the angels.[4] In 1704 John Dennis concluded that Milton 'was a little tainted with Socinianism, for ... 'tis evident that he look'd upon the Son of God as a created Being.'[5] Defoe, influenced perhaps by Leslie, decided (1726) that in his account of the begetting of the Son, 'Milton is not orthodox' but 'lays an avowed foundation for the corrupt doctrine of Arius, which says, there was a time when Christ was not the Son of God.'[6] Jonathan Richardson, the portrait painter, referred (1734) to a 'Conjecture which Some have made; I mean that *Milton* was an *Arian*; and This is built on Certain Passages in *Par. Lost*.' But Richardson anticipates much modern criticism in his reflection that some of those questionable passages 'are very Capable of Orthodox Construction, as All of them are for Ought I know.' Taking refuge in his own theological innocence and in the opinion of orthodox divines who have approved the poem (two of them 'very Lately'), he decides it is best to assume that the poet continued to the last to be faithful to the Trinitarian God invoked in the prayer at the close of his tract *Of Reformation*.[7] Once again there is the suggestion of a continuing current of criticism, perhaps partly oral, directed at Milton's attitude to the Trinity. In 1738-9 there was a flurry of concern about the subject in the *Gentleman's Magazine*. 'Theophilus' maintained that Milton 'has certainly adopted the *Arian* Principle into his *Paradise Lost*,' and although he does not explain precisely why he thinks so, his attack on the poet's sensualizing of spiritual truths and mingling of fiction and religion suggests that his opinion resembles Leslie's. 'Philo-Spec' replies by praising Milton for filling his story with 'so many surprizing Incidents, which bear so close an Analogy with what is delivered in holy Writ.'[8] The exchange continues, but while it throws an interesting light on eighteenth-century views of fiction, it does not bring us closer to the proof of Milton's Arianism. A decade later Thomas Newton notes that some have inclined to consider Milton an Arian, but concludes of Milton's supposed Arianism that 'there are more express passages in this work to overthrow this opinion than any there are to confirm it.'[9] By 1779, Dr Johnson can argue that the poet appears 'to have been untainted by any heretical peculiarity of opinion.'[10]

Thus for about seventy-five years after its publication, *Paradise Lost* raised a mutter of protest against its theology and specifically against its treatment of the Son. It is not much, particularly in an age of such theological nicety. Moreover the critics are not really certain whether the troublesome passages represent theological conviction or difficulties arising from the fiction. Leslie seems to treat the elevation of the Son in book 5 as an unintentional gaffe, the work of a bungler, not a heretic. On the whole, the poetry appears to have been relatively successful in escaping from theological controversy. John Shawcross observes that the question of Milton's Arianism is little discussed after 1739 until the publication of *De Doctrina Christiana* in 1825, 'when, as if for the first time, the possibility of Milton's having subscribed to anti-Trinitarianism arose.'[11]

The history of the response of readers to Milton's treatment of the Godhead should warn us against viewing the poem as a covert attempt to preach the unorthodox ideas of the theological treatise. Had this been Milton's aim, we should have to judge that he failed completely to accomplish it. Even modern critics, who possess the treatise, have been unable to agree whether the poetry emphasizes or suppresses some of the poet's more distinctive views. A crucial principle was asserted by Balachandra Rajan in 1947 when he observed that Milton 'does not consider *Paradise Lost* as a means of expounding a theological system which he would expound more openly in less dangerous circumstances.'[12] Milton is writing poetry, and his decisions concerning what to present and how to present it are made on artistic grounds. But it should be emphasized that this poet also believes in scripture as a comprehensive body of living truth about the condition of man. It is unlikely that he would treat as 'incidental'[13] any truth he believed to be based on scripture, even though it departed from orthodoxy. The problem, then, is to see how we are to reconcile his belief in the significance of scripture with his sense of the method and aim of poetry.

One kind of answer to this question begins by noting that the poetry, like the treatise, is filled with scriptural quotation and allusion.

According to this explanation, the poet ignores his own distinctive views, and allows scripture to speak for itself. Belief, whether orthodox or unorthodox, fades 'in a background of incantation,' or is covered 'by the flow of his verse and by Biblical language.'[14] The language and imagery of the poem evoke an orthodoxy which is more powerful than the poet's heresies. His biblical terms may be said to be 'hostages' to a theological system which he repudiates with his intellect.[15] Yet this way of proceeding begins to sound very unlike Milton, the poet of choice, the poet of deliberate and controlled artistry. If the quotations from the Bible 'reverberate orthodoxy,'[16] they surely do so only to the orthodox ear, not to that of the reader who comes to the poem in a more questioning mood, perhaps with *De Doctrina* fresh in mind. Milton's long effort to drive his readers from an implicit faith should prevent us from resting in traditional assumptions.[17]

While the poetry asks the reader to respond to the richness and variety of scripture, the poet does not take refuge in neutrality himself. The poetry, as Woodhouse observed, is positive in its affirmations.[18] These affirmations include beliefs about God's relation with man through creation and redemption, and about his sustaining providence. Although compressed biblical citation often brings with it the complexity and ambiguity of the Bible, not all interpretations are equally sound; the poem builds on right interpretations. These interpretations emerge from particular passages and both contribute to and draw strength from the larger patterns of judgment and decision through which the poet brings the reader. The reader seeks to follow the poet, and to live through the poem's argument. At the heart of the process is the basic principle of Milton's theodicy by which reason seeks to draw from scripture (internal as well as external) what is worthy of God as the highest moral nature. It is a principle repeatedly and explicitly invoked in *De Doctrina Christiana*, and it shapes the strategy by which the judgment of the reader is activated in *Paradise Lost*. Only by thinking of God in this way can man realize the godlike elements within himself.

Milton's avoidance of divisive formulations, then, is consistent with his aim of presenting Father, Son, and Spirit as beings who arouse in the reader the right kinds of response. In this Milton is doing something perfectly characteristic – pushing back behind the elaborate credal formulations to recreate in imaginative and concrete terms the subject matter of which they are but formal interpretations. His explicit comment, while pointing to his distinctive views, does so in a way that leaves the door open for more conventional interpretations. But the implied comment – and this must include what is conveyed by recurrent emphasis, by selection and omission, and by precise discriminations of feeling and sympathy – provides an imaginative experience that is designed to induce in the reader a correct set of responses to the Godhead.

And so my earlier conclusion stands in need of some modification: while the poet is under no obligation to justify the abstract conclusions of the theologian, he nonetheless seeks to present a renewed vision of God at another level, the level of aesthetic and literary experience. Nor is the poem hidden propaganda, filling the mind with conventional pieties while attacking feeling subliminally. On the contrary, Milton's treatment of God is a remarkably honest and open dramatization, and it provides the guidance of strong and significant pattern without hamstringing the reader's response by overly conceptual or too particular definitions and articles of belief.

In a sense, Milton was too successful. His poem has played such a continuous part in shaping English religious attitudes that we are in danger of missing the originality of his treatment of God. It stands out clearly, however, when the God of *Paradise Lost* is compared with other Renaissance or Reformation treatments of deity in prose or poetry. No doubt this distinctive quality arises partly from the fact that his poem is an epic (although some of the contemporaries who offer comparison were also handling heroic convention), but it also expresses certain deep-rooted convictions.

What might be called negative evidence, the omission of certain customary themes, is of some importance in shaping our reactions. An illustration of this can be found in the contrast between Milton's treatment of the Incarnation and his treatment of Father, Son, and Spirit. John Owen gave expression to the anxieties of the orthodox of the time when he wrote that 'the disbelief of the Mysteries of the *Trinity, and the Incarnation of the Son of God*, the sole Foundation of Christian Religion, is so diffused in the World, as that it hath almost devoured the power and vitals of it.'[19] The rejection of mystery became by the turn of the century one of the arguments of deists and Unitarians, although for somewhat different reasons.[20] We have already seen how Milton restricts the scope of mystery, insisting that biblical sanction is necessary for the identification of mysteries, and maintaining that the Trinity is on this authority wrongly identified as a mystery and the Incarnation rightly so. This distinction is reflected in *Paradise Lost*. In his account of the Incarnation of the Son in book 3, the Father clearly asserts the paradox of the Incarnation by which the Son will join divine and human nature, 'Son both of God and Man'(316). The same mysterious doctrine is stated more briefly by Michael in the final book of the poem (368-9). But one looks in vain for a complementary statement of the theme of the three persons in one God. There are, of course, a number of passages stressing the perfection with which the Son expresses the Father (most of them, as we shall see, intimating that this is a voluntary arrangement, a union of wills), but there is no extended passage clearly stating or celebrating the Trinity.

This fact becomes more remarkable when we remind ourselves of what an inevitable theme the Trinity provides in the religious poetry of the period.[21] Examples press in from all sides, and can be taken from the work of major poets of widely differing background and persuasion. Impressive treatments are found in the poetry of Dante, Spenser, and Tasso. While the Incarnation offered a more accessible theme to the religious poets of the seventeenth century, most paid their respects to that other, even more completely ineffable, mystery, the 'knottie Trinitie.'[22] Donne, Jonson, Herbert, Vaughan, and William Drummond provide obvious examples. The high churchman Joseph Beaumont sounds out the mystery in *Psyche* as he describes the triumphant return of the Son to heaven after his death and resurrection:

> *Three radiant Chairs of awful beauty* there
> Stand founded on secure *Eternity;*
> Which with such *mystick art united* are
> That 'tis *intirely One, as well as Three;*
> *Three equal and distinguish'd Seats, yet one*
> *Essential and everlasting Throne.*
>
> Down in the *midst the Father sate,* and on
> His *left hand* his all-quickning *Spirit;* but
> He at his *right* enthron'd his *mighty Son.* ... [23]

Even Milton approaches the subject in the opening of the *Nativity*, in the prayer in *Of Reformation* ('one *Tri-personall* GODHEAD'), and in the prayer to the Son as the 'ever-begotten light, and perfect Image of the Father' in *Animadversions upon the Remonstrants Defense against Smectymnuus* (*Works*, III, i, 76, 146). In these earlier years he appears to have given intellectual assent to Trinitarian orthodoxy, and thus in *Of*

Prelatical Episcopacy he condemned Tertullian for making 'an imparity' between God the Father and 'God the Son' (*Works*, III, i, 97).

It is all the more remarkable, then, that Milton nowhere gives whole-hearted expression to this topos in *Paradise Lost* or *Paradise Regained*. The mystery of the Incarnation is clearly established in *Paradise Lost*, but that of diversity within the unity of the Trinity is neglected. That Milton managed this without drawing more suspicion upon his theology in an age of intense concern for the articles of the faith is testimony to his narrative skill, which creates a strong sense of inevitability and propriety. The omission is symptomatic, however, and should prevent us from thinking that in its treatment of theological issues *Paradise Lost* 'is the poetry of Milton's age generally, not the expression of his personal belief.'[24] If the poem is representative – or better, expressive – of the age in which it was written, it is so in a distinctive and individual way.

The Spirit: Forms of Divine Power

Three radiant thrones shine out at the climax of Beaumont's account of the return of the Son to heaven, and there are three places at 'Heav'ns high council-table' in Benlowe's *Theophila*.[25] Milton's heaven appears to contain only two thrones. In *De Doctrina Christiana*, Milton argues that scripture nowhere expressly teaches the doctrine of the divinity of the Spirit, not even in such passages as those 'where God is either described or introduced as sitting upon his throne' (*Works*, XIV, 379). The easiest observation to make about the Godhead in *Paradise Lost* is that there is no clear role for the Holy Spirit as a distinct person, and, in this respect, the poem agrees with the theological treatise while avoiding its explicit and controversial language.

As we have seen, Milton holds that through much of scripture, both in the Old and New Testaments, the term *spirit* refers to the power and virtue of the Father, or of the Father through the Son. The Holy Spirit as a person, divine but inferior to the Son, appears for the first time in the New Testament as the Comforter who illuminates the faithful and sustains the church. In *Paradise Lost*, the Holy Spirit as subordinate person is revealed in the history of the foundation and development of the church in book 12. There Michael explains that the Son will send the Spirit to dwell within his followers, guiding them into all truth, and protecting them with 'spiritual Armour' (12.491). The first outpouring upon the apostles at Pentecost will be exceptional, enabling them to 'speak all Tongues, and do all Miracles' so that they can 'evangelize the Nations' (499-501). When the apostles die, they leave 'thir doctrine and thir story' in written form, and these records can now only be understood by that Spirit which, as *De Doctrina Christiana* put the same point, 'originally dictated them'(*Works*, XVI, 271). Throughout this section of his prophetic story, the angel repeatedly emphasizes the Spirit of God which was promised to all believers by the Son (John 15:26) and which is the source of grace, truth, and liberty. Closely linked with Father and Son, it seems here to be a distinct power, the Comforter, although the angel avoids identifying it as a distinct person or divine creature, and characterizes its presence in terms of enlightenment and living faith. The 'pouring' of the Spirit upon the followers of Christ might remind us of the outpourings from the Father received by the Son in earlier scenes. Nonetheless, we are in this passage (12.485-533) close to the third divine person as described in *De Doctrina Christiana*.

Throughout the rest of *Paradise Lost*, the term *spirit* is normally used in a way which recalls Milton's more general definition. Most, if not all, uses of the term can be easily accounted for in terms of the general sense in which *spirit* refers to the exercise of the divine influence of the Father, or of the Father through the Son. There are certainly points at which Milton's preference for this interpretation is expressed by omission, as when he neglects to mention the Holy Spirit in describing the conception of Jesus:

> A Virgin is his Mother, but his Sire
> The Power of the most High. ...
> (12.368-9; and again, 377-82)

So, too, there is no reference to the Spirit in the allusion to the 'wondrous birth' during the council in heaven (3.285). By contrast, other poets tend to choose this moment to celebrate the operation of the Holy Spirit, as Beaumont does in *Psyche*:

> For now that *Spirit* which first quickned her
> Return'd, and took his seat in *Mary's* breast.
> O what Excess of sweets and pleasure bare
> Him company into his virgin nest!
> O what pure streams of light, what glorious showers
> Of most prolific and enlivening Powers?[26]

But Milton's emphasis is quite in keeping with the argument of *De Doctrina Christiana* that the Sprit referred to at the annunciation is not to be understood 'with reference to his own person alone' (that person was in any case unknown to Joseph and Mary at the time), but principally with reference to the Father (*Works*, XIV, 389). It is notable that in *Paradise Regained* the references to the conception of the Son clearly follow the same pattern with one exception. Thus Jesus reports that his mother said to him 'Thy Father is the Eternal King' (1.236), and later Mary herself refers to 'that honour high / To have conceiv'd of God' (2.66-7). There is one passage, however, in which the conception is associated with the Holy Ghost, if ambiguously. The Father speaks to Gabriel:

> I begin
> To verifie that solemn message late,
> On which I sent thee to the Virgin pure
> In *Galilee*, that she should bear a Son
> Great in Renown, and call'd the Son of God;
> Then toldst her doubting how these things could be
> To her a Virgin, that on her should come
> The Holy Ghost, and the power of the highest
> O're-shadow her. ... (1.132-40)

But the passage from Luke 1:35 which Milton here paraphrases is one in which according to *De Doctrina Christiana* the Holy Ghost means the Father. The poem preserves the parallelism of phrasing by which in the Gospel 'power of the Highest' seems to interpret 'Holy Ghost.' It is symptomatic that Milton uses Luke's version rather than the alternative offered in Matthew 1:20, and in *De Doctrina Christiana* he notes that while in both passages Holy Ghost is 'without the customary article,' the Angel speaks 'in a more circumstantial manner in St. Luke' (*Works*, XIV, 389-91). The simpler statement in Matthew ('that which is conceived in her is of the Holy Ghost'), appears closer to the formulation of the Nicene Creed. Thus even in this exceptional passage the Holy Ghost may be taken as the power of the Father.

The scenes in *Paradise Lost* presenting Father and Son provide evidence of Milton's belief that the Spirit frequently signifies the virtue and power of the Father. This is particularly true of those revelations of power through the Son that occur at crucial points in the divine action. Thus after the Son's heroic offer to act as man's ransom during the council in heaven, the angel choir praises him as the manifestation of the Father:

> on thee
> Impresst the effulgence of his Glorie abides,
> Transfus'd on thee his ample Spirit rests.   (3.388-9)

Kelley's doubt that the Holy Spirit is here intended strikes me as justified.[27] Earlier in this scene the Son has been described as the 'radiant image' of the Father's glory (63), and the Father has spoken of him as 'alone / My word, my wisdom, and effectual might' (169-70). The reference to the Father's gift of his ample Spirit appears in this context to be simply another way of describing the spiritual gifts bestowed by God upon him. As in the passage on the Holy Ghost in *Paradise Regained*, parallelism hints at the right interpretation, suggesting that 'ample Spirit' is a variation of 'the effulgence of his Glorie,' and this point is given an interesting gloss by a passage in *De Doctrina Christiana* which states that Holy Spirit can imply 'that light which was shed on Christ himself' (*Works*, XIV, 363). And as Milton asks in this theological work (albeit in relation to a different scriptural passage), 'what could the Spirit confer on Christ, from whom he was himself to be sent, and to receive all things' (Works, XIV, 367).

The cryptic allusion is in any case not sufficient to evoke the idea of a third person participating in a heavenly triad. Any other poet of the period would surely have articulated the angels' song into three parts, reserving one for the Spirit, while Milton's anthem celebrates only Father and Son. Although the Trinitarian is free to read the passage in his own terms – for Milton as we have observed does not wish to use his poem to argue credal formulations – the emphasis of the passage subordinates Spirit to the Father's exercise of power and preserves at an experiential level the true relations of Father and Son as Milton understands them from scripture.

The next references to the transfer of divine power occur during the story of the begetting of the Son and his victory over the rebels. Throughout these two passages there are no significant references to the Spirit, that is, no references that evoke the idea of the third person of the traditional Trinity. The Father, we learn, permitted the war in Heaven in order to fulfil his purpose of honouring the Son, declaring 'All power on him transferr'd' (6.678). Instructing the Son concerning this epiphany, he remarks, 'Into thee ... Virtue and Grace / Immense I have transfus'd ... ' (6.703-4). As the Son sets out in the paternal chariot at the head of his army of faithful angels, 'Before him Power Divine his way prepar'd' (780). These are all ways of saying that the Spirit of the Father is expressed in the Son. It is in this sense that I would also understand the chariot of paternal deity which is 'instinct with Spirit' (752) and the four cherubic shapes in whom 'One Spirit ... ruled' (6.848). Virtue and power of the Father have been conferred upon the Son.

At the creation of the new universe the transfer of power is again stressed, and on this occasion there are several interesting references to the Spirit. Directing the Son to the work of creation, the Father assures him that 'My overshadowing Spirit and might with thee / I send along' (7.165-6). The 'overshadowing Spirit' invoked here appears to be the same as the 'ample Spirit' of 3.389, the modifiers drawing our attention to its comprehensiveness and all-sufficiency. The phrasing once again recalls Luke 1:35: 'the Holy Ghost shall come upon thee, and the power of the Highest shall overshadow thee.' As we have already seen, Milton considers that in the scriptural passage the Holy Ghost and the power of the Highest are the same being, the Father. Notice how precisely the poem's phrase 'overshadowing Spirit' reflects this gloss by its transference of the action of overshadowing from the 'Highest' to the 'Spirit.' Yet the theological tract does not offer a secret interpretation of the poem; it simply indicates intellectual grounds for the kinds of emphasis achieved in the poem through literary means.

Two significant references to the Spirit follow. The first, seemingly the most Trinitarian passage in the poem, occurs when heaven opens her gates

> to let forth
> The King of Glorie in his powerful Word
> And Spirit coming to create new Worlds. (7.207-9)

Assuming that 'King of Glorie' refers to the Father, these lines might suggest that God's work of creation can be described in terms of a triad of powers. However, the passage is quite consistent with Milton's comment on the creation in his theological work, where he observes that sometimes the term *spirit* signifies 'the power and virtue of the Father, and particularly that divine breath or influence by which every thing is created and nourished' (*Works*, XIV, 359-61). The poem's sequence 'King ... Word ... Spirit' expresses precisely the effect of creative influence exercised by the Father through the Son, an effect which makes us feel, as Alastair Fowler notes in his edition of the epic, that *Word* and *Spirit* are subordinate to God. As *De Doctrina* puts the matter, 'the power of the Father is inherent in himself, that of the Son and the Spirit is received from the Father' (*Works*, XIV, 393).

In the account of the creation, however, there is one passage which might be thought to provide a revelation of the Spirit as a distinct being. It occurs when the Son has circumscribed the new world with his golden compasses, and while darkness still covers the abyss:

> but on the watrie calme
> His brooding wings the Spirit of God outspred,
> And vital virtue infus'd, and vital warmth
> Throughout the fluid Mass. ... (7.234-7)

Yet while the passage evokes the traditional image of the third person of the Trinity expressed through the figure of a dove descending to brood, we know that for Milton the Spirit of God in the creation passage of Genesis 1:2 refers to 'the Son, through whom the Father is so often said to have created all things' (*Works*, XIV, 359-61). The 'divine breath or influence by which everything is created and nourished' originates in the Father, but is revealed through the agency of the Son. In the context of the poem, the close connection between the Son's delineation of the extent of the universe and the infusion of life into the abyss provides an emphasis in keeping with Milton's formal doctrine. Yet in *De Doctrina Christiana* he did not find it easy to reach a final conclusion about this mysterious event, and having argued that by Spirit is here meant 'divine power, rather than any person,' he adds that if after all a person is meant, it can have been only a subordinate minister, for 'God is first described as creating the heaven and the earth; the Spirit is only represented as moving upon the face of the waters already created' (*Works*, XV, 13-15). His hesitation perhaps arises from his strong sense of the typological parallels between this scene, the descent of the dove at the baptism of Jesus, and the work of the Spirit in the 'th' upright heart and pure.' The image of 'brooding wings' (7.235) lends some imaginative substance to the notion of a subordinate creature.

There are no other notable references to the Spirit in the account of creation. At the creation of man there is dialogue between Father and Son, and in composing this passage Milton would certainly have remembered that Trinitarians frequently cited as evidence of their doctrine the passage from Genesis 1:26 upon which his dialogue is based: 'Let us make man in our image.' The plural, it was urged, refers to the persons of the Trinity.[28] The Holy Spirit, however, takes no part in the deliberations of *Paradise Lost*. Moreover, it appears that either the Son or the Father breathes the breath of life into the nostrils of Adam (525-6), thus endowing him with that animating power frequently considered the gift of the Spirit.

There is, as we have seen, something tentative about Milton's theory of the Holy Spirit, and one suspects that he felt the scriptural evidence to be inconclusive. The main lines of his argument in the prose are clear enough, however, and these are repeated by the language and interpretations of the poem. Before the Gospel, the Spirit is normally the power and virtue of the Father: it merges with his wisdom, his Word, or his Son. The Holy Spirit as a distinct person, the Comforter, was promised by Jesus to his disciples, received by them after his death, and is now operative in the hearts of believers, writing there 'the Law of Faith / Working through love' (12.488-9). The office of the Spirit is thus to foster that inward and spontaneous order of love and obedience which is the essence of Christian liberty. This order becomes the norm in the Christian era, and renders less necessary those outbreaks of God's direct spiritual influence that mark the history of the Old Testament. Thus the poem is faithful to Milton's intellectual convictions concerning the Spirit without rigorously proclaiming them.[29]

In *Paradise Lost*, then, divine agency is presented principally in terms of Father and Son. It is time now to look at Milton's poetic strategy in presenting the pre-incarnate Son, leaving to a later chapter his treatment of the incarnate Son in *Paradise Regained*.

Impressions of the Son

Paradise Lost offers no clear-cut texts that establish the subordinationist view of the Son beyond doubt.[30] The problem of interpretation is part of the interest and significance of its treatment of deity. Like scripture, the poem provides a wealth of phrases that prompt interpretation. A number of these, often brief, may be read as implying the unity or equality of the Son with the Father: the Son is twice referred to as the 'filial Godhead' (6.722, 7.175); he is called by the Father the 'Heir of all my might' (5.720); he is said to sit by the Father 'imbosm'd' in bliss (5.597). Such language, of course, is also susceptible of interpretation in terms of Milton's view that the Father and Son are one in love, not essence, and that the Son receives as gift at the will of the Father all his attributes, including divine honours. A provocative passage occurs during the celebration of the Son by the angels after the council in heaven in book 3: 'Thee next they sang of all Creation first, / Begotten Son, Divine Similitude.' This has been considered suggestive of the subordinationist position at least since the time of Dennis.[31] The phrase echoes biblical texts (Revelation 3:14, 'the beginning of the creation of God'; Colossians 1:15, 'the firstborn of every creature') popular with the Socinians and to which *De Doctrina Christiana* gives a subordination-ist interpretation (*Works*, XIV, 191ff). While the lines from the poem are much less explicit than the prose treatise, it is worth noting both that Milton avoids the common interpretation by which such biblical passages as the two cited above are referred either to the beginning of the work of renovation in fallen man (the first born from the dead) or to the function of the Son at the creation,[32] and that his phrasing suggests that the Son is part of the creation, albeit prior to all the rest. The unusual impression made by the passage is furthered by the hymn as a whole, and particularly by the firm distinction drawn between the Son and the 'Eternal King' (374), and the evident feeling of the angels that the Son's act of unexampled love has elevated him so that his praise must henceforth never be disjoined from the praise of the Father.

A particularly interesting example of ambiguity is found in the passage in which the Father describes the Son as

> Thron'd in highest bliss
> Equal to God, and equally enjoying
> God-like fruition. ...   (3.305-7)

This is probably the most difficult single passage for those who, like myself, are convinced that Milton's subordinationism is important to the poem. C.A. Patrides views it as indicating a departure from *De Doctrina Christiana*, and urges that 'Equal' gets particular emphasis not only because it stands at the beginning of the line, but because as a trochee it calls attention to itself.[33] My own assumptions about what is happening in the council, however, draw me to agreement with Woodhouse, who argues that the crucial word is 'Thron'd,' and that the passage is not a statement of the Son's 'natural equality with the Father,' but rather 'of an equality in glory *bestowed* upon the Son by the Father.'[34] Commenting on the divine glory of the Son in *De Doctrina*, Milton remarks that 'the right hand of God primarily signifies a glory, not in the highest sense divine, but only next in dignity to God,' and notes that 'Christ has received his fulness from God, in the sense in which we shall receive our fulness from Christ' (*Works*, XIV, 337-9). These views seem in keeping with the tenor of the poem. A few lines after the account of the enthronement of the Son, the Father remarks that through his humiliation the Son will exalt 'thy Manhood also to this Throne' (3.314); if the throne were a symbol of equality of essence with the Father, such an elevation seems to run into the unhappy paradoxes which, according to Milton, face those who, identifying the Son with the Father and man with the Son, find they cannot evade the inference that man also is the same person with the Father (*Works*, XIV, 313).

Phrases and short passages take on differing significance, depending on the assumptions we bring to them. It is for this reason that the shaping of our assumptions and point of view by the larger elements of the poem is so crucial. Repetition with variation gives to certain motifs a cumulative significance. This is true of the image of the throne, and also of the motif of the paternal light illuminating the divine image expressed by the Son.

The use of the throne image throughout *Paradise Lost* strengthens the interpretation of the enthronement of the Son which sees it as an act of the Father and thus consistent with the Son's subordinate position. In the first place there is clearly only one 'supream' (5.670) or 'sovran' (5.656) or 'Impereal' throne (7.585), the seat of the almighty Father. Presumably it corresponds to 'the throne and habitation of God' mentioned in *De Doctrina Christiana*, the highest heaven that probably existed before the creation of the world (*Works*, XV, 31). Around this throne the angels circle and sing their hymns, here the Son returns after his victories (6.888-91 and 7.584-887), and it is against this throne, emblem of monarchy, that Satan directs his envy and his opposition. Satan claims, indeed, that his war shook God's throne, but later our doubt concerning this boast is confirmed, and we discover that even the chariot of the Father shakes 'All but the Throne it self of God' (6.834). The Son places the authority of this throne beyond dispute: 'O Father, O Supream of heav'nly Thrones, / First, Highest, Holiest, Best . ' (6.723-4). It is to this throne that Abdiel comes with the news of Satan's revolt (6.27), that the news of the Fall of man is brought (10.28), and that the Son presents the prayers of man repentant (11.20): it is the centre of power, communication and worship in heaven.

Repetition thus emphasizes the central idea that there is a single and supreme throne which expresses the absolute authority of the Father, who is God almighty. But there is a supplementary pattern of imagery expressive of the relation of the Son to the Father, a relation stated most simply by the way he takes his place at the right hand of the Father. Thus in the first scene in heaven the Father is 'High Thron'd above all highth' (3.58), and 'on his right / The radiant image of his Glory sat' (3.62-3). 'Sitting on the right hand of God,' Milton observes in *De Doctrina Christiana*, is 'a Hebraism signifying that he is exalted to a place of power and glory next to God' (*Works*, XV, 313). The idiom holds good in English. But in *Paradise Lost*, 6.742-5, Milton places the Son among the worshippers before God's throne, rather than 'in the midst of the throne' (Revelation 5:6).[35] Embosomed in the Father the Son is also said to share in the Father's throne, as when he is called 'Assessor' of his throne (6.679), an assessor being 'one who sits beside another, participating in his status and position.'[36] The throne appears to have two seats, then, as when the Son is said to rise from 'his radiant Seat ... / Of high collateral glorie' (10.85-6) (where, as Fowler notes, collateral may mean side by side, as OED, A1, or subordinate, as OED, A3). Clearly the Father could not be said to be 'assessor' of the throne of the Son, or to possess a seat of collateral glory, any more than he could be said to be embosomed in the Son. It is significant that the Father always possesses his throne, while the Son can leave his empty (7.141, 7.585-7, and *Paradise Regained*, 1.128, 4.596-9).

Calvin employs similar language, but to a different end. The comparison is instructive. Calvin, thinking particularly of the opening of Hebrews, argues that the setting of Christ at God's right hand implies that the second place was given to him.[37] He, too, speaks of the Son as 'vicegerent,' of the Father as 'assessor' ('the comparison is drawn from Kings'), and describes how he was 'invested with lordship over heaven and earth, and solemnly entered into possession of the government committed to him.'[38] Calvin thus draws attention to the subordination of the mediator. But as we have seen, for Calvin such subordination is consistent with the equality of the Son and the Father. Christ only holds the second place voluntarily through his assumption of human nature and his subjection of himself to the Father in order to redeem man. When the Son has accomplished the office of mediator, he will cease to sit at the right hand of the Father as vicegerent and his own Godhead will shine forth of itself.[39] Milton's handling of the relation of Father and Son in heaven is, by contrast, faithful to his view that what is true of the mediator is also true of the Son. Thus the council in book 3 shows him as subordinate and seated at the right hand of the Father before undertaking the mediation by which he became obedient to the Father in order to

[margin handwritten note: assessor = πάρεδρος]

save fallen man. And when he accepts that office of mediation, the process involves surrendering his place in heaven, as the Father observes: 'I spare / Thee from my bosom and right hand, to save, / By loosing thee awhile, the whole Race lost' (3.278-80). Again, by contrast, Calvin argues that the Son of God 'descended from heaven ... without leaving heaven.'[40] In short, for Milton 'sitting at the right hand of the Father' indicates the subordinate position of the Son which he will surrender during the period of his humiliation, while for Calvin it indicates the veiled and subordinate position of the mediator which will be given up at the completion of his office.

The heavy stress on the absolute authority of the Father encourages us to understand the divine status of the Son as a gift from the Father. In this light we should view the Father's assertion in book 3 that the Son has been throned in highest bliss equal to God. And at the close of that scene we find the most striking image of shared authority as the angels celebrate the power and love of Father and Son: 'lowly reverent / Towards either Throne they bow ... ' (3.349-50). It is, I shall argue, a dramatically appropriate moment for this image of joint authority.

Milton also stresses that the Son is the image of the Father. In *De Doctrina Christiana* Milton argues that if the Son is the image by which we see God, and the word by which we hear him, then precisely for this reason he cannot be one with God (*Works*, XIV, 401). *In Paradise Lost* the many passages referring to the Son as manifestation of the Father are usually couched in a way that implies, or is at least consistent with, the separateness of his being from that which it communicates: 'whom thou hat'st, I hate, and can put on / Thy terrors, as I put thy mildness on, / Image of thee in all things' (6.734-6), remarks the Son before meeting the rebels, and by his language suggests that he is image of God because he voluntarily assumes that which is given by his Father. Their unity is one of mind and will, as the Son emphasizes with characteristic humility:

> this I my Glorie account,
> My exaltation, and my whole delight,
> That thou in me well pleas'd, declarst thy will
> Fulfill'd, which to fulfil is all my bliss.

As in *De Doctrina Christiana*, it is a relation analogous to that which the Son will have with the regenerate, 'Made one with me as I with thee am one' (11.44), as we are told on several occasions.

The Father in turn delights in the Son's understanding ('All hast thou spok'n as my thoughts are, all / As my Eternal purpose hath decreed,' 3.171-2), and in his voluntary obedience ('And thou my Word, begotten Son, by thee / This I perform, speak thou, and be it don,' 7.163-4). But when the Father adds to his commands the claim that 'I am who fill/ Infinitude ... Necessitie and Chance / Approach not mee, and what I will is Fate' (7.168-73), we are made aware of an absolute power which dwarfs all else with the exception of goodness. Such divine attributes as omnipresence, omniscience, and omnipotence belong properly only to the Father (*Works*, XIV, 315-20): 'Thee Father first they sung Omnipotent, / Immutable, Immortal, Infinite, / Eternal King' (3.372-4). The angels do not make a parallel or similar statment about the Son, and this is in keeping with the sense given by the council as a whole that the Son is a secondary being of limited power.

Because of this union of mind and will, the Son is a perfect expression of the Father, a status conveyed sometimes by imagery of speech, but even more frequently by that of light. Thus the Father

> on his Son with Rayes direct
> Shon full, he all his Father full expresst. ... (6.719-20)

Significantly, the Son is here not the ray, as in much Trinitarian imagery, but the object illuminated. It has frequently been suggested that the light imagery in *Paradise Lost* contradicts the anti-Trinitarian position of the treatise, and that the use of the familiar metaphors of divine light to describe the generation of the Son inevitably recalls the orthodoxy of the past.[41] Yet what Milton says in the lines before us is quite unlike the traditional use of light imagery to express the Trinitarian view.[42] For Milton, light without an object is imageless. The Son, the nearest being to the Father, is the first image that the divine beam illuminates. Milton's use of light imagery here thus agrees with his rejection of the doctrine of the eternal generation of the Son; the rays emanating from the Father by an act of his will convey to the Son the divine gifts which enable him to express the Father.

This is not the only formula used by Milton in presenting Father and Son through light imagery, but it appears again distinctly during the heavenly dialogue concerning the judgment of man at the outset of book 10:

> So spake the Father, and unfolding bright

Toward the right hand his Glorie, on the Son
Blaz'd forth unclouded Deitie; he full
Resplendent all his Father manifest
Express'd, and thus divinely answer'd milde.   (10.63-7)

Other passages indebted to Hebrews 1:3 and 2 Corinthians 4:6 handle light imagery more simply:

Divine Similitude,
In whose conspicuous count'nance, without cloud
Made visible, th' Almighty Father shines. ...   (3.384-6)

This mild radiance, so different from the dazzling brightness that breaks from the clouds which dim the full blaze of the Father, is the adaptation of divine light to finite eyes through the medium of the Son, who acts as a kind of reflector. John Tombes, arguing a traditional concept of Christ's divinity against the incipient deism of the Socinians, urges that the phrase 'the brightness of Glory' from Hebrews 1:3 'doth not express what Christ was to others as a Looking-glass: ... but what he was in himself, and from whom, to wit, his Father, as the Beam from the Sun.'[43] The difference between the Son as the beam, and as that which the beam of God illuminates (the mirror in Tombes' illustration), is symptomatic of the difference in doctrine that separates Milton from the more orthodox Trinitarianism of the Baptist.

With these passages in mind, we are less likely to misunderstand one of the few texts which is capable of evoking Trinitarian dogma:

Beyond compare the Son of God was seen
Most glorious, in him all his Father shon
Substantially express'd. ...   (3.138-40)

As Maurice Kelley noted,[44] *substantially express'd* is consistent with the language of *De Doctrina Christiana*, where Milton argues that 'God imparted to the Son as much as he pleased of the divine nature, nay of the divine substance itself, care being taken not to confound the substance with the whole essence' (*Works*, XIV, 193). The original readers of the poem had of course no way of knowing the poet's distinctive view of the Son, and it must be admitted that the passage under discussion does use the language of orthodoxy. Nevertheless, the poet lends quiet support to the theologian by the association of the act of shining with the Father, by the adverbial position of 'substantially,' which conveys the reality and worth of the Son's expressive obedience, and by the view established elsewhere in the poem that all things are made of one first matter which has been endowed with various degrees of substance (5.469-79). Shortly after this passage, the song of the angel choir identifies the Father as the 'Fountain of Light' (375), noting that he is invisible amidst his 'glorious brightness,' and celebrates the way in which he is made visible by shining in the face of the Son: 'on thee / Impresst the effulgence of his Glorie abides' (3.387-8).

The individual phrase or image will not unlock Milton's view of God in *Paradise Lost*, even though it may link the poem with *De Doctrina Christiana*. Examining the treatment of the Son in *Paradise Lost*, we must attempt to locate the particular statement within the poem's larger patterns – narrative, dramatic, conceptual. We must be alert to patterns of emphasis, including the indications provided by significant omissions and silences, and allow our responses to be shaped by the implications of particular events. If we do so, we become aware of a strong suggestion of evolution or development in the Son's experience. To this we may add another point, more difficult to state: the control of the revelation of the Son as a distinct person by the decorum and structure of each particular dramatic episode.

The relations between Father and Son are repeatedly expressed in terms of the former's gifts of power and glory to the latter. The Father is said to 'honour' or 'appoint' his Son, and to 'transfer' or 'transfuse' power to him, while the Son 'assumes' the Father's gifts, and engages in action 'girt' with them. The great occasions in heaven are all moments at which the Son receives power, and seen in chronological sequence they suggest, as Stella Revard and John A. Clair have argued most persuasively, that the Son is involved in a process by which he is elevated to a type of coequality with the Father.[45] In himself mutable, he lacks the supreme power of the Father. As we have observed, it is the Father alone who is properly 'Omnipotent, / Immutable, Immortal, Infinite, / Eternal King' (3.372-4). But as an expression of the Father's will the Son becomes a 'Second Omnipotence' (6.684), and at the climax of his development, when he proves willing to be impaired by an act of love and obedience, he is given 'all Power' (3.317) by the Father and is told that he has become 'Head Supream' (3.319) and that he will be manifest as 'universal King' (3.317). Let us turn now to the sequence of scenes that present this development of the Son, taking them in the order of the story, rather than of the plot: the 'begetting' of the Son, his exaltation after overthrowing the rebels, his agency in the creation of the world, and his undertaking of the role of mediator during the council in heaven.

The Begetting of the Son

Chronologically the first stage in the process of the elevation of the Son occurs on a day in heaven when the angels are summoned to the throne of God and the Father utters a decree:

> This day I have begot whom I declare
> My onely Son, and on this holy Hill
> Him have anointed, whom ye now behold
> At my right hand; your Head I him appoint;
> And by my Self have sworn to him shall bow
> All knees in Heav'n, and shall confess him Lord.
> ...   (5.603-8)

The anointing of the Son as head of the angels is the occasion of Satan's rebellion, and thus initiates the action of the poem. Unlike books 1 and 2, this account of the rebellion stresses Satan's envy rather than his pride. Envy as the motive for the rebellion is found in a tradition of interpretation which reaches back to the medieval *Vita Adamae et Evae*. In this tradition, however, the envy of Satan is aroused by his foreknowledge of the Incarnation. English writers who employ this explanation include Joseph Beaumont, Thomas Heywood and – in a work taking issue with Milton – Charles Leslie. But no precedent has been found for Milton's precise location of the cause of Satan's envy in the 'begetting' of the Son rather than the announcement of the Incarnation. He appears to be the first to envisage such a scene, and his doing so may be taken in part as evidence of his powers as a dramatist.[46]

The advantages of his explanation of the rebellion are worth noting. In the first place, it establishes angelic experience as something that exists in its own right, rather than as merely auxiliary to man's trial. The dispensation under which the angels live includes an epiphany of the Godhead and a consequent testing of their obedience, and it thus stands in a relation of analogy to the various dispensations of God to men. Secondly, it allows a sharper differentiation between angelic and human responsibility. If the angels fall in response to God's treatment of fallen man, as in Leslie's version, then in terms of moral causation their sin appears secondary, man's primary, so that it would be even more difficult for us to accept the Father's argument that the angels 'by thir own suggestion fell, / Self-tempted, self-deprav'd' (3.129-30). Moreover, in the poem's world of dramatized motive there would be well-nigh insurmountable difficulties in presenting an event in which knowledge possessed by the rebel angels of God's treatment of fallen man prompted them to reject God and bring about man's fall. Milton's interpretation cuts economically through these difficulties; it establishes the significance of angelic experience as analogue to that of man, and it is built around certain key phrases in the Bible and expresses in typological fashion the continuity of the divine acts. The episode also accords in emphasis, in a manner Leslie did not see, with Milton's view of the nature of the Son.

Leslie's misunderstanding of the scene nonetheless points to certain of its implications:

> The folly of this contrivance appears many ways: To make the Angels ignorant of the blessed Trinity; and to take it ill to acknowledge him for their King whom they had always ador'd as their God; or as if the Son had not been their King, or had not been begotten till that day. This scheme of the Angels revolt cannot answer either to the eternal Generation of the Son, which was before the Angels had a Being, or to his temporal Generation of the blessed Virgin, that being long after the fall of the Angels.[47]

Leslie, knowing nothing of Milton's exegetical theory of the begetting, saw the episode as a clumsy invention that left the door open for heretical ideas of an Arian kind. Strangely, he was moving towards a correct view of the poet's position on what was technically the wrong evidence. The fact should make us see with fresh eyes the originality of Milton's treatment of the Son's elevation. It is not a device which would have recommended itself to someone for whom the mystery and paradox of the Trinity is a central fact of religious experience. So much Leslie sensed. On the other hand, he missed the evidence of the Son's prior existence emphatically provided by Abdiel during his debate with Satan, where he affirms that all angelic nature joined in one being would not be

Equal to him begotten Son, by whom

> As by his Word the mighty Father made
> All things, ev'n thee, and all the Spirits of Heav'n
> By him created in thir bright degrees,
> Crownd them with Glory. ... (5.835-9)

In spite of Satan's scoffing assertion that 'We know no time when we were not as now' (5.859), the reader is clearly to find in Abdiel's response an illustration of the way unfallen reason moves to the apprehension of truth: 'the good angels do not look into all the secret things of God, as the Papists pretend; some things indeed they know by revelation, and others by means of the excellent intelligence with which they are gifted; there is much, however, of which they are ignorant' (Works, XV, 107).

Of the quality of the Son's existence before the begetting we can say little, for all the manifestations of his nature dealt with in the poem are subsequent to that event. That he did exist previously, however, even Satan does not seem to deny, and the account of Satan's state of mind in rebelling implies that he knew the Son prior to his begetting (see 5.662-3), although Satan argues that the Son was then their equal (5.794 ff). Satan has an uncanny ability to distort reality, however, and when imagining the previous existence of the Son we are safer to be guided by the implications of Abdiel's observation that the Father created the angels by him 'As by his Word.'

After his begetting the Son is much more accessible to the minds and imaginations of the angels. His begetting, anointing, and kingship provide a kind of incarnation of the Son for the angels, and we are clearly meant to think of the analogy. The Father draws our attention to the fact that the angels have something corresponding to the doctrine of the church as the body of Christ when he observes that the faithful angels will be united in the Son 'as one individual Soule' (610). He is now the anointed one, a fact that looks forward to his identification as 'Christ.' The Son is head and Messiah of the angels as he is head and Messiah of mankind.[48] In Abdiel's remarks, there is even a suggestion of the act of humiliation by which the Son will in future exalt his manhood:

> since he the Head
> One of our number thus reduc't becomes,
> His Laws our Laws, all honour to him done
> Returns our own. (5.842-5)

These characteristics echo the Father's description of the Incarnation, humiliation, and resurrection of the Son during the council of book 3 (283-345).

The elevation of the Son is thus a critical event for the angels, and from it flows their testing, for it brings a new knowledge of God and opens up new possibilities for response. On many occasions both before and during the Son's acceptance of the role of mediator the idea of the pre-incarnate Son as the 'only begotten' of the Father is present, either explicitly or by implication (3.80, 3.384, 5.603-4, 5.835, 7.163), and the effect of such an emphasis is to link more firmly the exaltation over the angels with the Incarnation by way of parallelism.

Leslie lacked an important piece of information which is of some help in understanding the scene. In *De Doctrina Christiana*, Milton explains that there is a 'double sense' in which in scripture the Father is said to have begotten the Son, 'the one literal, with reference to the production of the Son, the other metaphorical, with reference to his exaltation' (*Works*, XIV, 181). Sir Herbert Grierson recognized the relevance of this passage to the poem, and argued that the begetting of the Son at book 5.600ff is metaphoric. By exalting the Son the Father is producing something new – a king.[49] Guided by the prose, we can find in the poem evidence that the metaphoric sense of begetting is intended. Thus Satan is said to feel envy of the Son of God who was 'that day / Honour'd by his great Father, and proclaimd / *Messiah* King anointed' (5.662-4). The lines suggest an elevation, not a creation. In his first conspiratorial speech, Satan complains not of the creation of a new being but of new laws and commands associated with 'our King / The great *Messiah*' (690-1). And throughout the discussion that follows – Satan's speech at the Mount of Congregation and his debate with Abdiel – the begetting scene is consistently referred to as an occasion when the Son was anointed, given power, and made King by the Father (5.774-7, 814-8, 842-5, 870).

The distinction between a metaphoric or figurative and a literal begetting is not unique to Milton's exegesis, but widespread in Protestant commentary. It was found to be particularly useful in explicating the passage from Psalm 2:6-7 upon which the entire episode of the begetting in *Paradise Lost* is founded: 'Yet have I set my king upon my holy hill of Zion. I will declare the decree: the Lord hath said unto me, Thou art my Son; this day have I begotten thee.' Three passages in the New Testament interpret these verses in terms of Christ (Acts 13:32-3, Hebrews 1:5 and 5:5). Patristic doctrine thus maintained that the begetting referred to in the Psalm is the eternal generation of the

Son. Protestants, as Stella Revard has noted, were dubious about this interpretation.[50] They considered it vulnerable to misrepresentation by those who wish to make the Son a subordinate being. Calvin, for example, teaches that the Psalm refers to the time when the Son is made manifest as mediator.[51] Many take the view, supported by Acts 13:32-3, that the verses apply particularly to Christ's resurrection from the dead and ascension. Thus William Perkins, clearly resisting Socinian interpretations, remarks that when 'the saying of the father, *This day have I begotten thee*,' is expounded of the time of Christ's resurrection, we must take care to distinguish between 'generation it selfe and the manifestation of it: and of the second must the place be understood, which may be brought to passe at the time of Christ's resurrection in which he was mightily declared to be the sonne of God, though in the meane season the generation itself be eternall.'[52] John Owen indicates the flexibility and richness of Calvinist interpretations of the passage. He observes that the exaltation of the Son described in Psalm 2 is assigned by some to the day of his Incarnation (by which he means the annunciation to Mary), by others to the day of his baptism when he was proclaimed Son by the voice from heaven, and by still others to his resurrection and ascension. All these interpretations are for Owen 'consistent and reconcilable with each other,' for he sees them in terms of the Calvinist conception of the career of the Son, in which the Son is exalted as his divine nature is made manifest.[53]

Milton's view is a version of the Protestant position. He asserts with unusual emphasis, as we have seen, the distinction between the literal and the metaphoric begetting of the Son, his production and his exaltation. He understands the 'Pauline' passages which employ Psalm 2:7 in terms of metaphoric meanings: Act 13:32-3 interprets the begetting as resuscitation from the dead, Hebrews 5:5 as a declaration of priestly power, and Hebrews 1:5 as a declaration of kingly power (*Works*, XIV, 183-5). The scene of begetting at *Paradise Lost* 5.600ff is in these terms not the literal generation of the Son; rather the word 'begot' is used figuratively to denote the calling into being of a new relationship and to evoke the ideas of rule and mediation associated with the gloss on Psalm 2:7 provided in the New Testament. The scene in heaven thus accords with the Reformed view of the exaltations of Christ, in which Psalm 2:7 is seen as referring to one of several possible occasions on which the Father granted special favour to his Son.

But while Protestant interpreters saw this manifestation of his divine nature in a sequence of events, we have yet to find a parallel for Milton's placing of a moment of exaltation *before* the Incarnation – indeed, before the fall of Satan and the creation of the world. Moreover, *De Doctrina Christiana* appears to omit reference to such an early event in divine history. In chapter 5 on the Son of God, 'metaphorical generation' is defined only in two forms, 'resuscitation from the dead' and 'unction to the mediatorial office' (*Works*, XIV, 183), and both of these, we must conclude, occur later than the scene in heaven, and not until man has fallen. Must we thus also conclude, with Maurice Kelley, that the episode in the poem is a fiction based on the transfer of the begetting from its proper place at the Resurrection to a time before the creation of the world?[54]

The answer is that while *De Doctrina Christiana* does not overtly specify an occasion corresponding to the scene in *Paradise Lost*, it does provide scriptural and theological grounds for the episode. To grasp this we must in the first place recall that in Calvinist theology it is possible to view the Son as mediator before the fall of man: 'Even if man had remained free from all stain, his condition would have been too lowly for him to reach God without a mediator.'[55] From this view theologians derived a double sense of the term mediator, for it could refer either to one by whom God bestows benefits and communicates himself to his creatures or to one by whom atonement for sin is made.[56] Milton prefers the term 'head' for the first function. Thus he speaks of the angels as being under Christ as their head, not their Redeemer (*Works*, XV, 101). Significantly, he rejects the Reformed view that the good angels retain their strength by the grace of God and are thus eager to participate in the mystery of man's salvation. On the contrary, he maintains, they are called 'elect' only in the sense of beloved or choice, and their contemplation of the mystery of salvation arises from disinterested love, since they have no need of reconciliation (*Works*, XV, 99). This reservation aside, however, Milton's position seems clearly related to the Reformed one: as the first of creation, the Son is, from the beginning, head of both men *and* angels. And since Milton believes the angels were created and tested before the world, it clearly follows that Christ, the anointed Son of God, had a function of headship before the creation of man. To this extent, at least, the begetting responds to a need of his theology.

Milton's use of the distinction between the literal and the metaphorical meanings of the begetting of the Son is complicated and apparently lacking in perfect consistency.[57] At one point he asserts that in scripture there are two senses in which the Father is said to have begotten the Son, one literal, the other metaphoric, while further on he remarks that

(a)

NB: "rationi consuntius videtur, stare suis viribus non minus angelos bonos quam stabit homo adhuc integer" (Doct. X cane 1,9).

b

nowhere in scripture is the Son said to be begotten except in a metaphorical sense (*Works*, XIV, 181,191). The explanation of the seeming contradiction is probably that the metaphorical sense does not exclude the simultaneous presence of a literal one. The Son was both literally produced and metaphorically exalted by the begetting of the Father, and both meanings can be found is Psalm 2:7. The two senses are inseparable so that the Son is never said to be begotten in a literal sense only. In scripture, the description of the production of the Son as a begetting by the Father carries with it inevitably an allusion to his exaltation and mediatorial work. The reason this metaphorical allusion is so important to Milton is because be believes, as we have seen, that the mediator is in no sense less than the Son. He rejects the traditional argument for the eternal generation of the Son which maintains that such generation is essential to the Father. Generation, he insists, has nothing to do with the essence of deity (*Works*, XIV, 187). While the language of begetting points thus to the exaltation of the Son and his mediatorial function, it can also be used to describe the production of the Son as long as care is taken to insist that God's act of generation is voluntary and does not arise from natural necessity. This permits a literal sense to Psalm 2:7, but one which is accommodated to human understanding, since God no more begets like a man than he is angry, repents, or forgets like a man. In this respect, then, Milton departs from Protestant exegesis by welcoming the literal sense of the passage from Psalm 2:7 and endorsing its subordinationist implications.

The begetting of the Son, like all God's acts of creation, has two stages. In the first, it is a decree in the mind of God, part of his internal efficiency. Milton calls it the first and most excellent of his special decreees. The execution of this decree took place within the bounds of time, and is an example of God's external efficiency: 'of his special decrees the first and most important is that which regards his Son, and from which he primarily derives his name of Father. Psal.ii.7' (*Works*, XIV, 89). The opening of chapter 5 of the first book of *De Doctrina Christiana*, in which Milton discusses the generation of the Son, does not manage with clarity the twin aspects of literal and metaphorical significance. It is nonetheless evident that Milton believes the Son was literally generated by the Father before all things but within the bounds of time, and that in the beginning he existed under the title of word or *logos*. At some later point, he was begotten metaphorically, that is, made manifest and exalted under the title of Son. Milton does not place the occasion on which this happened, but he emphasizes those texts

[left margin handwritten:] n/ ... that/

[right margin handwritten:] Neither produce nor exalt is a literal meaning of "beget," but begetting is a kind of producing; one step takes you there. To go from begetting Xp to exalting Xp a single step won't do the trick: you go to producing Xp, then from there to producing an exalted person who happens to be Xp. So produce is a less obviously fig. meaning of "beget" than exalt is.

which identify the Son as head of the angels (e.g. Ephesians 1:9-10), and he cites Hebrews 1:5 as evidence of the Son's exaltation above the angels: 'for unto which of the angels said he at any time. Thou art my Son, this day have I begotten thee.' Even more suggestive is the fact that Milton posits a special decree of God about the angels which he says is implied in scripture rather than distinctly mentioned (*Works*, XIV, 89). The context in which this observation is made strongly suggests that the special decree about the angels does not concern their creation (this is comprehended in God's general decree) but rather their government. As God's special decree concerning man centres on predestination to salvation in Christ, so his special decree concerning the angels should center on their election in the Son. One proof text for this decree is found in the reference to 'elect angels' in 1 Timothy 5:21, and we know Milton considered them elect in the sense that Christ is their head. He does not say when this decree was executed, but it, too, must have been fulfilled in time.

Thus we have reached the theological and scriptural grounds for the scene of the begetting in *Paradise Lost* 5.590ff. What is striking about this material is the way Milton has implied a scene of metaphoric begetting in which the Son becomes Messiah of the angels and yet has refrained from specifying when and how this occurred. At no point does he actually assert that the Son was exalted above the angels before the creation of the world, yet his language and proof texts are wholly consistent with the possibility of such an event and his conception of the governing role of the Son seems to call for it. The stage is thus set for the poem. The episode in *Paradise Lost* is not a deliberate fiction but is carefully founded on the evidence of scripture.

For Milton, as for many of the Reformed, the exaltation of the Son is a process; moments of exaltation occur repeatedly throughout his career, each being distinct yet related to the others.[58] The series includes the begetting, the encounter with the rebels, the undertaking of the office of Redeemer of man, the baptism, the resurrection and ascension, the last judgment. All these occasions involve both parallel and difference. Each triumph is discriminated from those before and after, although they are also complementary and cumulative. Thus while there is a close relation between the 'begetting' of the Son as Messiah of the angels in book 5 of *Paradise Lost*, and the exaltation of the Messiah as Saviour of mankind in book 3, the two events occur in remarkably different contexts, the one before the creation of the world, the other after the creation and as a response to the foreknowledge of the fall of man.[59]

The narrative forces the separation of the two events. The begetting sparks the rebellion of Satan; the rebellion leads to the temptation and fall of man and hence to the Son's voluntary acceptance of the function of atonement. The two events stand in the relation of occasion of action and consequence of action. And Milton uses other devices to show that they offer parallel with difference. We have already noticed how the language in which the Son is proclaimed head or Messiah of the angels anticipates his mediatorial function in relation to man. The Son is cast as mediator even without the Fall; this basic office arises from his function as a subordinate being who can communicate the Father by acting as his image. Another method of separating and paralleling the two events is found in biblical allusion. The two scenes appear to share only three biblical texts but these are of some importance:[60] Colossians 1:16, Ephesians 4:15, Philippians 2:10. All three texts have to do with the kingship and divine power of the Son. But the exaltation of the mediator in book 3 also draws on a range of New Testament passages pertaining to the Resurrection, judgment, and apocalypse. The begetting scene in book 5, on the other hand, looks back to Psalm 2:6-7 through the lens of Hebrews 1:3-5. Its two references to Genesis 22 are of particular interest, since they are drawn from the account of Abraham's willingness to sacrifice Isaac, and typologically introduce the priestly office which is thus quietly implicit from the start in the image of the 'only-begotten.' In this way the two passages share a common core of biblical allusion evoking the kingship of the Son, but are distinguished by the differing implications of the other texts cited. Thus Milton suggests biblical sanction for his separation of the two events.[61] By such discriminations we are invited to consider how the career of the Son is presented through his triumphs. While all time may be as one moment in the vision of God, there *is* time and real history in heaven as on earth, as Raphael is careful to point out to Adam (5.580-3).

The Son in Judgment

The next display of the relations between Father and Son occurs during the rebellion and war in heaven, an upheaval occasioned by the begetting. The Son is present at the beginning and the end of the war: at the beginning, he exchanges some ironic words with the Father (in terms of strict chronology his first speech) concerning the rebellion now gaining head under the leadership of Satan; at the end, he formally assumes the power given to him by the Father, explains his role to the faithful angels, and rides out in the paternal chariot to overthrow the rebels. The exact moment of the transfer of power by the Father occurs shortly before the Son's ascent of the chariot:

> ... Into thee such Vertue and Grace
> Immense I have transfus'd, that all may know
> In Heav'n and Hell thy Power above compare,
> And this perverse Commotion governd thus,
> To manifest thee worthiest to be Heir
> Of all things, to be Heir and to be King
> By Sacred Unction, thy deserved right.
> ...
> He said, and on his Son with Rayes direct
> Shon full, he all his Father full expresst
> Ineffably into his face receiv'd. ...   (6.703-21)

The impending conflict is thus presented as an occasion for the manifestation of the Son's merit, his title to rule. His merit makes him worthy of kingship.

This demonstration is couched in terms of unlimited power, but seemingly of power in a narrow sense – the exercise of a just vengeance. The Son makes this clear to his followers when he explains that the rebels will be defeated in battle, 'since by strength / They measure all' (6.820-1). As he observes to the Father, he is able to assume divine anger:

> ... whom thou hat'st, I hate, and can put on
> Thy terrors, as I put thy mildness on,
> Image of thee in all things. ...   (6.734-6)

So effective is the Son as the expression of the Father's wrath that he seems paradoxically to have put aside his usual function, for in changing his countenance to terror and becoming 'too severe to be beheld' (825) he ceases to mediate by making the Father visible as shining light 'without cloud' (3.385). Yet the Son is still the image of God; the terrifying image of power is not the infinite and invisible source. Moreoever, the Son's words to the Father clearly express his preference for love, and his sense that wrath is for him but a passing role, one that will shortly be laid aside. This first act of the Son, then, is limited to the use of power to express wrath, but enough is said to make clear that the episode is only a stage in the process of willed evolution leading to an apocalypse of divine love and union. And even as he approaches the rebels, his creative and organizing energy is evident as he gathers the faithful into unity and restores the landscape: 'This saw his hapless Foes, but stood obdur'd ... ' (6.785). The act of rejection is theirs, and even as they leave heaven, we are told that rather than being pushed, they throw themselves headlong down.

The dialogue of Father and Son makes it clear that the Son is a responsive agent, acting out of free obedience, not a kind of divine robot or celestial Talus. When the Father mocks his foes by adopting the stance of a temporal ruler who must be at pains to remain alert and provident, the Son relishes the joke, asserts the justice of his Father, and closes with a flourish which makes him sound a little like a young prince about to ride into his first battle in a burst of confidence, a youth 'eager to win his spurs,' as William Empson puts it:[62] 'and in event / Know whether I be dextrous to subdue / Thy Rebels, or be found the worst in Heav'n' (5.740-2). If we reject Empson's view that the episode reveals an appalling malignancy on the part of the Father, and see it as the whole poem urges us to do, the interchange becomes evidence of the vitality of awareness and tone that marks a relation based on free responses.

Glory is an important theme of the war in heaven. Satan speaks of this war as 'the strife of Glorie,' (6.290), but the angelic narrator dismisses with contempt the heroism of the rebels. Yet the rebellion is 'Matter ... of Glory' (5.738) to the Son, whose obedience leads to his triumph in 'ending this great Warr' (6.702). Memories of the language and imagery of classical heroic poetry merge with their scriptural analogues – arrows, divine thunderbolts, chariots, massive hosts, the single hero who appals his foes as he advances 'Gloomie as Night.' But traditional warfare is shown to be empty by this hero, who conquers without striking a blow, mastering his opponents simply by his spiritual authority. The Son is also quick to point out that the glory he wins redounds to his Father: 'thou always seekst / To glorifie thy Son, I always thee' (6.724-5). We feel the merging and union of 'God and *Messiah* his anointed King' (6.718). The Father's vision of the Son as King and heir of all things is answered by the Son's anticipation of the time when he will resign all things to the Father. This develops further the theme of unity intro-duced by the Father at the begetting (5.609-11) and fully stated later (chronologically later, that is, but earlier in the poem) at the close of the council in heaven (3.339-41).

Significantly, motifs from Psalm 2 are once again present in this treatment of judgment and exaltation. The Father speaks mockingly of the need to defend 'This our high place, our Sanctuarie, our Hill' (5.732), recalling how the king is set upon the holy hill of Zion. Like the 'kings of earth' in the Psalm, the rebels have taken counsel against the Lord and his 'anointed,' and as in the Psalm, the Lord laughs at these enemies and holds them in derision. A new word to describe the Son's role, not heard in the earlier scene of begetting, is 'heir,' which is repeated in an emphatic way four times. The word recalls the first chapter of Hebrews, in which the Son is 'appointed heir to all things' (1:2), his claim being established by reference to the begetting of Psalm 2:7. The same chapter of Hebrews is recalled at the close of the triumph of the Son, when he returns to his place at the right hand of the Father (Hebrews 1:3).

The narrative of the triumph of the Son provides the most sustained description of his appearance and outward behaviour in the poem. Yet little is anthropomorphic about this visual representation. Milton's pre-existent Son is most like a man when he speaks, least so when he acts. What we see – although without much visual clarity – is a warrior figure, fully armed in 'Celestial Panoplie' (6.760), and seated on a throne in a mysterious chariot, his bow and quiver full of thunderbolts hanging beside him. This figure leads the thousands of chariots of God, and the faithful angels rally to his blazing ensign. His countenance, once bright with the glory of the Father, is now too severe to be beheld, but we do see his hand grasping the thunders, and these bolts are sent against his opponents while the eyes in the living wheels of the chariot shoot lightning until he checks his strength in mid-volley. In a grim parody of his work of salvation, he raises the overthrown, then drives all before him like a herd of goats until they hurl themselves from the verge of heaven. The Son then returns to the courts and temple of his Father and to his seat of glory. The whole process is difficult to visualize, and is meant to be. The spectacular and panoramic effects recall the splendid multitudes in baroque paintings of the judgment or the ascension, but the repeated invitation to imagine the Son in human form as a warrior is difficult to accept because of the mysterious and emblematic images which surround him.

The account of the Son's triumph is remarkably rich in biblical allusion. The texts woven together by Milton with such coherence and point show how profoundly his mind was stirred and shaped by the great statements concerning judgment and glorification which are scattered throughout scripture. Ezekiel's vision of God in a machine (1:4ff) provides the central imagery of whirlwind, fire, lightning, wings, wheels, eyes, creatures, spirit and throne. Significantly, the voice of the Lord that accompanies Ezekiel's vision reveals to him the sin and idolatry of Israel and the punishment that overtakes the wicked. This exemplification of divine power in judgment is linked by Milton with others, especially Isaiah's visions of the wrath of God, such as that (5:13-16) in which a multitude descends into hell and the Lord is exalted (*Paradise Lost*, 6.874-91; see also 6.770 and Isaiah 66:15). Supporting such major allusions are more glancing ones, such as those to Job's vision of the might of God, which is able to shake the heavens with a power beyond comprehension (6.833; Job 26:11), and to Daniel's Ancient of Days sitting on his fiery throne in Judgment (6.832; Daniel 7:9-10). Milton also employs imagery of smoke, fire, and storm of the sort found in psalm describing God's exercise of power against his enemies (6.765-6; Psalms 18:8ff; 50:3). The Son's command, 'Stand still in bright array ye Saints' (6.801), recalls Moses' injunction to his people, 'stand still, and see the salvation of the Lord' (Exodus 14:13), shortly before he leads them across the Red Sea to witness from the other side the destruction of their enemy. 'Vengeance is his' (6.808) echoes the claim attributed to the Lord in the Song of Moses (Deuteronomy 32:35, cited Romans 12:19), that impassioned celebration of the power and judgments of God. Milton was well aware of how these Old Testament passages were answered and overgone by apocalyptic texts of the New Testament. Passing allusions to the latter include references to the unquenchable fire in Jesus' parable about cutting off the offending member in Mark 9:43-5, to the sign of the Son of Man in Heaven that heralds the last judgment in Matthew 24:30, and to the terrible example of the punishment of the sinning angels in 2 Peter 2:4 (see 6.876-7, 776, 739). But the most pervasive source of New Testament reference, present both in phrase and image, is Revelation. Specific references – which increase in number as the episode moves to its climax – include the chaining of the rebels in the underworld (6.738-9; Revelation 20:1-2), the cry of the wicked that they might be hidden by mountains from the wrath of the Son (6.842-3; Revelation 6:16), and the celebration of the Son on his return to heaven (6.880-92; Revelation 4:11; 7:9; 5:12). Milton counts on our recognition of the way Revelation gathers up Ezekiel's imagery of lightning, eyes, fire, throne, and mysterious creatures, so that its account of the last things echoes and elaborates upon the earlier prophecy of God's power and justice.

The allusions I have cited are representative in their stress upon the judgment and condemnation of the wicked. Several also recall the exaltation of the judge. While the greater number of references are to the Old Testament, there are several to the New, so that we sense the consistency of the divine action, which is brought out particularly by the heavy use of Revelation towards the close. But what is most striking about the episode as a whole is the New Testament context provided by the Son at the outset as he responds to the will of the Father:

> this I my Glorie account,
> My exaltation, and my whole delight,
> That thou in me well pleas'd declar'st thy will
> Fulfill'd, which to fulfil is all my bliss.
> Sceptre and Power, thy giving, I assume,
> And gladlier shall resign, when in the end
> Thou shalt be All in All, and I in thee
> For ever, and in mee all whom thou lov'st. ...   (6.726-33)

Before proceeding to act as judge of the wicked, the Son asserts the importance of obedience and love. In doing so he alludes to two occasions, one at Jesus' baptism, the other at his transfiguration on the mount, when the voice of the Father testifies that 'This is my beloved Son, in whom I am well pleased' (Matthew 3:17; 17:5). The headship of the Son, his gathering in of the faithful, is the subject of a number of Milton's favorite Christological passages (here, 1 Corinthians 15:28; in line 779, Romans 12:5, Colossians 1:18). A moving aspect of the passage is the way it echoes Jesus' prayer to his Father shortly before his betrayal, when he knew the end was approaching (John 17:1-23). The echo is particularly clear in the emphasis on the unity of love which recalls these words from the prayer: 'as Thou, Father, art one in me, and I in Thee, that they also may be one in us.' The responsive speech of the Son thus establishes a connection between his exaltation in the overthrow of the rebels and certain crucial events in the life of Jesus, including his baptism, his transfiguration, his casting out of spirits from the possessed (6.856-8), and his sacrificial death and resurrection (see especially 6.746-9). While the Old Testament references dominate the body of the narrative, linking the Son's act with its judgment and prophecies, the Son's opening speech on love prepares us for the closing emphasis on Revelation and invites us to see this first act of judgment as a prefiguration of the last.

The varied imagery describing the transfer of power from Father to Son is revealing. Some images imply an internal transaction, others present the process in a more external manner. The internalizing images include those of pouring, the ingredients being poured having about them a degree of abstraction ('Into thee such Vertue and Grace / Immense I have transfus'd,' 6.703-04), and of light, which communicates the Father's nature to the Son. The father-son metaphor itself, while capable of various implications, seems basically to belong to the class of internalizing images. But there are many which imply a relation of a more external nature. Such are the images of investiture, as when the Son is commanded to 'Gird on' (6.714) the panoply of the Father, and of a legal transfer through which the Son becomes assessor, heir, or vicegerent. There is much ceremonial and political language – the Son being anointed, honoured, appointed – and this suggests the external modes by which the exchange of authority is manifest in society. In the scene in which the Son overthrows the rebels, we are left in no doubt that his essential resource is the inward transfusion of virtue and grace. But we are also very aware throughout of the martial and political language and imagery employed to express the delegated power which he exercises. Indeed, here more than anywhere else in the poem the divine virtue seems to have materialized to the point where concrete images, mysteriously qualified, can be used in its presentation. It is worth emphasizing, too, that the celestial panoply, the chariot, and the lightning bolts are all manifestations of the Father which are employed by the Son.[63]

The Son and Creation

The role of the Son during creation in book 7 reveals further aspects of his relation to the Father. An important feature of Milton's narrative of the creation is the impression that it produces of two strata, one simple, direct, in a sense primitive, the other more complex and speculative. The middle section, with its beautiful and concrete elaboration of the hexameral material, has something of the directness and visionary simplicity of ancient literature; the opening and closing scenes in heaven, by contrast, continue to express the nature of the Godhead in the complex terms already established. Thus at the beginning and the end we hear of Father, Son, and even Spirit, but throughout the central portion only of God. One might almost be tempted to argue that this middle section represents a different stage of composition, and that the change of manner marks the joins. Yet the effectiveness of the passage as a whole supports the assumption that the variety in the treatment of

God is deliberate and expresses Milton's views of God's agency. Such an assumption is made by Leland Ryken, who perceptively notes that the creative act is variously attributed to the Son, the Father, the Spirit, and the Godhead, and concludes that this is part of a deliberate technique of blurring: 'The dramatic illusion is that the divine agents and their actions are too remote to yield a clear and definite impression to human view.'[64] Perhaps there is an effect of what Ryken calls 'distancing' here; certainly we are meant to feel the wonder of the harmony of will and purpose uniting Father, Son, and Spirit. However, I think we will understand the narrative better if we start with the hypothesis that Milton sought not to confuse us in order to distance the transcendental realm but to convey something about the nature of God's agency.

A glance at *De Doctrina Christiana* reveals at once how closely the presentation of creation in the poem conforms to Milton's theological views. 'Creation,' Milton begins, 'is that act whereby God the Father produced everything that exists by his Word and Spirit, that is, by his will, for the manifestation of the glory of his power and goodness' (*Works*, XV, 5). Throughout the theological argument that follows he insists on the primacy of the Father in the act of creation. The Father is the principal cause, the Son the instrumental or less principal cause: 'the Father is not only he "of" whom, but also from whom, and for whom, and through whom, and on account of whom are all things ... ' (*Works*, XV, 9). The creation, then, is not a work performed jointly or collectively by Father and Son. Nor, as we have seen, does the Spirit participate on equal terms in the creation; for either the Spirit is simply the power of God the Father, or, if it is a distinct person, it is 'only a subordinate minister' (*Works*, XV, 15).

These ideas lie directly behind Milton's handling of the creation in the epic. They are reflected with precision in the speech in which the Father instructs the Son:

> begotten Son, by thee
> This I perform, speak thou, and be it don:
> My overshadowing Spirit and might with thee
> I send along. ... (7.163-6)

Milton's intention is not to blur the relations within the Godhead, but rather to show how the Father comprehends the creation that is executed by the Son, how he is its origin, cause, archetype, and end. This comprehension is not merely stated in theoretical terms, but is brought home to the reader through his experience of the action. Close attention to the creation narrative will make this evident.

As the creation begins, we watch the Son setting out in his chariot surrounded by the numberless host. He is the perfect medium for his Father, and since 'all his Father in him shon' (196) we should not be surprised to find that 'the King of Glorie' is also said to be present, embodied in 'his powerful Word / And Spirit' (208-9). Imagination apprehends the visible manifestation, the more or less anthropomorphic image of the Son in the chariot, but we are aware, too, of the other presence, the 'Paternal Glorie' (219) that is felt as a quality of the Son's person rather than a separate identity. As the Son stays his chariot in the chaos, and turns the golden compasses to circumscribe the universe, we are further prompted to visualize his agency in the creation. His voice, too, holds our attention, for when God speaks the utterance is at once effective as the 'Omnific Word' (217). In short, on the instant that the Father manifests himself in creative action, the Son is present as instrument of that action.

Although in this sequence the word 'Son' is used once only (at the outset, 192), the pronouns, syntax, and narrative movement assure us that he continues to be the agent. There is thus an edge of surprise in the shift that occurs nearly forty lines later: 'Thus God the Heav'n created' (232). Nonetheless it is a shift perfectly in keeping with the notion that the Father, King of glory, goes forth *in* the Son, creating *by* his agency. The creation is the act of God the Father operating by his word and Spirit (*Works*, XV, 5). Of course the narrative method now also echoes the simple and magnificent language of the biblical account: 'Let ther be Light, said God,' 'God saw the Light was good,' 'God said, let ther be Firmament / Amid the Waters,' 'God made / The Firmament,' 'God said, / Be gather'd now ye Waters under Heav'n,' and so on. Aesthetically, Milton was right to realize that a departure from the traditional formula would entail a loss of authority in his account of the creation and detract from the element of ritual repetition. As the work of the sixth day draws to its climax, however, there is a reference to 'the great first-Movers hand' (500), and by its human quality this image turns us back towards the divine Son and prepares us for the transition that is about to take place.

As we have noted before, the passage in Genesis where God says 'Let us make man in our own image' (1:26) was frequently used as evidence for the Trinity. While Milton cannot accept this argument, he nonetheless admits that in this passage God 'speaks like to a man deliberating'

(*Works*, XV, 37). In the poem the episode brings us back to the recognition of the roles of Father and Son:

> therefore the Omnipotent
> Eternal Father (For where is not hee
> Present) thus to his Son audibly spake.
> Let us make now Man in our Image, Man
> In our similitude. ...   (7.516-20)

The moment of decision humanizes God, separating the two powers only to show how the Father acts in the Son.

The subsequent passage reveals a subtle modulation and ambiguity in the manner in which the divine actor is indicated. The speech of the Father is followed at once by the creation of man: 'This said, he formd thee, *Adam* ... in his own Image hee / Created thee, in the Image of God / Express' (7.524-8). Since the speaker was the Father, it is natural to assume that the pronoun takes him as antecedent ('This said, he ... '), from which it follows that the image of God in man is also that of the Father (but it is not as simple as this, see below, p 126). Next we hear of the creation of male and female, the blessing of mankind, the leading of man to the garden, and the prohibition, all seemingly performed by the same divine agent. But now a change occurs:

> Here finish'd hee, and all that he had made
> View'd, and behold all was entirely good;
> So Ev'n and Morn accomplish'd the Sixt day:
> Yet not till the Creator from his work
> Desisting, though unwearied, up returnd
> Up to the Heav'n of Heav'ns his high abode,
> Thence to behold this new created World
> Th' addition of his Empire, how it shew'd
> In prospect from his Throne, how good, how faire,
> Answering his great Idea.   (7.548-57)

The first 'viewing' follows the formula, and is comprehended within the ritual of the sixth day. But the second viewing takes place from the vantage point achieved by the Creator upon his ascent to his throne in heaven. While the 'Empire' answering the 'great Idea' suggests the Father, the ascent itself seems appropriate only to the Son, who alone descended in localized fashion. As we proceed, everything contrives to bring us almost unawares to the view that the agent throughout has been the Son. The divine actor leads his glorious host of angels through the blazing gates of heaven, and along the starry road to the holy mountain which is the throne of Godhead, and there

> The Filial Power arriv'd, and sate him down
> With his great Father (for he also went
> Invisible, yet staid[:] such priviledge
> Hath Omnipresence) and the work ordain'd,
> Author and end of all things. ...
> (7.587-91, punctuation as emended by Fowler)

The sequence of events since the creation of man has thus been controlled by a divine agent identified initially with the Father, but by the close located in the 'Filial Power.' Pronouns and descriptive epithets create a seamless continuity, so that one figure dissolves insensibly into the other. The passages at the beginning and end of this sequence (517-18, 588-90) provide the key, both emphasizing that the Father is omnipresent and therefore can be with the Son and yet still in heaven.

It is noteworthy, also, that the hymn sung by the angels on the seventh day in heaven refers to the Son yet does not sharply distinguish his agency from that of the Father:

> Great are thy works, *Jehovah*, infinite
> Thy power; what thought can measure thee or tongue
> Relate thee; greater now in thy return
> Then from the Giant Angels; thee that day
> Thy Thunders magnifi'd; but to create
> Is greater then created to destroy.
> Who can impair thee, mighty King, or bound
> Thy Empire? (7.602-9)

Here and through the remainder of the hymn God's omnipotence and omniscience are stressed in a way that evokes the Father, yet the notion of a 'return' to heaven and the reminder of the victory over the 'Giant Angels' seem appropriate rather to the Son. Milton concludes in *De Doctrina Christiana* that the term 'Jehovah,' like 'God,' may be applied to the Son as well as the Father (*Works*, XIV, 251). The angels in this hymn of creation appear to celebrate a divine being who includes both Father and Son.

At the beginning of the creation we are aware of the Son's departure from heaven and his descent into the Chaos to begin the work of creation; then as divine agent he becomes simply 'God,' until with the climactic creation of man he seems for a moment to have given place to the Father; finally, the divine agent returns to heaven as the Filial Power, and is received by the omnipresent being that has, paradoxically, been awaiting him.[65]

The ambiguity has been carefully controlled throughout, and the final effect is not to blur the relations of Father and Son, but to demonstrate that the Son is the instrumental cause ('by thee / This I perform,' 7.163-4) and the Father the principal cause ('Author and end of all things,' 7.591). Thus the creation achieves a different emphasis from the rout of the rebel angels, for while the latter narrative draws attention to the Son as an individual being, albeit expressing the will of his Father, the former emphasizes the way he is the Father made visible.

The Son as Mediator

The climactic event in the pre-incarnate history of the Son is the one we witness at our first introduction to heaven in the council of book 3. Foreseeing that man will fall, the Father calls for an act of sacrifice that will atone for sin; the Son offers himself, and in the sequel the Father gives the Son 'all Power' (317) and makes him 'Head Supream' and 'universal King.' The Son's assumption of the Father's omnipotence at this point, as Revard has suggested, fulfils the progressive realization of his divinity displayed through the chronologically earlier episodes.[66] From the begetting through the acts of vengeance and creation to the present expression of obedient love the Son has shown an increasingly comprehensive mastery of his role, and proved himself to be the Son of God 'By Merit more then Birthright' (3.309). As we have seen, Milton's theology makes the merit of Christ a cause of his exaltation. The poem states the case with vigour, showing a Son who successfully puts his virtue on trial and whose mediatorial office is not separable from his divine nature.

Readers have differed in their estimate of Milton's success in dramatizing the Godhead during the council, but it would be impossible to deny the impact of this scene and its important place in the design of the poem. Acknowledging the difficulty of the scene, Northrop Frye stresses its centrality, observing that 'the better we know the poem, the more important become these passages that we cannot fully understand without possessing the poem.' After the persuasive performance of Satan in the first books, the challenge to the reader now is to turn the universe inside out with 'God sitting within the human soul at the centre and Satan on a remote periphery plotting against our freedom'; there is nothing that can be done with the disagreeable God of *Paradise Lost* except to 'swallow' him.[67] This forcefully expresses the demands made upon the reader by the violent shift in perspective effected through the council. Much good criticism over the last thirty years has recognized the crucial nature of the scene and has sought to explore its mode of presentation, and we have as a result become much more articulate about the council.

Before the deliberations of the council begin, the Father looks down on his works, sees Adam and Eve 'Reaping immortal fruits of joy and love' (3.67) in the garden, and notes how Satan prepares to 'stoop with wearied wings, and willing feet / On the bare outside of this World' (73-4). His speech is directed to his Son, who sits on the throne at his right hand, although one gathers that this is a plenary session of the heavenly council with multitudes of angels in attendance. The simple physical relationships are suggestive – the Father at the centre, the Son to his right; far below, the world, approached by Satan, and containing within its outer shell the garden and its inhabitants, Adam and Eve. The Father then speaks, and tells the Son that Satan will pervert man and man will fall. The divine vision comprehends all space and all time, and we realize the finitude of man as we view Adam and Eve through the eye of God. This heavenly 'height' characterizes the entire council.

Thus we approach the Incarnation by a kind of *a priori* method: granting the fact of the Fall, here is the logic that shapes the strategic response of providence. It is interesting how little of the Gospel narrative is present. The dialogue draws heavily on the Bible, and especially on the New Testament, for its language, but the passages echoed and paraphrased generally have to do with theological principles rather than historical detail. True, we are told that the Son will be made flesh of 'Virgin seed, / By wondrous birth' (284-5), but we are not told the name of his mother, nor that of the chosen race, nor the country of his birth. We learn that the Son will become the head of mankind, but nothing is revealed about his life, teaching, and miracles, nor about the paradox that his kingship will involve adopting the form of a servant. His death is foreseen and discussed, but no mention is made of the cross, and apart from one cryptic phrase ('be judg'd,' 295), there is no reference to his enemies or to the nature of his death as a malefactor. The historical detail of the life of Jesus has been screened out, leaving only the large theological abstractions.

The reader must make an effort to grasp the general causes and intentions behind the fact of the Incarnation. The discussion emphasizes the way this second Adam makes satisfaction for the sins of the first, the union of two natures in the person of the Son, and the final triumph over Satan, Sin, and Death. Biblical citation is principally devoted to supporting these theological positions: 'As in Adam all die, even so in Christ shall all be made alive' (1 Corinthians 15:22, cited 3.287-8); 'the Word was made flesh' (John 1:14, cited 3.283-4); 'at the name of Jesus every knee should bow, of things in heaven, and things in earth, and things under the earth' (Philippians 2:10, cited 3.321-2). Milton has taken the interpretive passages about Christ's nature and office from the Epistles and the Gospels (especially the Johannine Gospel) and woven them together into a theoretical explanation of what is still to happen. The decorum governing the debate, however, requires that the pre-existent Son be kept distinct from the historical Christ, and one is given a strong impression that the Son's awareness of the future does not extend to a detailed knowledge of his future Incarnation.

The deliberations of the council in heaven, however, are not remote from human modes of feeling and response. Father and Son discuss man's future with an intense concern that is coloured by a wide range of emotion. Divine causation is thus brought within reach of judgment and interpretation. Allusion to the Old Testament encourages this process. Abraham and Moses both provide types or figures of the Son's intercession on man's behalf. The accommodation of God's ways to human understanding is exemplified by Abraham's argument for the preservation of Sodom (Genesis 18, referred to in lines 153-4 of *Paradise Lost*), and this in turn might recall Moses' arguments for the preservation of the Israelites after the offence of the golden calf and after the disaffection following the return of the spies (Exodus 32, Numbers 14). John E. Parish remarks that in these episodes God knew the solutions in advance, but used each occasion to test his chosen saints and to clarify their minds.[68] Adam's conversation with the divine presence about his desire for a mate (*Paradise Lost*, 8.357-451) is an illuminating illustration of the way Milton understood this process of education by disputation with God. The colloquy of Father and Son, while more mysterious, contains elements of a similar sort: the Son acts as man's intercessor, and elicits from the Father the justification of his ways while simultaneously proving his merit by his responses to these ways.[69]

Such elements contribute to the scene's affective power, and bring heaven closer to human modes of awareness. But, as we have seen, they are also placed within a context provided by repeated references to the New Testament, and particularly to passages in the Epistles on the role of the Son, and to passages of a metaphysical and eschatological kind from Revelation and the Gospels. The reader is led from the real but prophetic and anticipatory vision of God in the Old Testament *towards* the fully realized vision of the New Testament. But the crucial figure in that process of realization, the Jesus of the Gospels, is not directly present. Instead we are shown the pre-existent Son, whose love displays the source of the love to be realized in history through the Incarnation.

An important analogue to Milton's treatment of the council is found in the tradition of the debate among the four daughters of God whose reconciliation is anticipated in Psalms 85:10-11.[70] John Evans suggests that this tradition caused some of the embarrassments of Milton's scene, for 'in spite of Milton's explicit statements to the contrary,' the Father and Son are associated with their allegorical predecessors, Justice and Mercy.[71] But this judgment ignores the success with which Milton creates the effect of a dialectic taking place within an all-encompassing unity. His achievement can be measured by comparison with the stiffness and artificiality of Joseph Fletcher's treatment of the same subject in the third part of *The Historie of the Perfect-Cursed-Blessed Man* (London, 1629). Fletcher's speakers are such personified attributes of deity as Justice and Mercy, and like sophomores in a debating society they urge very limited and exclusive points of view. God stays outside the debate, resolving it at the close in a way not anticipated by even the most perceptive speakers. Milton's council does not suffer from this sense of shadow boxing. As Father and Son speak, all the attributes dealt with by Fletcher are touched upon, but they appear quite naturally as part of the seamless texture of the dialogue. Justice, Mercy, Truth, Peace, Wrath, Pity, and the others are there as ingredients in an ethical situation, not members of allegorical teams. This means that most attributes belong equally to the Father and the Son: both praise mercy and love, both insist upon justice and righteousness.

Our awareness of the relation between Father and Son grows in subtlety and richness as the council progresses. Shifts in style and tone serve not only to distinguish the speakers,[72] but to indicate the progress of the discussion. The council must be seen as a whole, as an unfolding process which moves through stages to a climax and which is framed by the light imagery of the invocation at the opening of book 3 and of the angel choir at the close. The progress in the revelation of the divine responses leads from restrained to exalted love, from logical analysis to ecstatic feeling. The distance between God and man narrows throughout the scene.

Initially the Father is incisive, cool, aloof; he brusquely clears his justice, but makes us aware of that 'distance and distaste' (9.9) now separating fallen man from God. His defence of his treatment of his creatures, while not really egocentric in its righteous condemnation, nonetheless provides an expression of the justice which is the reality behind the Satanic parody.[73] This, as Irene Samuel has put it, is 'the omniscient voice of the omnipotent moral law,' and 'speaks simply what is.'[74] The paradoxes arising from God's foreknowledge are daunting to the intellect, and his tendency to speak of the Fall as now in the past, now in the future, now present, leads to the feeling that this malign event is corrupting all time. Only at the close do we catch the bright flash of mercy. The Son's reply at once indicates his role as intercessor as he praises the Father's decision to offer man grace. Here, as Samuel notes, are 'the distinctive tones of a quite different voice ... the independent being speaks his own mind.'[75] But his celebration of divine mercy emphasizes that it is consistent with the goodness and glory of the Father. Mercy is the reasonable conclusion. The very attempt to show the decision worthy of the Father in this manner brings his ways closer to man.

The second speech by the Father outlines the process by which his grace will renew those who sincerely attempt to respond to it. Milton's God, as Gary Hamilton observes, is rejecting certain aspects of rigid Calvinism, and in declaring the Arminian view of general redemption he wishes to show that it is 'no more a threat to the sovereignty of God's grace than is the doctrine of absolute predestination.'[76] Renovation brings the recognition of total dependence on God, but it also restores the powers of mind and will. The extraordinary feature of this speech is the sudden turn that takes place two-thirds of the way through, introduced by 'But yet all is not don ... ' (203). Until this point, the scheme of salvation has been presented without reference to the Son. The theology of the first part of the passage is strikingly liberal, and without further qualification has about it an aura of deism. The implication is that universal grace will be sufficient to restore all men who make the effort to respond. If there is a touch of inscrutability about the Father's decision to choose some of 'peculiar grace / Elect above the rest; so is my will' (183-4), this is a prerogative which does not undermine the principle that the remainder of mankind will be given a perfectly fair trial.[77] The passage narrows still further the gap between God and man, for it shows God operating upon principles that are easily assimilated into the human ethic of responsibility. But this effect is now qualified, for at the turning point in the speech the Father reveals that salvation for man is possible only if someone is found willing to pay the penalty of death for man and thus to satisfy justice.

The manner in which the necessity of a sacrifice is introduced is in keeping with Milton's view that the ultimate object of saving faith is the Father, not the Son (*Works*, XV, 403). This is the reason that he can develop so fully the picture of man's salvation without reference to the Son. But this does not mean that the doctrine of Christ's satisfaction for sin is a pious and conventional afterthought; as we have seen, Milton considers it a central doctrine, integral to his conception of the Incarnation. One of the questions we should ask of this moment in the argument is whether it makes God's ways more or less understandable, more or less accessible to human evaluation. Does it encourage us to think what is most worthy of God? The answer will vary according to the presuppositions of the reader and the particular portion of the event he seizes upon. In one way, it appears to ignore our desire for rational explanations. Expiation for Adam's sin may only be made by a heavenly power willing to become 'mortal' in the fullest sense. It is a mysterious doctrine, and theologians were quick to point out that Timothy calls it the great 'mystery of godliness' (1 Timothy 3:16). John Owen, reflecting on the Son's 'condescention' in accepting humiliation as man's saviour, remarks that it is a mystery 'that becomes the Greatness of God with his Infinite Distance from the whole of Creation, which renders it unbecoming him, that all his ways and works should be comprehensible by any of his Creatures. ... '[78] Milton himself, although cautious in positing mysteries, observed that the Incarnation is frequently spoken of as a mystery in scripture (*Works*, XV, 265). As the subject is brought into the dialogue in heaven, we become aware of the weight of that mystery. The sudden introduction of the issue, its cryptic and formulaic presentation, come as a shock after the reasonable vision of salvation that preceded. Like the earlier argument about foreknowledge and free will, the problem of satisfaction is simply stated, not rationalized, as if the Father wished to challenge the reader's responses. Having offered an intellectual account of the operations of providence, the Father now reveals that those operations are provisional upon an act that while explicable in legalistic terms, is curiously opaque to moral feeling:

> Dye hee or Justice must; unless for him
> Som other able, and as willing, pay
> The rigid satisfaction, death for death.   (3.210-2)

Yet at the same time, the episode has the effect of making us aware of the extent to which the Father is concerned about man's predicament. He cannot tidy up the situation without himself becoming involved in it. His freedom, like man's, involves the affirmation of a moral order: 'Dye hee or Justice must' – there is no ignoring the dilemma. The effect is to remind us that God cannot simply dissipate the tragedy, for that would mean suspending the moral order which he himself created as an expression of his nature; rather he must comprehend it. In this way he approaches closer to us, not now through illuminating man's reason, but by participating in the irrational and tragic results of man's defection. Here we might feel the truth of Joan Webber's assertion that 'it is creation, it is sheer love of becoming, despite all the pain and frustration intrinsic to the process, that justifies the ways of God to men.'[79] The full force of the divine strategy is felt when the Son responds to the call for love. At this point there is a powerful release of feeling, and the mood created by it dominates the rest of the conference. Divine love is not irrational, of course, but it acts according to the higher logic of faith. A Christian, a deist, and a secular humanist would state the problem in different ways, but all would likely agree that the heightened emotion connected with love and self-sacrifice has altered the tone of the dialogue and introduced a range of response different from the energetic, but morally oppressive, mood of the Father's initial reflections on salvation, or the reasonable and encouraging tone of his preliminary account of salvation.

The dialogue creates a clear context for the response of the Son. The role adopted by the Father is one which, as Barker observes, challenges the Son 'to induce from him a loving and sacrificial response' and to show 'what the Father is confident he will show, that justice is essentially an instrument of mercy.'[80] In offering to act as man's ransom, the Son demonstrates that he understands in broad outline the nature of the task. He perceives that by being made mortal he will be exposed to humiliation and death, but he has faith that the Father will raise him from the grave and enable him to triumph over his foes. His speech gathers power as it moves to a climax in the triumphant vision of his return to heaven at the head of the multitude of the redeemed. The 'human' qualities apparent in the previous speeches of Father and Son – the pity, anger, logic, and love – are fulfilled here in the adoption of human nature by the Son, who gathers all into his expression of the divine nature. We could apply to the scene the argument employed by John Owen in his account of the progressive revelation of God in history: 'it had been absurd to bring in God under perpetual Anthropopathies, as grieving, repenting, being angry, well-pleased, and the like, were it not but that the Divine Person intended, was to take on him the Nature wherein such Affections do dwell.'[81]

It is worth noticing that the formal explanation of the Incarnation is left to the Father; indeed, part of the drama here lies in the gradual unfolding of the meaning of that act. 'Which of ye will be mortal to redeem / Mans mortal crime' (214) is the first statement of the matter by the Father, and this suggests that the volunteer may lose his immortality. The Son, offering himself, thinks in terms of legal substitution, requesting his Father to 'Account mee man' (238). He knows that this process will involve putting off, for a time (he seems uncertain about the length of the process),[82] the glory that he enjoys at God's right hand. But it is the Father who explains the theological implications of this transformation:

> thy Humiliation shall exalt
> With thee thy Manhood also to this Throne;
> Here shalt thou sit incarnate, here shalt Reign
> Both God and Man, Son both of God and Man,
> Anointed universal King. ...   (313-7)

The whole scene has been moving to this mystery of the two natures in one. What had first seemed an unpleasant but necessary device, the 'accounting' the Son to be man, is turned by providence into a positive and integrating principle. The poem suggests that the Son had not foreseen this outcome, that it is a surprising turn displaying God's power to change all to good. This final speech by the Father is a splendid and joyful celebration of the merit of his Son, who will gather all the faithful, both men and angels, into his person. The dryness of tone, rational and restrained, that marked the Father's earlier speeches has now given way to a mood of rapt contemplation.[83] The shifting tenses that in the earlier speech produce an uneasy sense of circling around the

Fall are now replaced by a firm thrust towards the future. The apocalyptic events unfold before our eyes with an effect of ease and inevitability. At their centre, exerting divine power to guide and dispose all things, is a figure who is incarnate God. The distance between God and man vanishes at this point, and God at last becomes 'All in All' (341).

The relations between Father and Son have been manifested through the debate, and grace, mercy, and peace have been anchored in the love of the Son. We have found that no easy separation of the debaters in terms of mercy and justice is possible. The Father initiates, the Son responds. The Father is not the spokesman for stern justice, for it is he who first introduces the concepts of mercy and love, and his final speech provides a vision of things hoped for. The Son is not simply the spokesman for mercy, since he is concerned throughout to rescue man in a way that clears the Father's justice.[84] The richness of tone humanizes the deity, making us aware that his ways are accessible to our minds and hearts. The climax of the process achieves the integration of man with God through the Son.

Milton's emphasis in the entire scene, then, falls on the Son's voluntary assumption of the role of mediator and redeemer. Through his response to the occasion offered by the Father, he proves himself 'By Merit more then Birthright Son of God' (309). The fact that he can take merit to himself, controversial but not in itself unorthodox in Reformed theology, is consistent with Milton's subordinationist view.[85] Freely responding to God's call in faith, and holding in perfect concord the love of God and Man, the Son becomes both the ransom for man and a model of true heroism. He has fulfilled the types offered by the intercession of Abraham and Moses.[86] The Son's trial of virtue and proof of goodness arises out of his continuing unity of will with his Father as expressed in his interceding love, obedience, and self-sacrifice; unlike the earlier scenes, in which there is a transfusion of power to the Son that enables him to overthrow the rebels or create the new world, in the council the Son shows a perfect response that lies in an act of renunciation achieved through his own will and 'fulness ... of love divine' (225). Now all power is conferred on the Son until that time when the 'regal Sceptre' shall no longer be needed for 'God shall be All in All' (340-1). Power is thus put in its place as the effect rather than the cause of the Son's victory, and as the instrument rather than the goal of providence. What the developing action of the scene throws into relief is the final importance of the state of loving obedience achieved by the Son.[87]

At the close of the council, the Father bids the angels 'Adore the Son, and honour him as mee' (343). The angel chorus which follows celebrates the Son's achievements and his exaltation. At the climax of the hymn, the chorus pays tribute to the act of humiliation by which the Son reconciles Mercy and Justice, and concludes that 'henceforth' the praise of the Son shall never be separated from that of the Father. The celebration of divine love strikes a note of Christian devotion: 'O unexampl'd love, / Love no where to be found less then Divine' (410-11). The angels have thus received a further revelation concerning the nature of their Messiah, and they stress how they now know that he who 'sat second' to the Father is at one with him. We are at liberty to infer that a change has been achieved not only in the awareness of the angels but in the status of the Son.

As we have seen, an emphasis on the voluntary assumption of the role of mediator by the Son is not uncommon in Reformed theology. Present in Calvin, it is given prominence in the writings of the later Calvinists such as John Owen by the use of the language of covenant theology. For Owen, the ground of the Gospel dispensation is 'that *compact, covenant, convention*, and Agreement, that was between the *Father,* and the *Sonne*, for the accomplishment of the worke of our Redemption by the Mediation of Christ. ... The *Will* of the Father, appointing and designing the Son to be *Head, Husband, Deliverer*, and *Redeemer* of his *Elect* ... with the *Will* of the *Sonne* voluntarily, freely undertaking that *worke*, and all that was required thereunto, is that *Compact*. ... '[88] Milton's council is clearly a representation of the making of such a covenant. Yet the covenant is for Owen eternal; for Milton, its sealing occurs at a particular time in heaven. Owen, like Calvin, envisages an agreement by which the Son undertakes the subordinate role of mediator: Milton believes the Son can act as mediator because he is by nature subordinate to the Father, not one in essence with him.

Reformed theology frequently pointed to the merit of the Son as a factor in his exaltation, although usually with a careful discrimination of the human and divine natures. Richard Baxter develops this idea in a fairly radical manner when he writes that the covenant is a revelation of the merit of the Son which impresses angels as well as men: 'Angels themselves desire to pry into this mysterie (1 *Pet*. 1.12). . And here a very *great truth* appeareth, which very many overlook, that *exaltation* of the *person of the Redeemer*, and the *glory* that God will have in *him*, is a *higher* and more *principal* part of Gods *intent* in the sending of him to be *Incarnate* and *Redeem* us, then the *glorifying of man*; and God *by us.*'[89]

So much the orthodoxy of the day permitted: a covenant by which the Son is exalted and glorified. But Baxter is able to view the office of redeemer as entailing subordination and yet affirm that the Son is not by nature a subordinate being. Where Milton is original is in his suggestion, fostered by the overall pattern of his treatment of the Son, of an earned Godhead.

While the overthrow of the rebel angels suggests the Son's capacity for individual separate action, and the creation his unity in act with the Father, the council reveals him to be both developing individual and perfect image. The sense of evolution in the Son's role is very marked when we place his actions in chronological sequence, starting with the begetting and moving through the expulsion of the rebels and the creation to the climactic events of the council. But this is not the order in which the poem presents his acts, and the effect of beginning at the end is to disguise the possibility of seeing him as an evolving character. The blaze of love and power which illuminates him by the climax of the council stays in memory, and provides the background that colours our response to the acts subsequently narrated. Milton has thus muted the unorthodox idea of the Son's evolving heroism, but he has done so in such a way that the careful reader will respond to the implication of the sequence of scenes, a sequence that invites him to design a hypothesis appropriate to its form. The presentation of God in *Paradise Lost* is consistent with the theological treatise, and yet unfolds in a mode which is persuasive rather than polemical, a mode involving the reader in interpretative judgments which are assisted but not controlled by the poet. An important difference between treatise and poem is that while the former is organized in terms of logical categories, the latter unfolds in time through the reader's experience of the narrative. This unfolding is crucial to the presentation of deity in the poem, for the reader grows in knowledge as he follows the poet-narrator through contexts for judgment.

CHAPTER FOUR

The Image of God in Man: Before the Fall

Calvin opens the *Institutes* by observing that all true and sound wisdom consists of two parts: the knowledge of God and the knowledge of ourselves. These parts are intimately related. Knowledge of ourselves arouses us to seek God and leads us on to find him. Yet paradoxically man never achieves a clear knowledge of himself unless he has first looked on God's face. From the contemplation of God, he can then pass to the scrutiny of himself and the recognition of fallen man's imperfection.[1] Milton's method in *Paradise Lost* reveals the same twin concerns, the same action and reaction. While the epic introduces us to God before turning to the dramatization of man, we are repeatedly made aware that knowledge of one is closely related to knowledge of the other, and while the perfect image of the Father is located in his divine Son, man also is made in the image of God and seeks after the Fall to restore that image. In the next two chapters I shall examine the epic's treatment of sonship as this is presented in terms both of unfallen and fallen man. In developing this topic it will be important to continue to bear in mind the role of the Son of God, who in both pre-existent and incarnate forms provides models as well as guidance for Adam and Eve.

Milton's treatment of prelapsarian experience has produced some of the liveliest moments of controversy in recent criticism. Indeed, the progress of this protracted debate through statement and counter-statement is impressive evidence of the power of *Paradise Lost* to arouse conflicting responses that effect a kind of dialectic. C.S. Lewis, in his glowing and reverential picture of Adam and Eve, the King and Queen of earth who were 'created full-grown and perfect,' restored them to their proper dignity; in doing so, however, he left Milton's state of

innocence open to the charge, prosecuted with considerable zeal by
A.J.A. Waldock, of being 'effortless,' 'blank,' and 'featureless.' Psychological interest was then discovered in the portrayal of Adam and Eve by
such critics as E.M.W. Tillyard and Millicent Bell, but at the cost of the
poem's theology: Adam and Eve, it was urged, were falling or fallen long
before the plucking of the fruit in book 9, perhaps even before the
opening of the narrative.[2] Innocence, it seemed, was either august and
dull, or secretly corrupt. Both views tended to the conclusion that real
virtue – the kind of virtue relevant to the wayfaring and warfaring
Christian – became possible only with the Fall. Rejecting the horns of
this dilemma, a number of students of the poem have now urged that far
from praising a fugitive and cloistered virtue, Milton in his presentation
of Adam and Eve is offering a dynamic image of experience before the
Fall. His treatment of unfallen man is no less controlled and consistent
than his treatment of Satan, and the theology and psychology work
together, not against each other.

A significant advance was made in the recognition that Milton is not
committed to the Augustinian view of our first parents. While Augustine acknowledges that there was in man a secret and private declension
of the will before the public act of eating the fruit, his usual emphasis is
on the serenity of Adam and Eve before the Fall, when they were
'agitated by no mental perturbations.'[3] Unlike Augustine, Milton
allows Adam and Eve to feel uncertainty, doubt, even the play of
contrary impulses, while at the same time insisting that they are still
unfallen. As A.S.P. Woodhouse argues, he permits an unusually wide
range of experience, including inner conflict, to man in the state of
innocence, and he clearly means us to see in this variety the potential for
further growth and evolution. Arthur Barker's essays dealing with this
subject are of central importance, and direct our attention to the way in
which every prelapsarian incident in the poem 'involves ... a "calling"'
and 'illustrates the possibility of refusal,' so that 'what is significant
about these incidents is not that they forbode the Fall but that they
illustrate the kind of active response that is according to the norm of
right.'[4]

Meditating on childhood memories in *The Mill on the Floss*, George
Eliot remarks that 'there is no sense of ease like the ease we felt in those
scenes where we were born, where objects became dear to us before we
had known the labour of choice, and where the outer world seemed only
an extension of our own personality.'[5] This evokes a powerful mood,
and one that appears frequently in the seventeenth-century longing for a

golden age. Such an approach to Eden was open to Milton, but he did not take it. Adam and Eve are presented as figures who develop through the labour of choice, and who move to a proper evaluation of what is dear to them only by recognizing the limits of the individual personality. Neither white thoughts from infancy nor green thoughts of pre-sexual ecstasy absorb this Adam, but rather the 'sweet ... labour' (4.328) of confronting reality. Adam's final aim, like that set out for all of us by Milton in his tract *Of Education*, is 'to know God aright, and out of that knowledge to love him, to imitate him, to be like him' (*Works*, IV, 277). Since his reason and will are not, like ours, in need of repair, his evolution is rapid. Knowledge of God, however, requires self-knowledge, and man's development is thus directed towards establishing a true sense of his identity. Baldly stated, progress depends upon the discrimination and right evaluation of three things: the 'I' or self as centre of impulse, feeling and thought; God, as the source of life and reason; and nature, or the 'other' (including other selves), that which is nether God nor self but contains notable expressions of both. These aspects of the quest are related in a way that is complementary, even dialectical. The self achieves definition through the recognition of its limits, and wholeness through an understanding of the harmonies that link it to that which is external to it.

The catalyst in the process is trial, for Adam is required to adjust to the perspectives and pressures of shifting contexts and a widening pattern of relationships. The problems he confronts are perfectly real, and cannot be solved by the automatic appeal to a formula: they require fresh responses, a willingness to make discoveries, an alert but open stance towards experience. And experience brings clarifications. Adam moves towards a living awareness of the meanings of love and obedience, and towards a seasoned knowledge of the faculties and powers of the personality, and of the ways in which they combine to produce truth or illusion.

Before the Fall, Adam and Eve take great strides towards the realization of their identities. Tillyard was right, I think, to sense 'the gradual freeing of the wills of Adam and Eve till by the time of uttermost trial the process is complete,' although wrong to conclude, as he came to do, that this movement is part of a strategy to purge an evil that is already latent.[6] Between their first moment of consciousness and their ominous separation at the outset of book 9, Adam and Eve increase in maturity. The stages of Adam's evolution are indicated by the figures with whom he works out his problems: the 'Presence Divine' (8.314), with its parental love and comprehension of his nature; the angel Raphael, a superior yet limited intelligence; his human mate, Eve, less than his equal and yet a fully individual and free agent. The movement is from the kind of intimacy with God which precedes real independence to the condition of responsibility in which the free being loves and judges for itself. In an instant God created an earth that 'self ballanc't on her Center hung' (7.242), but a similar result is achieved in the moral sphere only through time and experience. In order that Adam may freely stand, there is a sense in which he must stand free of God.

Whatever happens, Adam and Eve cannot remain as they are. Time will bring change. Repeatedly we hear that if they are obedient they will grow more and more spiritual, ascending to heaven by merit, while if they disobey the prohibition they will fall towards death and non-being. There is nothing static about life in Eden; its pleasures require energy, concentration and poise. Thus Adam and Eve assert their superiority to the beasts by labouring in a garden where vitality constantly threatens order. They trim erring branches, prop flowers that are in danger of being overcome by their own weight, clear paths of gum and blossoms, and wed the vine to the elm. As J.M. Evans argues, such activity suggests how they must also control their own development, supporting feeling with its proper object and pruning excessive curiosity or desire.[7] But more than restraint and reinforcement is involved. The garden itself will be outgrown by mankind, as Michael indicates in a surprising glimpse of what might have been:

> this had been
> Perhaps thy Capital Seate, from whence had spred
> All generations, and had hither come
> From all the ends of th'Earth, to celebrate
> And reverence thee thir great Progenitor.   (11.342-6)

Thus even the garden is not itself integral to the happiness of unfallen mankind. Rather it offers a subject for the art of man, the same art that will eventually create a much larger culture. In a similar way, human responses are not merely to be lopped, propped, and pruned; rather, the powers of the personality are to be integrated in the fresh and demanding contexts provided by the expanding pattern of relations.

Milton is thus at pains to make us realize that unfallen experience, like fallen, is involved in process. That is why we are given such a strong sense of the passage of time – psychological time – before the Fall. By flashback we are shown Adam and Eve in their first moments of life, we see (from both points of view) their courtship (however brief) and marriage, we catch glimpses of their domestic conversation and the simple ritual of their days, we sense their concern for their future children, and we become aware of the increasing maturity of their relation to each other. While the literal passage of time between our first meeting with Adam and Eve in book 4 and the fall in book 9 is very short, a matter of perhaps eight days, the narrative has managed to convey, by a variety of techniques, the sense that we have followed them through a significant period of their lives.[8] We have watched them grow, observing their responses to 'passions within ... and pleasures round about' (*Works*, IV, 319), and their efforts to temper the forces of the personality into an increasing perfection of virtue. And until book 9 brings the moment of their parting, they are successful. They proceed along a path of self-realization which is simultaneously the realization of God through his image. The unfallen experience of man is thus an initiation into the meaning of sonship or filial freedom.

In Our Image, after Our Likeness

The growth of Adam and Eve is founded upon their creation in the image of God: 'Let us make now Man in our image,' says God, 'Man / In our similitude ... ' (7.519-20). This is the first thing stressed when we meet Adam and Eve in book 4 of *Paradise Lost*:

> in thir looks Divine
> The image of thir glorious Maker shon,
> Truth, wisdome, Sanctitude severe and pure,
> Severe but in true filial freedom plac't. ... (4.291-4)

Milton thus gives a central place to the doctrine that man was made in the image of God. His treatment of the doctrine conforms in many respects to Reformed teaching, but shows distinctive elements which are often a result of his unusually strong emphasis on the trial and growth of prelapsarian Adam and Eve.

All the works of God reflect his glory, of course, but traditionally those which are 'images' hold a pre-eminent position. 'Things without intellect,' as Thomas Aquinas observes, 'are not made to God's image.' Only rational creatures, which imitate God through the possession not merely of being and of life, but of intelligence, can according to Thomas be said to be images.[9] Calvin would agree, and he remarks that when God's image is placed in man 'a tacit antithesis is introduced which raises man above all other creatures and, as it were, separates him from the common mass.'[10] Despite his emphasis on the unity of nature, Milton also restricts the term 'image' to free agents that are capable of expressing divine attributes with special intensity. All the creation shows 'goodness beyond thought, and Power Divine,' but in the lower works God is 'dimly seen' (5.157-9); in the work of the six days, Adam and Eve alone possess 'the image of thir glorious Maker' (4.292).

The image is said to shine 'in thir looks Divine,' and the phrase suggests that it has a sensible and external manifestation. Their tall, erect shapes are 'Godlike,' Adam's forehead and eyes declare 'Absolute rule' (4.301), and it is such physical expressions of the divine image that enable Raphael to speak of it as 'Inward and outward both' (8.221). Eve's beauty is a softer, more sensuous version of divine virtue, although Adam recognizes that her outward gifts are – like her inward ones – an inferior resemblance of God's image (8.540-6). Adam's assessment appears to be supported by the poem as a whole. This judgment is less qualified than the usual assertion of the subordination of Eve to Adam. Calvin, expressing a common view, states that when Paul called man, in contradistinction to woman, 'the image and glory of God' (1 Corinthians 11:7), he was referring to the domestic relation, but that Moses did not restrict the personal image to Adam.[11] This view makes the first couple equal in original righteousness, but not in the conjugal order. Milton clearly sees them as equal in innocence, but goes out of his way to emphasize that, as he put it in *Tetrachordon*, 'the woman is not primarily and immediatly the image of God, but in reference to the man' (*Works*, IV, 76). While other Renaissance commentators hint at this opinion, Milton states it firmly.[12] Milton's position is consistent with his belief that true social authority depends entirely on superior reason. Thus unlike Calvin he must stress the difference of Adam and Eve in terms of reason. (In the divorce tracts, where he seeks to explain marriage in a fallen world, Milton remarks that in cases where the wife has more reason than the husband, she should have authority.)[13] Yet Eve is fully human, possessing reason and will, and Adam's judgment that she resembles less 'His Image who made both' (8.544) needs to be balanced by the recognition that she is, as Adam requested, 'fit to participate / All rational delight' (8.390-1).

Milton's sense of the continuity of body and spirit allows him to handle the external aspects of the image more emphatically and with fewer reservations than most commentators; believing that 'the whole man is soul, and the soul man' (as he puts the matter in *De Doctrina*, *Works*, XV, 41), he does not share Calvin's fear of the heresy of the anthropomorphites, who 'were too gross in seeking this resemblance in the human body.' Calvin does not deny that the whole man bears signs of the divine creator, but he distinguishes outer from inner signs: 'For although God's glory shines forth in the outer man, yet there is no doubt that the proper seat of his image is in the soul.'[14] Milton, by contrast, does not hesitate to speak of the outward image, and he does so without appealing (as do some theologians) to the sanction given to the body by the Incarnation. Thus Raphael, in a passage which echoes Adam's praise of Eve's beauty, speaks of how God has poured his gifts on Adam, 'Inward and outward both, his image faire' (8.221), while Satan, characteristically, stresses the way the divine resemblance shines in their outward shape (4.363-4). Yet Milton agrees with Calvin, and with a long tradition of exegesis, that it is in the properties of the soul that 'our likeness to God principally consists' (*Works*, XV, 37-9), the physical reflection being of secondary importance.

Reformed theologians tend to see the image in terms of the active response of the full personality to God, and to react against the view which limits the image more narrowly to intellect. They hold that the image, while located principally in the mind, finds expression in the whole man, and in all man's faculties and inward powers. A lively passage in Calvin's commentary on Genesis gives expression to this position:

> That Paul makes the image consist in 'righteousness and holiness' is by the figure synecdoche, for though this is the chief part, it is not the whole of God's image. Therefore by this word the perfection of our whole nature is designated, as it appeared when Adam was endued with a right judgment, had affections in harmony with reason, had all his senses sound and well regulated, and truly excelled in everything good.[15]

While the seat of the image is the mind and heart, its influence is pervasive in the whole personality. Here is a view of the image in keeping with the dramatic reading of the Genesis story developed by Reformed exegesis.[16]

For Milton also the image involves the whole man. It is founded on reason, but as the Father remarks during the council in heaven, 'Reason also is choice' (3.108). The animals, we are told later on divine authority, also 'know / And reason not contemptibly' (8.373-4), but they lack the free spirit that is characteristic of God's image. Man is both continuous with the rest of nature and yet distinct from it. When God 'breathed into his nostrils the breath of life' (Genesis 2:7), man received 'that measure of the divine virtue or influence, which was commensurate to the capabilities of the recipient' (*Works*, XV, 39). The same divine influence animates every living thing, but in man it is 'fitted' for the exercise of reason as well as life (*Works*, XV, 41). As has often been noted, the thrust of this analysis is towards a kind of monism: 'man is a living being, intrinsically and properly one and individual, not compound or separable, not, according to the common opinion, made up and framed of two distinct and different natures, as of soul and body, but ... the whole man is soul, and the soul man, that is to say, a body, or substance individual, animated, sensitive, and rational' (*Works*, XV, 41). It is this individual rational substance which expresses God's image. Milton is clearly comfortable with the Protestant emphasis on the way the image engages the heart as well as the mind.[17]

The image affects the responses of the whole man:

> he formed thee, *Adam*, thee O Man
> Dust of the ground, and in thy nostrils breath'd
> The breath of Life; in his own Image hee
> Created thee, in the Image of God
> Express, and thou becam'st a living Soul. (7.54-8)

The lines manage to convey a sense of the integrity of Adam's nature with its fusion of body and soul. By conflating the two accounts of creation in Genesis (1:27, which mentions 'image'; 2:7, which mentions dust and breath), Milton implies that earthly substance and divine energy and form merge in the individual 'living soul.'

There is a long tradition of exegesis, going back at least to Irenaeus, which distinguishes sharply between the 'image' and the 'likeness' of Genesis 1:26: 'Let us make man in our image, after our likeness.' Various explications of this passage were developed. One of the most popular, accepted by many Fathers and by such scholastics as Lombard and Thomas Aquinas, held that the image consists in man's natural endowments, such as reason, free will, and memory, while the likeness to God is found in such supernatural gifts as sanctity, justice, and innocence. The earlier Reformed commentators, however, refused to accept the traditional distinction between the two terms (later Reformed commentaries invented a new one).[18] Their uneasiness was increased by the scholastic argument that man lost his likeness to God at the Fall, but retained the image of God in the natural faculties which are essential to his being. This latter position, sometimes also fathered upon Irenaeus, seemed to Reformed theologians to weaken the meaning of original sin by leaving human nature and reason more or less intact, and thus undermining belief in justification by faith alone.

Calvin and Luther, who both deny the distinction between image and similitude, conclude that man lost the divine resemblance at the Fall. While some traces or remnants of the image of God may remain, they are insufficient to enable fallen man to recover. Through sin the image has become so corrupted and obscured that we cannot grasp it with the intellect.[19] In view of the importance attributed to this exegetical crux in the age, then, it is significant that Milton agrees with Calvin that the distinction is based on a non-existent difference.[20] His agreement is apparent in *Paradise Lost* during the account of man's creation in book 7, where parallel phrasing makes it clear that one term glosses the other: 'Let us make now Man in our image, Man / In our similitude. ... ' (519-20). It is clear also from 4.291-4, cited above, in which the image is identified primarily with mental and spiritual virtues, and not with the faculties. Reason may be the eye of the image of God, but only when it is right and holy. Milton is like Luther, particularly, in his belief that the image consisted in a righteous and holy way of life.

The identification of likeness and image did not resolve the problem of the character of Adam's original perfection. The controversy about the proper reading of Genesis 1:26 was only an aspect of a larger issue with which Reformed writers were preoccupied. This concerned the natural and supernatural elements in the endowment received by Adam at the creation and the question of the operation of grace before the Fall. Protestant writers frequently endorsed the doctrine that original righteousness was in some sense natural to man. Those who did so found themselves taking issue with what is probably the dominant view of original perfection in scholastic thought, the view stated by Thomas Aquinas. Thomas distinguishes sharply between the qualities of Adam's nature which were proper to him as a man, and the supernatural qualities which represent a *donum indebitum*. The free gift of qualities not essential to human nature – such as perfect sanctity and mighty intellectual powers – is what raised man from the first moment of creation to the supernatural plane. The loss of the *donum supernaturale* at the Fall entailed man's descent from the supernatural plane to the natural.[21] In the sixteenth century the Council of Trent did not give its official approval to this view, but rather found a wording which left room for the Franciscan view that man was created in a state of pure nature and, as Duns Scotus had argued, achieved righteousness progressively. Protestants, however, single out the Dominican view of original righteousness (or some version of it) as the one against which to set their distinctive emphasis on natural perfection.

This does not mean that the Protestants agreed on the best way to define the first perfection of nature. Calvin opens his discussion of Adam's gifts by appealing to St Augustine (a writer who could be used by all sides since his mind does not seem to have been decisively made up concerning this point).[22] Calvin approves Augustine's opinion that sin corrupted man's natural gifts, and that his supernatural gifts were stripped from him. Beginning in this way, Calvin is committed to a distinction between natural and supernatural endowments. The gifts beyond nature include faith, love of God and man, and zeal for holiness and righteousness. Now extinguished, these may be recovered through Christ. Natural gifts, such as soundness of mind and uprightness of heart, were withdrawn at the same time, but since reason and will are inseparable from man's nature, they are not completely wiped out, but rather corrupted and put to evil uses. Calvin clearly wants to remove all temptation to rely on human powers.[23]

Some Reformed theologians follow Calvin's lead. Thus Wollebius asserts that the gifts of the image of God were partly natural, partly supernatural. The natural gifts were the simple and invisible substance of the soul, and its faculties of intellect and will. The supernatural gifts were clarity of intellect, freedom and rectitude of will, the conformity to reason of the whole person, and dominion over the lower creatures.[24] As Wollebius' list of supernatural gifts implies, and as his subsequent commentary suggests, the attributes consist in large measure in the right functioning of the natural faculties. Such gifts are supernatural only in so far as they are out of reach of corrupted nature unless it is restored by grace. For this reason, much Reformed theology departs from the language of Calvin on this issue, and calls such gifts natural to unfallen man. The important distinction, this school of thought concluded, is between the faculties of mind and will which are diminished by the Fall but cannot be totally obliterated without the destruction of man, and those gifts of wisdom and righteousness which were wholly lost in the Fall. But even the latter may be considered natural gifts proper to man in his unfallen state. They were created along with man's nature, they were necessary to the end for which he was created, and but for the Fall they would have been transmitted from Adam to his successors. As Johannes Hottingerus put it, in a work published in 1660, 'this original righteousness and immortality of the first man were natural gifts, not supernatural, so far as that is *natural* which the first man received with his actual nature; while *supernatural* is what is above the intact nature and its condition.'[25]

Protestants often associated the distinction of supernatural from natural gifts with Catholic apologetics. They feared it because it seemed to invite the Dominican interpretation of the Fall in which supernatural gifts are lost but nature left intact. Thus John Weemse, a Scottish divine, insists that original righteousness was natural to man, not supernatural. He rebukes the theology of the Roman church, and particularly the arguments of Bellarmine, for maintaining that Adam's holiness was supernatural, and thus that man as a natural being was 'void both of grace and sinne.'[26] This view struck Weemes as failing to justify the ways of God or to account for man's present evil plight. John Davenant, Fellow and then Master of Queen's College, Cambridge, and one of the King's delegates to the Council of Dort in 1618, argued in the scholastic manner that 'pronitas ad malum non fluit ex principis naturae integrae' (an inclination to evil does not originate in principles of unfallen nature), and reproved some Catholic writers for suggesting that in the state of innocence the inferior part of man's soul was restrained by a supernatural rein, and that otherwise he would have possessed a propensity to evil caused by too great a favouring of sensitive objects. Davenant concludes, echoing Hugh of St Victor, that in such a noble being as man was in his native and original condition, neither rein nor spur was required. Before the Fall, the sensitive appetite was sanctioned by God and functioned under the sceptre of reason.[27]

Milton does not distinguish the gifts of Adam into natural and supernatural kinds. That Adam enjoyed grace before the Fall is assumed in *De Doctrina* (*Works*, XV, 205), and evident in *Paradise Lost*. But his faculties before the Fall are in themselves morally sound and give expression to his 'native righteousness' (9.1056). Man is created in a state of natural and holy integrity, endued with 'sanctitie of Reason,' and thus self-knowing, magnanimous, and devoutly grateful to his maker (7.508-16). His faculties are sanctified but natural, nature being the art of God. As the Father explains the matter, 'I made him just and right, / Sufficient to have stood, though free to fall' (3.98-9). There is no suggestion here that the sufficiency is supernatural in character.[28] Thus

Raphael explains that he is 'perfet within,' and should require no 'outward aid' (8.642). Raphael encourages Adam to be heroic in resolution, to stand fast, drawing strength from 'self esteem, grounded on just and right / Well manag'd' (8.572-3). While Adam owes his happiness to God, his continuation in it he will owe to himself, 'That is, to thy obedience; therein stand' (5.522).

This emphasis on man's natural virtue is of course important to Milton's theodical purpose, since he wants to make it very clear that sin arises from the abuse of freedom, not from the withdrawal of supernatural support. The Father, justifying his providence at the heavenly council, puts the matter clearly when he explains that Adam and Eve are 'Authors to themselves in all / Both what they judge and what they choose' (3.122-3). Only through this radical freedom of both will and deed can they demonstrate true allegiance, constant faith and love.[29] It is this lesson which the Father wants Raphael to bring home to Adam:

> advise him of his happie state
> Happiness in his power left free to will,
> Left to his own free Will, his Will though free,
> Yet mutable. ... (5.234-7)

Milton's treatment of Adam's sanctitude thus derives from the particular Protestant position in which original righteousness is held to be natural. He does not accept Calvin's account in which such gifts are characterized as supernatural. His stress falls on the goodness and the freedom of man's created nature. Positions concerning unfallen experience are ultimately derived from the theologian's conception of fallen and renovated experience. Calvin is clear-headed about this, pointing out that the true nature of the image of God in man is to be derived from what scripture says of its renewal through Christ. Looking at Milton's position in this light, we can see his consistency. The Arminian tendencies in his treatment of the process of renovation emphasize the role of choice and free response in the regenerate, and thus offer a parallel to the emphasis on freedom in the trial of unfallen Adam. The renovation of the natural image of God restores the law of nature and enables man once more to apprehend it through reason and freely express it in action. Sanctitude in the regenerate, as well as in the unfallen, has a natural base.

Those who held that the state of original righteousness was natural to man did not deny the role of grace in prelapsarian life. Such grace, they argued, was bestowed upon man from the beginning and would have been transmitted to posterity had he remained sinless. Reformed writers could thus hold that it was natural, if not essential, to his soul.[30] Grace was required to preserve Adam in the integrity of his nature and to move him to action. All agreed, however, that such grace did not restrict the freedom of man's will. Adam received grace by which if he would he might not sin, but he did not receive grace by which he was unable to sin.

Milton makes it clear that God's providence supports Adam in the state of innocence, but he does not suggest that Adam needed actual grace as an inward incentive and aid to the performance of specific good actions. Grace activates his nature, and thus activated he is able to exercise reason and free will. As Sister Ira Corcoran concludes, Milton implies that if Adam had grace, it was habitual, not actual and efficacious.[31] Prelapsarian Adam lives in a state of sanctity which is natural to him in the sense that it accompanies his creation in the image of God. No infusions of special grace are necessary to make reason holy and the will free. Adam's habitual sanctity springs directly from God's love for his image, a love which enables man to enjoy the filial freedom of a Son.

Yet Adam in *Paradise Lost* does receive guidance and education from God. Much of this is given in the form of external graces. External graces were thought to include such aids as instruction, spiritual books, and good example. Adam is well provided with such help. Normally it is communicated by speech and thus addressed to his judgment. Revelation may take the form of command (as in the injunction concerning the tree of knowledge), of example (as in the 'terrible Example' – 6.910 – revealed by Raphael), or of debate (as in Adam's colloquy with his maker). In these encounters Adam is often told of 'Things above Earthly thought' (7.82), as in Raphael's story of the war in heaven, a story beyond the reach of human knowledge (7.75). Yet the matters that are revealed to him are accommodated to his understanding so that he can judge in terms of the moral and spiritual values which are developing in him. At other times, as in Adam's dialogue with the celestial presence about a mate, contact with God challenges reason in such a way that Adam is led to a fuller understanding of his situation. Grace, as Adam points out to his maker, can raise the creature to 'what highth thou wilt / Of Union or Communion, deifi'd' (8.430-1). In the colloquy, Adam's earthly nature is finally overpowered by the heavenly nature with which he holds converse, so that having strained his thoughts to the height he sinks down exhausted in sleep. Yet the revelation has not consisted in the passive reception of a contemplative vision, but has developed from a conversation in which Adam plays an active role and defines his status as a creature. Experience has been heightened by the activation of reason.

Revelation does occur through vision, as well as voice. At first encounter, this might seem a more internal operation of grace. At the creation of Eve, as earlier during his introduction to the garden, Adam receives influence which works on 'Fancie my internal sight' (8.461). These dreams lead to awakenings in which all that was dreamed is found to be real, and their appeal to feeling and sensation is finally capped by an appeal to conscious judgment. If the visions are initially more subjective than the voices, they nonetheless initiate an experience which is to be assimilated by the individual in terms of a rational response to God's judgments. And even the voices do not achieve their impact at one stroke, but as parts of a cumulative and increasingly judgmental process.

In the episode of the naming of the animals, grace again appears to be working internally to create a supernatural effect, for Adam is suddenly endowed with a knowledge of their nature. It is significant, I think, that he knows their 'Nature' rather than their natures. What he is given does not appear to be knowledge of a scientific kind, but a recognition of his relation to the animals, including a sense of his intermediate position as a creature not 'Brute as other Creatures, but endu'd / With Sanctitie of Reason' (7.507-8).[32] To be given knowledge about the animals is thus to be conscious that man alone is fully endued with reason. The astronomy lesson of book 8 provides ample evidence that Adam's understanding of nature develops along normal lines of inquiry and analysis, and does not show supernatural insight.

Illumination thus comes not through a voice, but through the inward working of divine influence. Yet the understanding achieved in this way can be given rational and public expression, as it is when Adam distinguishes himself from the animals during his subsequent colloquy with God. The epic contains a number of other prelapsarian episodes in which grace appears to operate in a purely internal manner without using as medium the voice of an angel or some other outward manifestation of divine presence.

This internal operation of grace is to be observed particularly when man prays. There are several examples. The grace of inspiration enables Adam and Eve to pray morning and evening with a 'prompt eloquence' which is stimulated by 'holy rapture' (5.147-9). Man reflects God's glory back to its origin through hymns of praise and thanksgiving, thus revealing his possession of the image of God. Adam grows more like his maker as he prays to him in gratitude. But *Paradise Lost* also contains prayers which are pleas for help. Adam's first prayer is a request directed tentatively to the creation for information about the creator (8.273-82). The pause that follows, which leaves Adam untroubled, is simply a prelude to the guidance provided by the divine being who proves to be the author of all things. Adam's request for a mate is answered almost immediately, and the first couple's plea for offspring will clearly be answered in due course. In these situations, prayer reveals man's wish for the fulfilment of providence. But there is another example of prayer before the Fall which is of a different kind and looks forward more directly to uses of prayer after the Fall. This occurs at the close of the morning hymn, when Adam and Eve ask that if any evil gathered during the night in connection with the dream of temptation, it be dispelled 'as now light dispels the dark' (5.208). The response to that prayer includes not only God's delegation of Raphael as instructor, but also the achievement of harmony within:

> So pray'd they innocent, and to thir thoughts
> Firm peace recoverd soon and wonted calm.   (5.209-10)

The cathartic sense of the achievement of calm of mind, accompanied by the imagery of light overcoming darkness, points forward very clearly to the experience of renovation after the Fall. Yet here there is no need of prevenient grace to take 'The stonie from thir hearts,' as when they are moved to prayer after the Fall: they do not require 'implanted Grace' (11.4, 23), for the whole law is still implanted and innate in them. The narrator's comment on their prayer, indeed, suggests that the very act of inspired praise and thanksgiving has proved the agent by which they recover peace.

The image of God is in man by way of creation. Original righteousness, while leaving room for growth, does not require special support of a supernatural kind. Adam knows what is intrinsically good from inner law, and his disposition is naturally good and holy and thus inclines him to do what is right (*Works*, XV, 115). Not only is there no need to invoke supernatural gifts which run counter to nature, but there is nothing missing from nature which must be supplemented in a supernatural manner. 'Grace' in its full theological sense is a word not applied to Adam's life until after the Fall. Yet as we have seen, there is a kind of grace at work in the garden. Whether it operates in an external manner or more subjectively, grace activates, heightens, and intensifies Adam's natural powers, especially that of reason, and prepares him for the trial that will shortly take place. According to Weemes, Adam in the state of innocence had no need of a 'preventing grace,' yet he did need stirring up, he did need a 'preparing grace' that would arouse him not from sin or sluggishness but from the intermission of action.[33] Milton seems to hold that such preparing grace provided an education concerning the conditions of trial. The trial itself had to be undertaken in complete freedom.

Perhaps the most remarkable aspect of Milton's treatment of the unfallen state is the way he invokes yet qualifies and even undercuts the ancient notion that Adam's perfection placed him beyond nature as we normally understand it. This maximal theory of original perfection has a long history stretching back to Genesis itself, where interpreters find two views of the first man: in the so-called Priestly document, man is a demi-god; in the Jahwist document, on the contrary, he is a childlike creature.[34] Elaborated by rabbinical commentary, the maximal theory of the godlike man finds expression in the exalted conception of Adam's original condition developed in the East by Gregory of Nyssa and the Cappadocians in the fourth century, and by St Ambrose in the West at almost exactly the same time.[35] Opposed to this is the minimal conception which emphasizes Adam's immaturity and capacity for growth. This is endorsed by the early Patristic writers, most notably Irenaeus, and it becomes an element in the Augustinian synthesis, in which, as John Evans makes clear, there is a blend of maximal and minimal ideas.[36] Milton, too, draws on both traditions, but he does so in such a way as to humanize the qualities attributed to Adam by the two traditions, thus accommodating them to moral and rational life.

There are repeated evocations of the maximal tradition in *Paradise Lost*. Thus man dwells in a garden containing 'pure, immortal Elements' (11.50), he talks face to face with God, he is endowed with knowledge, and he is exempt from worries and enjoys a choice of 'manifold delights' (4.435). Yet all these wonders are made comprehensible: the garden is continuous with the rest of nature (of which it is a part), man's conversations with God make strenuous demands on his intelligence, the infused knowledge of nature proves less than magical, and the happy life does not exclude doubts and trials. But while Adam is not exalted above nature, neither is he submerged in it. It is true that, like the Adam of the minimal tradition, he must learn about his world through experience, discovering not only the delights of sensation, but the disturbing power of feeling and the demanding nature of obedience. But he is no innocent child, rather a man fully responsible for his behaviour. Milton seems to be suggesting that the maximal and minimal views of Adam each contain a certain amount of imaginative truth, but that the important thing is to realize that such truth is not literal. We are given glimpses now of one pattern, now of another, so that we are led to an awareness that these are ways of speaking of the moral integrity and heightened consciousness of the state without chronic sin. The result is to create in the reader a shock of recognition. Perfection is not completion, and is thus still potentially in human nature and capable of renewal; what seems beyond our reach is actually waiting within each one of us, being already known in part. The image of God consists in free will, rational judgment, and love, and these are essentially the same at every point on the scale leading from the simplest rational innocence to the highest spiritual perfections. Evans rightly observes that Milton goes out of his way to refute the two most popular beliefs of the maximal commentators – that men fed and procreated like angels.[37] Yet Milton also draws attention to the similarities of angelic and human behaviour in these two areas. Angels can eat like men, and even digest human food in the usual way, and they enjoy erotic experience that consists, like human love, in unity. Here, as elsewhere, Milton is suggesting that what is important is not the level of being but the free choice of service and love. Heaven is more like to earth than we might think.

Perfection is consistent with limitations, incompleteness, and mutability. The likeness to God is not static and definitive: man's creation in the image of God leaves lots of room for growth. This, too, is both a traditional view and a common Reformed one. Calvin, for example, admits that the image of God was only shadowed forth in man until he should arrive at perfection. In Gospel times, the approach to perfection can only be determined by what scripture says of renovation in Christ. But while Calvin assumes parallels between the state of Adam and that of the Christian, he does not pursue these as far as does Milton, for Calvin thought of Adam as living under a covenant of works. Thus he approves Augustine's suggestion that the tree of life was a figure or a sacrament of Christ, since Adam depended on the Son of God to enable him to fulfil the covenant.[38] Later Reformed theology endorsed this view and gave it systematic elaboration. Wollebius puts the matter succinctly, noting that before the Fall man lived under a covenant of works which was confirmed by a twofold sacrament, consisting of the tree of life and the tree of knowledge, the purpose of which was to signify eternal happiness for those who obeyed, and the substitution of evil for good for those who disobeyed. While theologians argued about the number and nature of the sacraments in Paradise, they agreed that the covenant promised eternal life and required perfect obedience to the law inscribed on the heart as well as to the positive and probative law forbidding the eating of the fruit of the tree of knowledge. It was thus sometimes called the covenant of nature. The covenant of works established at Sinae was simply a re-enactment of the covenant first made with Adam in Paradise.[39]

Milton may once have held a similar view, for in *Tetrachordon* he describes Adam as having 'a law without him, as a guard set over him,' and contrasts this condition with that of the Christian, who has been set over the law by Christ (*Works*, IV, 74). However this may be, in his later remarks on unfallen life, Milton attributes to Adam much of the freedom enjoyed by the Christian. In particular he rejects the orthodoxy of the Westminster Confession by denying that Adam lived under a covenant of works.[40] Adam, he observes in *De Doctrina Christiana*, was not required to perform any works – he was merely forbidden to do one thing. Adam, like the regenerate, enjoys the liberty to fulfil the inward law through love. For Milton, this is essential to the state of sonship. The poem makes this clear in dramatic terms. The passage in book 8 in which God tells Adam the conditions on which he will be happy in Paradise (8.317-33) is not a description of a covenant being struck (Adam makes no reply), but rather of what Milton calls a declaration of power (*Works*, XV, 115). Adam, in his first speech (4.411-39), reflects on that declaration, and rightly concludes that apart from one easy prohibition, he and Eve enjoy 'Free leave so large to all things else, and choice / Unlimited of manifold delights.' The dispensation under which Adam lives is analogous to that of the Gospel in its offer of liberty.

Thus Adam's sanctitude is said to be founded in 'true filial freedom' (4.294). This links Adam both to the regenerate and to the Son. As the Son himself tenderly puts the matter during the council in heaven, Adam is God's 'youngest Son' (3.151). There are, of course, enormous differences between these two beings, the 'onely Son' (3.79) or 'radiant image' (3.63) in whom the Father shines 'without cloud / Made visible' (3.385-6), and 'Gods latest Image' (4.567), created by the Son and subordinate to other 'Sons of God' (5.447). Nonetheless, the Son is the ultimate model of man's nature, as the various references to Adam's filial position suggest. Our awareness that man is created in the image of God through the image of the pre-existent Son is shaped by the repeated emphasis which the epic places on the Son as *the* image in whom God's deity is 'beheld / Visibly' (6.681-2). If he is the only adequate image of God, it follows that he is the model for Adam's reflection of deity. Interesting witness to this is provided by the phrase describing man as made in 'the Image of God / Express' (7.527-8), which recalls a passage in Hebrews 1:3 that identifies Christ as the *express* image of God. St Augustine remarks that since the Son is like the Father by equality of essence, then that which is made in the likeness of the Son must also be made in the likeness of the Father.[41] But Milton, we know, denies the identity of essence of Son and Father. The Son is united to the Father through obedience and love, and thus provides a living paradigm of the wisdom, holiness, and righteousness which are reflected in Adam. This filial Adam lives in freedom and not under a covenant of works, for he has the law of nature within him.

Calvin, by contrast, conducts his discussion of the creation of man without much reference to sonship. Calvin does not think the *imago dei* in man should be referred directly to Christ. He sharply rebukes Osiander for his contention that Adam was made after the example of the incarnate Christ, and he condemns those who, like Servetus, claim that Adam was created in God's image because he conformed to Christ, who is the sole image of God. The latter position seems close to Milton's. Calvin maintains, on the contrary, that unfallen man reflects as in a mirror the wisdom, righteousness, and goodness of God the creator.[42] This is the usual emphasis of Reformed theologians, who consider Adam to have lived under a covenant of works and reserve 'sonship' for discussion along with adoption.[43] John Weemse makes a helpful distinction when he argues that Adam was created according to the 'essential image' of God in the holiness and righteousness common to all three persons of the Trinity, and that the personal image of the Son is achieved only by the regenerate.[44] Certainly Calvin reserves the idea of sonship for his discussion of renovation since it is a privilege of Christ's kingdom; although Christ's rule was present from the beginning, it is clearly manifest only under the Gospel. Calvin argues that men became sons by free adoption because Christ is the Son of God by nature. By becoming Son of Man with us, he made us Sons of God with him, thus providing the likeness, the image of righteousness and holiness, to which God would have us conform.[45]

But Milton treats Adam before the Fall as a Son of God, and writes as if the model for his likeness to God were found in the pre-existent Son. He avoids the metaphors which imply that the divine image is externally imposed on man's nature, like a seal on wax, and employs instead the metaphors of reflected light and of sonship. Thus he not only establishes a close connection between unfallen man and the pre-existent Son, but also an important element of continuity between the unfallen and regenerate states. The integrity of Adam's being, and the continuities of the monistic universe he inhabits, suggest that his relation to the Son involves a real conformity of will and virtue. In this way the poem implies that Adam's relation to the Son before the Fall has a striking similarity to that of the regenerate man to Christ under the Gospel. And while Milton accepts the widespread tradition that before the Fall Adam could not have known of the Incarnation, he nonetheless, as we shall see, gives his Adam enough clues to enable him to realize that his future development lies in his relation to the Son as head. Far from being remote, then, prelapsarian experience has much in common with the experience of the Christian wayfarer.

Growth, the development of man's powers in God's image, involves encounters and relations with nature. A long tradition, often attributed by commentators to Chrysostom, locates the image of God in man's rule over the animals and the lower orders of nature.[46] The description of man's dominion in Genesis 1:26-8 provides the basis for this view ('and let them have dominion'), and further support is often found in Psalm 8, with its apparent echo of the Genesis passage and its celebration of man's lordship over nature. Milton's translation of the Psalm underlines the parallel between the power delegated to man and the power of God. In *Paradise Lost*, the theme of man's original dominion is reiterated many times, being formally asserted at the creation (7.510-23, 523-34; 8.339-41) and recalled by Adam (4.430-3; 8.545). Yet like Calvin, who also emphasizes unfallen man's lordship, Milton stresses that this authority is derived from man's inward gifts. It is an effect rather than a source of his conformity to God's image. While we are not given much detail of this aspect of unfallen life, there is enough comment to indicate that in a sense Adam's empire is increasing. This is seen particularly in his practice of the art of gardening, by which he brings order into the wilderness. The world below his mountain, his nether empire, awaits his attention, the home of 'Nations yet unborn' (4.663). The animals, too, frisk about Adam and Eve and entertain them, and appear to be seeking a relation with man. While Adam knows that he cannot through converse make them 'erect /

From prone' (8.432-33), the gesture of fealty made by birds and beasts at the naming ceremony indicates their incorporation in man's sphere of activity. While a talking serpent is clearly surprising and ominous, God's assertion that the animals 'reason not contemptibly' holds promise for further development.

But it is society that provides the testing ground in which man can best grow in likeness to God. Adam recognizes that he cannot achieve that likeness in isolation:

> Man by number is to manifest
> His single imperfection, and beget
> Like of his like, his Image multipli'd,
> In unitie defective, which requires
> Collateral love, and deerest amitie.   (8.422-6)

Man's growth in the image of God requires the exercise of human love in societal relations, both 'deerest amitie' of marriage and 'all the Charities' of family relations (4.756). Adam and Eve look to the fulfilment of God's promise of 'a Race / To fill the Earth' and to 'extoll / thy goodness infinite' (4.733-4). To 'multiply a Race of Worshippers' (7.630) is also to create a context in which man may conform more closely to the maker whose image he bears.

Growth, then, involves the exercise both of rule over nature and of domestic and other societal relations. The inner law seeks expression in stewardship and in love of man. It also, of course, finds fulfilment in love of God. Adam is progressing up a scale and becoming more 'spiritous, and pure' as he tends closer to God (5.475). In terms of interior psychology, his likeness to God is located in the exercise of his natural faculties, such as reason, will, memory, and imagination. Many theologians argue that the image of God in man reflects the Trinity. Augustine was the chief source for such speculation: 'we ... recognize in ourselves the image of God, that is, of the supreme Trinity, an image ... nearer to Him in nature than any other of his works, and ... destined to be yet restored, that it may bear a still closer resemblance. For we both are, and know that we are, and delight in our being, and our knowledge of it.'[47] More specifically, the Trinity is reflected in the three faculties of the soul – the understanding, the will, and the memory.

The idea became a commonplace in the speculation of subsequent thinkers. John Donne's elaboration of the correspondence in his second sermon on Genesis 1:26 ('And God said, Let us make man in our image, after our likeness') provides a useful gloss. The three faculties, Donne explains, image the attributes of the Persons of the Godhead. Power, the attribute of the Father, is proper to the understanding: 'for no man can exercise power, no man can governe well without understanding the natures and dispositions of them whom he governes.' Donne's example is Adam's naming of the animals. Wisdom, the attribute of the Son, is imaged in the will: 'for wisdome is not so much in knowing, in understanding, as in electing, in choosing, in assenting.' Goodness, the attribute of the Holy Ghost, is best realized in terms of memory: 'to remember, to recollect our former understanding, and our former assenting, so far as to doe them, to Crowne them with action, that's true goodnesse. The office, that Christ assignes to the holy Ghost, and the goodnesse, which he promises in his behalfe is this, that he shall bring former things to our remembrance (John 14:26). ... all goodnesse is in remembring, all goodnesse, (which is the Image of the holy Ghost) is in bringing our understanding and our assenting into action.'[48]

Milton would not allow this kind of argument in a defence of the orthodox doctrine of the Trinity, and he would probably have agreed with Calvin that Augustine 'speculates with excessive refinement, for the purpose of fabricating a Trinity in man.'[49] Yet, using the terms in his own way, it is likely he could also have acknowledged with Calvin that there is something in man which refers to the Father and the Son and the Spirit, even though a definition of the image of God should rest on a firmer basis than such subtleties. Milton's subordinationism does not prevent him from thinking of divine power as triadic, as we have seen. The triadic pattern that we have been exploring is present in his treatment of Father, Son, and Spirit: in the omniscience and omnipotence of the Father, in the love revealed by the Son, whose voluntary obedience makes him the perfect image of the Father, and in the fostering goodness of the Spirit. It is this pattern, perhaps, that lies behind the description of the image of God in man as consisting in 'Truth, wisdom, Sanctitude' (4.293), that is, in knowledge, love, and holiness.[50] Understanding and will will produce knowledge and love, and serve, as we have seen, to distinguish man from the lower creation; they operate together in the unfallen experience of Adam and Eve. Adam exercises his understanding in the naming of the animals, in the analysis of dreams, and in speculations about astronomy, and his will (which of course cannot be completely isolated from understanding) is particularly evident in his preservation of temperance in knowledge and affection. Eve likewise shows judgment, as in recognizing the superiority of wisdom to beauty, and obedience, as in rejecting the satanic dream.

Sanctitude, the third aspect of the image, can thus be seen as the crowning virtue arising from the harmonious interplay of truth and wisdom. Here Donne's reference of goodness to memory is helpful, since it emphasizes the autonomy proper to virtue, the way it is expressed through the actions of a consistent personality. Recollection, the drawing together into a coherent unity of all that is known and approved, is a creative act of memory that gives meaning to freedom. It is just such a meaningful freedom that Adam and Eve seek to realize. The effort to imitate God by making the faculties responsive to his will, truly knowing God with the mind and loving him with the heart, thus leads to the active life of good works.

The experience of Adam and Eve in the state of innocence holds certain analogies with that of fallen man seeking to become regenerate. While they are at no time blinded by the letter, their apprehension nevertheless grows more spiritual. They, too, are under the obligation of 'closing up truth to truth' (*Works*, IV, 339) as experience becomes more complex and varied. The ideal is an alert poise that rises above the dependencies that nourish it. Such a condition suggests the creative use of memory described by Donne, that act of recollection by which we draw together 'our former understanding and our former assenting so farre as to doe them, to crowne them with action.' Short though Adam's life is before the Fall, he has much to recall as the moment of testing approaches, not only the direct awareness of pleasures without and passions within, but also the experience of evil and creation made available indirectly by Raphael's narrative. Adam's story of the creation of Eve at the end of book 8 is a real climax to his education, and reveals the central place of recollection in the ethical life.

Education for Trial

My purpose now is to explore the growth in consciousness by which Adam and Eve realize more and more fully the divine image. Man gradually takes possession of filial freedom by expressing it in choice and action. This process is worth examining in some detail. As in the case of the Son, the presentation of the changes in man is managed through a sequence of dramatized moments, each one showing a response to testing. The beginning of this process is located in the accounts of the first moments of consciosness provided by Adam in book 8 and by Eve in book 4. Milton shows how from these beginnings there is a progressive evolution of the unfallen couple which involves a testing of their relations with each other, with their world, and with God. Milton dramatizes the discoveries by which they learn to judge, and shows them increasing in knowledge about the significance of law, love, evil, and grace. They participate in their education with vigour, gaining insights into the rhythms of their experience and the poise essential to an adequate response. Milton emphasizes how they grow through time towards wisdom. Over them stands the figure of the Son, whose example in filial obedience is made known to them through Raphael's narratives and whose presence in the garden gives Adam his most direct contact with God.

The place to begin the discussion is with the account that Adam gives of his creation to Raphael in book 8. His first impressions as he awakens into consciousness are of the 'flowerie herb' on which he lies and the 'Balmie Sweat' on his skin that is rapidly drying under the sun (8.254-5). Tactile, thermal, and olfactory sensations dominate, and bring a fugitive awareness of self that gives way almost at once to wonder as he gazes awhile at the expanse of heaven above him, absorbed in the perception of space. He next leaps to his feet, led by instinct to realize that his posture is erect, not supine, and stares in delight at the varied, animated scene about him. The pleasure he feels at this smiling world draws his attention back to himself, so that he peruses his body and tries out his physical powers, walking and running with 'supple joints':

> But who I was, or where, or from what cause,
> Knew not. ... (8.270-1)

The responses of the first few moments of life culminate in the question of his identity – who am I? – and this leads him back to external nature with a new urgency as he asks for instruction: 'Tell, if ye saw, how came I thus, how here? / Not of my self; by some great Maker then ... ' (8.277-8). The use of direct speech creates a vivid sense of the mood of excitement and probing. Adam's first speech is a request for illumination concerning the creator of nature and the self, and ends with a revelation of the impulse to worship. He displays cogency as a natural theologian: unlike Satan, he grasps the limitations of his knowledge (compare Satan's claim to be 'self-begot, self-rais'd' in 5.860), and moves at once to a recognition of God's power and goodness, basing his judgment partly on the sense that the beauty outside him must be the work of some 'great Maker,' but even more on the vitality he feels within himself. The arguments for the existence of God from design and 'conscience' are both adumbrated in the brief scene, but so too is the doctrine that man cannot have a satisfactory knowledge of God on the basis of nature or reason alone. Adam needs a revelation.

The scene of the awakening creates a superb image of the vitality of unfallen life. Adam's intellectual pleasure arises from his restless, energetic search for the meaning of existence. He leaps into life, crying for contact with the unknown God and consequent self-knowledge. The terms of his search – self, God, nature – have now been firmly established, the rhythm of the episode being a characteristic one in which a tendency outward to nature is played off against an inward, self-oriented movement, and the resolution of the tensions thus generated is left to providence.[51]

Adam is now granted an interview with his maker. The terms used to describe the appearance of the deity are suggestively vague, but the brightness of the vision does not quite hide some human characteristics. The divine shape is able to take Adam by the hand, to raise him with feudal courtesy, to hold a 'cleer aspect' or to increase in intensity in a way that suggests a smile, to emerge in brightness from the shade of trees, and to perform the surgical operation by which Adam gives birth to Eve. One senses that a power more than human has taken this form in order to accommodate itself to man's perceptions. Adam's alternation between sleep and waking suggests the manner in which the presence quickens the powers of the personality, both conscious and unconscious. The divine shape is unaltered in dreams, and this achieves an effect of surprise by reversing the fallen experience of dreams in which (as in Milton's Sonnet XXIII) bright figures vanish as the dreamer awakens.

God's presence is most fully realized as a voice,[52] a voice that is always gracious but that increases in intimacy as the divine colloquy continues. God begins by observing that he has come in response to Adam's call, so that the first lesson taught by grace is the efficacy of prayer. Adam's response is to fall prostrate in adoration. God graciously raises him, and the scene develops in an atmosphere of ceremony and benevolence as the Maker gives Paradise to Adam 'to Till and keep, and of the Fruit to eate' (320), warns him not to touch the prohibited fruit of the tree of knowledge, 'The Pledge of thy Obedience and thy Faith' (325), wills the entire earth to Adam and his heirs, and finally confers upon him dominion over the beasts. Adam is silent during this speech, for no immediate response is required on his part. As we have seen,

Adam is not under a 'covenant of works'; as a being naturally good and holy, he does not need to covenant to perform that to which he is himself inclined, while the prohibition on the tree is an exercise of God's judicial power that does not need ratification by Adam's consent (*Works*, XV, 113-5). God's testament is thus couched in a style succinct and legal; Adam's gradual recognition of its full meaning – as an invitation to reason and a challenge to faith – demands further thought and experience.

Analogues are already beginning to teach Adam that he is made in the image of God. As God is 'Author of all this,' so Adam is 'first Father' (4.495) of mankind; as God is 'Universal Lord' (8.376), so Adam holds the inferior creation in subjection. While the birds and beasts pay fealty to him, he finds his understanding quickened:

> I nam'd them, as they pass'd, and understood
> Thir Nature, with such knowledg God endu'd
> My sudden apprehension. ...   (8.352-4)

Natural wisdom, as Milton remarks in *De Doctrina Christiana*, is a consequence of the image of God in man (*Works*, XV, 53). The extent of Adam's knowledge before the Fall was a subject that aroused some controversy, but Renaissance commentators generally agreed in pointing to its limits. Edward Reynolds was fairly representative in remarking that Adam had 'so much of *Natural Knowledge* as should dispose him for the Admiring of Gods Glory, and for the Governing of other Creatures over which hee had received Dominion. ... '[53] Such knowledge would not involve the ability to perform an anatomy or account for the circulation of the blood. Milton's Adam, I have suggested (above, p. 122) is cast in this tradition. His understanding of the animals is not exhaustive scientific knowledge but the 'lowly' wisdom that enables him to see their inferior place in the scale of being and their contribution to the providential order. Adam's previous naming of the sun and moon does not mean that he grasps astronomy, nor does his naming of woman indicate more than a recognition of her role and origin.

The 'sudden apprehension,' in fact, is an intuitive short-cut, divinely fostered, to knowledge that was accessible through the ordinary processes of reason. In the normal course of things, those processes depend on the response to sensation and other external stimuli. Indeed, one of the remarkable traits in Milton's portrait of Adam is the way he avoids suggesting that Adam's development is governed by innate ideas.

Creation in the image of God does not entail such knowledge. Adam establishes his identity, not by introspection, but by engagement with the world around him. In this, Milton's treatment seems more Aristotelian than Platonic, at least in the sense those terms held for the seventeenth-century reader. Nathaniel Culverwell, for example, rejects the innate ideas of the Platonists, and argues for the Aristotelian view that the soul, entering the world as an *abrasa tabula*, arrives at common notions or seminal principles by responding to sense impressions: 'we will look upon the understanding as *speculum non coloratum*, a glasse not prejudic'd nor prepossest with any connate tinctures, but nakedly receiving, and faithfully returning all such colours as fall upon it.'[54] As John Weemse put it, 'first principles are not actually written in the heart of man, but potentially: the minde of man is not like a seminarie, which containeth in it diverse sorts of seedes. ... but it is like unto the eye, which being inlightened by the Sunne, hath that naturall facultie in it to discerne colours; So the minde frameth these principles when the objects are layd before it.'[55] It is in this spirit that Milton portrays Adam's responses. He is not fully equipped with ideas, but shows the operation of the law of nature implanted in him by his ability to draw the right conclusions from his experience.

The naming ceremony has heightened Adam's sense of the grandeur of God, and he appeals now for a name by which to praise him, admitting that the deity 'Surpassest farr my naming' (359). Yet the very transcendence of God seems to lead him back to his own finitude and incompleteness: 'but with mee / I see not who partakes' (363-4). What follows is a lively demonstration of Adam's ability to think for himself, and to draw inferences from what he has seen and been told. The divine voice observes, not without a smile, that Adam has all the creatures for company; Adam replies that they are unequal to him, and hence cannot provide true fellowship; God questions this repudiation of solitary pleasures, and points out that he has himself been alone for all eternity, and Adam rejoins, yes, but you are God, infinite and perfect, while I am a man, 'in unitie defective' (425) and perfect only 'in degree' (417). God is delighted by the vigorous intelligence of his creature:

> Thus farr to try thee, *Adam*, I was pleas'd,
> And finde thee knowing not of Beasts alone,
> Which thou hast rightly nam'd, but of thy self,
> Expressing well the spirit within thee free,
> My Image, not imparted to the Brute. ...   (8.437-41)

Adam's response to the dialectic of argument has led him to recognize his intermediate position in the scale of being; he is superior to the animals by his possession of reason, God's image, yet in relation to God he is finite and incomplete. This new awareness of his nature has been won through the effort at comprehension occasioned by God's challenge, and it brings with it a more penetrating awareness of God's nature. The divine omnipotence has been recognized by reference to God as creator and ruler, and reinforced by the analogy of Adam's limited empire. God's transcendent attributes – his unity, incomprehensibility, infinity, and eternity – are grasped with only a little prompting and realized through contrast with man's limited nature. Goodness and justice, two attributes of crucial importance in the operation of God's ways to man, are brought home to Adam through the experience of the debate itself. The climax of the revelation lies in God's identification of his image in man – the free spirit that acts on reason. Not simply transcendent Maker and Lawgiver, this God is pressingly immanent, and insists on being known through participation in ethical relationships. And by creating Eve in Adam's image, God gives him further evidence concerning the workings of divine love. At the close of the episode, Adam searches once more for a name by which to express his response, and comes up with 'Creator bounteous and benigne' (492).

Eve describes her birth into consciousness in book 4 of the poem, so that as we listen to Adam's story we are able to compare it with that of his wife. The similarities and differences are instructive. She awakens in shade, and this seems appropriate to her gentler, less direct, confrontation with the world, and her association with dream and illusion. Like Adam, she wonders 'what I was, whence thither brought, and how' (4.452), but she does not make the imaginative leap to 'some great Maker.' The murmur of water, in Adam's story only one of many signs of life, here exerts a compelling music that leads her to the pool. Looking into this illusory heaven, she is greeted by her reflection:

> I started back,
> It started back, but pleas'd I soon returnd,
> Pleas'd it returnd as soon with answering looks
> Of sympathie and love. ...   (4.462-5)

This 'smooth watry image' (480) is a cheat, since it lacks the free spirit that characterizes a true image. Eve is rescued from its mimicry by the voice which explains that she is looking at herself, and which then leads her to her true image, Adam. Even then she has a moment of hesitation, finding Adam less soft and mild than the compliant shape in the water. Adam's speech explaining her origins and their unity, reinforced by his firm yet gentle touch, changes her mind. Dennis H. Burden points out that Eve's hesitation dramatizes her free choice of Adam.[56] Presumably this is the same brief pause that Adam describes to Raphael later, throwing the incident into quite a different light by stressing how it revealed Eve's innocence and honour (8.501-10). A comparison of the two accounts of the event, both true, reveals the subtlety of Milton's treatment of the relationship. Eve remembers the moment as one in which she shrank from masculine vigour, Adam as a just expression of her dignity and of the value of her love. Each is aware of having grown by the other, and each is aware that the reconciliation of opposites has been brought about by the persuasion of reason.

To view Eve at the pool only as an ironic anticipation of the Fall is to misread the poem badly. The humour, irony and charm of the story are qualities of the story-teller, and her articulate speech stands in contrast to the silence of the childlike nymph she describes. Eve is looking back at an earlier period of her life, a time when she lacked her present maturity, and the effect of the story is thus to emphasize the degree to which she has developed. Her recreation of the past event shows how fully she has mastered its implications. The original narcissistic impulse was of necessity innocent, since until the voice speaks she does not realize that she is looking at herself. The experience concerns a basic phase of the process of individuation in which self discovers its separateness as a centre of perception and feeling. Her first impulse is towards a comfortable solipsism, in which the ego and the other merge, and thus she is drawn back to the 'smooth watry image.' The awareness of her individuality aroused by her meeting with Adam is at first alarming, but uneasiness gives way to pleasure as she realizes her place in a larger reality. Her instinctive groping towards completion in another self finds its echo and fulfilment in Adam's cry: 'Part of my Soul I seek thee, and thee claim / My other half' (4.487-8). Thus Eve, like Adam, begins life with a drive away from isolation and towards the discovery of self through relationships, and like him she confirms her impulse by a choice.[57] But all this was in the past, and she tells the story now in order to convey her present love.

The two flashbacks that we have examined stand at the beginning and end of the Edenic portion of the story. They give prominence to the theme of the growth of unfallen consciousness which is central to this portion of the story. Even as we encounter Adam and Eve for the first time in book 4, we are made to feel that they have already lived long enough to establish a normal pattern of behaviour. They have a past, and they have increased in knowledge and experience. The sequence of events in their day is no longer surprising or novel to them, but has the satisfying familiarity of ritual. No longer directly guided by divine voices and shapes, they appear to have achieved a degree of valid independence. They are beginning to stand on their own. Adam's easy reference to the 'nature' that through night 'bids us rest' (4.633) indicates how they have come to accept the ordinary workings of God's providence. Eve's beautiful lyric celebration of their love finds it woven through 'All seasons and thir change' (640). Adam's first speech (4.411-39) in the poem is cleverly designed to suggest how experience has begun to open up the meaning of their state. This is clearly not the first time he has spoken to Eve of the terms set out in God's testament ('for well thou knowst'), including the prohibition. He is not instructing her, but sharing his meditations with her. As he rehearses the conditions of their life, he glosses and amplifies, showing the effort he has made to understand them. The 'power' that made them must be infinitely good. Everything is grounded on that. They have done nothing to merit his favour, for the only service required by God – obeying the prohibition on the tree – has proved easy. He has clearly now some experience of the 'manifold delights' open to them, and he has discovered that their garden tasks, too, are full of pleasure. The prohibition, which has aroused his concern to the extent that he has speculated on the meaning of death ('Som dreadful thing no doubt'), seems a small price to pay for the bounty they have been shown. This is perhaps the most insecure point in Adam's review, for he fails to comment on knowledge, and speaks of obedience in terms only of the natural bent of inclination ('easy,' 'hard') rather than of the freedom of the will. What the speech reveals, then, is Adam's effort to draw his experience together in a manner that justifies God's ways to him. He has learned much; he has more to learn.

The contrast between Adam and Eve in this first scene clearly emphasizes her subordinate but individual role. Adam's attention is on the providential order that shapes their lives, giving them dignity and purpose. He is forward looking, his eye already on the morrow's work (he mentions it twice) and future developments that may be in store for them (the 'Nations yet unborn,' 663). Eve's speeches are intensely personal, subjective, particular, inward looking, a kind of descant on their love sounding over Adam's reflections on their relation to nature and heaven. Her single question concerning the world around them ('But wherefore all night long shine these ... ?' 657) is almost comically abrupt, and obviously designed to prolong Adam's speculative mood. The very harmony of their relation suggests how far they have come since Eve's momentary hesitation on being shown Adam. Yet the moods of paradisal life are not unchanging. A week later Eve will awaken filled with unease about the progress of their work in the garden, worried lest together in their work they 'forget all time' and lose the day, and Adam will find himself arguing that there is no need to be anxious, for nothing without her is sweet. It is as if their former words to each other had undergone a strange transmutation in memory, producing unforeseen responses and half-conscious qualifications. Growth through time holds these sudden turns, challenging achieved poise and integration.

The catalyst of further development is the demonic dream inspired by Satan in the sleeping Eve. It is a characteristic anxiety dream 'reflecting waking concerns,' in which Eve imagines herself performing the act that has been forbidden.[58] Her account of the dream reveals a split reaction: on one hand is the attraction (difficult to admit) felt during the dream towards the experience of self-transcendence and the guide who makes it possible (the beauty of the evening, the fairness of the tree, the angelic qualities of her guide, and the wonder of her sudden 'exaltation'); on the other hand is her horror at the deed, her passivity and reluctance to participate, and her subsequent relief that it was only a dream. There is here the same division between the compelling charm of the desirable and the reservations of the intellect that marks Adam's later description of his feeling about Eve. The dream thus brings an awareness of the kind of conflict possible within the self, an experience of the meaning of disobedience that should put both Eve and Adam in a better position to resist temptation when it is offered.[59]

The distress caused by the dream is extensive and difficult to shake off. The sadness includes Adam, for as he explains this trouble 'Affects me equally' (5.97). For him, as for Eve, it is a first experience of evil. For both, too, it brings home the fact of their separateness. Adam was absent in Eve's dream, and their conversation and kisses now are an attempt to effect their reunion. Adam succeeds in cheering his wife and himself, and all being thus 'cleard' they emerge into sunlight and praise their maker with 'prompt eloquence' (149). Having done their best to settle the problem by reason and affection, they turn to God in prayer. Even now the dream is not forgotten, however, for the prayer ends with an appeal to God, who called light out of darkness at the creation, to disperse any evil that might have gathered during the night. Now at last they recover firm peace and calm; but the dream continues to have repercussions, for it is in response to their prayer that God sends Raphael down to instruct them. Their attempt to adjust to Satan's incursion into their world has taught them not merely about themselves, but about the importance of prayer. The process established, by which a problem is worked out on the human level to the point at which an appeal can be made to God, is neglected during the scenes leading to the Fall, but revived thereafter.

Adam's analysis of the dream is perceptive. He recognizes that it contains echoes from their talk of the previous evening, and he uses this as evidence to support his view that it was a product of fancy. During the period when reason is dormant, he explains, fancy imitates her, misjoining shapes and creating 'Wilde work' (112). Yet this account, as Adam recognizes, is not adequate. Eve's virgin fancy, like that of nature, should have produced a 'Wilderness of sweets' (294), not this demonic vision of evil. Adam, of course, has no way of knowing the source of the 'addition strange' (116) that his theories leave out of account. He can see, however, that there is no sin without responsibility:

> yet be not sad.
> Evil into the mind of God or Man
> May come and go, so unapprov'd, and leave
> No spot or blame behind: Which gives me hope
> That what in sleep thou didst abhorr to dream,
> Waking thou never wilt consent to do.   (5.116-21)

This is sound advice as far as it goes, and it points to the educative value of the dream, with its experience of moral alternatives. Yet many readers have felt that there is something a bit facile about Adam's optimism. As Balachandra Rajan observes, Adam evades the warning which he ought to deliver.[60] He dismisses the dream as if it were totally innocuous, instead of seeing it as a challenge requiring a concentration of all their powers. Perhaps he is too solicitous in his own distress to allay the perturbations of Eve's mind. In short, his speech lacks a sense of the reality of evil. Mimic fancy, playing in reason's absence, is a figure as innocent as Eve flirting with her watery image. Of the way reason may be surprised by 'some faire appeering good' (9.354) he has nothing to say. His psychology is abstract and theoretical, based on the kind of artificial separation of the powers of the soul characteristic of an introductory text book. The ethical life is assumed to be a highly intellectual operation involving joining and disjoining, consent and approval, but lacking in that sense of trial, crisis, and engagement which makes the will a real power.

It is precisely to illuminate Adam on these issues that Raphael is now sent by God to visit him. He is not merely to warn Adam of the presence and intentions of Satan, but also to teach the doctrine of freedom (5.233-8). Adam must be made to comprehend the process by which the wrong choice may be made by the conscious mind.

Raphael proves a deft teacher, clever at leading the discourse on by a natural progression to his central theme. In response to Adam's question about food in heaven, Raphael describes the scale of being and reveals that man may progress up it, may become more refined, more like the angels, and perhaps turn at last 'all to Spirit' (5.497) if he remains obedient and thus retains God's love. Adam's reply is symptomatic:

> What meant that caution joind, *if ye be found*
> *Obedient*? can we want obedience then
> To him, or possibly his love desert
> Who formd us from the dust, and plac'd us here
> Full to the utmost measure of what bliss
> Human desires can seek or apprehend?   (5.513-18)

Adam's words reveal that his ideas about obedience lack clarity and psychological perception. He simply cannot imagine the process that would lead to disobedience. I do not mean, of course, that he fails to see the importance of the fruit of the forbidden tree as the 'sign' of obedience: this has already been emphasized by the testament of God himself. But Adam must progress into a living awareness of the way obedience is a fully human condition dependent upon a harmony among the powers of the soul. Even in Paradise, man cannot rest in what *Areopagitica* calls an 'implicit faith' (*Works*, IV, 333).

Raphael in his answer places emphasis on free will: God requires voluntary service, and would find no pleasure in creatures who were bound by fate or necessity. Man, though perfect, is mutable, and trial will determine the quality of his love for God. Like the angels, man holds his happiness through his obedience; 'freely we serve, / Because wee freely love' (538-9). It is the doctrine of *Areopagitica*, adapted to the unfallen state. To Adam it is divine philosophy, more delightful than angelic music,

> nor knew I not
> To be both will and deed created free. (548-9)

Richardson provides an incisive gloss here: 'nor was it unknown to me that my will and actions are free. I knew I was free. Two negatives make an affirmation.'[61] While this is the logic of the statement, its emotional effect is somewhat different. (The very fact that the commentator considered a gloss appropriate points up the danger that two negatives may *feel* like simple emphasis.) No doubt Adam thinks the double negative in this context more polite than a blunt affirmative, less likely to seem arrogant or critical. We also might sense, however, that Adam is just perceptibly on the defensive; the omission of the doctrine of freedom in his previous speech, these words imply, should not be taken to mean that this doctrine was unknown to him. More important, the remark makes it clear that Raphael has brought Adam a step closer to a full understanding of the nature of freedom. What was once not unknown is rapidly becoming more and more clearly defined and known. Yet even now that knowledge is too theoretical. Adam draws back from the possibility of temptation, taking refuge in the reaffirmation of the view that love is the only imaginable response to God's goodness. He has more to learn.

(8)
<> This is arbitrary. A. says his freedom isn't news -- period. He doesn't say it is "more known."

Raphael's cryptic allusion to 'some' who are fallen has, not surprisingly, aroused anxious curiosity. Adam is like a younger son who, learning of the rejection of the parents by an older brother, suddenly becomes aware of his voluntary relation to them. Raphael now has the opportunity to develop his argument through the story of one who was created free but proved disobedient and thus broke 'union' (5.612) with God. Satan's career is presented as a 'terrible Example' (6.910) of what happens when the growth of the self becomes diseased. His rejection of God entails the loss of contact with external reality and a consequent regression into solipsism and paranoia. In rejecting his sonship, he loses his freedom; the revolt against dependence leads to servitude, 'Thy self not free, but to thy self enthrall'd' (6.181).

(b), (c)
[ ] A isn't confident at 5.550-53 because he doesn't know his will can go wrong (5.548-49) but because he's sure it won't. Whatever the basis of that assurance, the existence of somebody who both could & did it doesn't shake it -- esp. if the somebody was <> caused to go wrong by a disease of the self.

By the close of the story of the war in heaven, the narrative has presented Adam with a powerful demonstration of the tragedy of the self-enclosed individual. In order to bring history to the point where Adam's memories begin ('that posteritie / Informd by thee might know,' 7.638-9), Raphael now provides an account of the creation of the world that takes up most of book 7. As well as revealing how divine energy is expressed in the variety, fertility, and order of the cosmos (and thus making explicit what Adam had sensed from the earliest moment of life), the story of the work of the six days emphasizes the difference between man and the rest of the creation, reiterating in the speeches of God and the angel choir the special status of man as 'image' and 'similitude' of God. As the 'Master work,' man acts as a kind of mediator between the rest of the creation and God, being set off from the rest of the creatures by 'Sanctitie of Reason' (7.508). Self-knowledge is the key to man's important position: from this he draws his authority, and from this arises the love that enables him to communicate with God (7.505-16). The answer to Satan's solipsism lies in the recognition that identity is achieved through acceptance of relations and dependencies.

The disturbing qualification of Raphael's early speech, 'if ye be found obedient,' has expanded into a comprehensive treatment of the meaning of obedience. The demonic form of selfhood has been contrasted with the institution of the image of God in man. Adam, who has been listening with diminishing doubt and burgeoning delight, has been taught of good and evil by the vicarious experience offered through imaginatively presented history. Disobedience, once inconceivable, has been dramatized in the story of Satan in a way that is vivid and searching. He has also been given an image of goodness in the revelation of the Son, the 'filial Godhead' (6.722), in whose exercise of freedom Adam is to find a model to help him realize his own sonship. Milton, it should be remembered, wants us to bear in mind the distinction between our own knowledge and Adam's. Indeed, the discrimination of the two is part of the imaginative discipline of the poem, by which the reader is led into a fresh awareness of what he thought he knew. Adam, of course, lacks the revelation of the incarnate Son made in book 3 in the context offered by God's overview of all time. He does not yet require a ransom, and it would be most inappropriate for him to be given a glimpse of that act of humiliation by which the Son will exalt manhood to God. The Son he learns about is the avenger and creator, the Son who sallies forth in the splendid chariot of his Father to overthrow evil and turn it to good. The embodiment of perfect obedience and love, he is seen to merit the divine powers transferred to him by the Father. Thus he offers a model by which Adam may direct his growth by degrees of merit to a more spiritual condition. Learning that this is God's 'onely Son' (5.604) and the image of the Father 'in all things' (6.736), Adam can better understand his own role as *a* son of God made to his image in *some* things.

Yet the speeches in heaven presented by Raphael suggest that the relation of the Son to man may be more intimate than that of example. There is food for meditation in the Father's remark that all the inhabitants of heaven will unite in the Son to form something like 'one individual Soule' (5.610). More explicit is the Son's adumbration of his glorification by the Father:

> Sceptre and Power, thy giving, I assume,
> And gladlier shall resign, when in the end
> Thou shalt be All in All, and I in thee
> For ever, and in mee all whom thou lov'st. ...   (6.730-3)

This, indeed, echoes the conclusion of the council in heaven in book 3; the eschatological climax foretold by the Son will be the same whether man stands or falls. Adam, of course, cannot now understand its full implications, for he is not taught all things at one time. But he should be able to place this vision of ultimate unity in relation to what he has learned about the possibility of progress up the scale of being to states 'more spiritous, and pure' (5.475), and from this to guess that the future will bring some further manifestations of the Son as man's Messiah. In this economical way Milton solves the vexed problem of whether Adam had knowledge of the Incarnation. He retains the enriching idea that Adam foresaw his union with the Son ('for the excellencie of the mysterie, and because he was to bee the head of mankinde,' as John Salkeld put it),[62] yet without the embarrassing possibility that Adam also foresaw his Fall. He does not go as far as Osiander, who aroused Calvin's scorn by maintaining that Christ would have become a man even if the Fall had not occurred.[63] But he manages to affirm the unifying function of the Son apart from the process secured through the Incarnation.

The Adam of book 8 is, in the best sense of the words, a more sophisticated being than the musing figure we met early in book 4.[64] His progress is indicated during his account to Raphael of the 'rigid interdiction, which resounds / Yet dreadful in mine eare,' by the ease with which he adds the qualification 'though in my choice / Not to incur' (8.334-6). The last of the Edenic books shows Adam now participating in the educational process, first setting the terms in which the astronomy lesson is to be conducted, then offering his own account of Eve for the consideration of his angelic mentor.

The first of these discussions shows a preoccupation with the stars far more abstract than in the early conversation with Eve, although here the sophistication does not seem quite satisfactory. As he considers the vastness of the universe and the enormous distances travelled by the heavenly bodies, Adam feels for a moment that the cosmos is alien and incomprehensible. The seeming anomalies of a geocentric universe suggest that nature herself is capable of disproportion and superfluity. It is as if Adam were scanning 'this goodly Frame' (15) in search of his reflection; failing to find the outlines of the familiar image, he suffers a vague sense of dislocation. The anxiety concerning space, characteristic of the seventeenth century and recalling Pascal,[65] comes as a surprise so shortly after the lyric animism and anthropocentric bias of the creation story in book 7. (In the first edition of *Paradise Lost* the two books are one, and the effect of strangeness even more pronounced.) Adam's question may have been triggered by the song of the chorus, as Barbara Lewalski suggests,[66] but it also seems to be an uneasy reaction to the magnificence of his position of 'Master work' celebrated in the account of creation, a kind of vertigo which momentarily dries up his powers of imaginative response. As Adam puts it later, summing up what he has learned, 'apt the Mind or Fancie is to roave / Uncheckt, and of her roaving is no end' (188-9). The intrusion of fancy into the arena proper to judgment recalls Eve's dream. Significantly, Raphael says to Adam, 'Dream not of other Worlds' (175). The imagination, one contemporary writer put it, is 'a Facultie boundlesse, and impatient of any imposed limits, save those which it selfe maketh.'[67] The mind's dangerous power to wander 'beyond all limit and satiety' (*Works*, IV, 320) is a result of the promptings of 'fancy'.

Raphael begins his reply by admitting that heaven is 'as the Book of God before thee set, / Wherein to read his wondrous Works' (67-8), but quickly goes on to underscore the opportunites for pride implicit in Adam's question. Man is not the measure of all things, and must realize that what is beyond his comprehension, far from being meaningless, is contained within God's providence: 'the great Architect / Did wisely to conceal, and not divulge / His secrets to be scann'd by them who ought / Rather admire' (72-5). Here is wisdom and frugality of a different order from that sought by Adam. The angel has recognized the vein of uncontrolled imagination in Adam's question, and his comic but charming story of the antics of future astronomers shows what can happen when the faculty is given free rein. These men will 'model Heav'n,' 'calculate the Starrs,' 'weild,' 'build,' 'unbuild,' like mock gods, their inadequacy revealed by the desperate need to save appearances that makes them 'contrive,' 'gird,' and scribble (79-83). They set out to find the reflection of their minds in the universe, but end like frustrated children defacing their copy-books.

If touched by satirical banter, Raphael's correction remains genial. His criticism is directed, not against natural philosophy or science as such, but against the inversion of the priorities of knowledge. Self-knowledge is the prime wisdom, and should not be clouded by conjecture and speculation concerning matters that are hidden. By prying into the secrets of God, man can jeopardize his understanding both of himself and of 'That which before us lies' (8.193). As Barbara Lewalski argues, the implication is that humanistic values must not be displaced by scientific speculation or activity.[68] The vigour and lucidity with which Raphael juxtaposes the geocentric and heliocentric views, on the other hand, makes it clear that scientific discussion of such matters is not in itself reprehensible.

Viewing man against the abyss of nature, Pascal concluded that the only remedy against alienation is to know our limitations; 'nous sommes quelque chose, et ne sommes pas tout.'[69] The lowly wisdom recommended by Raphael is similarly an exercise in true humility. The angel first takes the geocentric scheme for granted, and proceeds to dismiss Adam's criticisms of it as flaws in his own perception. Size and brightness are less significant than more 'solid' good, as Adam should know. The place of honour in the creation belongs to men: 'not to Earth are those bright Luminaries / Officious, but to thee Earths habitant' (98-9). But this emphasis on man's importance is at once qualified:

> And for the Heav'ns wide Circuit, let it speak
> The Makers high magnificence, who built
> So spacious, and his Line stretcht out so farr;
> That Man may know he dwells not in his own;
> An Edifice too large for him to fill. ...   (8.100-14)

True humility must avoid the excess of false humility as well as the defect of pride. The service of earth by heaven declares the importance of man, the masterwork; the vast size and incomprehensible energy of heaven reveals his finitude and dependence. Adam requires a precisely adjusted sense of proportion: he should acquire the confidence to receive the ministration of the heavens as his right, and the realism to accept his insignificance in comparison with the grandeur of God.

Having drawn upon the geocentric cosmos for the material of his argument, Raphael now admits that in fact the universe may be heliocentric. He proceeds to sketch the outlines of this new hypothesis with enthusiasm and easy accuracy. Surprisingly – for the modern reader, at least – the heliocentric system seems less austere and alien than its predecessor, being characterized by economy, simplicity, and reciprocations of light and vitality. The evocation of a more sympathetic universe reaches its climax in the suggestion that the moon and many other planets may be inhabited by 'living Soule' (154). Raphael, recognizing Adam's imaginative difficulty in balancing between all and nothing, now gives him the reassurance that he is part of the history of 'living Soule.' Adam has found the self-reflection that he sought as he gazed into the sea of space, but it is no sooner glimpsed than withdrawn as a matter hid (167) that is beyond his experience. Even the angel choir, speculating that every star is perhaps a world of 'destind habitation,' concluded that only God knows their seasons (7.622-3). Raphael ends on the same note, telling Adam to acquire self-knowledge, rather than dream of other worlds.

Raphael refuses to tell Adam which cosmology is true, if either, and his aim is partly 'to make the point that it is not his province as angelic instructor in metaphysics, theology, and ethics to resolve questions of natural science for man.'[70] Questions of fact should not in any case be injudiciously employed in the search to understand God's ways. By allowing the two hypotheses about the heavens to confront each other without resolving their contradiction, Raphael illustrates the difference between quantity and quality, fact and value. Each hypothesis becomes the vehicle for expressing something true. From the geocentric view, we gain an awareness of man's central role, served as he is by a creation in which enormous quantities express the power and mystery of the creator; from the heliocentric view, the picture of man as inhabitant of an animistic universe in which, under the providence of God, the scale of nature seeks repeatedly to rise to the production of living soul. One picture is static, the other dynamic, one stresses hierarchy, the other fertility and growth. Each is true, whether or not the scientific structure providing its symbolism is true. Together they suggest the complexity of man's situation, his position as an individual, separate and unique by virtue of his freedom and rationality, yet linked by vital harmonies to the larger context of nature.

Towards the close of the day, Adam takes up the creation story by describing his first moments of life and the way in which he collaborated with God in the creation of Eve. She is, as God promised, 'Thy wish exactly to thy hearts desire' (8.451), both different and yet an *alter ego*, 'Bone of my Bone, Flesh of my Flesh, my Self'(495). Adam now seriously disturbs Raphael by confessing that his self-control is threatened by the beauty of Eve. The other delights of Eden do not affect his mind, but her beauty transports him and awakens the commotion of passion. Perhaps 'Nature faild in mee' (534), speculates Adam, thereby revealing again his dangerous neglect of the principle that 'God and Nature bid the same' (6.176). His state of mind anticipates that disastrous moment to come when he will be 'not deceav'd, / But fondly overcome with Femal charm' (9.998-9). Elaborating on the 'charm of Beauties powerful glance' (8.533), he describes how it works upon him even though he knows full well that woman bears a less direct resemblance to God than man. As he admits, his panegyric on Eve presents a picture only of that which 'seems,' an illusion, not a reality. It is the picture of a monarch whose power is absolute. The main current of imagery evokes a presence chamber in which beauty receives the submission of virtue, reason, and wisdom, and creates an effect of awe like an angelic guard. Fancy is again producing 'Wilde work,' this time by misjoining masculine and feminine qualities, the former being made contributory to the latter. The speech develops rather in the manner of a day-dream in which reason is restrained while the imagination builds an image under the pressure of feeling. The appeal of the image lies in its completeness, its self-sufficiency, its fusion of masculine and feminine attributes. The image is himself, but perfected, and he feels the admiration we all give to those who appear invulnerable:

> when I approach
> Her loveliness, so absolute she seems
> And in her self compleat, so well to know
> Her own, that what she wills to do or say,
> Seems wisest, virtuousest, discreetest, best. ...   (8.546-50)

The devotion is touched by a narcissism reminiscent of Eve by the pool. Adam's 'hearts desire' is his 'other self' (8.450-1), and there is a danger that he will treat Eve as idol, not image.

Why does Adam expose his feelings to Raphael in this way? Arnold Stein in a passage of great perceptivity suggests that Adam's panegyric on Eve is an adventure in illusion paralleling Eve's dream. Adam, he argues, deliberately presents his extravagant praise of Eve as an illusion that he presumes to control 'by formal, daylight knowledge.'[71] This, perhaps, makes the episode too wilful, too sinister. Adam is led into the panegyric quite naturally by the story of his marriage. It develops as a spontaneous outpouring in which the initial awareness of the truth established by the twice repeated 'seems' tends to be forgotten in the surge of wonder (although peeping out again in 'As one intended first, not after made / Occasionally'). Like Eve's account of her dream, this is an attempt to clarify and master a complex psychic event by putting it into words. And like Eve, Adam directs his words to a being of superior intelligence, whose advice is trusted. The analogy is seen to be even closer when we recall that Raphael by virtue of his superior nature adopts a masculine role in relation to Adam's relatively feminine one. (Thus Raphael describes Adam as God's image fair, attended by 'all comliness and grace,' 8.222). The intimacy of the occasion is conducive to self-revelation, although of course there are restraints that prevent the kind of direct appeal made by Eve.

Raphael now balances the previous injunction to 'be lowlie wise' (8.173) by an exhortation to 'be not diffident / Of Wisdom' (562-3). Self-knowledge, leading to a proper self-esteem, will prevent Adam's authority and freedom from being eroded. True love is a process of self-discovery, not self-abandonment; it reinforces reason and will, making outward shows give way to inward and spiritual realities. Adam has understood much of this, and his reply, only 'half abash't,' contains a vigorous defence of their love as a union of mind and soul. There is nothing here to subject him. Why, then has he spoken as if there were?

> I to thee disclose
> What inward thence I feel, not therefore foild,
> Who meet with various objects, from the sense
> Variously representing; yet still free
> Approve the best, and follow what I approve. (8.607-11)

As has frequently been noted, this looks like the doctrine Adam unfolded to Eve when, in an effort to comfort her after her demonic dream, he explained that evil may come and go in the mind without blame if it is 'unapprov'd' (5.118). But how much more positive is the

present expression of the doctrine, with its assumption that virtue is
something actively sought! Adam now *knows* himself 'both will and
deed created free' (5.549) in a way that was beyond his understanding
before Raphael's visit. I see nothing glib or facile in Adam's explanation.
Obedience is no longer an abstraction to him, but is known in terms of
the act of ordering the inner world of psychic forces. The angel's reproof
has acted as a challenge, and through his defence of himself Adam's
understanding of freedom is strengthened and confirmed. Having
brought him to this point Raphael can do no more:

> to stand or fall
> Free in thine own Arbitrement it lies.
> Perfet within, no outward aid require;
> And all temptation to transgress repel. (8.640-3)

This dialogue of love avoids the excesses of aspiring romanticism and
the defects of bleak rationalism. The aspiration of the lover is seen to be
in itself neither transcendent nor delusory, but a force which should be
integrated in the whole personality. Rich in sensation and feeling, its
true form is found in the moral life that develops out of the relations of
husband and wife. Raphael emphasizes reason, Adam (in his final
speech) will, and their commentary stresses how love exercises these
powers and thereby refines the image of God in man. As we know from
the earlier hymn, wedded love has as one of its ends the creation of a
community of individuals bound together by 'Relations dear, and all the
Charities / Of Father, Son, and Brother' (4.756-7). The 'two great Sexes'
(8.151) thus animate the ethical life, as well as the cosmos. They are
reconciled in a relation that avoids both aggression and surrender,
seeking a communion that preserves individual differences of response.
The process is one in which strong, sensuous impulses are transmuted
into graceful decencies without losing their differentiating qualities.
But the process may refine Adam and Eve beyond their present state; it
offers a scale leading to heaven, and this means that human love may
provide an increasingly satisfactory context for the love of God. Adam's
final question concerning the sexuality of angels, far from being a
diversion, is the logical climax to the debate. Having been told earlier
that in future 'men / With Angels may participate' (5.493-4), it is natural
enough that Adam should seek enlightenment concerning the upper
reaches of eroticism. What he is given is a brief glimpse of a form of
communion that is free from all sub-rational restraints and impedi-

ments. This vision of the 'union of Pure with Pure' (8.627) should remind us of how the whole historical process is leading to a time when the faithful will be 'United as one individual Soule' in the Son (5.610), that Son whose relation to the Father is the ultimate example of voluntary union.

On the very morning that Satan returns to the garden and enters the body of the snake, Adam and Eve have their first disagreement. It opens with a strained discussion of the most appropriate way to pursue their work, Eve urging that they will get more done if they separate, but it quickly moves, with compelling emotional logic, to an uneasy debate concerning their relation to each other. The debate proceeds by a kind of dialectic of feeling, and while the participants become increasingly alarmed at the turn it has taken they are unable to regain their balance. The psychological richness of the scene is remarkable, and critical language is scarcely capable of catching, much less exhausting, the drama of its casuistry.[72]

Because the dispute ends in the separation of Adam and Eve, we think of it as the beginning of the Fall. No doubt we are right to see in it proof that the hour of temptation is upon them. Further, the episode seems to invite our judgment of the characters. In the large outline offered by hindsight, the pattern appears to be clear enough. As the outcome surely proves, Adam is right in urging that they are safer together, and in advising Eve not to seek out temptation. His 'leave not the faithful side / That gave thee being' (9.265-6) is a plea, an exhortation, and a command, and Eve should have responded. Instead she reveals an ominous impulse towards self-sufficiency. But it is tempting to see a weakness in Adam, too, when at the end of the argument he releases Eve from obedience to his ruling by giving her permission to go if she sees fit. His dilemma is a real one, for he does not want to deprive her of freedom. But is it necessary for him to suggest the excuse that justifies her departure? As Anthony Low has concluded, 'his appeal to the principle of freedom is in its way as flawed as Eve's earlier appeal to the value of trial and experience.'[73]

Such a weighing of responsibilities is a necessary phase of our reaction to the scene, and criticism has tended to focus on it. Yet turning from these considered judgments back to the text, one is likely to feel all over again the complexity of the position in which Adam and Eve find themselves, and to sympathize with their inability to light upon a ready solution. Milton has created a subtle mimesis of a moment of discovery. The new experience evolves with inevitable logic, testing the judgment of the participants and resisting any simple reduction by formula. Here it will be useful to emphasize two points concerning the debate. First, the outcome surely cannot be evil; whatever the decision, it will be innocent and capable of eventual assimilation into the rhythm of challenging pleasures in Eden. Their disagreement does not bring the experience of evil, but only a degree of distress compatible with the learning process before the Fall. The separation does not make the Fall necessary, but reveals in a striking fashion that unfallen man learns by trial and error.[74] Of the argument that follows, Addison observed long ago that 'it is such a dispute as we may suppose might have happened in Paradise, had Man continued happy and innocent.'[75]

The second point is that Adam and Eve are real individuals, not allegorical abstractions. The image of God, Milton insists, is present in both man and woman; they do not together make one individual, but two distinct beings, each sufficient to stand, each free to fall. Their unity, like that of Father and Son in heaven, arises from the unity of their wills.

The scene is thus a dramatization of a crucial step in the process of individuation. This, in fact, is the moment at which Adam and Eve recognize that they are *not* allegorical parts of a whole, but rather separate entities united by willed relationships. Their early experience established their interdependence, the manner in which they complement, even complete, each other; so much is evident in the very language used about them and by them: 'Thy likeness, thy fit help, thy other self' (8.450), 'Whose image thou art' (4.472), 'my other half' (4.488), 'Bone of my Bone, Flesh of my Flesh, my Self' (8.495). But this intimacy, while nourished by instinct and feeling, is to be grounded in the will. The present scene shows them growing in awareness of the separateness that makes their voluntary love meaningful. The catalyst of this growth, the argument, is in itself distressing, but its final outcome should have been an increase in joy. Adam's later preparation of a crown of flowers as a peace offering points to what might have been the happy reunion that brings with it a growth in love. That hurt feelings play an important part in this domestic crisis, as in its more mundane counterparts, can be seen from a passage placed in the middle of Adam's first reply to Eve:

> But if much converse perhaps
> Thee satiate, to short absence I could yield.
> For solitude somtimes is best societie,

And short retirement urges sweet returne.   (9.247-50)

If Adam had stopped before speaking these words, the disagreement might have been averted. The first half of his speech was a masterly defence of the principle that in Paradise labour is subordinate to delight. But he is too upset to ignore the possibility that there is some personal implication in Eve's words. Perhaps she is satiated with his presence? The query provides a glimpse of insecurity arising from the uneasy sense that Eve has been less than candid – has indeed, been using the garden as an excuse. Behind this immediate anxiety looms an even more important issue. Adam, who is observant concerning the rhythms of their existence, sums it up sententiously: 'solitude somtimes is best societie / And short retirement urges sweet returne.' Personal fulfilment is achieved by being sometimes alone, sometimes in company. Adam knows the complete cycle, for he was alone both before and immediately after the creation of Eve. Granting the principle, he proceeds to argue in the second half of the speech that this is not the time for its application, since a malicious foe waits his opportunity to trap them.

Now it is Eve's turn to be hurt. Since violence cannot harm them, Adam must fear that she will be deceived by Satan, her faith and love 'shak'n or seduc't' (287) by his fraud. The difficulty of communicating concerning this subject is becoming increasingly evident. Adam now tries with 'healing words' to soothe his wife; admittedly external force cannot harm them, but the very attempt itself would be an affront to Eve. This chivalric niceness sounds off-key in a poem in which faithful angels and even the Son of God do not shrink from confrontation with evil. But the next moment Adam admits that more than the possibility of insult disturbs him: 'Suttle he needs must be, who could seduce / Angels ... ' (307-8). He himself feels stronger and more virtuous when in her presence, sustained by her influence: 'Why shouldst not thou like sense within thee feel / When I am present' (315-16). One can sympathize with the difficulty he feels in pressing his case. He hopes that by stressing his dependence on her, he will stir her to a similar declaration.

His tact is wasted. The argument from insult, if we can so name it, is quickly dismissed by Eve: 'his foul esteeme / Sticks no dishonour on our Front,' she rightly says, 'but turns / Foul on himself' (329-31). By advancing a rather shaky argument in order to take the sting out of his earlier words, Adam has weakened his entire position. His statement of reliance on Eve appears to succeed in allaying her distress, but fails to lead her into a similar declaration. Instead, she proceeds to talk about the problems posed by 'our' condition. How are they happy, if they live in fear of trial, 'not endu'd / Single with like defence' (324-5)? Adam's deference to her feelings has only succeeded in leading her to treat their relationship as one of equality. There is a strident note in the rhetoric with which she now attacks what she considers to be the implications of Adam's position:

> Let us not then suspect our happie State
> Left so imperfet by the Maker wise,
> As not secure to single or combin'd.
> Fraile is our happiness, if this be so,
> And *Eden* were no *Eden* thus exposed.   (337-41)

This seems far indeed from the Eve of book 4, who declared that none of the joys of Eden were sweet without Adam.

Eve's contempt for 'unassaid' virtue has reminded many readers of the attack on 'cloister'd' virtue in *Areopagitica* (*Works*, IV, 311). The similarity, however, does not prove that Milton speaks through Eve at this point in the debate. As J.S. Diekhoff has argued, we must take care to distinguish the ethic proper to fallen man (the subject of *Areopagitica*) from that proper to Adam and Eve before the Fall.[76] Eve, yet innocent, does not need to purify herself by trial. Yet, as we have seen, there is a close analogy between unfallen and fallen experience. Trial will come unsought, as Adam observes, and will serve as the occasion for further development. Adam and Eve will progress, not indeed from impure to pure, but 'by degrees of merit' (7.157) to heaven. Eve's appeal to the individual conscience is thus not irrelevant. She is, in fact, simply echoing Raphael's final words to Adam, words that she confesses to having overheard:

> Perfect within, no outward aid require;
> And all temptation to transgress repel.   (8.642-3)

Are we to condemn her for seeking to realize such inward perfection? I think not. Orders and degrees do not jar with liberty, and Eve's virtue is no less free and interior than that of Adam, her superior and head. Already the dream has shown that separate experiences of a distressing kind are possible. We do less than justice to this awakening individualism in Eve if we fail to see it as her response to what she has experienced and been told in the preceding books. Their lives are to develop in complexity, and the rhythm of short retirement and sweet return will undoubtedly bring moments of solitude. She cannot be dismissed with the advice that as she is already pure she should not worry. Nor does Adam attempt to do so. Rather he admits the relevance of her remarks, and tries to provide them with an appropriate context.

The alert poise which in *Paradise Lost* is essential to the ethical life must adjust to the shifting winds of circumstance. Timing is crucial. To force the issue may be as useless as to evade it. The right act accepts the providential context for choice. Adam in his reply to Eve tells her to wait and watch. This last speech is a distillation of all he has learned from the angel concerning the freedom of 'both will and deed' (5.549) that is proper to man. The severity of Adam's tone tends to disguise the fact that he is confirming one of Eve's most important assumptions – she is correct in thinking the choice of good and evil lies in the will of the individual:

> within himself
> The danger lies, yet lies within his power:
> Against his will he can receave no harme. (9.348-50)

Eve was right, then, to think that they are not exposed to danger from outward force, right to conclude that trial is important in their development, and right to believe that the individual must decide according to his conscience. This awakening individualism is a process that parallels Adam's development into freedom, and to this extent it is benign. At this moment in her evolution, however, she seems too literal-minded and doctrinaire in her viewpoint. She continues to neglect the way in which they are exposed to danger from within: 'Firm we subsist,' as Adam remarks, 'yet possible to swerve' (359). Happiness does not depend upon being self-sufficient, as Eve implies that it does. Further, her wish to prove her inner freedom by single trial is involved in a corrosive and subtle contradiction, for it attributes to Adam's presence a compulsive force that threatens her individuality. If she is free, she is so in Adam's presence, as well as in his absence. In any case, he offers collaboration, not restraint: 'Not then mistrust, but tender love enjoynes, / That I should mind thee oft, and mind thou me' (357-8). Eve's response points to a further symptom: her impatient desire to prove herself neglects the order created in her life by providence, and

(a) [ ] Then she is no safer - unless freedom is consistent with being inhibited from sinning.

(b) Then how sinless? Or how well equipped to avoid sin?

particularly her role as Adam's helpmate. Eve has achieved a partial insight into the meaning of freedom, but her intense yet narrow interpretation of it threatens to isolate her from the rest of reality, and Adam's crash course in ethics fails to release her.

Milton describes Adam in the argument to book 9 as one who yields 'at last.' Before the yielding comes the moment at which he seems on the point of issuing a command:

> Trial will come unsought.
> Wouldst thou approve thy constancie, approve
> First thy obedience; th' other who can know,
> Not seeing thee attempted, who attest? (366-9)

Tenderness has prevented Adam from issuing an unqualified command, but now it appears that what he has been saying should not be looked on merely as advice, but rather as an order. Yet as soon as the imperative mood crystallizes, Adam draws back from it, as if feeling he has gone too far, and offers another possible resolution to balance against the first:

> But if thou think, trial unsought may finde
> Us both securer than thus warnd thou seemst,
> Go; for thy stay, not free, absents thee more;
> Go in thy native innocence, relie
> On what thou hast of vertue, summon all,
> For God towards thee hath done his part, do thine. (370-5)

Adam is undoubtedly right to seek to persuade Eve rather than to confront her with bare commands. His task is to convince her of the reasonableness of his request and, as he will explain later, 'force upon free will hath here no place' (1174). But his weakness lies in a failure of confidence, as can be seen in the emotional curve of his final speech. It builds to a climax, then suddenly loses all authority. The admission that she may consider her reasons for parting superior to his reasons for staying would have been possible at the outset, but at the end creates an anticlimax that reveals his timidity. He does not believe in the relevance of the argument that he provides for her (that it is easier to be alert if you actively seek trial) and he should have left her to think of it herself. For the third time in the debate, Adam has retreated from the possibility of Eve's disapproval. First came the pang at the thought that she might be temporarily satiated by his company; then the attempt to explain away the danger she might meet alone in terms of insult and dishonour; now, finally, this withdrawal of his command out of fear that Eve will not willingly obey it. He should have had greater 'self-esteem' (8.572), but like Eve he feels his identity threatened by the dispute.

When the decision to part is recalled after the Fall, Eve will bitterly remind Adam of this moment, saying he did 'permit, approve, and fair dismiss' (9.1159). This distorts Adam's closing words by taking them out of context. Adam replies that he 'warn'd ... admonish'd ... foretold / The danger,' and that 'beyond this had bin force' (1171-3). This seems closer to the truth, but it is dishonest in its assumption that a command is the equivalent of 'force.'[77] In any case, these acrimonious after-thoughts arise from understandings already darkened by the Fall. If separation and trial had been successfully undergone, a different analysis of the parting would have been possible, one in which each party admitted neglecting the true interests of the other. The truth would then have been seen to lie neither in Adam's 'beyond this had bin force' nor in Eve's 'fair' dismissal.

The debate is at once symptomatic and open-ended. It reveals the origins of weakness, but leaves the participants intact. It mobilizes human resources, but fails to achieve a decisive resolution. The demanding nature of unfallen existence, suggestively built up by the earlier episodes, is here given its most powerful statement. Adam and Eve are confronted by questions that are perfectly real, but that do not seem susceptible of immediate, formal solution. Important questions, they concern such things as authority, timing, and decorum, and they come all in a rush. Unfallen man cannot taste evil, but in this crisis of casuistry we can see that moral decision before the Fall has an urgent tempo suggestive of our own experience. Yet Adam's uncertainty is not the paralysis of a Hamlet, nor does Eve display the insatiable thirst for dominance of a Faustus. Compare with the present scene that in which the importunate realism of Lady Macbeth overwhelms her husband's inhibitions on the night of the king's murder, or that in which Antony is fondly overcome by female charm before the battle of Actium, and you become aware of a difference more basic than the parallels. Adam and Eve are not fatally flawed; rather they marshal what they know to meet the emergency, they struggle to communicate about subjects dangerous with feeling, they endure risks in the hope of new insight. Fully engaged in the act of choice, they keep their freedom.

Hindsight, the chronic perspective of the fallen, inevitably leads us to see the shape of things to come in the argument. Even the narrator is caught by this regret, crying out at the moment of parting 'O much deceav'd, much failing, hapless *Eve*, / Of thy presum'd return!' (404-5). But Eve is still innocent as she sets out. It is hard for us not to see in her present concern with independence the shape of her later Satanic question: 'inferior who is free?' (825). In the same way, it is hard for us not to see in Adam's acquiescence the shape of his later self-abandonment: 'with thee / Certain my resolution is to Die' (906-7). But at the moment of parting these things are only potentially there. Along with them, in the potency of the moment, is the possibility of growth to higher goodness, of an increase in knowledge and love emerging from a testing of relationships, of a strengthening of identity through the rhythm of separation and return, which in *Paradise Lost* is the rhythm of all growth. Through such process man moves to a more and more adequate realization of the image of God within him.

CHAPTER FIVE

The Image of God in Man: After the Fall

The Object of Saving Faith

The ancient controversy concerning the possibility of salvation outside the church, which had revived in the age of Calvin, became increasingly intense in seventeenth-century England as a result of the conflict between orthodox Calvinism and the new rationalism. At Cambridge in the middle of the century the Reformed view of faith and salvation was ardently defended by Anthony Tuckney.[1] Tuckney is particularly anxious to insist that there can be no salvation apart from Christ. His position is that embodied in the Westminster Confesion of Faith, a credal statement which he helped to formulate: 'much lesse can men, not professing the Christian Religion, be saved in any other way whatsoever, be they never so diligent to frame their lives according to the light of *Nature*, and the Law of that Religion they professe. And, to assert and maintain, that they may, is very pernicious, and to be detested.'[2] In his tract *None But Christ*, Tuckney provides a vigorous polemical defence of this doctrine:

> because *salvation is only by Christ*, therefore in all matters of *salvation*, with a single eye let us look to *Christ*, and to *God* in him, and at ourselves as receiving all from him, as *Elected* in him, *Redeemed* by him, *Justified* by his grace, and the imputation of his righteousness, in which is the ground of our comfort, and *Sanctified* by his *Spirit*, not by a *Philosophical faith*, or the use of *right Reason*, or a *virtuous morality*, too much nowadays admired and

cried up. As of old, *The Temple of the Lord, The Temple of the Lord.*
So now, *The Candle of the Lord, The Candle of the Lord.*[3]

Tuckney's mockery of those who rely injudiciously on the candle of the
Lord mentioned in Proverbs 20:27 is undoubtedly a reference to
Nathaniel Culverwell as well as Benjamin Whichcote, and to the recent
Cambridge habit of interpreting the candle as the light of reason. Such
doctrine, stressing nature and morality, was in Tuckney's view a sure
way to turn men into deists, not Christians.

Although Tuckney would prefer to let the heathen sleep in the dust,
he finds it necessary to speak out and repudiate a view that fails to
distinguish between morality and divinity. Unless the ancient philosophers knew Christ, they are 'fallen irrecoverably.' Nor is he willing to
speculate about ways in which the heathens might have known Christ
without scripture; certainly such knowledge was not available through
the contemplation of creation or providence, or by the 'improvement' of
natural reason or the agency of angels or Sybils. With consistency
Tuckney also denies that persons incapable of faith, such as infants or
madmen, can be accepted 'for *Christ's sake without faith in Christ.*' We
must restrict our attention to the way of salvation that has been
revealed, refusing to be led astray by speculations which offer a hope for
the non-Christian world, and recognizing that God's justice 'is as
infinite and incomprehensible as his mercy.'[4]

Against such dogmatic views we can see more clearly the position
which emerges in the works with which Milton was concerned in the
fifties, *De Doctrina Christiana* and *Paradise Lost.* In the theological
tract his view is clearly different from Tuckney's, more liberal, even
though the formulation is quiet and undramatic:

as was shown in the fifth chapter, the ultimate object of faith is not
Christ the Mediator, but God the Father; a truth, which the weight
of scripture evidence has compelled divines to acknowledge. For
the same reason it ought not to appear wonderful if many, both Jews
and others, who lived before Christ, and many also who have lived
since his time, but to whom he has never been revealed, should be
saved by faith in God alone; still however through the sole merits of
Christ, inasmuch as he was given and slain from the beginning of
the world, even for those to whom he was not known, provided they
believed in God the Father. Hence honorable testimony is borne to
the faith of the illustrious patriarchs who lived under the law, Able

[sic], Enoch, Noah, etc. though it is expressly stated that they believed only in God, Heb.xi. (*Works*, XV, 403-5)

The reference to the illustrious patriarchs offers a biblical source to disarm criticism. In the eleventh chapter of the Epistle to the Hebrews, the author celebrates that faith which is 'the substance of things hoped for, the evidence of things not seen,' illustrates its operation by a roll-call of Old Testament saints who triumphed 'by faith,' and concludes that these patriarchs 'received not the promise, God having provided some better things for us, that they without us should not be made perfect.' Milton has this conclusion in mind when he asserts that 'they believed only in God.' The promises, as the author of Hebrews notes, were seen 'afar off.' But while awareness was shaped through prophecy and typology, sustaining faith, in Milton's view, was placed in God the Father.

This position is quite unlike Calvin's doctrine. Calvin devotes several sections of the *Institutes* to demonstrating that from the beginning of the world, Christ was set before all the elect, and that the patriarchs 'participated in the same inheritance and hoped for a common salvation with us by the grace of the same Mediator,' for they 'knew Christ as Mediator, through whom they were joined to God and were to share in his promises.' Agreeing with the 'common saying' of the schoolmen that God is the object of faith, Calvin insists that it requires qualification, for 'unless God confronts us in Christ, we cannot come to know that we are saved.'[5] Milton, by contrast, considers salvation by faith in God the Father without a knowledge of the Son to be possible not only for the Jews but even for Gentiles, and after as well as before the birth of Christ. The merits of Christ make salvation possible, but it is not necessary for the recipient of such benefit to know its source: 'by unbelievers ... those only can be meant to whom Christ has been announced in the gospel; for "how shall they believe in him of whom they have not heard?" Rom.X.14' (*Works*, XVI, 123).

The allusion in the passage cited above to chapter 5 of *De Doctrina Christiana*, the chapter elaborating a subordinationist view of the Son, indicates the radical context in which the doctrine of faith in God the Father is to be placed. Since the Son is divine but not one in essence with God, he is not the object of saving faith. Milton's statement would have disturbed less rigidly conservative Protestants than Tuckney. Milton is radical in his assertion that the possibility of regaining to know God aright and thus of renewing the mind and faculties exists in all ages and dispensations. A precisionist like Tuckney would consider Milton's position on this issue dangerously inclined in the direction of deism and the abhorrent and profane opinion 'that every man may be saved in any Religion, if he be true to it, and live orderly in it.'[6]

Other passages in Milton's writing lend support to this view of the process of salvation, and amplify its significance. Thus his rejection of the Calvinist interpretation of election and predestination leads him to deny that Christ made satisfaction for the elect alone, and to insist that he died for all mankind (Works, XV, 319-23). Not only is the atonement for all men, but all men are invited to a knowledge of the true God:

> It may be objected, that all have not known Christ. I answer, that this proves nothing against the doctrine, that all are called in Christ alone; inasmuch as, had he not been given to the world, God would have called no one: and as the ransom he has paid is in itself sufficient for the redemption of mankind, all are called to partake of its benefits, though all may not be aware of the source from which the benefits flow. ... how much more ought we to believe that the perfect sacrifice of Christ may be abundantly sufficient even for those who have never heard of the name of Christ, and who believe only in God? (Works, XV, 349)

The proposition that Christ died for all men was condemned by the Calvinists at the synod of Dort, and defended by the Arminians. But the idea that the sacrifice of Christ may be sufficient even for those who have never heard of his name goes beyond the usual Arminian position.

Milton thus makes God the Father the ultimate object of faith, affirms that the Son acts as a ransom for all mankind, and argues that all are called to partake of the benefits of his death, even though they may not be aware of the source from which these benefits flow. Michael's history of the world in the last books of Paradise Lost implies this doctrine and is throughout consistent with the position found in De Doctrina Christiana, but it avoids the controversial issue of whether a person can be saved if he lacks not only clear revelation of Christ but also all knowledge of Old Testament prophecy and teaching. It is evident, however, that the saints who lived before the coming of Christ were saved in spite of their inability to perceive the redeemer openly. It would have been possible to suggest (as others had done) that a knowledge of Christ was available to them either through the instruction of Adam or by some other method. The impression left by Michael's narrative, however, is that most of the knowledge revealed to Adam was not communicated to his descendants.[7] Presumably Adam will explain to his sons enough about the covenant between God and man to enable them to make the kind of sacrifices recorded in the opening vision of Abel and Cain. This accords with the instructions the Father gives to Michael when he bids him to intermix in the narrative of the future 'My Cov'nant in the womans seed renewd' (11.116). But the worship of Abel and Cain is so simple that it appears almost instinctive, and it is not until God instructs the Israelites through Moses that a more elaborate and self-conscious program of worship will be established and followed (12.227-44).

The illustrious patriarchs who were saved before the calling of Abraham leave no impression of having received special knowledge of the Incarnation through tradition or new revelation; they are, rather, concentrated intensely on the reformation of contemporary corruption.[8] Thus Enoch spoke

> much of Right and Wrong
> Of Justice, of Religion, Truth and Peace,
> And Judgment from above   (11.666-8),

and was treated with violence by the people as a result. According to *De Doctrina*, the last judgment was predicted first by Enoch and the prophets (*Works*, XVI, 339). Thus Noah, too,

> preachd
> Conversion and Repentance, as to Souls
> In Prison under Judgements imminent.   (11.723-5)

Such reformers sought to restore purity of faith and manners to a corrupt world, and their teaching centres on repentance and the imminence of destruction. Not knowing Christ, they are saved by their trust in the Father, the ultimate object of faith, and without knowing it they typified the life of Christ. Even Abraham and those who followed him knew Christ only by the promise and by types and shadows, although the promise is gradually clarified by new revelations, and particularly by the discovery of the office of mediator in Moses. As Milton remarks in *De Doctrina*, 'honorable testimony is borne to the faith of the illustrious patriarchs who lived under the law, Able [sic], Enoch, Noah etc. though it is expressly stated that they believed only in God, Heb. xi'

(*Works*, XV, 405). Under the law salvation was through Christ alone, 'equally as under the gospel, although he was not then revealed: Acts xv,10, 11' (*Works*, XVI, 111; see also XV, 405). Even Christian liberty, the peculiar fruit of adoption and the special privilege of the Gospel, was not unknown during the time of the law (the meaning, of course, and not the name – see *Works*, XVI, 153), and in the poem it can be seen in the actions of Enoch, Noah, or Abraham.

According to the opening sentences of Milton's theological tract, Christian doctrine 'is that divine revelation disclosed in various ages by Christ (though he was not known under that name in the beginning) concerning the nature and worship of Deity. ... Under the name of Christ are also comprehended Moses and the Prophets, who were his forerunners, and the Apostles whom he sent' (*Works*, XIV, 17-19). In this sense the revelation of Christ was present from the beginning, since 'there was a promise made to all mankind, and an expectation of the Redeemer, more or less distinct, even from the time of the fall' (*Works*, XV, 257). This first manifestation of the covenant of grace through the Son is dramatized in the epic at the scene of judgment. As Georgia B. Christopher has shown, Milton's view may be profitably compared with Luther's idea of the eternal new testament, or Calvin's concept of the perpetual sense of scripture.[9] However, it is also necessary to stress the way in which the revelation of Christ is progressive, taking forms appropriate to the varying dispensations of God's relation with men. It is not until the arrival of the Gospel that Christ and his office are explicitly understood (*Works*, XVI, 99-101). This view is emphasized by the poem, as well as the treatise, for it describes how the figure of the Messiah was only gradually understood and realized through history. In spite of special insights, the patriarchs and prophets do not have a clear and full knowledge of Christ, but with faith they follow particular leadings and discharge particular tasks. I think it probable that Milton preserves the decorum of progressive revelation more easily than some of his contemporaries because of his belief that salvation depends on faith in God, not Christ. Certainly his story has none of the exclusiveness of the dogma concerning salvation by Christ alone developed by Anthony Tuckney.

We are left with an anomaly. Adam appears to discover more about Christ, and about the significance of the Incarnation and the Crucifixion, than any of the Old Testament patriarchs and prophets who lived after him. Not until Gospel times will such explicit knowledge be again

given to mankind. True, Milton clearly believes that the prophets who
sang of the Messiah and forecast the Nativity were given insight into the
future. But the revelations which they received were partial compared
to the overview of God's plan given to Adam. It is Adam's literary
dimension, supported perhaps by traditional exegetical speculations,
that allows Milton to treat him in a way that departs from the decorum
governing the representation of other Old Testament figures. Adam's
experience contains the experience of mankind. If Milton had written
one of those treatments of such Old Testament prophets as David and
Elijah which he projected in the forties, would he have felt at liberty to
give his subject knowledge of a sort comparable to that received by
Adam? It seems most unlikely, except possibly in the case of Moses. The
only full treatment of an Old Testament 'saint' provided by Milton is
that of Samson, and while Samson appears – at least to some readers – to
move to the possession of the equivalent of Christian liberty, he does so
apparently without the aid of the promise contained in the *protevangelium*. Unlike the Jesus of *Paradise Regained*, Samson does not seem to
have devoted himself to close study of scripture. The language of the
play is full of echoes of scripture, and especially of the Psalms, but
Samson is not an interpreter of biblical history at large. Rather his
powers of interpretation are concentrated on his own history and
situation.[10] In Adam, however, Milton found a figure whom he felt at
liberty to treat both as an individual and as the representative of
mankind's response to the revelations of Christ through history. From
either perspective, his education is remarkable evidence of the manner
in which regeneration can proceed a long part of the way to its goal
without explicit recognition that all its benefits flow from Christ.

Reconciliation and Regeneration

Chapter 3 drew attention to the importance in Reformed theology of the
distinction between the two major aspects of the work of the Son,
reconciliation and regeneration. Calvin's judicious handling of the
distinction assumes the final inseparability and integration of the
functions. In the seventeenth century, however, the distinction became
a source of controversy. Some, like Tuckney, felt obliged to defend the
doctrine of reconciliation from what they perceived to be the incipient
Pelagianism of the rationalists. Others, like Whichcote, sought to place
a vital emphasis on the inward process of redemption by which the

believer is renewed in God's image. Milton, we saw, preserves the distinction between the formal doctrine of satisfaction, upon which rests man's reconciliation with God, and the inward realization of Christ. The external and internal aspects of regeneration are carefully handled throughout *De Doctrina Christiana*. The distinction contributes support to the argument that men who have not heard of Christ's act of redemption may yet conform inwardly to his image. But Milton also affirmed without hesitation that the internal process was made possible by the act of satisfaction. He would have found it easy to agree with Whichcote's observation that the Son of God is 'a principle of divine life within us, as well as a Saviour without us.'[11]

Another – and related – distinction important to Milton's view of regeneration is that between the functions of Father and Son. It would not be appropriate to assign to one person the more 'external' process of bringing about the satisfaction of justice, and to the other the 'internal' task of renewing the mind and heart of the Christian. On the contrary, each person is involved in both aspects of the process; there is no division of the work, but rather mutual participation in each stage. Indeed, in each effect of regeneration – repentance and saving faith, ingrafting in Christ, justification, adoption, fellowship with Christ, glorification – the parallel contributions of Father and Son are stressed.[12]

This elaborate and balanced pattern provides a challenge to the art of the epic poet. Salvation as a process in divine history, a process that concerns God's attributes and the relation of eternity to time, is to be placed in conjunction with salvation as a process within the human spirit, a process through which will and mind are strengthened and clarified. The cooperation of Father and Son in the first process is to be related to their cooperation in the second. The entire action must thus be shown as an image of harmonious order, and in aesthetic terms this can of course be achieved only by a statement that uses art to convey the excellence of the operation of divine will. Firmness of emphasis, economy of statement, tact in eliciting relationship, integration of the parts in dramatic terms – such aesthetic properties become expressive of the providential control of human experience. Internal and external dimensions of regeneration are to be held in a single view, the former having reference to the experience which characterizes the individual, the latter evoking the larger reality that is beyond the full understanding of the individual and provides the context for his activity; in each dimension we must see the operation of the transforming powers of both Father and Son.

'A Saviour Without Us'

The external function of the Son, his role as a 'saviour without us,' is particularly evident during the council in heaven in book 3 of *Paradise Lost*, where the Father outlines the strategy for man's salvation. We have already noticed the dramatic approach to the Incarnation provided by this scene. The Father develops a firm and rational statement of the operation of saving grace, and only after establishing the prospect of man restored and freely following the dictates of conscience does he make the process dependent upon a redeemer. The effect of this pattern is in keeping with the view that the Father is the ultimate object of faith and that many may be saved through faith in God alone. As so often, the theological position is not overtly stated in the poem, but gives shape to the argument nonetheless:

> I will cleer thir senses dark,
> What may suffice, and soft'n stonie hearts
> To pray, repent, and bring obedience due.
> To Prayer, repentance, and obedience due,
> Though but endevord with sincere intent,
> Mine ear shall not be slow, mine eye not shut.
> And I will place within them as a guide
> My Umpire *Conscience*, whom if they will hear,
> Light after light well us'd they shall attain,
> And to the end persisting, safe arrive. (3.188-97)

All men will be called, and to all will be given grace sufficient to arrive at the goal; only those who scorn the invitation will be excluded from mercy. As Gary Hamilton has seen, the Father is here 'declaring the Arminian view of general redemption.'[13] But it should be emphasized that the Father forsees all this and explains it without reference to the Son. Yet all is soon acknowledged to be dependent upon the Son's satisfaction for sin. In the Father's concluding speech to the council, there is no doubt that the Son is the source of redemption to all mankind: 'Be thou in *Adams* room / The Head of all mankind' (3.285-6). As Milton put the matter in the prose passage cited earlier, 'all are called in Christ alone; inasmuch as, had he not been given to the world, God would have called no one.' The exclusiveness of 'without thee none,' however, should be understood in terms of Milton's belief that all who

[handwritten margin note: [] The pt. is that the sinner can resist grace.]

are called to partake of the benefits of the Son's sacrifice 'may not be aware of the source from which the benefits flow' (*Works*, XV, 349). Once again the poetry eludes controversy by avoiding the explicit and formal statement of a liberal doctrine, while yet managing to achieve the *effect* of the doctrine: the Father's first promise of salvation to all who endeavour 'with sincere intent' to respond to grace requires a generous reading of the Son's atonement in which it is understood to be truly effective for all mankind: 'So Man, as is most just, / Shall satisfie for Man' (3.294-5).

To some extent, then, the atonement is an enabling action – it releases the mercy of God, which would otherwise have been inhibited by his justice. It does this through the legalism of the Calvinist doctrine of imputed righteousness:

> thy merit
> Imputed shall absolve them who renounce
> Thir own both righteous and unrighteous deeds,
> And live in thee transplanted, and from thee
> Receive new life.   (3.290-4)

As Milton observes in *De Doctrina Christiana*, 'man, paying nothing on his part, but merely believing, receives as a gift the imputed righteousness of Christ' (*Works*, XVI, 29). In his way the Son effects the release from bondage to sin of all believers, both those who know him and those who are unaware of his sacrifice. The Son thus appears to be the mediating agent or secondary cause of man's salvation, while the Father is the principal cause: man is called *by* God the Father, but called *in* Christ the Son.

The roles of Father and Son here are analogous to their roles in the creation of the world (as Milton explicity recognizes – *Works*, XIV, 323). As we saw earlier, the account of the creation in book 7 of *Paradise Lost* exemplified Milton's view that the Father 'comprehends within himself all lesser causes; whereas the Son is only he by whom are all things' (*Works*, XV, 9). A similar pattern shapes the operation of divine powers at man's recreation after the Fall. And as at the creation the Son circumscribes with his compasses the area in which the act is to occur, so his death is said by the Father to 'compass' (3.342) the whole process of salvation for man.

The Son formally became 'a saviour without us' (in Whichcote's language) at that moment when he 'renewd' (3.226) his mediation in order to accept the office of redeemer. This is a truly voluntary act, and has a definite beginning. The importance of this external aspect of his task is kept before us throughout the poem. It is evident, for example, in the long and tragic soliloquy spoken by Adam after the Fall (10.720-844), in which he seeks to exculpate himself from sin but ends (like Satan earlier) by recognizing his own responsibility and the justice of God's ways. We watch him groping towards the recognition of the theology already revealed during the council in book 3:

> Will he, draw out,
> For angers sake, finite to infinite
> In punisht man, to satisfie his rigour
> Satisfi'd never. ...   (10.801-4)

This kind of speculation about divine behaviour is dangerously like the theology of Hell, and it is to Adam's credit that he shortly realizes his inability to solve the problem. Nonetheless, such passages show the approach of the natural understanding to religious truth, and if put in a less self-regarding and querulous fashion Adam's observation would have a place in the debate of justice and mercy in heaven.

The soliloquy is both subtle and moving, and invites us to see the contrast between Adam and Satan at the very moment when Adam himself is convinced of their likeness, even identity. Overwhelmed by the logic of moral reality, Adam laments his powerlessness:

> first and last
> On mee, mee onely, as the sourse and spring
> Of all corruption, all the blame lights due;
> So might the wrauth. Fond wish! couldst thou support
> That burden heavier then the Earth to bear,
> Then all the World much heavier, though divided
> With that bad Woman?   (10.831-7)

Adam understands that atonement can be achieved only through the satisfaction of God's justice, and he sees also his own inability to make reparation. Painfully, he is moving towards comprehension of the need for a redeemer. As the Son observed earlier, Adam cannot provide 'Atonement for himself or offering meet, / Indebted and undon' (3.234-5). It was the prospect of such helplessness that aroused the Son's pity during the council in heaven, and inclined him to appease God's wrath by offering himself (3.405-6). Although Adam does not yet know it, he has already benefited from the Son's intervention. At the judgment the Son came as both judge and intercessor, deriving his authority to mitigate the doom of man directly from his agreement to bear the punishment of man's sin (10.73-5). Adam's hesitant progress towards an understanding of atonement is the result of grace extended to him through the mediation of the Son, and there is thus a kind of benign irony about the limits of his vision.

In the final book of *Paradise Lost*, too, the external aspect of the atonement is repeatedly emphasized as Adam is shown the plan for man's restoration.[14] Thus he learns the Pauline doctrine that 'Law can discover sin, but not remove' (12.290), and is led on to perceive that the 'shadowie expiations' (12.291) made in the blood of bulls and goats are testimony to the need for a better covenant: 'Some bloud more precious must be paid for Man ... ' (12.293). The clue put into Adam's hand at this point leads shortly to a full statement of the Protestant version of the doctrine of satisfaction. The Son of God saves man not only by fulfilling the law, but also by suffering man's penalty, death; his merits are imputed to all who believe in his redemption. Sin is now powerless 'to hurt them more who rightly trust / In this his satisfaction' (12.418-19), and the ransom paid redeems from death 'as many as offerd Life / Neglect not, and the benefit imbrace / By Faith not void of workes' (12.425-7). This last passage is reminiscent of the language used by the Father in introducing the scheme for redemption at the council, and recalls Milton's Arminian belief in the need for sincere endeavour on the part of the individual. Woven through the account is a stress on the universal significance of the events of Christ's life which also might recall the views stated more explicitly in *De Doctrina Christiana*. This Godlike act involves man or all mankind:

> from that day
> Not onely to the Sons of *Abrahams* Loines
> Salvation shall be Preacht, but to the Sons
> Of Abrahams Faith wherever through the world.
> ...   (12.446-9)

'*Abrahams* Faith,' as Alastair Fowler notes, has now been given a more precise definition, yet it remains what it always was, a faith in the 'living God' (12.118). The account of the Incarnation in book 12 is thus consistent in emphasis with the picture drawn from *De Doctrina Christiana* and the council in book 3 of *Paradise Lost*: God the Father is the ultimate object of faith, and offers grace to all who sincerely attempt to live by faith; the Son makes salvation possible, acting as a ransom sufficient for the redemption of all mankind, through his merits resolving the conflict of justice and mercy that threatened to paralyse the process of redemption.

'Divine Life Within Us'

But Milton would also have agreed completely with Whichcote that the Son is 'a principle of divine life within us.' In describing the repentance and renovation of man in *Paradise Lost*, Milton repeatedly draws attention to the role of the Son and what might be called the internal operation of his influence. In order to examine this second aspect of the Son's work, let us return briefly to the council in heaven. We saw when examining the external operation of the process of redemption that it is possible to view the sacrifice of the Son by the Father as a piece of enabling action which provides the legal justification for extending mercy. But it is of course much more than this. The emotional atmosphere of the council is altered strikingly when the Son offers himself as a ransom for man's sins. While the Father's initial account of salvation conceives of the process in terms of the conscientious response of the repentant individual to a grace that restores the powers of will and reason, the somewhat later passages devoted to the Son's triumph over death emphasize the transforming power of love and associate love with heroic deeds. Again, the Father speaks of salvation in terms appropriate to the effort of the individual, but the reconciling agency of the Son creates a new sense of community, a gathering of the righteous into brotherhood, a glorious intimacy fulfilled when God once more will be 'All in All' (3.341). The Son is no mere 'Saviour without us,' then, but during the council he adds love to conscience, reveals the heroism which provides a model for mankind, and thus creates that communion of mind and heart which is Milton's version of the mystical body of Christ. He is a principle within, as well as without, as *De Doctrina Christiana* makes clear (italics mine): 'The effect and design of the whole ministry of mediation is, the satisfaction of divine justice on behalf of all men, *and the confirmation of the faithful to the image of Christ*' (*Works*, XV, 315).

Milton does not, of course, think in terms of a sharp division between external and internal functions, between the 'satisfaction' and the 'confirmation,' the event and the response. No doubt he would have sympathized with Benjamin Whichcote's criticism of Tuckney as one who appeared 'to insist on Christ, less as a principle of divine nature in us; than as a sacrifice for us,' when 'both speak the rich grace of God in Christ to man: I mean, expiation of sinne, in the bloud of Christ, and true participation of the divine nature ... and I ... dare not, compare them: both being the provision of Heaven, to make us capable of happiness. ... ' Whichcote was afraid of a 'canting' affirmation of Christian dogma and urged that faith in Christ's satisfaction is best confirmed by the surrender of the self to the divine will, and the 'real transformation of man into the spirit[,] image and nature of Christ.' In these Gospel times, when Christ is known and freely professed, 'let him also be inwardlie felt, and secretlie understood.'[15] Whichcote is thus led at times to speak as if the progress of the Gospel has reached a point where inward feeling and understanding are all-important: 'Christ is not to be as in Notion or History; but as a Principle, a Vital Influence.'[16] Milton, too, speaks always as if faith in the satisfaction made by the Son were inseparable from the renewal of the image of the Son within.

As Milton explains regeneration in *De Doctrina Christiana*, the discovery of Christ as a principle of life within is intimately connected with the recovery of the law of nature. His argument suggests a doctrine of recollection, for the law of nature was given originally to Adam in unwritten form, being imprinted on his heart, and even after the Fall a remnant continues to dwell in the hearts of all mankind. This law is progressively renewed in the regenerate. The source of such renewal is identified by Milton with Christ, although he also speaks of the agent of renewal as the Spirit. The metaphors through which Milton repeatedly describes the process by which Christ gives back the unwritten law to the believer use the biblical imagery of writing on the heart (Isaiah 51:7; 2 Corinthians 3:3. etc). As Christ and the spirit write upon the heart or renew the writing on the heart, the regenerate gradually regain the understanding and freedom once possessed by Adam.

What is re-established in this way is of course not an elaborate body of prescripts such as the written law, but an attitude or mode of responding and understanding.[17] As the image of writing on the heart suggests, the 'unwritten' law is internal and not merely intellectual. Milton characteristically stresses the inward aspect by contrast with the written law of Moses. Like the antinomians, but for his own reasons, Milton insists that the whole Mosaic law was abrogated by Christ, including the moral parts. The regenerate are no longer bound to follow the written prescripts of the decalogue. The sum and essence of the written law, however, is preserved by the command to love God and neighbour.

While the outward tablet of the law is abolished, the end of the Mosaic law is fulfilled through love.]

The contrast of written and unwritten law is central to Milton's explanation of the Gospel. The covenant of grace frees men from servile obedience to outward prescription, making them sons instead of servants, perfect men instead of children. Liberty was known in Old Testament times, for the covenant of grace was announced obscurely by Moses and the prophets, but Christ establishes it in the clearest terms. Under Christ, the fruitless effort to be obedient to prescription is replaced by free choice guided by love and the spirit of truth (*Works*, XVI, chapter xxvi).

The regenerate are led by Christ to a life which is morally active. While works of the law lead away from Christ, works of faith are directed by love and conform to the unwritten law. These may deviate from the letter of Gospel precepts, in order that the spirit of love may more effectively be fulfilled.[18] At one point Milton even speaks of an 'internal scripture' provided by the spirit which is superior to the written word and offers a more certain guide (*Works*, XVI, 273).

The inward presence of Christ thus releases the individual from bondage to outward prescriptions so that he can act freely and spontaneously in the spirit of love. A creative inward order is made manifest in outward actions. While release from the written law is a precondition of any genuine spiritual development, understanding of the unwritten law is progressive. The great images of learning as process employed by Milton is *Areopagitica* years before – the gathering of the pieces of the slain god, the sorting of the confused pile of seeds, the joining of like to like as the seeker passes from known to unknown – are still applicable to his later view of the development of the regenerate. The unwritten law is not a code to be memorized but a pattern of relationships to be mastered through experience, through ceaseless attempts to realize love in thought and action. The regenerate person who engages in this effort not only gains a heightened sense of moral consciousness and identity, but is at the same time associated more and more closely with others through fellowship in the Son, so that love of neighbour and love of God find fulfilment in unity.

At first sight it is perhaps surprising that Milton can speak of this progress in the mind of Christ in terms of a recovery of what was known to Adam before the Fall. It might appear that the knowledge possessed by the Christian is radically different from that granted Adam, including as it does the story of 'how man fell / Degraded by himself' (*Paradise*

Regained, 4.311-12) and of the response by which the Son makes possible his redemption. Adam originally had no need of a mediator to make satisfaction for sin. In that sense the internal scripture of the Christian draws on a knowledge of God's decrees not relevant to Adam's version of the unwritten law. It provides wonderful evidence of the mystery of God's love. But in *Paradise Lost*, at least, Adam has abundant evidence of God's love presented in terms suitable to his unfallen state. While he does not know of the Son's act of mediation, other acts of judgment and creation performed by the Son are revealed to him, and this knowledge enables him to grow in awareness of the inner law. The Christian's perception of the unwritten law through the mediation of the Son brings out even more intensely and fully its qualities of charity and freedom.

Moreover, as we have seen, Adam is engaged even before the Fall in a process of trial which develops his comprehension of the unwritten law by requiring him to live by it in a variety of challenging circumstances. Like the Christian, he perceives that responsive action leads to a union of free agents in the performance of God's will. *Paradise Lost* follows out the implications of Milton's somewhat unusual view that Adam did not live under a covenant of works. Like the regenerate under the Gospel, Adam must exercise his freedom and through choice seek to move from theory to practice, fulfilling the spirit rather than the letter of the law and seeking to know himself and to express his love of God and man. The analogy between the life of the Christian and the life of Adam before the Fall is founded on a significant core of common experience. But the exploration of parallels and connections between unfallen and fallen experience must wait until we have examined the renewal of man in the last books of *Paradise Lost*.

The repentance and gradual renewal of will and understanding in Adam and Eve offer a dramatic treatment of the internal process of regeneration. The developing experience of Adam as he finds new life within is coordinated with his discovery of the covenant made by God with man through the Son for the satisfaction of Sin. Adam, moreover, provides an unusually challenging figure in whom to portray the regenerative process, since at the outset he has no knowledge of Christ as Redeemer, and it is only at the end of the process that his spiritual rebirth is given final confirmation by the revelation of the nature and significance of the Incarnation. At the close, faith in the expiation of sin by the blood of Christ and participation in the divine nature are perfectly integrated, so that we become aware that each is supported by the other.

Judgment by the Son begins the internal process of renovation in Adam. It produces two quite different effects in him. Initially it reinforces his sense of guilt and his agonizing regret. The Son's manner throughout the judgment scene is stern, and while he does remove the stroke of death into the future, and allude to the bruising of the serpent by the seed of the woman (the promise which constitutes the *protevang-elium*),[19] his emphasis is not encouraging as he reveals the pain and labour that will characterize man's life until his eventual return to earth. His last words suggest that Adam should meditate upon his death:

> for thou
> Out of the ground wast taken, know thy Birth,
> For dust thou art, and shalt to dust returne.   (10.206-8)

Adam knew before that he is 'dust of the ground' (7.525), but now he is commanded to meditate on the significance of his origins. And the next time we see him he has indeed abandoned himself to reflections on the many meanings of death, his self-condemnation turning the stay of execution into a nightmare of horrid possibilities:

> how gladly would I meet
> Mortalitie my sentence, and be Earth
> Insensible, how glad would lay me down
> As in my Mothers lap?   (10.77-8)

This speech, unlike his soliloquy on first awakening into life, represents an Adam who is convinced that he is unheard, that he is talking to himself, and his gestures in the direction of an audience – 'Did I request thee, Maker' (10.743), 'Fair Patrimonie / That I must leave ye, Sons' (818-19) – simply draw attention to his intolerable feeling of isolation, his sense of being self-enclosed and abandoned. Thus he ends appropriately by addressing himself ('coulds't thou support,' 834; 'concludes thee miserable,' 839).

But other things happen at the close of the judgment episode of which Adam is not directly aware. As soon as the Son has passed sentence he assumes the form of a servant and begins his work of mediation, clothing their 'inward nakedness' with the 'Robe of righteousness,' and then returning to heaven to make intercession for man (10.220-8). The inward work of the Son in the process of renovation begins here. Adam is now to receive benefits from Christ's death, even though it has not yet occurred in history, and although he is not aware of 'the source from which the benefits flow' (*Works*, XV, 349). And in his misery and despair, of course, he is at first totally unaware of the beneficent influence that has begun to act in his favour. The 'dreadful voice' in the garden sounded to him like a kind of thunder in his ears (10.779-80), and we are likely to remember how Satan heard the thunder 'bellow though the vast and boundless Deep' (1.177). Expecting nothing but justice, his despair causes him to cry out in exacerbation of spirit:

> Shall Truth fail to keep her word,
> Justice Divine not hast'n to be just? (10.856-7)

The reader, however, can see that already something restorative has begun to take place, and that the law's delay is really mercy in disguise. For we can understand that Adam's conclusion is wrong, and that at the very moment when he decides he is 'to *Satan* only like both crime and doom' (841), he has begun to display striking differences from Satan. We possess the advantage, of course, of having listened to Satan's soliloquy on Mount Niphates at the opening of book 4. Both Satan and Adam twist and turn in an effort to evade responsibility, and each concludes by recognizing that his effort at self-justification leads only to his conviction. But there the similarity ends. Unlike Satan, Adam does not reaffirm his opposition to God, but wishes rather that he could pay for his sin and thus save his descendants if not himself. And while the 'Fond wish' (834) expresses Adam's despair, it also reveals that his egoism is not, like Satan's, perfect, and it anticipates, if uncertainly, the discovery of the redemptive act of the Son.

The subsequent reconciliation of Adam and Eve is a moving episode in which the dialectic of human responses leads the fallen couple towards new self-understanding. Adam's excessive tirade against women in general and Eve in particular fails to repulse her. Falling at his feet like a defeated Homeric warrior — 'thy suppliant / I beg, and clasp thy knees' (10.917-18) — she proceeds to pray, not for life, but for peace and the restoration of his love. As Joseph Summers has perceptively observed, 'it is a speech of human love after man's fall, and it marks an end to the battle between man and woman.'[20] Love introduces the idea of forgiveness. No doubt there remains in this speech, as in the interchange as a whole, the insistence on the first person noticed by some readers.[21] This points to the egotism of guilt and the fallen sensibility, and Adam and Eve will not be free of it, or able to speak of the self without the false notes of melodrama, until much later. There is nonetheless a great deal that is promising about Eve's plea. Prompted perhaps by Adam's attempt to identify her with sin in the phrase 'thou Serpent' (10.867), she recalls, as Adam has failed to do, the 'doom express' (10.926) by which the cruel serpent is their foe, in this way tactfully reminding him that their judge did not distinguish her guilt from his. Although she does not seem to recall the hopeful aspects of that doom very clearly, she does hit upon the fortunate idea of going to the 'place of judgment' (932) to pray, an idea that will shortly be adopted in revised form by Adam.

Eve feels that her double responsibility makes her guilt worse than Adam's:

> both have sin'd, but thou
> Against God onely, I against God and thee,
> And to the place of judgment will return,
> There with my cries importune Heaven, that all
> The sentence from thy head remov'd may light
> On me, sole cause to thee of all this woe,
> Mee mee onely just object of his ire.   (10.930-6)

She is wrong, of course, in her assessment of responsibility, and there is a touch of extravagance in her grief. As Adam is quick to point out, the fact that she finds his displeasure so hard to bear should convince her that she is 'ill able to sustaine / His full wrauth whose thou feelst as yet lest part' (10.950-1). The comparison between Eve's testimonial of her concern for Adam and Adam's earlier 'Fond wish' that he might make atonement for sin by bearing God's wrath is a subtle one. Eve's remark is less guarded, more rhetorical and emotional than Adam's; it has less to do with an intuition concerning the operations of God's will than with a desire to regain Adam's affection. As Adam's soliloquy wrestled despairingly with his alienation from God, so Eve more hopefully seeks to reunite herself with her husband:

> bereave me not,
> Whereon I live, thy gentle looks, thy aid,
> Thy counsel in this uttermost distress,
> My onely strength and stay.   (10.918-21)

Her language – reminiscent of the Psalms – reinforces her statement of dependence, and recalls their relationship before the Fall. It is a faith that will be tested by the traumatic events which are to follow, but will emerge resolutely at the final moment of exile: 'with thee to goe, / Is to stay here' (12.615-16).

By reassuming her proper attitude to Adam, Eve shows that the tide has turned. Perhaps her nature prevents her fall from being as profoundly tragic as Adam's. Certainly the poem gives the impression that she initiates the restoration as well as the Fall. The turning point is marked by domestic events, and only after some order has been restored in their relations to each other can they seek to repair their relations with God. Here at the close of book 10 we suddenly feel the re-emergence of the pattern that characterized their relation in book 4, when we first met them – the man meditates on justice and obedience, the woman expresses love for her husband.

The process of renovation has of course only begun, and the next speeches continue the dialectic of responses. As his heart relents, and he learns by experience about forgiveness, Adam finds himself, like his wife, 'disarmed.' But while he has been moved by her love for him, his overt response is to subject her words to analytic, and rather negative, criticism:

> If Prayers
> Could alter high Decrees, I to that place
> Would speed before thee, and be louder heard,
> That on my head all might be visited,
> Thy frailtie and infirmer Sex forgiv'n,
> To me committed and by me expos'd.   (10.952-7)

Adam recognizes his responsibility, even exaggerates it, but still has not caught on to the possibilities of prayer. There is something competitive in his assertion that he would outgo Eve in seeking to bear the blame if he thought it would do any good, but the underlying motive in these remarks is his frustration at the thought that the way back to God is blocked. For a moment he entertains the hope that by striving to assist each other in offices of love they may make woe more bearable, a policy more humane than that put forward by Mammon during the council in Hell, but tainted by the same erroneous assumption that life without God is possible. He has not yet seen that prayers are not inconsistent with 'high Decrees,' that 'God decreed nothing absolutely, which he left in the power of free agents' (*Works*, XIV, 65) and that his conditional decrees permit man to achieve regeneration by responding to the grace that is offered to all.

Eve's reply is clearly wayward, yet serves as a catalyst which produces a surprising revival in Adam. Her suggestion that they remain childless or, if that prove too difficult, that they commit suicide, provides a stoic parody of true heroism. She is said to recover 'heart,' but the energy so gained is turned into gestures that only appear self-denying, being in reality grounded on egoism. Her state of mind is consistent with the tendencies revealed in her experience with her reflection in the pool, for she accepts a sterile and self-regarding isolation. Having regained Adam, she appears to care for nothing else. The picture drawn of abstention from sexual relations ('with desire to languish without hope, / Before the present object languishing / With like desire,' 10.995-7) recalls the 'vain desire' (4.466) with which she languished at her image in the pool, and what follows seems the narcissistic plunge into the depths. Her concern over their 'hapless Seed' (10.965) is suicidal, being motivated by 'vehement despaire' (10.1007).

Adam is 'nothing sway'd' by her counsel, having raised his labouring mind to 'better hopes' (10.1010-11). He sees that while her 'contempt of life and pleasure' (1013) has the appearance of self-transcendence, it is basically self-destructive. His own speech swings in the opposite direction, developing to a conclusion in which life is accepted, a life of prayer, quiet effort, 'many comforts' (1084), but no real heroism. True patience is still to be learned by Adam, and its lessons will include both 'Nor love thy Life, nor hate' (11.553) and 'Judg not what is best / By pleasure' (11.603-4). *Paradise Lost* is a poem which ultimately affirms both life and pleasure; before that affirmation can emerge, however, the true forms of each must be separated from false or lesser forms.

Nonetheless, the speech by Adam at the close of book 10 with which we are presently concerned marks a turning point. It begins in memories of God's justice and 'vengeful ire' (10.1023), but ends by recognizing that through his anger shine 'favor, grace, and mercie' (1096). The blocked lines of communication are now opening: 'I' and 'me' change to 'we' and 'us'; God's 'ear' is understood to be open to prayer; and memory returns, recalling the gracious temper of the judge and his enigmatic yet hopeful promise concerning the bruising of the serpent's head by the seed of the woman. As Georgia B. Christopher observes, Adam makes a 'great interpretive leap' and 'hits upon the correct referent for "serpent",' thus connecting 'the Serpent with the Grand Enemy of cosmic wars that

Raphael had warned of.'[22] Adam has begun to think, to use his understanding, and the result is a telling analysis of the effects of the curse, the nature of the revenge on Satan, and the operation of mercy. It is a superbly imagined episode, dramatically presenting the process of 'natural renovation' by which Adam, his mind and will partially renewed by divine impulse, seeks knowledge of God and undergoes an alteration for the better (*Works*, XV, 355). Part of Milton's achievement lies in showing this process as one that is psychologically plausible, integrated at the natural level. Part also lies in showing how pre-Christian man under the influence of grace can move towards faith and the recognition of Gospel values, yet without fully understanding the source from which these benefits flow.

Adam thus moves to a perception – accurate as far as it goes but partial – of the reconciliation of justice and mercy, the feat negotiated in the heavenly council of book 3, but to be fully revealed and finally accomplished at the Incarnation. He sees that God's 'ire' (10.1023) is what the proud call the effects of his justice, that it is best to serve him by accepting his 'just yoke' (1045), and that their judge showed mildness, not anger. Adam's memory of the judgment begins to shape the image of Christ as he adopts the form of a servant out of pity in order to clothe fallen man. Even the sentence of the Son now appears in a more positive and hopeful form, as Adam realizes that labor will bring its own rewards, and that the pain of childbirth will be recompensed by joy.

But Adam misses important things too. Symptomatic is his inability to recognize that he has been clothed not only outwardly with the skins of beasts, but inwardly with the 'Robe of righteousness' (10.222) provided also by the Son. The missing clue is the story of his redemption by the Son; of this, he has only figurative hints, like the 'Fruit of thy Womb' (1053) that will recompense for pain with joy (cf Luke 1:42; John 16:21). Lacking this clue, he is not aware of the tragic aspect of the reconciliation of justice and mercy. This limitation colours his view of the future, which rapidly develops into a narrow optimism with a materialistic emphasis, not entirely unlike the visions of false repose offered to Samson by Manoa and Delila.

After his fine perception of the judge whose ear is open and heart inclined to pity, Adam goes on to speculate that this benevolent figure will teach them how to survive the inclement seasons which now threaten:

> such Fire to use,
> And what may else be remedie or cure

> To evils which our own misdeeds have wrought,
> Hee will instruct us praying, and of Grace
> Beseeching him, so as we need not fear
> To pass commodiously this life, sustain'd
> By him with many comforts, till we end
> In dust, our final rest and native home.   (10.1078-85)

Such modest Promethean aspiration is anticlimactic, and the account of the possible ways of creating fire (1072-8) is contrived to suggest the clumsy and laborious nature of the process, unlike the sure and graceful movements of unfallen man. No doubt Adam's concern for their survival is genuine, for he is quick to perceive how things are changing and protection against the elements will be necessary if the seed of the woman is to bring their revenge to pass. But it is wrong, I think, to accept Adam's remarks at face value at this point, as if Milton were using him to express his own views concerning the acceptable uses of technology. While it is true that Adam's humility offers a protection against the excess so frequently associated with technical achievement (the building of Babel, or the arts of the sons of Seth), the chief point to be made about his response at this stage is surely that it is self-centred and in a sense unimaginative. Only symbolically, by the opposition of darkness, cold, and discord to the light and heat of sun or fire, does the passage speak of Adam's spiritual plight. But Adam is not in a state of mind to read the meaning of such figures. He has much to discover. Grace has not been given to Adam that he may live in comfort, and the distance between his present mood of easy if narrow optimism and his final heroic stance at the close of the poem is a measure of what he still must learn. Only at the close will he understand how the unbearable vision of justice elaborated so powerfully in his soliloquy at night and the intuitions of mercy in the present meditation are to be reconciled.

By the close of book 10, then, Adam and Eve have completed only a stage in their recovery. Filled with remorse, they are penitent, and pray for forgiveness with hearts contrite. This change appears to go beyond attrition or what Milton in his theological study calls the 'secondary species of repentance,' which is that 'whereby a man abstains from sin through fear of punishment, and obeys the call of God merely for the sake of his own salvation' (*Works*, XV, 359). While such secondary repentance is associated with natural renovation, it is also a legitimate element in the condition of the regenerate. Although Adam's night soliloquy displays his fears, his subsequent conversation with Eve reveals the beginnings of the 'higher species' of repentance, associated with supernatural rather than natural renovation, 'whereby the regenerate man perceiving with sorrow that he has offended God by sin, detests and avoids it, humbly turning to God through a sense of the divine mercy, and heartily striving to follow righteousness' (*Works*, XV, 379). Adam and Eve are thus passing through the 'progressive steps in repentance' mentioned in *De Doctrina Christiana*, 'conviction of sin, contrition, confession,' and while the later steps, 'departure from evil' and 'conversion to good,' are still to be realized, they are drawing closer (*Works*, XV, 385).

These later stages of repentance will not be realized until Adam has been disciplined by the visions of history. Alastair Fowler is certainly right to find in the final words of Adam at the close of book 10 a reminder of Milton's belief that mercy leads to repentance, and repentance to faith; as Milton puts the matter in *De Doctrina Christiana*, presumably thinking of Calvin among others, 'repentance, in regenerate man, is prior to faith. ... Therefore that sense of divine mercy, which leads to repentance, ought not to be confounded with faith, as it is by the greater number of divines' (*Works*, XV, 387).[23] It is unlikely, however, that Milton thought of the two aspects of regeneration as completely separate in time. Adam has clearly developed the kind of faith appropriate to natural renovation, which lies in a trusting response to God. This is particularly evident in his assent to the prophecy concerning the bruising of the serpent's head, which contains the degrees of faith (historical and temporary faith, and faith in miracles) that Milton associates with the natural mode (*Works*, XV, 361).

But what of saving faith, which is 'a full persuasion operated in us through the gift of God, whereby we believe, on the sole authority of the promise itself, that whatsoever things he has promised in Christ are ours, and especially the grace of eternal life' (*Works*, XV, 393)? In respect to such faith, Adam has made only a beginning. He has much to learn about the ways of God, but his recognition that God is merciful as well as just prepares for a right understanding of the promise concerning the woman's seed. Faith may spring, Milton tells us, from what in the first instance is an imperfect knowledge of God,[24] and this is clearly Adam's case. He does not yet have a 'full persuasion,' for he is in the position of those converts 'whose faith must necessarily be for a time implicit, inasmuch as they believe even before they have entered upon a course of instruction' (*Works*, XV, 397). One of the chief things to be revealed in that course of instruction is the promise that is especially crucial to saving faith, the promise of eternal life. Of this Adam presently has no knowledge at all. He sees that providence has prepared vengeance for the serpent, but not that death will be the gate of life. And since Christ has not yet been revealed to him, his faith at present is placed in the Father alone, the ultimate object of all faith. At the close of book 10, then, Adam has shown the kind of repentance and faith comprehended within natural renovation, but the higher forms of these conditions are also incipient in him. It is clear that he and Eve have made substantial progress towards renovation without a direct knowledge of Christ. They are, as Mary Ann Radzinowicz had observed, free again at the moment when they pray.[25]

[handwritten margin note:] [ ] On what def of "free"? Is it possible for them to sin? If not, terms are sliding here.

Milton's handling of repentance once more demonstrates his skill in presenting psychic growth and process. The movement to repentance occurs in terms of the interplay of personalities in the context of domestic relations. Each partner contributes to the dialectic, and the unity of their marriage is affirmed as a result.[26] Milton shows a lively sense of how Adam can know something and yet not know it experientially, and how he can partially lose his knowledge only to regain it subsequently in a new and stronger form. The shape of the episode reveals some of the categories of Milton's theology concerning repentance, but there is no strain about this, and one does not feel that experience has been distorted to fit the categories. The discriminations among stages of repentance and faith, and particularly the provocative distinction between natural and supernatural renovation, are used as imaginative guidelines to ethical experience. As so often, theology offers a means for adapting the great mythic features of Milton's story to his ethical intelligence.

But now the reader comes to one of the most surprising turns in the narrative. Having seen repentance in terms of human motive and response, we suddenly stand back from the episode and at the beginning of book 11 see it from the vantage point of heaven:

> Thus they in lowliest plight repentant stood
> Praying, for from the Mercie-seat above
> Prevenient Grace descending had remov'd
> The stonie from thir hearts, and made new flesh
> Regenerate grow instead, that sighs now breath'd
> Unutterable, which the Spirit of prayer
> Inspir'd. ... (11.1-7)

The event we have been watching was not entirely what it appeared to be. Prevenient grace made possible both the human reconciliation that we have just witnessed and the movement to prayer. No less than the pride of Satan, the humility of Adam and Eve occurs only with the will and high permission of all ruling heaven. Further, the prayers of the repenting couple make their way to the throne of God only because of the intercession of the Son.

The Father's words to the assembled angels concerning man's repentance are even more disconcerting:

> He sorrows now, repents, and prayes contrite,
> My motions in him, longer then they move,
> His heart I know, how variable and vain
> Self-left. (11.90-3)

This leaves no room for vanity about human effort.[27] Without the sustaining grace of God, Adam and Eve would be irrecoverably lost. It is worth recalling how the process of natural renovation is characterized in *De Doctrina Christiana* as variable and uncertain. At this level the feelings of faith and repentance 'may be either the genuine beginnings of conversion, or the mere effect of nature, or, lastly, they may be altogether fictitious' (*Works*, XV, 357). Such repentance and faith may prove transient and vain, 'owing to the remains of human frailty still inherent in us' (*Works*, XV, 363). In view of our sense that Adam and Eve in the repentance scene appear to be moving to and even beyond the limits of natural regeneration, it should be remarked that the later and supernatural phase of regeneration also depends continuously on God's grace, for a saving faith is 'operated in us through the gift of God' (*Works*, XV, 393), and even the saints must persevere with the assistance of the Spirit until the end. The Father's description of Adam's heart as 'variable and vain / Self-left' would apply to all men absolutely, although perhaps relatively it would apply less to the seasoned Christian than the novice.

As Jackson C. Boswell has observed, Milton's use of prevenient grace emphasizes that while men have freedom of choice, God is the author of all things, including the impulse to salvation: 'salvation does not lie within the natural capacity of man but in God's will. Even man's decision to strive for grace is the gift of God.'[28] Boswell is right to stress that this doctrine has not always been sufficiently recognized by critics. Grace is not a response to human effort, but the ground of it. But like some Arminians, Milton posits a synergism by which the human will co-operates with grace in the process of regeneration. As the Father remarks during the council, men who respond to grace will be saved:

> I will cleer thir senses dark,
> What may suffice, and soft'n stonie hearts
> To pray, repent, and bring obedience due. (3.188-90)

This process, well under way in Adam and Eve by the close of book 10, is in Milton's view available to all men, as we have seen. Since the effect of prevenient grace is to clear the understanding and free the will so that effort is once more possible, human responses are as important after the Fall as before. On the one hand, then, dependence on prevenient grace exhibits the frailty of the human condition, man's inability to escape from bondage to the self, his total dependence on God for his deliverance from sin. On the other hand, the effect of such grace is to encourage man to work out his salvation with diligence through the use of his human faculties of will and reason, trusting to his renewed natural responses to bring him through the dust and heat of the day. Prevenient grace enables man to act rightly once more. It can work this effect without being recognized by the recipient, as Adam's progress reveals, and the chief benefit of knowing of its operation would seem to be that such knowledge induces humility and removes the possibility of glorying, like Satan, in recovered strength.[29]

The scene in heaven that opens book 11 also contains a further manifestation of the Son. The sequence here firmly recalls that of the council in book 3. First there is a description of the operation of the grace of the Father, then the Son reveals the act of redemption which has released that grace. It is suggestive that the Son here speaks first, taking the initiative as he presents the prayers of Adam and Eve to the Father, offering himself as propitiation for man's sin:

> Accept me, and in mee from these receave
> The smell of peace toward Mankinde. ...
> ...
> To whom the Father, without Cloud, serene.
> All thy request for Man, accepted Son,
> Obtain, all thy request was my Decree. ... (11.37-47)

The immediacy of the scene is noteworthy: this offering takes place in the present, an event happening before our eyes. The Son now exercises his priestly or sacerdotal function, for as priest he does not simply offer himself once as a sacrifice for sinners but also 'has always made, and still continues to make intercession for us ... "appearing in the presence of God for us," Heb ix. 24 ... ' (*Works*, XV, 291-5). The act of self-sacrifice which is to be accomplished at Calvary centuries later is timelessly present in this ritual of heaven.

The speech also marks, as it were behind the scenes, an advance in the progress of Adam and Eve towards regeneration, for the Son now introduces into his relationship with them the process of communion described through the image of ingrafting. It is still somewhat formal, being presented in terms of the doctrine of merit:

> all his works on mee
> Good or not good ingraft, my Merit those
> Shall perfet, and for these my Death shall pay. (11.34-6)

The passage does not touch on the new spiritual life in Christ which is the effect of being planted in him. Such 'newness of life' involves both the comprehension of spiritual things and that charity which brings forth good works spontaneously (*Works*, XVI, 3ff), and the education of Adam and Eve in these two prime matters is just about to begin and will not finish until the close of Michael's visit. But already the Son anticipates that union and fellowship which is the goal of the process, observing that death

> To better life shall yeeld him, where with mee
> All my redeemd may dwell in joy and bliss,
> Made one with me as I with thee am one. (11.42-4)

Here, too, the immortality of the redeemed, their triumph through death, is again strongly stated; this theme was introduced at the first council in heaven, but has been suppressed during the period of man's gradual repentance when death bears down on Adam like a monstrous enigma. Now the theme of resurrection is strongly sounded (although not yet in Adam's hearing), and it will continue to be recalled until its triumphant statement at the close of the world's history.

The next phase in the renewal of Adam and Eve commences when

Michael is sent to banish them from Paradise and to offer consolation and instruction. Reveal, says the Father,

> To *Adam* what shall come in future dayes,
> As I shall thee enlighten, intermix
> My Cov'nant in the womans seed renewd;
> So send them forth, though sorrowing, yet in peace. ...
> (11.114-17)

As Michael is given his instructions, Adam and Eve awake and say their morning prayers. There is a suggestion here of that earlier moment when morning prayer brought firm peace to their thoughts after the distress caused by Eve's Satanic dream, but now the mood is tense with paradox and strife as they feel

> Strength added from above, new hope to spring
> Out of despaire, joy, but with fear yet linkt. ...
> (11.138-9)

These are some of the great motifs that will echo throughout the education of Adam.

The terrible night of repentance is past. The sacred light that now breaks and the morning dew that embalms the earth suggest the grace that has illumined Adam's mind and softened his heart. His first speech to Eve is full of wonder at the discovery he has made through the experience of prayer:

> For since I saught
> By Prayer th' offended Deitie to appease,
> Kneel'd and before him humbl'd all my heart,
> Methought I saw him placable and mild,
> Bending his eare; perswasion in me grew
> That I was heard with favour; peace returnd
> Home to my Brest, and to my memorie
> His promise, that thy Seed shall bruise our Foe. ...
> (11.148-55)

The key is the promise that lies in memory. Here as elsewhere grace is seen as recalling what was known yet unrecognized, enabling the mind to grasp its significance.

The 'offended Deitie' is more and more clearly taking the form of the Son, even though the saviour has not yet been revealed to Adam. He is persuaded that he has been heard, and while his condition is a great distance from that firm persuasion called assurance of salvation and founded on the testimony of the Spirit (*Works*, XVI, 71), communication with God is now possible. The promise concerning the seed of the woman 'Assures me that the bitterness of death / Is past, and we shall live' (11.157-8). Under the impulse of grace, Adam's understanding is tending in the right direction. But too much must not be read into his words. As his remarks a few lines later remind us, he knows nothing yet of that 'second Life, / Wak't in the renovation of the just' (11.64-5) of which the Father spoke to the Son. His words grope towards a solution that has not been revealed to him yet, but their primary meaning is simply that the fact of death no longer robs life of significance since they look forward to becoming the instruments of God in the destruction of their enemy.

Adam and Eve now display a touch of overconfidence in their assumption that the worst is over. The experience is a familiar one: shock gives way to relief at the avoidance of immediate disaster. Thus Eve, taking her cue from Adam's earlier remarks on the commodious life, concludes 'Here let us live, though in fall'n state, content' (11.180). Although their determination arouses pity and even respect, their trust is clearly vain because they have not confronted the way in which their act has changed reality. This optimism gives point to the Father's observation that they would be variable as well as vain if left to themselves. While the lapse may be minor, containing only a trace of similarity to attitudes found in hell, it nonetheless underlines the importance of their coming exile from the garden. Adam, to do him justice, quickly perceives in the mute signs in nature a warning that they have become 'too secure of our discharge / From penaltie' (11.196-7). The fluctuation of mood, the alternation between groundless confidence and despairing anxiety, is characteristic of their present state.

The limitations of Adam's view are further emphasized by the way he unconsciously provides a parody of the annunciation in his celebration of Eve:

Whence Haile to thee,

Eve rightly call'd, Mother of all Mankind,
Mother of all things living, since by thee
Man is to live, and all things live for Man.   (11.158-61)

He is no doubt recalling the angel Raphael's earlier use of the 'holy salutation us'd / Long after to blest *Marie*, second *Eve*' (5.386-7). But Raphael's *Ave* was directed to Eve as the principle of vital fruitfulness in the human world, surpassing in plenty the fruitfulness of the trees of Paradise, while Adam tries to express a more subtle role in which fallen Eve becomes mother of mankind no longer through simple fertility, but rather by providing the seed that will restore life to man. Once more Adam is groping, letting his mind play over the implications of the promise. Only much later will Adam come to an understanding of the promise through the words of Michael, at which point he is able to praise Mary directly: 'Virgin Mother, Haile' (12.379).

At the descent of the angel, moments later, Adam's words again have figurative significance beyond his understanding:

Eve, now expect great tidings, which perhaps
Of us will soon determin, or impose
New Laws to be observ'd. ...   (11.226-8)

Unlike the tidings of great joy to be announced at the Nativity, the 'New Laws' anticipated by Adam are stringent. As the tone indicates, Adam's state is still uneasy, and there is much about which he needs to be enlightened. His attitude is far from Satan's sneering observation to Beelzebub at the moment of conspiracy: 'New Laws thou seest impos'd' (5.679). But it is removed also from the faithful Abdiel's response to the Satanic doctrine: 'His Laws our Laws' (5.844). Without a knowledge of the Incarnation, Adam cannot recognize the pattern in his experience.

Although Michael's first speech is forthright and compact, it tempers the sentence of banishment by reference to the promise:

thy Prayers are heard, and Death,
Then due by sentence when thou didst transgress,
Defeated of his seisure many dayes
Giv'n thee of Grace, wherein thou may'st repent,
And one bad act with many deeds well done
Mayst cover: well may then thy Lord appeas'd
Redeem thee quite from Deaths rapacious claime;

> But longer in this Paradise to dwell
> Permits not; to remove thee I am come,
> And send thee from the garden forth to till
> The ground whence thou wast tak'n, fitter Soile.
> (11.252-6)

Repentance is a continuing process, and the 'conversion to good' can only be fulfilled through deeds. Michael is putting the matter very simply, placing the responsibility for good works on Adam, and for the moment ignoring the factors which Adam does not know – the inability of man in himself to 'appease' God, the ingrafting of works on Christ, and the distinction between works under the law and works of faith. Even more striking is the announcement of redemption from death, which is of necessity made without reference to Christ, so that the 'Lord' whose wrath is appeased is also he who redeems. Michael's statement thus reveals the possibility of renewed life in a way that can be apprehended by the natural man (or, indeed, the deist) who lacks the revelation of Christian truth.

It is worth stressing that this is the first sounding to Adam of the great truth that man will be redeemed from death. The original judgment, while it hinted at revenge upon the powers of evil, did not mention the possibility of escape from mortality and dust. At first it may appear surprising that Adam fails to perceive the full significance of the angel's remark. His shock at the news of his exile from the garden prevents him from absorbing the promise of redemption. At the close of his reply, he refers only to 'life prolongd and promisd Race' (11.331), apparently taking redemption from death in natural terms as the survival of the race. But this has repeatedly been Milton's way of dramatizing psychic development: the truth seems to be misunderstood on first acquaintance, or to be lost again because of the inadequacy of the recipient or the stressful context in which it appears; later it is rediscovered through enlightened memory, and finally apprehended in a lively and imaginative fashion. As Calvin remarked, the seed of a hidden faith may lie as if dead in the heart, and then burst forth with vigour.[30]

Absorbed in the present loss, Adam and Eve appear to miss the great promise at the heart of the angel's tidings. Critics have rightly drawn attention to the errors in Adam's response to Michael. Melancholy has overtaken him, and he speaks of his loss of the garden in a manner resigned and hopeless:

> here I could frequent,
> With worship, place by place where he voutsaf'd
> Presence Divine, and to my Sons relate;
> On this Mount he appeerd; under this Tree
> Stood visible, among these Pines his voice
> I heard, here with him at this Fountain talk'd:
> So many grateful altars I would reare
> Of grassie Terfe, and pile up every Stone
> Of lustre from the brook, in memorie,
> Or monument to Ages, ... (11.317-26)

In ethics as well as poetry, this is a subtle and fascinating moment; what was natural and right is on the point of becoming false and delusory, a perversion of memory. Turning to prayer during the past night, they went without hesitation to the 'place' where they had been judged in order to seek pardon. That act indicates the happy simplicity and directness of their religious practices and worship. For Adam before the Fall God is the 'sovran Presence' (10.144) with whom he has talked on several occasions, as the Son implies at the beginning of the judgment scene: 'Where art thou *Adam*, wont with joy to meet / My coming seen far off?' (10.103-4). As we have seen, the presence appears to have a 'count'nance' (11.317) and other visual properties (although not distinct ones as is the case with the angels), and it is particularly identified as a voice ('My voice thou oft hast heard, and hast not fear'd,' 10.119). It is decidedly associated with the garden, and also with the early stages of experience. While its divine colloquies with Adam press him to an exacting use of his reason, the presence has something of the character of the parent as experienced by the child.

Intellectually, of course, Adam is aware of God's omnipresence. It is a matter upon which Raphael touched at points in his narrative, and particularly when describing the creation. Adam's natural bias, however, has been to see God present in his works as the maker in the thing made: this is the theme of the morning hymn praising the creator of the 'universal Frame' (5.154). Remembering how human communion with God has been established only in the garden, his imagination now fails him and he concludes that in losing the garden he is also being deprived of the 'blessed count'nance.'

The passage is so highly charged and evocative partly because it recalls the intensity of childhood experiences, and the nostalgia which sometimes makes us seek to revive them in recollection. Such clinging to the past is for Milton the false form of memory, opposed to that true form by which the forgotten knowledge returns at the appropriate occasion to transform judgment. Adam is clearly wrong to think in terms of a pastoral religion that restricts God to times and places, and his mistake will recur in the future among the patriarchs. His fanciful wish that he be allowed to raise altars of turf or stone in memory of the past opens a door that leads finally to the demonic concern with a memorial to fame shown by the builders of Babel. Adam must learn that a melancholy attachment to the past will not help, that God is everywhere and prefers the upright heart and pure before all outward temples and places of worship. Holiness is an inward state, not a property of places, and God cannot be placated by external ritual. But the angel's reply is 'benigne' for he understands the desire in Adam's words. Outside the garden God will be

> found alike
> Present, and of his presence many a signe
> Still following thee, still compassing thee round
> With goodness and paternal Love, his Face
> Express, and of his steps the track Divine. (11.350-4)

Michael is already leading Adam from flesh to spirit, as he points out that the 'Express' face of God and his footsteps are not to be thought of as localized phenomena, but rather as his encompassing love and goodness. If the new spiritual life is to lead to a paradise within, the husk of the old world must be cast away.

In order to confirm Adam's faith in divine benevolence, Michael now takes him to the hill of the visions of God to show what will happen in the future to man. The history lesson advances the process by which Adam, being ingrafted into Christ, achieves newness of life, so that Adam may learn

> True patience, and to temper joy with fear
> And pious sorrow, equally enur'd
> By moderation either state to beare,
> Prosperous or adverse: ... (11.361-4)

Faith will be the dominant issue in the revelations that follow, but as 'pious sorrow' suggests, the process of repentance will continue, leading as it does through the later states of 'departure from evil' and 'conversion to good' (*Works*, XV, 385). The great theme of 'suffering for Truths sake' (12.569) is muted here, for Michael is adjusting his language to the present understanding of Adam, and thus stresses moderation as the key to endurance. Adam's response shows how quickly he is learning, and with what zeal he takes up the role of the novice who is about to be initiated:

> Ascend, I follow thee, safe Guide, the path
> Thou lead'st me, and to the hand of Heav'n submit,
> However chast'ning, to the evil turne
> My obvious breast, arming to overcom
> By suffering, and earne rest from labour won,
> If so I may attain.   (11.371-6)

He is on the right track: 'arming to overcom / By suffering' is a real insight, based partly on what the angel has already told him, but also on the emerging pattern of his own experience. While he does not know the realities behind the terms he uses, his language foreshadows the truth, and his gesture is the first unconscious step towards the imitation of Christ. He is willing to strive and to suffer, and although his confidence may show a certain lack of self-knowledge, it clearly affirms his good intentions. The process of regaining the image of God within has been initiated and developed, but progress towards fulfilment now depends on further revelation.

The Image of God and the History of the World

The visions of human history in the final books of *Paradise Lost* are marked by parallel and contrast, and centre on the gradual revelation of the Son as the incarnate Christ.[31] The basic pattern of fall, judgment, regeneration, and renewal is repeated cyclically from age to age, each new world being born out of the ruins of the old. Yet there is progress too, a movement from implicit to explicit, 'From shadowie Types to Truth, from Flesh to Spirit' (12.303). The dominant feature of this typology is the Pauline and Augustinian emphasis on the men of faith as prefigurations of Christ. Abel, his faith approved, shall lose no reward, 'though here thou see him die, / Rowling in dust and gore' (11.459-60); Enoch is 'The onely righteous in a World perverse' (11.701); Noah is 'the onely Son of light / In a dark Age' (11.808-9); Abraham is the 'one faithful man' (12.113) through whom all nations will be blessed; Moses is a figure of the mediator. The model for such typology is to be found in the histories of the saints in the Epistle to the Hebrews (11-13), and Stephen's speech before the Sanhedrin in Acts (7:1-53). The author of the Epistle to the Hebrews sets out to illustrate the doctrine that faith is 'the substance of things hoped for, the evidence of things not seen.' His examples comprise a short history of the world. Beginning with Abel, Enoch, Noah, and Abraham, he sweeps down history through a cloud of witnesses to Christ, the 'author and finisher of our faith,' and concludes by hinting at the second coming. It is in terms of the lonely men of faith who realize that in this world God has no continuing city that Milton, like the writer of the Epistle to the Hebrews, records the history of the world.

This history completes the education of Adam. By the close, the process of regeneration is well advanced, and Adam is on the way to regaining the image of God, now in the form of 'my Redeemer ever blest' (12.573). The process has two main movements. The initial movement is primarily designed to expose the spiritual bankruptcy of natural man, and its religious teaching seldom goes beyond that natural theology which, in a liberal view, is available to all men through the light of nature. The closing movement, which entails a change in method, is concerned with spiritual regeneration through grace, and its emphasis falls on the revealed truths of Christianity. Together the two movements form the main thesis and antithesis of the dialectic.

Michael's first task is to help Adam to achieve patience. With this end in view, he dwells on the loss of those 'two fair gifts' with which Adam was endowed, Happiness and Immortality (11.57-9). Death is the chief theme of the vision of Abel, the subsequent allegorical vision of the Lazar House, and the picture of war in the heroic age. The treatment of the sons of Lamech and Seth centres on the theme of pleasure, and pleasure is again considered in the picture of the 'luxurie and riot' (11.715) of the heroic age. Through these scenes, Michael manipulates Adam's mood in such a way that he fluctuates between extremes of emotion. Adam, for example, has shown a tendency to slight death and to assume too easily that its bitterness is past. In order to understand the spiritual sense in which this is true, he must first realize the fleshly sense in which it is false. His chief reaction to the story of Abel is one of sheer horror at the fact of death, and this horror is increased by the subsequent vision to the point where he trembles on the verge of rebellion or despair. Having led Adam to this brink, Michael now, in a series of steps, persuades him to adopt an attitude of stoic disdain towards death:

> Nor love thy Life, nor hate; but what thou livst
> Live well, how long or short permit to Heav'n.   (11.553-4)

Michael also wishes to correct Adam's tendency toward hedonism. Again he leads him to an extreme, this time an extreme of false joy. First Adam is shown two examples of the 'Arts that polish Life' (11.610), music and metal work, and then a scene which combines revelry, music, and ceremony to form an image of sensual and civilized delight. 'True opener of mine eyes, prime Angel blest' (11.598), exclaims Adam, unaware of the ironic overtones of his remark, 'Here Nature seems fulfilld in all her ends' (602). Having elicited this crystallization of error, Michael delivers a swift and crushing condemnation of Epicureanism. Adam's earlier Robinson Crusoe-like hope that God would provide shelter and fire did not extend to such refinements as metal work, but the 'arts that polish life' emerge very naturally out of the attempt 'to pass commodiously this life' (10.1083), and Michael has now checked the tendency to see the significance of history in terms of the mastery of environment.

The next scenes are drawn from a later and more decadent historical epoch. The nomadic period gives way to a civilization of villages and walled cities. Adam, who can be deceived by pastoral delights, lacks the corruptions of sophistication, and he sees at once the falsity of martial heroism and the true courage of Enoch. Being less concerned with immediate problems, he has more thought for the future, and his reactions are now partly those of a father for his children, particularly when he is shown the flood:

> How didst thou grieve then, *Adam*, to behold
> The end of all thy Ofspring, end so sad,
> Depopulation; thee another Floud,
> Of tears and sorrow a Floud thee also drown'd,
> And sunk thee as thy Sons; till gently reard
> By th'Angel, on thy feet thou stoodst at last. ...
> (11.754-9)

In his illuminating observations on this movement, Raymond Wadding-ton points to the traditional view that the flood marks the end of the age of Adam, and suggests that the story has reached the moment of the death of Adam. The flood, a type of baptism, is associated with Adam's tears, and this confirms the symbolic significance of the pattern expressed by Adam's sinking only to be 'gently reard' by Michael.[32]

Certainly the story of the flood is resonant with typological implications. Crucial is the prefiguration of Christ by Noah. Michael hints at this theme by calling Noah 'The one just Man alive' (11.818), but it is Adam who establishes it clearly when, at the triumphant conclusion of the voyage, he expresses his sense of happy relief:

> Farr less I now lament for one whole World
> Of wicked Sons destroyd, then I rejoyce
> For one Man found so perfet and so just,
> That God voutsafes to raise another World
> From him, and all his anger to forget.
> But say, what mean those colourd streaks in Heavn,
> Distended as the Brow of God appeas'd,
> Or serve they as a flourie verge to binde
> The fluid skirts of that same watrie Cloud,
> Least it again dissolve and showr the Earth?   (11.874-83)

The rhythm of his response anticipates his later, more assured expression of the paradox of the fortunate fall (12.469-78), just as his response to the idea of one just man causing God to raise another world anticipates the language and doctrine of the atonement. 'Dextrously thou aim'st,' says the angel of Adam's speculation concerning the rainbow, and explains that it is the sign of God's covenant by which he undertakes not to disturb the natural order again until 'fire purge all things new, / Both Heav'n and Earth, wherein the just shall dwell' (11.900-1). The understanding which Adam reaches at this point is far from complete: he still thinks in terms of restoration to an outward paradise through justice. Yet the language he is learning is capable of sudden transfiguration when the truth is finally revealed, and the reader is aware that Adam is being prepared without his knowledge for the Incarnation. Michael's prophetic addition to Adam's interpretation of the rainbow – that the world will be purged by fire – underlines the need to restrain optimism by a realistic appraisal of humanity. The alternation of joy and despair in Michael's history brings home to Adam not only the ramifications of his own sin, but the surprising and bewildering ways in which providence brings good out of evil.

After he has finished the story of the flood, Michael pauses to see if his pupil has any comments. Adam remains silent. The brief event (it was added only in 1674) mirrors perfectly both Adam's bafflement (the complexity of the problem is beyond any solution he can suggest), and his expectant sense that some further revelation is to be made. This sets the stage for the counter-movement, in which Michael will reveal the matters of faith which make supernatural renovation possible. As he resumes the story, however, one has at first a strong sense of continuity. Once again we are shown a fairly blameless pastoral world, living according to the law of nature, but sacrificing cattle and crops to God, which is corrupted and destroyed by city dwellers. This new era, however, is not a new heroic age, but the age of empire, and Nimrod and his crew represent a form of evil far worse than anything encountered earlier.[33]

Adam is quick to see the degrading effects of this new form of evil, but powerless to overcome it, since it stems from his own sin. Everything about the building of the tower of Babel, from the bitumen of hell used as mortar to the punishment visited upon the builders, reminds one of Hell. The episode shows mankind becoming Satanic, turning earth into both an empire and a bridgehead for the invasion of heaven.[34] The chaos and violence of the heroic age could be met by a flood which, appropriately, suggests the 'dark / Illimitable Ocean' (2.891-2) of Chaos; the perverted order of Babel – to be reasserted again and again in history – requires a different kind of answer.

It is to this answer that Michael now proceeds. As he describes the election of Abraham a new sense of direction and urgency enters the narrative. Adam, listening to the 'gracious things' (12.271) that follow, quite understandably has little comment to offer. But his brief remarks serve to reveal the angel's strategy in leading him from flesh to spirit. His exclamations of joy indicate the growth of awareness and his vast relief that all is not lost ('O sent from Heav'n, / Enlightner of my darkness,' 12.270-1); his questions, and his tendency to overleap the mark, suggest the difficulties of spiritual vision. 'Now first I finde / Mine eyes true op'ning' (12.273-4), he exclaims on learning of the entry into Canaan. This time the words convey no irony, for he is right. Yet his conception of the blessing which Abraham will bring to all nations is clearly too literal, as he will find later (12.446ff), and like the younger Milton he obviously believes that the end of history is imminent. These misconceptions give piquancy to the question in which he asks why the Israelites, with whom God now dwells, have need of so many laws, for these argue 'so many sins' (12.283). In order finally to see the need for a redeemer, he must learn that 'by the law is the knowledge of sin' (Romans 3:20).

The next resting point in the narrative occurs when Adam is told of the Incarnation. The angel's story, which has carefully recalled the prophecy concerning the seed of the woman at point after point, has fostered in Adam a strong desire for a redeemer, and now that the good news is announced his joy is almost unbearable and must be given expression:

> O Prophet of glad tidings, finisher
> Of utmost hope! now clear I understand
> What oft my steddiest thoughts have searcht in vain,
> Why our great expectation should be call'd
> The seed of Woman: Virgin Mother, Haile,
> High in the love of Heav'n, yet from my Loynes
> Thou shalt proceed, and from thy Womb the Son
> Of God most High; So God with man unites.
> Needs must the Serpent now his capital bruise
> Expect with mortal paine: say where and when
> Thir fight, what stroke shall bruise the Victors heel.
>   (12.375-85)

This is Adam's moment of discovery, when the glad tidings of the Gospel are plainly revealed to him. In describing the birth of Christ, Michael has said that 'A Virgin is his Mother, but his Sire / The Power of the most High' (12.368-9). It is Adam who first uses the title 'Son of God,' recognizing in a sudden flash that their 'great expectation ... / The seed of Woman' (12.378-9), whose identity his thoughts have searched in vain, is none other than the divine being known to him through Raphael's accounts of the war in heaven and the creation. There is in this passage an extraordinary sense of things falling into place. Adam's comprehension of the heart of the mystery of the Incarnation is contained in the brief statement 'so God with man unites' (12.382); it is this truth which vivifies memory, uniting at a stroke all he has learned into a significant design. The thrust of the historical revelation has been the rediscovery, in a new context, of the God already known.

And yet the mysterious truth of the God-man is difficult to keep steadily in mind, and Adam's final words indicate that his response to Michael's account has been too literal. He knew that the Messiah was born 'Barr'd of his right' (12.360) and he should have been more alert to the possibility that the Kingdom to be established is not of this world. Michael now has the perfect opportunity to emphasize the spiritual nature of the conflict:

> Dream not of thir fight,
> As of a Duel, or the local wounds
> Of head or heel: not therefore joynes the Son
> Manhood to God-head. ...   (12.386-9)

And he proceeds to reveal to Adam the obedience and suffering by which the Son satisfies the Father and makes atonement for man before ascending to heaven.

Adam has at last glimpsed the goodness infinite and immense that is expressed through the grace of God. For a moment he is ecstatic at this new creation of light out of darkness. So moved is he, indeed, that he suggests that the Fall may finally be a cause for rejoicing. He seems in danger of losing sight of the cost of the affair. But now it is not necessary for the angel to prevent him from lapsing into complacency. Adam's new realism about mankind prompts him to ask the right question about the fate of the followers of Christ after the Resurrection:

> who then shall guide
> His people, who defend? Will they not deale
> Wors with his followers then with him they dealt?
>   (12.482-4)

He is, apparently, remembering the supernatural aid which was given to the Israelites by angelic powers and by the pillar of fire and the cloud. The penultimate truth of the dialectic is established when he learns that the Christian's armour is spiritual, his consolations inward, and that he worships in living temples (12.485ff). The earlier passage describing how the doom of Adam is annulled by the Godlike act of the Son is now balanced by a passage stressing the inwardness of true faith; the Son is within us as well as without.[35]

At the close, man and angel summarize, in antiphonal chorus, the lessons of history. This is the most fully and explicitly Christian moment in Adam's story. His view now touches and becomes the true vision of life. The last step in Michael's argument is that in which he urges Adam to transform knowledge into deeds and active virtues. The final realization of the spirit lies in the ideal of the 'paradise within':

> onely add
> Deeds to thy knowledge answerable, add Faith,
> Add virtue, Patience, Temperance, add Love,
> By name to come call'd Charitie, the soul
> Of all the rest: then wilt thou not be loath
> To leave this Paradise, but shalt possess
> A paradise within thee, happier farr.   (12.581-7)

As *De Doctrina Christiana* indicates, the love of God here intended results 'from a consciousness and lively sense of the love wherewith he has loved us, and which in theology is reckoned the third after faith and hope.' Such responsive and answering love is 'the offspring as it were, of faith, and the parent of good works' (*Works*, XVI, 11). The lively sense of God's love for man is now possible for Adam, who has at last heard of the redeemer 'ever blest.' The long history of the future has thus furthered the process by which Adam is ingrafted in Christ. The resulting 'newness of life' brings a comprehension of spiritual things, and a love of holiness, for the understanding is restored in large part to its original clearness and the will to its original liberty (*Works*, XVI, 5). It is at this point that Adam becomes aware of the way the unwritten law is being restored to him. The new spiritual life in Christ has brought enlightenment, so that he knows what is necessary for true happiness of life and for eternal salvation (*Works*, XVI, 7). The 'heavenly things' made known to Adam concerning the history of God's redemptive love for man enable him to aspire to a life of service and love in the eye of God. Such knowledge requires commitment and action. Faith itself is a kind of interior action (*Works*, XV, 407), and for this reason it is placed side by side with 'deeds' in the angel's final exhortation. The emphasis in Michael's final words has shifted from the comprehension of spiritual things to the process of living by that knowledge. The awareness of divine love which is produced in the hearts of the regenerate by the spirit will enable Adam to bring forth good works spontaneously and freely (*Works*, XVI, 9).

In calling charity 'the soul / Of all the rest,' Michael reminds us of the Miltonic doctrine, maintained since the time of the divorce tracts, that the whole Mosaic law is abrogated by the coming of Christ, and its essence summed up in two injunctions – love God, and love your neighbour. Adam has now reached the point at which he can begin to live in accordance with the Spirit within, participating through expectation in the Gospel. His lost sonship will eventually be restored as adoption, and his alienation from his race replaced by fellowship with the regenerate in Christ. Milton achieves a remarkable effect of beauty and fulfilment by giving the last speech of his great story to Eve. Propitious dreams have made her aware of the nature of Adam's experience, and she has developed in faith, love, and hope:

> though all by mee is lost,
> Such favour I unworthie am voutsaft,
> By mee the Promis'd Seed shall all restore.   (12.621-3)

Adam is pleased, 'but answer'd not,' for the moment of departure has arrived. There is at this moment a faint echo of that other occasion on which Eve had the last word, the disastrous moment of separation from Adam when she also willingly went forth to meet trial, but without Adam. Adam's silence indicates that the dialectical process is complete, and as his vision has merged with that of the angel, so Eve's understanding now touches his. The last voice of *Paradise Lost* is that of a woman in love who is confident that her descendant will renew the world. Indicative of her spiritual development is the way in which her closing words emphasize, not revenge (the understanding of the prophecy worked out by the fallen pair during the first stage of repentance), but restoration.

Dialectical development is basic to the education of Adam. An interesting theoretical account of such process is to be found in the divorce tracts. There, in an attempt to circumvent the most obvious interpretation of Christ's injunction against divorce (Matthew 19:6), Milton evolves a significant theory of Christ's method of teaching. Christ, he argues, employed in his teaching a strategy of indirection. He did not teach all things at all times, and on occasion he even allowed his audience to mistake his meaning; yet he did not 'omitt to sow within them the seeds of a sufficient determining agen the time that his promis'd spirit should bring all things to their memory' (*Works*, IV, 188). He spoke often in monosyllables, rather than in continued discourses, leaving the work of drawing together his remarks to 'the skilfull and laborious gatherer' (*Works*, III, ii, 491). This method, along with other devices of a literary sort,[36] makes demands on the responses of his followers, and drives them from the letter to a spiritual apprehension of the truth. Thus Christian liberty is not simply a precept of the New Testament; it is expressed in the very texture of the Gospel, in its 'drift and scope' (*Works*, III, ii, 184).

A comparable strategy is found in Michael's education of Adam, and an awareness of its operation increases one's sense of dramatic conflict and psychological complexity in the last two books. Michael's aim is to bring Adam to a full and spiritual understanding of the Son's prophecy concerning the war between the seed of the woman and the serpent. He leads Adam towards this goal by a series of graded steps, each one but the last inconclusive, and each consequently capable of misinterpretation. Yet as he proceeds he does sow within Adam 'the seeds of a sufficient determining,' so that by the close of the story every part takes its place in a total design.

The events themselves, whether presented in vision or simply recounted, provide the material on which he and Adam must practise the art of gatherers. He employs ambiguity, sometimes appearing to mislead Adam deliberately in order to crystallize the false interpretations which must be rejected, and he uses the 'art of powerfull reclaiming' employed by Christ in which excess is administered against excess, bending the crooked wand the contrary way, 'not that it should stand so bent, but that the overbending might reduce it to a straightnesse by its own reluctance' (*Works*, IV, 174). Christian liberty is the 'drift and scope' of Michael's narrative, and by the close Adam demonstrates that he has learned its nature. While his first reactions to the visions of history are extreme and need strong correction, he soon begins to get closer to the mark, responding to each surprising turn in the story in a manner which shows he has learned from the past. His memory of the experience of sin and judgment is illuminated and transformed, so that he is at last able to comprehend how good is brought out of evil by the ever-present God who inspires obedience and love. Thus with the assistance of the spirit, and under the tutelage of the angel, Adam proves a 'skillful and laborious gatherer,' capable of joining truth to truth, and arrives at the point where all his perceptions are unified by the figure of 'my Redeemer ever blest' (12.573).

Adam's experience in the last books is remarkably comprehensive, spanning either directly through encounter or vicariously through vision and story the full range of human situations and historical dispensations. Yet he is located at one definite point in time, the beginning. He is the wayfaring Christian only by anticipation. He leaves the garden resolved to live by what he has learned, but like other Old

Testament saints and prophets, he will conduct his life in accordance with truths which are seen 'far off.'

The Analogy of Fallen and Unfallen Experience

The patterns within this comprehensive body of experience are richly suggestive, susceptible of analysis in a variety of ways. Note has often been taken of the manner in which some of the visions answer the sins of Adam and Eve, pointing to his effeminate uxoriousness, her ambition. What needs stressing, however, are the many parallels and contrasts between experience before and after the Fall. Some are obvious correspondences of theme or event, others more elusive properties of language and imagery. One of the chief effects of this process of parallelism is to draw attention to the continuities of the learning process, the way movement towards understanding is similar in different dispensations.

An important parallel is found in the similar kinds of education provided by the two angels. Raphael and Michael both teach that love arises out of obedience to God, and that in this process the Son plays a crucial role in producing unity. Both present the trial of obedience within a context of conflict, loss, and triumph, in which the creative and destructive powers of God are made manifest, and both stress the free response of the individual will as the source of growth. The angelic teachers encourage class participation, so that Adam demonstrates his understanding of providence to Raphael in his account of his creation, while to Michael he proves his mastery of the lessons of history.

Similar challenges and temptations appear in the unfallen and fallen worlds. Dreams – sleeping or waking – are of particular importance in both. Sometimes dreams support truth and virtue, sometimes oppose them. Dream is throughout associated with fancy, desire, and the irrational realm of passion. The transitions between sleep and waking are always significant moments of psychic change. Satan prompts aspiration at night, conspiring with Beelzebub at the time 'Friendliest to sleep and silence' (5.668), seeking in the night to reach the organs of Eve's fancy in order to forge illusions and dreams. Dreaming is often a figure for false imaginings, the roving of fancy without check, and it is in this sense that Adam understands the truth of the angel's injunction, 'Dream not of other Worlds' (8.175). While Adam does not use the term 'dream' in describing his passion for Eve, he does use language ('transported,' 8.529, 'charm,' 533) which implies that the experience he seeks to describe is not controlled by waking reason but arises spontaneously out of feeling. Dreams expressing desire can also be lively shadows of the truth, such as those which are given to Adam at the beginning of his life when he dreams of the garden and of the creation of Eve. In both instances fancy is moved, and in the latter its internal sight is said to create an effect of trance. Here Adam's experience clearly has a relation to that of the narrator, who nightly visits the sacred mount of the Muses and prays that he will be inspired and given inward sight by the heavenly Muse, rather than by the empty dream of classical tradition.

After the Fall, Adam must be taught to abandon false dreams. Thus the Father decrees his removal from the garden lest he eat of the tree of life 'And live forever, dream at least to live / For ever' (11.95-6). The delusion of self-sufficiency must be destroyed if there is to be any hope of passing from solipsism to renewed faith in God. An important step is taken when Adam prays and is given in return an inward vision ('Methought I saw') of a forgiving God. Further dreamlike scenes follow, as Michael takes Adam up in the visions of God to a high mountain, and there purges his sight, both his 'visual Nerve' and his 'inmost seat of mental sight' (11.415-18). Once again Adam sinks down in sleep, his spirits entranced, this time to be raised by an angel who directs his attention to the future. These visions, rightly used, are materials for his re-education, but in themselves the scenes of book 11 are full of characters ruled by empty dreams of false passion and aspiration. Thus Adam is attracted by the vision of feasting and erotic love, and has to be taught that such pleasure is empty of real good. The depictions of roving looks and sensual beauty, the strong appeal to ear and eye, imply the surrender of rational control and recall Eve's dream and Adam's confessional revery about Eve. A similar dreamlike effect of abandoned action is apparent in the accounts of the heroic age, with its 'infinite / Man-slaughter,' of the luxury and riot of peace, and of the vain effort to build the tower of Babel.

In the last book, however, the visions – now at one remove from Adam since only the angel can see them – drop the sensual dream-modes of appetitive roving and enchanted fixation, and declare with increasing clarity the promises of God, using shadows and types to anticipate the truth but moving firmly on towards the recognition of the spiritual reality. Michael's warning to Adam concerning the manner in which the Son will defeat Satan – 'Dream not of their fight, / As of a Duel,' (12.386-7) – shows how deeply ingrained in fallen nature are the false values of romanticized conflict. The angel's account of the inward law of love engraved on the heart by the spirit, of the inward consolations and outward gifts bestowed on the regenerate, and of the living temple in the heart, provides a rich survey of the spiritual reality of the regenerate. It is a reality which makes carnal power illusory and all outward rites merely empty forms. This is the substance of the paradise within, that condition 'happier far' which develops when deeds of love are added to faith. Not a state of fantasy, but a condition of the fullest consciousness and spiritual awareness, it nonetheless looks to completion when 'the Earth / Shall all be Paradise, far happier place / Then this of *Eden*' (12.463-5), so that, like Adam's dream, it will some day be found 'all real' (8.310).

As this discussion of dream and consciousness suggests, the structure of Adam's experience both before and after the Fall expresses Milton's sense that the growth of psychic awareness is dynamic. The development of the relations of self, God, nature, and society are preoccupations of both periods. In both, memory and judgment are tested as new circumstances require new interpretations and imaginative applications of what is known. In both, opportunities are provided for self-discovery through the exercise of the will in response to trial, although after the Fall this is only possible with the assistance of grace. Adam's growth before the Fall, it will be recalled, led from theoretical knowledge into practice. It brought insight into the varieties of egoism and thus fostered a proper sense of the self. Through dreams, stories, interchanges with Eve, and encounters with manifestations of God, Adam was encouraged to 'judge of fit and meet' (8.448) and freely express the image of God within him. After the Fall, Adam's growth and transformation are even more marked as he passes from near despair to faith. A few illustrations of correspondence between the patterns of development will bring out the unchanging elements in the learning process.

Uncertain and moody even after his prayer of penitence, Adam's response to the visions of death and desire in book 11 is by fits despondent and elated. At first the visions provoke and puzzle him; checked and corrected in his superficial interpretations, he gradually starts to use his faculties of memory, imagination, and judgment. The prolonged contemplation of the Flood represents a turning point. Adam emerges from this testing vision not only aiming more 'dextrously' (11.884) in his interpretation, but having begun to sense the rhythm of God's providence, the rhythm which brings good out of evil, a new world out of one just man. But shortly before this recovery of faith he is near despair; overwhelmed by grief and tears, he concludes the visions to be 'ill foreseen' (11.763). His small taste of God's foreknowledge is nearly too much for him. His reaction shows not only his anxious care on behalf of his descendants, but his lack of trust. He was shown the preparation of the ark, and should not have leaped to the conclusion that all aboard would be consumed 'wandring that watrie Desert' (11.779). Such an outcome would make bitter irony of Michael's earlier promise to show 'what reward / Awaits the good, the rest what punishment' (11.709-10), and the example of Enoch might have furnished the needed clue. (To be fair to Adam, he does, although full of doubt, ask the angel to finish the story.) The experience of doubt and reassurance brings Adam to a better understanding of himself and of his limits and dependence upon God.

The passage contains a curious resemblance to Adam's discussion of the heavens with Raphael in book 8. There, looking out at the sea of space, Adam ends in thinking of his own nature as the measure of all things. His suggestion that there is a disproportion in nature contains a criticism of the art of God which was displayed for him in the story of the creation. As we saw, Raphael uses the occasion to teach Adam a sense of proportion. So in the later passage, Adam looks at the great flood and thinks he sees the loss of all human measure as his sons are overwhelmed by nature. His judgment implies a distrust of God's providence in giving him foresight of this tragedy. And in the unhappy context of a fallen world, an angel is again trying – with some success – to establish in Adam a proper sense of proportion which will enable him to accept and appreciate God's judgments and covenants.

Another major shift in Adam's awareness occurs during the account of the mission of Moses. This vision of the blessing on the seed of Abraham is received by Adam as an unmerited favour providing true knowledge in place of the forbidden knowledge which he fell in seeking. He now humbly accepts the benign nature of his education. Although his understanding remains only partial, he is given an introduction to the theology of law, grace, and mediatorial atonement. The account is notable for the way it stresses the merely transitional function of the laws ordained on Mount Sinai. The voice of God which is mediated through Moses is full of terror and the laws which it proclaims seem to demand obedience in servile fear. Adam's education at this point is perfectly consistent with the views of *De Doctrina*. There Milton repudiates the widely held Protestant view that the law has many uses for Christians. Any effort to live by the works of the law, he maintains, leads away from Christ. The most he will admit is that a knowledge of the law (as opposed to an attempt to live by it) can lead on to awareness of sin and acceptance of God's grace. Thus in the epic (12.300-6) Adam is led at once from impotent works of the law to works of faith. It is made clear to him from the start that the promulgation of the moral law was intended to discover sin and to make man aware of his need for grace, and that the ceremonial law is incapable of making the needed satisfaction but points through types and shadows to the better covenant of the Gospel. At no point, not even as a passing trial, is Adam invited to imagine a life of works under the law.

The experience of Adam before the fall again provides a parallel. As we have seen, Milton maintains that Adam was not required to perform any works, but was merely forbidden to perform one particular action. He needed no other commands, for the law of nature was innate in him and taught him whatever is intrinsically good (*Works*, XV, 113-17). The purpose of the single prohibition was thus to give man an opportunity to make his obedience evident, for in all other areas of choice he was disposed to do right by natural impulse and reason without a command. Milton emphasizes that this prohibitin was a matter of positive right, a command from a lawful power concerning a matter which otherwise would be indifferent. There was nothing in the nature of the fruit that called for a prohibition.

Milton seems to create unnecessary difficulties here as a result of his eagerness to bring out the special nature of the command and to repudiate the idea of a covenant of works. What he neglects to affirm at this stage in his argument is that a significant act of disobedience must by definition involve an infraction of the innate law. Obedience to the prohibition is a pledge of obedience to God, but such a response is itself evidence of an inner state of harmony with the unwritten law planted in man's mind (*Works*, XV, 179-80). By the same token, the breaking of the prohibition makes evident something which has already occurred within, a contravention of the unwritten law commanding the love of God and man. Milton's subsequent discussion of the way our first parents were guilty of evil desire which in turn led to evil action helps to restore the proper emphasis. Indeed, with his account of the Fall, Milton makes the importance of the infraction of innate law perfectly clear as he lavishly illustrates the way the first offence broke every point of the law.

In the epic, these views are conveyed in dramatic terms. Adam's first words to Eve in book 4 set out the conditions of their happiness in a manner which closely approximates *De Doctrina*. As we have seen, the life of Adam in the garden brings home to him the inward nature of the law which directs his actions and the importance of his assessment of each case in terms of its particular circumstances so that he can 'Approve the best, and follow what I approve' (8.611). Love, as Raphael observes, should be his reason for keeping the 'great command' (635). Central to the act of disobedience in book 9 is the loss of the inner law of love, and the consequent surrender of liberty. This entails looking at the prohibition as if it were a law of works, a law to be obeyed in servile fear. Thus Eve is led to see in the prohibition a denial of freedom and virtue, while Adam comes to think of it as inconsistent with love. Michael's lesson concerning the distinction between works of the law and works of faith thus has a real bearing on the truth that Adam approached earlier but failed to secure and thus lost at the Fall.

The last great change in Adam's awareness in book 12 – his recognition of the saviour and his discovery of the spiritual nature of the quest for salvation – has already been considered. It does not, in any case, deal with the events that exhibit a close connection with prelapsarian life. Yet the quality of freedom before the Fall is strikingly similar to that enjoyed by Adam restored. The root of freedom is in both cases the same, namely the unwritten law, although for the proto-Christian Adam of the last book the love which is the heart of innate law has been greatly clarified by the action of God and his Son.

There is one other connection between the two dispensations which deserves comment by way of conclusion, and this concerns society. In spite of their isolation, Adam and Eve in paradise give the impression of looking towards a larger community. They anticipate children, 'more hands' (4.629) and 'younger hands' (9.246) to help control the wanton growth of the garden (4.628). Adam's prayer to God for a companion is more than a request for a helpmate, since he hopes that out of 'Collateral love' man may beget 'Like of his like, his Image multipli'd' (8.423-6). This important speech echoes the narrator's earlier hymn to wedded love as the true source of human offspring and of 'all the Charities / Of Father, Son, and Brother' (4.756-7). Michael's remark that if the Fall had not occurred Eden would have been a 'Capital Seate' (11.343) from whence generations would have spread to the ends of the earth is striking evidence of the potential hope of prelapsarian society. With the Fall, of course, Adam's anguish gathers around the 'Fair Patrimonie' that he has now left his sons (10.818). But he rightly refuses to consider dying childless, and the angel leads him out of the swamp of self-recrimination and self-pity to the point where he recognizes that some of his sons deserve his anger ('O execrable Son' 12.64), and some his admiration and humble love. Book 12 emphasizes the godly society stemming from the seed of Abraham, but achieving fulfilment in the sons of his faith 'wherever through the world' (12.449). This is the spiritual society of the church, in whose members the spirit writes the law of faith working through love. The seed of the woman is the 'great deliverer' (12.149) who will gather this society into a new and comprehensive paradise to enjoy fruits of joy and eternal bliss. Milton returns very forcefully at the close to Eve, who in the marriage bower has been taught by a propitious dream concerning the promised seed. And here is the last fine connection between unfallen and fallen experience, for in each dispensation human fruitfulness prepares for the emergence of a community of love, 'one Kingdom, Joy and Union without end' (7.161). The final goal for man, the kingdom, is set by the Father even before creation, and remains unchanged by the Fall. Before and after the Fall, the growth of the human community, the multiplying of the image, is a condition of movement towards that goal. Mankind must imitate God's creativity and accept the trials of the community in history.

The divine image in man is not fixed and static. Its development takes analogous forms in unfallen and fallen experience. The way man learns as he undergoes renovation parallels with variations the learning process of unfallen man. The similarities are manifold and can be seen in a number of areas – the function of angelic teachers, the interplay of dream and consciousness, the questioning of God and nature, the importance of rooting freedom in inner law, the testing of the memory, the imagination and the judgment of the individual, and the significance of the development through time of the kingdom. In both worlds, the fallen and the unfallen, the image of God is fostered and developed by self-knowledge and knowledge of God and nature.

CHAPTER SIX

The Doctrine of the Incarnate Son

The treatment of the Son in *Paradise Regained* provides a contrast and yet a complement to that in *Paradise Lost*. The two poems present companion views. *Paradise Lost* centres attention on the pre-existent Son and yet repeatedly anticipates and reflects upon the Incarnation. In the final books, in particular, Adam is seen gradually conforming to the image of Christ, and when this process is well advanced it is strengthened by the revelation of the patience and heroic martyrdom of Christ's life and death, and thus too by the discovery of the ransom paid to redeem man from Sin and Death. In *Paradise Regained*, on the other hand, the pre-existent Son is seldom mentioned. This epic centers on the trial of the incarnate Son in the wilderness, a trial which provides the opportunity for him to lay down 'the rudiments / Of his great warfare' (1.157-8). Jesus defines the terms of man's conflict with Satan and vividly expresses the freedom of the regenerate condition. Yet while Satan is worsted in the encounter, the anticipated victory over Sin and Death is still in the future by the close of the poem, and it has been apprehended only obliquely by prophecy and foreshadowing. The emphasis here thus falls in a different manner from that of *Paradise Lost*. *Paradise Regained*, it has been argued, does not pay the same close attention to the theology of satisfaction and atonement that marks the earlier epic. It has even been suggested that the importance of such Pauline doctrine to Milton waned as he grew older, and that he consequently ignored it in his last treatment of the Son.[1] But the consistency of his religious views, reaching even to *Of True Religion, Haeresie, Schism, Toleration and the growth of Popery* in the year preceding his death, renders such a conclusion highly improbable, and it is more sensible to consider the presentation of the Son in *Paradise Regained* as an adaptation of the views found in *De Doctrina Christiana* to a particular dramatic and aesthetic context. I hope to make the coherence of Milton's position evident by first discussing the theory of the incarnate Christ in *De Doctrina Christiana* and then proceeding to the treatment of the Son in *Paradise Regained*. Once again it is important to assess Milton's views within the context of Reformed theology.

The Christology of the Reformed theologians was orthodox in its stress on the settlement of Chalcedon. That council, held in 415, sought to bring to a peaceful resolution more than a century of controversy concerning the nature of Christ, controversy which had flourished after the agreement concerning the Trinity at Nicea. The council of Chalcedon was anxious to rule out the errors of the past age, and particularly the doctrines associated with the names of Nestorius and Eutyches. Nestorius is generally considered the author of the view that there were in Christ not only two natures, but also two persons. Thus he saw the person of Jesus as the result of the conjunction of the person of the Logos and the person of man. Emphasizing the distinctness of the two natures, Nestorius did not reach a clear expression of their unity.[2] Eutyches, on the other hand, is historically the founder of an extreme form of monophysitism in which the Lord's humanity is thought to be totally absorbed into his divinity.[3] This view achieved unity, but at the cost of the full manhood of Jesus. Eutyches himself seems to have become a kind of doctrinal scapegoat, for the surviving evidence of his thought suggests that he was somewhat incompetent rather than dogmatic and radical. Behind him in the monophysite tradition, however, stands the much more imposing figure of Apollinaris, who argues that in the Redeemer the divine spirit of God the Son was substituted for a human mind, so that Christ had a single nature composed of flesh and divinity.

In the face of such diverse opinion, the Council of Chalcedon reaffirmed the Nicene Creed, setting beside it the Creed of Constantinople and adding glosses by Cyril of Alexandria and Leo of Rome. It also set out a formal confession of faith in which equal recognition is given to the unity and the duality in the God-man. According to this formulation, the two natures joined in Christ participate in an unequal manner. God the Logos constitutes the one person and the one hypostasis in Jesus, while the humanity in him is only a nature.[4] The incarnate word thus exists in two natures, each complete and each retaining its distinctive properties and operation unimpaired in the union, 'unconfusedly, immutably, indivisibly, inseparably.' G.L. Prestige points to the negative and abstract quality of the Chalcedonian settlement: 'The formula states admirably what Christ is not.'[5] A safeguard against heresy and perversion, it failed to confront the problem of how two distinct and complete natures are combined in one Christ, and ignored the indications of a positive solution provided by such thinkers as Cyril of Alexandria.[6] A compromise, the settlement lacked the vigorous insights into the significance of Jesus to be found in the writings of the individuals, orthodox or not, whose debate led to its devising.

Discussion of the nature of Christ by Reformed theologians characteristically grows out of the terms established by the Chalcedonian settlement. Calvin sets the pattern clearly. In the person of Christ, he argues, divinity and humanity are united in such a way that each retains its distinctive nature unimpaired.[7] Thus the two natures are neither fused nor separated in the union. Separation is identified as the error of Nestorius, who pulled apart the nature of Christ and thus devised a double Christ made up of a human and a divine person. Fusion is called 'Eutyches madness,' for he destroyed one of the natures in his attempt to show the unity of the person. Truly considered, the person of the mediator is Son of man according to the flesh, and Son of God with respect to his divine nature.[8] In achieving a balanced statement of these aspects of the Son, Calvin repeatedly finds it useful and important to define orthodoxy against the heresies which emphasize one aspect or the other. His discussion of Christ's nature thus begins with a discussion of docetism, the view that Christ only seemed to take flesh and that his body was a phantom or mere appearance. Against the ancient Manichees and Marcionites, and probably, too, against contemporary followers of their doctrine such as Menno Simons the anabaptist, Calvin argues that the Son took on a nature truly human and suffered according to the infirmity of the flesh. Before leaving the subject, he closes his discussion by repudiating the opposite heresy, the belief championed by his contemporary, Servetus, that the Son of God was not eternally begotten but came into being with his birth as man. This, in Calvin's view, is to confuse the flesh with divinity; rather, the flesh should be recognized as the temple of divinity.[9] The truth which Servetus failed to grasp is that at the incarnation the eternally begotten Son of God was manifested in the flesh. Heresy is thus balanced against heresy, so that the orthodox position appears to be one of moderation which recognizes the importance of both flesh and spirit.

Calvin's approach is repeated, refined, and elaborated by subsequent theologians of the Reformed church. There is agreement that the divinity of Christ is not the divine nature common to the three persons of the Trinity, but consists in the person of the Logos. The humanity is not a person, but the nature common to all human personalities. In the Incarnation, then, the human nature was assumed into the person of the mediator without altering the Logos.[10] Reformed dogmatics continued the ancient practice of affirming against Nestorius that there is in Christ only one person, the eternal Son of God, who assumed human nature, and of maintaining against Eutyches that the two natures are united in such a way that they are indivisible and without confusion. Thus theologians sought to avoid the two rocks, one dividing the person, the other confounding the natures.[11]

Turning from Calvin and his successors to chapter 14 of the first book of *De Doctrina Christiana*, the chapter 'Of Man's Restoration and of Christ the Redeemer,' one is likely to feel that within a recognizable pattern of argument there are unfamiliar elements. It is noteworthy that Milton does not repeat the full formula derived from Chalcedon by which the Reformed tried to steer by the twin dangers of Nestorianism and Eutychianism. He seems, rather, to be concerned to stress the positive perception which lies at the heart of each one-sided view, namely, the Nestorian concern to ensure the full humanity of Christ, and the monophysite emphasis on the unity of his person. Modern critics, indeed, have found traces of both heterodoxies in Milton's argument. Some justification for such speculation is provided by the tone and stance of the chapter as a whole, which defiantly links its position with the subordinationism of book 1, chapter 5, and contains passages of rebuke which recall the belittling of abstract theological speculation in the earlier chapter. Although less polemically than in chapter 5, Milton seems to be warning the reader that his views are not entirely conventional.

Much, however, is either commonplace or expected in view of the positions already adopted. Milton affirms the orthodox belief that at the Incarnation the Son became fully human, and he cites the traditional proof-texts. With equal firmness he denies that Christ is merely human, insisting on his divinity and noting that in the beginning he was the Word through whom all things were made in heaven and earth. Here the reader is referred back to chapter 5 for an account of the way the Son's divinity is of a secondary order: 'from whence it follows, that he by whom all things were made both in heaven and earth ... he who in the beginning was the Word, and God with God, and although not supreme, yet the first born of every creature, must necessarily have existed previous to his incarnation, whatever subtleties may have been invented to evade this conclusion by those who contend for the merely human nature of Christ' (*Works*, XV, 263). There is no room for adoptionism in Milton's theology of the Son, nor does he have sympathy with the Servetian doctrine that the Son comes into being at the Incarnation.

Christ's being is double, divine and human. Unlike *Paradise Lost*, *De Doctrina Christiana* moves away from orthodoxy in its reflections on (a) the two elements in Christ. Here a tendency to Nestorianism has been pointed out by W.B. Hunter, who draws attention to Milton's lack of orthodoxy in asserting that in Christ there are not only two natures but two persons.[12] Milton's ironic amazement at the metaphysical theories used to support the orthodox view of a union of two natures in one person is reminiscent of his mockery of the doctrine of the three-in-one Trinity. He directs his argument specifically against the position of Reformed theology, for which he takes Zanchius as spokesman. Zanchius, in a passage cited by Milton, states that the Logos assumed human nature by forming for itself a body and soul in such a way that neither one existed independently but only in the Logos. Milton responds by asserting that when human nature ('the form of man in a material mould') comes into existence at the Incarnation, it must bring a whole man into existence too, a man with no part of his essence or personality missing (*Works*, XV, 267). Milton's phrasing leaves open the possibility that this whole man existed before the union with the divine person and nature, but it is not his intention to emphasize this possibility.[13] His position, rather, is that *nature* and *person* are close in significance, and that in the Incarnation the two things signified are (b) inseparable. By making the terms *person*, *nature*, and *hypostasis* into variations on a central meaning (an analysis for which there is much justification in the history of their usage),[14] Milton creates a situation in which he may affirm that two natures, two hypostases, and *two persons* unite to form the single person or being of Christ, the God-man. This position is quite different from the orthodox view, for in the latter the Logos is the sole person of the Son and the humanity is only a nature.[15]

Once Milton has firmly made the point that the union of two intelligent natures is a union of two persons, he drops the subject. In the succeeding argument he reverts to referring to the two *natures* rather than the two *persons* of Christ. The doctrine of the union of two persons is not found at all in the Christology of *Paradise Lost*. But if some of the language through which he states the doctrine is of only passing interest to him, the rejection of the orthodox view is clearly of primary significance in his treatment of the humanity of Christ. His reasons for resisting the orthodox doctrine are made evident in the course of the argument. Philosophically he found unacceptable the view that the humanity of Christ is a universal. Richard Hooker stated the orthodox position clearly when he wrote that the Word 'built her house of that *nature* which is common unto all, she made not *this or that man* her habitation, but dwelt *in us.*'[16] Milton could not accept this realist approach to universals: it seemed to him to reduce the humanity of Christ to a mere collection of properties. The human nature of Christ, he believed, was realized in an individual: 'It is certain that the Logos was made that which he assumed; if then he assumed the human nature, not man, he was made not man, but the human nature' (*Works*, XV, 269). Such an outcome would be totally implausible. Manhood is not simply a collection of properties or attributes, but must have its own specific identity. Milton's impatience about this point may well have arisen from the very elaborate analyses by which Zanchius and others sought to rationalize the doctrine of the human nature. The account provided by Wollebius is relatively straightforward, and for that very reason throws the problem into relief: 'The human nature of Christ has no individuality other than the hypostasis or subsistence of the Logos; that is, of the Son of God. In this respect, Christ differs from all other men.'[17] For Milton, a rationalist sceptical of the scholastic handling of universals, Wollebius' argument amounts to a denial that Christ was truly man.[18]

An important feature of Milton's position thus lies in the way it resists the Chalcedonian Christology adopted by the Reformed churches and reaffirmed in such credal statements as the Thirty-nine Articles and the Westminster Confession of Faith. According to the latter formulation, the two natures are represented in Christ in an unequal manner. God the Logos constitutes the one person and the one hypostasis in Jesus, while the humanity in him is only a nature.[19] But Milton rejects the assumption that Christ could have a real and perfect subsistence in his human nature without that nature having a subsistence of its own. According to him, it was by such a separate subsistence of the human nature that Christ became a real man. Strikingly unequal in essence, the divine and human natures, nonetheless, bring similar kinds of ingredients to the union, each contributing a person. Milton thus attempts to reinforce the importance of Christ's humanity; underlying his effort is his belief that the individual person is defined in

[handwritten marginal note:] The orthodox point seems to be that what becomes (and is) the man Jesus is the Logos, not the man Jesus—not that the incarnate Word = < the Word, the property of being human >. But if so, M was driven by a misreading into a theory of two persons fused.

action by rational choice so that it is futile to try to express the human nature of Christ simply in terms of abstract properties.

The parallel with Nestorian teaching is clear yet apparently of no deep significance in itself. Like Nestorius, Milton thinks of each of the natures as subsisting in its own person. His concern, like that of the Antiochene school to which Nestorius belonged, is to bring out the full humanity of Christ. But Nestorius rejected the term 'hypostatic' to describe the joining of the two natures, and was uneasy about the term 'union,' preferring 'conjunction.' Milton, on the contrary, stresses the hypostatic union or coalescence of the natures. Authorities differ in their account of the way Nestorius derived the single being of Christ from the two persons, but it appears that he believed the persons complemented each other in the union, becoming component parts of one person. Their union is thus unlike that of the two natures, which does not result in a new nature.[20] Milton speaks without discrimination of the union of the natures and persons in the single person of the mediator, and in the same breath he affirms that the properties of each remain distinct after the union (*Works*, XV, 271). He seems to be moving in quite a different direction from Nestorian teaching.

But the important thing about Milton's speculations at this point is the way they are checked by his recognition that the union is a mystery. This is to some extent conventional. Cyril of Alexandria, for example, took a characteristic stand of the orthodox when he urged that the manner of the union is entirely beyond understanding.[21] But many theologians, ancient or modern, were prepared to go further than Milton in characterizing the mode of union. It was compared to the union of body and soul, or of iron and fire. For Wollebius, the union is like that of metal and fire in a red-hot sword.[22] Among the Reformed it was also common to define the type of union by negation, denying that it is like the union of essence in the Trinity, or of essence and power in the Son's omnipresence, or like the relation of friend with friend, or of Christ and the elements of the sacramnt. These lists end by reaffirming that the relation is hypostatic and personal, usually repeating by way of gloss the Chalcedonian formula.[23] Milton's sense of the mystery of the Incarnation prevents him from using such analogies even to define by negation. It is better, he urges, for us to remain wisely ignorant, and to say simply that the Son of God, our Mediator, was made flesh and is both God and man (*Works*, XV, 273).

While Milton's theory of two persons in Christ recalls Nestorianism, his emphasis on the coalescence of the divine and human natures and persons of Christ has led at least one critic to suggest a link with monophysite heresy.[24] At first sight, the evidence seems to make this association improbable. Certainly there is no suggestion of the Apollinarian denial of the existence of a rational soul in Jesus. On the contrary, Milton is at pains to affirm not only that one element of the union was the intelligent substance of his manhood, but also that he was made up of body and soul. Milton also, as we have seen, acknowledges the Chalcedonian formula's affirmation that each of the two natures in the union retains its distinctive properties.[25]

While seeking to respect the mystery of the Incarnation, however, Milton nonetheless stresses the coalescence of the persons and natures. Even in the midst of denying that we can know much about this, he hints at his own position, and the result is a passage full of interest for readers of *Paradise Regained*:

> That Christ therefore, since his assumption of human flesh, remains one Christ, is a matter of faith; whether he retains his two-fold will and understanding, is a point respecting which, as Scripture is silent, we are not concerned to inquire. For after having 'emptied himself,' he might 'increase in wisdom,' Luke ii.52. by means of the understanding which he previously possessed, and might 'know all things,' John xxi.17. namely, through the teaching of the Father, as he himself acknowledged. Nor is this twofold will implied in the single passage Matt. xxvi.39. 'not as I will, but as thou wilt,' unless he be the same with the Father, which, as has been already shown, cannot be admitted. (*Works*, XV, 275-7)

The reproof directed at the spirit of the question does not prevent a kind of answer. Since the Bible does not mention a twofold will or intellect, we should not invent them. The implication is that Christ had one will and one intellect, and that these were finite. The process of kenosis by which he 'emptied himself' at the Incarnation (Philippians 2:7) led to the loss of knowledge proper to his pre-existent state, and now a single mind, a finite and human one, is responsible for his growth in response to the instruction of the Father. It is the same mind, now human because emptied, which was his in heaven before the act of kenosis.

The orthodox view maintains that each nature retains the power of choice, so that the Son has a twofold will. Milton, stressing that there are two persons involved in the union as well as two natures, implies that volition is proper to the former, the persons, rather than the latter, the natures, and that consequently the merging of the two persons results in a single will. The assumption of a single will in Christ shows clearly the unusual situation created by Milton's subordinationism, for he is under no obligation to distinguish between an infinite and a finite will. Thus he can assume a continuity of willing and of rational activity which connects the pre-existent and incarnate states. The faculties remain the same, but their power is restricted to human scale by the Incarnation. The reference to Matthew 26:39 is interesting in the light of the importance of this and a few similar texts in the arguments by which the dyophysites supported their doctrine of two wills and two operations (other texts they employed, apparently considered of no relevance at all by Milton, include John 5:30, 6:38, Mark 14:36).[26] By contrast, Milton's subordinationism leads him to a position in which the two natures are united in the single will and intellect of the one person of the mediator. His position in this matter is also clarified by his assertion that the two persons, each presumably with intelligence and will, also merge into the single person of the mediator.

Calvin's dyophysite position provides a revealing contrast:

> But he [Christ] is called 'the servant of the Father' ... he is said to have 'increased in age and wisdom' ... and not to 'seek his own glory' ... 'not to know the Last Day' ... not to 'speak by himself' ... and not to 'do his own will' ... he is said to have been 'seen and handled.' ... All these refer solely to Christ's humanity. In so far as he is God, he cannot increase in anything, and does all things for his own sake; nothing is hidden from him; he does all things according to the decision of his will, and can be neither seen nor handled.[27]

Here is a recognition that two natures include two wills and two operations, the human will freely following the divine will. Here too, by implication, is the idea that there are two intellects in Christ, one limited and the other not. Calvin considers Christ's human intellect to be perfectly real and natural. Those who say that Christ's growth in knowledge was an appearance are 'over-timid.' Luke's statement that Christ grew in knowledge may be taken literally, for his soul was subject to ignorance as a result of kenosis (Luke 2:40). He was, for example, genuinely ignorant of the date of the *parousia* (Matthew 24:26). On the other hand, Christ exhibited an extraordinary knowledge due to his divinity, as when by divine rather than human sight he became aware of Nathaniel under his tree.[28] With respect to will, Calvin again wants a fully human Christ as well as a divine Christ, one who, in words from

Hebrews 4:15, 'in every respect has been tempted as we are, yet without sinning.'[29] This is brought out well in the *Institutes* in the seminal discussion of the suffering and death of Christ, where Calvin argues that since Christ suffered voluntarily and voluntarily held himself within the bounds of obedience, he showed a weakness which included the passions of sorrow, fear, and dread, and yet was pure and free from all vice. His struggle arose not simply from the encounter with death, but from the sense of being forsaken by God. Calvin finds a refutation of Apollinaris in the recognition that Christ's obedience arose from this soul, and a refutation of the monothelite belief in one will in the recognition that Christ 'did not will as man what he willed according to his divine nature.'[30]

Kenosis is for Calvin concealment rather than annihilation or alienation of the divine majesty of the Son;[31] the incarnate Son freely concealed himself and witheld his divine powers. He laid down his glory not by diminishing it but by supressing it before the gaze of men.[32] During the period of his manifestation in the flesh, he also continues to perform without cessation or diminution his other work of divine ordering of the universe. On earth, however, his divinity was normally concealed behind the flesh as a 'veil.' Yet his divine glory did occasionally break through, most notably at the transfiguration but also in his performance of miracles.[33] Calvin is quick, however, to check any suggestion of docetism, of a divine being who only *seems* to adopt the likeness of man. He emphasizes that the divinity expresses itself also *through* the flesh, for the veil is itself a reality of the person of the Son. Even in his character as a servant, and in his human nature, heavenly power is evident.[34]

Milton, by contrast, writes that the divine nature of Christ is manifested when the Son is exalted after his death (*Works*, XV, 315). Normally Milton does not seem interested in the possibility of occasional outbreaks of divine glory during Christ's ministry. His theory of kenosis differs from Calvin's in its emphasis on the laying aside, rather than the concealing, of divine power and glory. In *De Doctrina Christiana*, Milton glosses the crucial passage from Philippians 2:7 by observing that the Son 'emptied himself of that form of God in which he had previously existed' (*Works*, XIV, 343). As Milton notes elsewhere, 'form of God' in this context seems to be synonymous with 'image of God' (*Works*, XIV, 275). But what Milton's commentary is clearly saying is not that the Son gave up entirely the image of the Father but that he gave up those powers and prerogatives which he enjoyed in heaven, and that he did so in order to express the love and mercy of God through humility. The image of God is not lost and restored by this process, but continues to shine through the obedience of the incarnate Son. The changes that occur are a result of the varying dispensations through which the form or image is expressed.

In its technical sense, kenosis or emptying thus refers to the Son's voluntary surrender of the place of glory at the right hand of the Father. But this does not mean the loss of anything integral to his identity, for his glory is not self-derived (*Works*, XIV, 339), being a gift from the Father from whom he received the fullness which was subsequently emptied. Along with glory, he renounced superhuman knowledge and the memory of his exalted life in heaven, with its exercise of divine powers conferred by the Father. Such a temporary withdrawal of gifts, however, does not in any way affect his fundamental identity, which resides in perfect obedience. He is the express image of God because of that obedience, which rests on perfect faith, and is altered neither by humiliation nor by exaltation.

In a primary sense, indeed, 'emptying' is to be seen as an act of love and compassion. In this light we can understand Milton's observation that 'as Christ emptied himself in both his natures, so both participate in his exaltation' (*Works*, XV, 315). Both natures are emptied and suffer humiliation through the passion and death. The moral nature of kenosis as an act of service and self-sacrifice is of central importance. Thus the process is also seen in operation in the scene in which Adam and Eve are judged when the Son still has the knowledge and attributes of his pre-incarnate state. If the 'emptying' and humiliation can be seen in the Son's human nature during his life on earth and also in acts undertaken in heaven in his divine nature, then it is a moral process not restricted to the surrender of divine powers at the Incarnation.

But thinking of the process in terms of the transformation of the pre-existent Son into the incarnate Son, we should note how the moral emphasis enables Milton to stress the humanity of Jesus and to merge this with the divinity. Christ, he writes, embodies the 'fulness of the Godhead' in his human nature as 'the entire virtue of the Father, and the full completion of his promises' (*Works*, XV, 261). This, rather than the preliminary surrender of divine honours and powers, is the true act of humiliation by which he redeems mankind: the entire person of Christ, both human and divine, expresses the image of God through actions of service and self-sacrifice. The analysis in *De Doctrina* of particular events in the life of Christ provides further support for the conclusion that the divinity of Milton's Son of God is fully accommodated to his humanity. A supreme prophet, he is united to God through love and obedience, that is, by a harmony of wills, and because of this virtue, as well as his birthright, he is in a sense present with the Father in heaven even when ministering on earth in the body (*Works*, XIV, 315). But his more than natural insight is a gift arising from voluntary union with the Father, not an indication of supernatural powers possessed in his own right. Milton explains events such as Christ's awareness of Nathaniel under his tree (John 1:48) in terms of gifts rather than, as Calvin would have it, of the exercise of divine power. Even at the moment of death, when Jesus exclaims 'my God, my God, why hast thou forsaken me?' he does not find in his divine nature a vantage point superior to suffering, and thus both human and divine natures are comprehended in the unity of his person. The seam is still invisible at this climactic point (*Works*, XV, 305-7; XIV, 331).

In all this there is nothing of Calvin's characteristic emphasis on kenosis as concealment. While in a line from *Paradise Regained* (4.599) Milton uses the ancient image of the flesh as shrine or tabernacle, on the whole he avoids speaking of the flesh as if it were some kind of veil. Nor does he believe that the Son continued to exercise divine power in heaven while incarnate on earth. His conception of the unity of Christ prevents such a division of operations. He does not balance the limitations of Christ as man against his omnipotence or omniscience as God, for he rejects the Calvinist view of his divinity, nor is there any suggestion that what Christ wills in one nature he would, if possible, avoid in the other.

A further piece of evidence is provided by Milton's mortalism. According to this view, the whole man dies, body and soul being inseparable and thus dying and rising together (*Works*, XV, 219), and even Christ is not excluded from this process: 'on the testimony of the prophet and the apostle, as well as of Christ himself, the soul even of Christ was for a short time subject unto death on account of our sins ...' (*Works*, XV, 231). Nor was it merely in his human person that he died, for according to Milton 'he yielded to death in his divine nature likewise' and was raised 'not ... in his human nature alone, but in the whole of his person' (*Works*, XV, 307). Such an argument suggests the close integration of natures in Christ.

There appears to be some tension in Milton's position concerning the incarnate Son. He insists that Jesus is both man and God, and in orthodox manner he refers to the way the properties of each nature remain distinct after the union. Yet his affirmation of the Son's unity of being appears to lead him towards the monophysite conception of a single will and mind. But there is less contradiction here than might at first appear, for his insistence that nothing useful can be said of the natures in separation means that their importance to man lies entirely in their union in the person of the mediator. Christ has a divine nature which makes him one in being with the pre-existent Son, but it is accommodated to human understanding through its coalescence with human nature. Milton's position here can be explored in terms of his handling of the doctrine known as the *communicatio idiomatum*, which concerns the interchange of properties of the divine and human in Christ.

This is an ancient doctrine which was endorsed in a particular version by Reformed theology and was affirmed by the Second Helvetic Confession.[35] Calvin's treatment of the subject is representative and influential. Like others before him, Calvin uses the doctrine as a hermeneutical tool for keeping in balance the varied scriptural witness to the unity of the person of the mediator. He illustrates the *communicatio idiomatum* by four kinds of statements,[36] each type being closely related to the others. When Christ said about himself 'Before Abraham was, I am' (John 8:58), he was claiming for himself what is proper to his divinity, that is, qualities utterly alien to man. On the other hand, when Christ is said to have been 'seen and handled' (Luke 24:39), the reference is solely to his humanity. Such statements, however, may be transferred improperly, although not without reason, to his divinity. Thirdly, when John teaches 'that God laid down his life for us' (1 John 3:16), a property of humanity is shared with the divinity as a result of the union. Following upon this is the last category, which is comprised of statements that comprehend both natures at once, such as the Johannine account of the office of the mediator as expressed in such passages as 'he received from the Father the power of remitting sins' (John 1:29). Such statements are not spoken simply of the divine nature or the human.

The fact that Milton accepts the idea of the *communicatio idiomatum* is itself interesting, for anti-Trinitarians saw it as a device by which their opponents tried to evade the contradictions of their position. Servetus, for example, repeatedly attacks the doctrine.[37] It is thus not surprising that Milton's use of it is guarded and not very enthusiastic. He illustrates briefly the transfer in a manner consistent with Calvin's analysis (*Works*, XV, 279). Certain things said about Christ in an

περιχώρησις κυκλοφορά ἐστιν.

unrestricted sense, he notes, have to be applied to one or other of the two natures. To put it another way, a characteristic proper to one of the two natures is, by idiomatic licence, transferred to the other. His two illustrations, employed also by Calvin, involve 1) a claim by the incarnate Son to what is proper to the divinity ('Before Abraham was, I am,' John 8:58), and, pointing in the reverse direction, 2) the attribution of a property of the human nature to the divine nature ('he that came down from heaven, even the Son of man, which is in heaven,' John 3:13).

Milton's argument, briefly and elliptically stated, appears to follow the general line of Reformed thought on the subject. The Reformed avoided the ancient doctrine of perichoresis or interpenetration, by which the early Fathers spoke of the union of the two natures,[38] and stressed instead that the properties of the natures are shared by the person of Christ the mediator. It is the personal union, according to Reformed thought, which gives the attribution of properties reality, since both natures truly subsist in the Son of God. The properties of each nature are bestowed upon this unique person, so that anything said of either nature is also said of the person. As theologians were fond of pointing out, the figure involved in all these operations is a form of synecdoche by which what is proper to one nature in Christ is attributed to the person which is itself called by the name of the other nature.[39]

Milton, too, stresses the importance of the person of the mediator to a proper understanding of the *communicatio idiomatum*. While acknowledging the licence that permits the interchange, he affirms the underlying truth that all such properties belong to the person of the mediator, who unites man and God. Milton's emphasis falls on this unity, rather than on the presence of two natures. Indeed, he departs from his Reformed contemporaries in his belief that nothing useful can be said about the two natures. Thus while Milton's brief account of the *communicatio idiomatum* in De Doctrina I, 14 appears conventional, it contains an important reservation: Christ is both man and God, but of his two natures and their union speculation is useless. When we turn back to I, 5, 'Of the Son,' it becomes clear that Milton repeatedly echoes the kind of attack directed by the anti-Trinitarians against the evasive use of *communicatio idiomatum*. In these passages he does not employ the technical term, but speaks rather of the kind of equivocation by which Trinitarians misuse the appeal to different aspects of Christ's nature and office and thus distort scripture to suit their own purposes:

after the hypostatical union of two natures in one person, it follows that whatever Christ says of himself, he says not as the possessor of either nature separately, but with reference to the whole of his character, and in his entire person, except where he himself makes a distinction. Those who divide this hypostatical union at their own discretion, strip the discourses and answers of Christ of all their sincerity; they represent every thing as ambiguous and uncertain, as true and false at the same time; it is not Christ that speaks, but some unknown substitute, sometimes one, and sometimes another; so that the words of Horace may be justly applied to such disputants: 'With what noose shall I hold this Proteus, who is ever changing his form?' (*Works*, XIV, 229)

Since little or nothing can be said of the natures, what is important is the biblical account of the single person resulting from the hypostatic union.

Repeatedly Milton comes back to the attack against such equivocators. In the following passage, Proteus is replaced by Vertumnus, another shape changer. The passage is reflecting on the assertion by Jesus that all things have been given to him by the Father:

But here perhaps the advocates of the contrary opinion will interpose with the same argument which was advanced before; for they are constantly shifting the form of their reasoning, Vertumnus-like, and using the twofold nature of Christ developed in his office of mediator, as a ready subterfuge by which to evade any arguments that may be brought against them. What Scripture says of the Son generally, they apply, as suits their purpose, in a partial and restricted sense; at one time to the Son of God, at another to the Son of Man, now to the Mediator in his divine, now in his human capacity, and now again in his union of both natures. (*Works*, XIV, 303)

A similar technique is used by Milton to bring out the subordinationist meaning of passages in which the Son acknowledges that the Father is greater than he, for here again Milton insists that Jesus spoke not merely as man but as man and God at once (*Works*, XIV, 223). Many glosses employ the same hermeneutical device, finding in the Son's statements evidence of his subordinate position by refusing to distinguish a human from a divine speaker. As we saw earlier, his basic line of argument in setting out the biblical witness to the Son is to insist that all the things said in scripture of the mediator are also said properly of the Son.

There is a remarkable consistency to Milton's views on the incarnate Son. All the beliefs I have discussed in this chapter lead in the same direction, for all contribute to the description of Christ as a unified being in whom the divine and human are one. Milton shows no real interest in the formulae for differentiating between the two aspects of Christ which were developed at Nicea and Chalcedon. In this he is quite unlike Calvin and his successors. Of the danger of Eutychianism or Apollinarianism he has nothing to say, presumably because the notion that Christ's humanity was completely absorbed into his divinity is a way of thinking quite foreign to him. He does reject the other extreme, the adoptionism associated with Servetus and the Socinians, and clearly he makes this point explicitly in order to distinguish his emphasis on Christ's humanity from theirs. [His seeming Nestorianism is a result of his desire to emphasize the full, particular, and rational individuality of Christ, but unlike Nestorius, he insists on the coalescence of the two persons.] His apparent monophysite tendency brings both human and divine together in a being who is finite and unified, without the disjunction of the two natures conveyed by the Calvinist notion of concealment, or even the reservations implied by the similes of union used by Reformation theology. This leads Milton to stress the moral aspect of kenosis, that act by which the Son emptied himself of divine honours and prerogatives. Since the divine nature of the Son is rooted in his filial relation with the Father, his essential identity remains unchanged after the act of emptying. The dyophysite strategies employed in Calvin's discussion of this topic have no relevance to Milton's position. Since Milton stresses the moral significance of kenosis as an act of love and humiliation, he can speak of the sacrifice by which the Son empties himself in his human as well as his divine nature. This emphasis on the unity of the incarnate Son means that Milton finds only a limited role for the practice of *communicatio idiomatum* or interchange of properties, and he forcefully attacks its abuse by those who seek by equivocation to tear apart the unity established in the Incarnation. Only a Son who is divine but not God, and whose humanity takes existential and individual form, can act as mediator.

CHAPTER SEVEN

Initiation in the Wilderness

Milton achieves a strong sense of perspective in *Paradise Regained* by his choice of the temptation as the event by which to interpret the character of the Son. This perspective gives prominence to the Son's human qualities. The poem presents a young but rapidly maturing man who is engaged in understanding his vocation. It is worth emphasizing the preliminary nature of the experience Jesus undergoes. He is being put to the proof, initiated: the overthrow of the devil in the wilderness is an experience that stands at the threshold dividing private from public life. It is clearly so in the Gospel accounts, where it is followed by definite announcements that his public mission has now begun: 'From that time Jesus began to preach, and to say, Repent: for the kingdom of heaven is at hand' (Matthew 4:17; see also Mark 1:14, and Luke 4:18). The temptation in the wilderness thus comprises a short period of withdrawal in which the hero retires to the desert in order to prepare his soul for heroic action.

Milton's handling of the immediate context is tactful and suggestive. The brief history of the Nativity and the early growth of Jesus is told by Mary and by Jesus himself. At the beginning of book 2 further context is provided by the appearance of the disciples, Andrew and Simon, and 'others though in Holy Writ not nam'd' (2.8). Their doubts, complaints, and reassertion of faith establish an important pattern, one that not only anticipates the events after the crucifixion but also provides a too literal yet innocent interpretation of the Messiah's kingdom which counterbalances Satan's too literal and corrupt conception. Milton's effort to harmonize the Gospel accounts through his narrative involves a shift at this point from Luke. It is Luke who gives the rich account of the birth and early life of Jesus (the annunciation, the angel choir, the prophecy of Simeon, the boy Jesus in the temple) which provides the basis for Jesus' soliloquy in book 1 and for the meditation of Mary that follows hard upon the lament of the disciples in book 2. But Luke writes as if the temptation took place before Jesus drew the disciples to him. In his account the conversion of Simon at Gennesaret does not take place until Jesus has preached and healed the sick. In Matthew and in Mark, also, the temptation precedes the meeting with Simon, Andrew, and the others. It is in John alone that Milton finds evidence of an earlier gathering of disciples. John, of course, does not mention the temptation in the wilderness at all, but his account makes it clear that in the day following the baptism two or more disciples, including Andrew, talked with Jesus and lodged with him, and that the next day more followers gathered around him. As Ira Clark has remarked, 'only in John is Jesus surrounded by disciples this early, only in John 1:41 does Andrew talk to others about finding the Messiah, and only in John is the list of twelve disciples lacking.'[1] By thus drawing on John, Milton created a chronology in which Jesus begins to live more openly immediately after the baptism but before the temptation, gathering friends and disciples around him, yet still, as in Matthew, delaying the formal and public announcement of 'his God-like office now mature' (1.188).[2] Thus when he enters the desert to combat Satan, the thoughts of this band of believers grapple with the sense of loss arising from his sudden absence; his initiation, while not public like his later acts, has also an initiating effect on the nucleus of believers already drawn to him.

Milton's choice of the private moment when Jesus stands at the threshold of his life's work as the subject of his poem is immensely interesting. There is a degree of analogy between the poet and the disciples meditating on the absence of the Messiah: like them, he must employ faith, reason, and imagination to apprehend the process by which the Son overcomes Satan.[3] The student of Milton is also likely to feel that there is something highly appropriate, even a kind of inevitability, about his selection of this episode. Milton's concern with choice and vocation, evident from his early writing onward, here finds a fitting subject. Nor is it inappropriate that towards the end of a long career the poet should write about beginnings, the threshold of action. For Milton, the root of the matter lies there, and anyone who wishes to avoid lapsing into an 'implicit faith' must return repeatedly to the springs of action, the emergence of private impulse into public word and deed.

This is not to deny the extraordinary range of reference and implication achieved through the treatment of the temptation episode. As Frye, Lewalski, Christopher, and others have amply demonstrated, the temptation in the wilderness is placed within a large context by means of type, example, and allusion.[4] That context includes not only the Gospel history, but the unfolding revelation of the Bible as a whole. Implicit in this episode is the full significance of the Incarnation. Other critics, such as E.M. Pope and Patrick Cullen, have taught us to see how the repudiation of the 'infernal triad' of world, flesh, and devil is a comprehensive experience that defines the norms and values of the wayfaring Christian.[5] The initiation lays out the rudiments of Christ's great warfare. Yet this range of vision, this effect of comprehending history, does not weaken the sense that the poem shows a particular moment in which the Son crosses the threshold and prepares to assume his Messianic office. There is a displacement of the larger, Gospel meaning to accommodate this precise stage in the evolution of Jesus.

The shaping force of the particular moment is srongly felt at the end, as well as the beginning. In the closing lines, it is the humanity of Jesus which receives the final emphasis:

> Thus they the Son of God our Saviour meek
> Sung Victor, and from Heavenly Feast refresht
> Brought on his way with joy; hee unobserv'd
> Home to his Mothers house private return'd. (4.636-9)

The mixed feelings this passage arouses and curiously blends, the sense of near paradox, is reminiscent of the effect achieved by the close of *Paradise Lost*, although more reassuring. The angel choir, which has sung for Jesus' ears alone, accompanies him in a manner visible to his eyes only. The phrase 'Brought on his way' suggests that the angels withdraw before he re-enters his mother's house. The divine revelry, recalling the nativity, is balanced by the outward calm, meekness, and isolation of the human figure. The phrase 'his Mothers house' reminds us of his humanity and mortality: 'his Mother then is mortal.' It also suggests a return to the circle of human affections. The final emphasis on his isolation in 'unobserv'd' and 'private' stresses that this has been an inward and spiritual triumph. But there is also something portentous about this quietness: it recalls that the period of withdrawal will shortly end and Jesus will commence his public mission. The three Gospels that treat the temptation agree that it is a prelude to action.

The angel choir has itself anticipated the opening of his mission in prophetic words of encouragement that mock the impotence of Satan and his crew:

> Hail Son of the most High, heir of both worlds,
> Queller of Satan, on thy glorious work
> Now enter, and begin to save mankind.   (4.633-5)

It is Matthew and Mark, and perhaps Matthew in particular,[6] that Milton follows at the close of the poem, for Luke does not mention the service of the angels. While all three evangelists agree that the work of ministration now begins, Matthew's account provides the best frame of reference in which to assess the mood of Milton's close. There the temptation in the wilderness is followed almost at once by the Sermon on the Mount. The sayings and parables uttered by Jesus concerning his kingdom give public and positive expression to issues which in Milton's story are considered by Jesus during the temptations. The sermon teaches the new righteousness with its law of love that makes men into sons of God. The beatitudes, which open the sermon and were described by Calvin as a discourse on 'true blessedness,'[7] contain little or nothing that is not present directly or by implication in the thoughts and words of Jesus in Paradise Regained. Matthew concludes his description of the Sermon on the Mount by noting the astonishment of the people at the doctrine of Jesus: 'For he taught them as one having authority, and not as the scribes' (7:29). Milton's Jesus, on the verge of engaging with Satan, notes the interpretations of the scribes, whose views he has already transcended ('searching what was writ / Concerning the Messiah to our Scribes / Known partly' 1.260-2), and concludes that his baptism indicates that he must now 'openly begin, as best becomes / The Authority which I deriv'd from Heaven' (1.288-9). The temptation in the wilderness is a final trial and clarification of his views which confirms his authority. By thus stressing the temptation as initiation, we gain at least part of the answer to the objection that the Christ of Paradise Regained is cold, aloof, and too negative. He is, rather, gathering his extraordinary energy and swarming thoughts in order to introduce the kingdom first publicly announced in the Sermon on the Mount.

The Son's Mode of Consciousness

The perspective offered by the choice of the temptation as subject is one which stresses the Son's humanity. Milton was being quite traditional when he observed in *De Doctrina* that Christ underwent the temptation in his human nature (*Works*, XV, 305). *Paradise Regained* appears on first acquaintance to take this perspective for granted, and to direct attention to the office or mission of the Son, rather than to his nature. Jesus retires to the wilderness in order to meditate on the best way to begin his work of saviour and to 'Publish his God-like office now mature' (1.188). But the question of his office cannot be separated from that of his nature. What he does must express who he is. And in spite of Milton's warnings against fruitless speculation, it is clear that in undertaking the subject of the brief epic, he accepted the challenge of finding a way to dramatize the nature of the incarnate Son.

Critical opinion concerning this important issue is various. One theme which provides a critical focus is that of identity. According to a number of readers, a source of dramatic interest in the poem lies in the manifestation of the nature of the Son. Many years ago A.H. Gilbert offered a clear and persuasive interpretation of the tower temptation in terms of this theme: 'On the part of Satan, the last temptation is a final test of identity. ... He has felt only human power to resist his wiles, and cannot perceive that perfect humanity is nothing less than divinity.'[8] It is perhaps not only Satan who receives this revelation, however, for the identity of Christ is also importat to all his followers. E.M. Pope finds in medieval and Renaissance exegesis of the biblical account of the temptations a preoccupation with the theme of identity, so that Milton follows a strong tradition when he views the temptations, especially that of the tower, as a revelation of Christ's true nature.[9] Barbara Lewalski takes the argument a step further, arguing that the discovery of the filial nature is for Jesus a process of self-discovery. When Satan receives his unexpected answer on the pinnacle, Jesus 'completes his journey to self-understanding' by comprehending his nature as image of the Father, and exercises divine power 'in standing where standing is impossible.'[10]

The view of the poem which holds that identity is a significant theme has not been universally accepted, however. For Thomas Langford, Satan's doubts about the identity of the Son are mere strategy, and 'the view that Christ finally demonstrates his divinity by superhuman behaviour undercuts the whole purpose and effect of the Temptation experience.'[11] Irene Samuel protests against viewing *Paradise Regained* as a '"Who am I" poem' rather than a '"How am I to live" poem.' The identity of the protagonist is 'a main concern of Satan, as though if he could just discover exactly who this man is he would then have the advantage of him; but God, the angels and the man himself put their emphasis elsewhere,' and so, the implication is clear, should the reader, for the Son of God 'takes his stand *not* on his special nature at all, but on his common bond with all humanity.'[12]

The question of identity, as these comments suggest, is intimately related to the problem of the function of the natures of Christ. Does Jesus act entirely through his human nature, or does he sometimes draw on his divine nature? And does he recognize and understand his divine identity, or is this something he discovers through experience? This issue, clearly of importance to our reading of the drama of *Paradise Regained*, also has obvious relevance to the Christology adopted by the poet. While there have been minority reports like that of Irene Samuel, criticism has, until recently, favoured a dramatic reading based on the assumption that throughout Milton draws attention to the two natures. For example, a sense of the tonal differences in the speeches of the Son led Don Cameron Allen to conclude that throughout the poem Jesus fluctuates between his divine and human natures:

> The fluctuation in this man's knowledge of himself and of his mission is what makes *Paradise Regained* more taut in action than Johnson perceived. In his divine nature Christ knows his identity and foresees his course, but in his human nature the 'exalted man' is often uncertain of both. As we read the epic, we watch him as he crosses and recrosses the boundary between the two persons, for it is out of this wandering to and fro, out of the humanly uncertain and the divinely sure that Milton gives validity to the test and extracts from it a highly dramatic conclusion. It is also Milton's way of expressing the union of the two natures in Christ. ...[13]

By this analysis, the Son's divinity is present spasmodically, appearing, vanishing, and reappearing in a providential pattern. His moment of self-discovery on the tower is only the climactic event in a series of experiences through which he is enabled to speak in a higher strain, that is, in a manner beyond what might be expected from his human understanding alone. Yet this seems a strange way to express the union of two natures in Christ, and one that would not be likely to recommend itself to a poet who considers the natures of Christ to be such a mystery that nothing can usefully be said of them in separation. A somewhat similar, but more elaborate and persuasive, position is adopted by Barbara Lewalski, who argues that in *Paradise Regained* 'the incarnate

Christ is the occasional recipient of special illumination activating the divine in himself, and may revert to the merely or nearly human on other occasions.'[14] She offers a detailed reading of the poem in support of this view, and links it with her fine insight into the way the mediatorial office of Christ is envisaged in terms of Calvin's threefold pattern of prophet, priest, and king. This last connection is undoubtedly correct and its discovery was a major contribution to our understanding of the poem; but I see no reason to make it dependent upon a spasmodic or discontinuous activation of the Son's divinity.

The initial difficulty is that all Jesus' words are authoritative. It is fruitless to seek to isolate certain moments when he speaks in tones which indicate he has achieved certainty or experiences a flash of divine understanding. Even the first soliloquy is incisive and definite, and while he there reviews various states of mind experienced in the past, the state in which he meditates is not really characterized by 'doubts and hesitations.'[15] The disciples 'doubt' in the absence of Jesus (2.11), and even Mary experiences 'cares and fears' and 'troubl'd thoughts' (2.64-5), but Jesus himself, led by the Spirit, has no uncertainty about his progress, and gives himself to 'deep thoughts' (1.190) and 'holiest Meditations' (2.110). Moving forward from this soliloquy, I do not find the fluctuations in manner that have been remarked by other critics. Four critical passages in the poem should clarify the nature of the problem of interpretation.

Jesus' speech on prophecy at the end of the first temptation brings into focus a major theme:

> No more shalt thou by oracling abuse
> The Gentiles; henceforth Oracles are ceast,
> And thou no more with Pomp and Sacrifice
> Shalt be enquir'd at Delphos or elsewhere,
> At least in vain, for they shall find thee mute.
> God hath now sent his living Oracle
> Into the World, to teach his final will,
> And sends his Spirit of Truth henceforth to dwell
> In pious Hearts, an inward Oracle
> To all truth requisite for men to know.   (1.455-64)

These words close a very strong speech in which Jesus exposes the weakness of Satan's claim to be the agent of God and in doing so gives a vivid and telling picture (all the more striking because the language used

U.S.A. - 33 EAST TUPPER STREET, BUFFALO, NEW YORK 14203
TEL. (716) 852-0342

340 NAGEL DRIVE, CHEEKTOWAGA, NY 14225
TEL (716) 683-4547

5T8

SOLD TO	VENDU À	PAGE

INDIVIDUALS
CASH WITH ORDER
PAYMENT RECEIVED

1

PLEASE QUOTE INVOICE NO. WHEN MAKING ENQUIRIES. * * * * *
S'IL-VOUS-PLAÎT CITER CE NUMÉRO DE FACTURE POUR TOUTE DEMANDE DE RENSEIGNEMENTS

OUR REF. NO. E NO DE RÉFÉRENCE	CUSTOMER CODE CODE DU CLIENT	AO	INVOICE DATE DATE DE FACTURE	INVOICE NO. NO DE FACTURE
94681	999993	28	14/08/87	4/63975

'RE	ISBN	CUSTOMER'S ORDER NO. NO. DE COMMANDE DU CLIENT	LIST PRICE PRIX LISTE	DISCOUNT ESCOMPTE	AMOUNT MONTANT
	8020-90236		.00		
4S OF	8020-56792		35.00		

TOTAL BOOKS TOTAL DES LIVRES	B/O CANCEL DATE DATE DE CANC. DE COMM. À SUIVRE	INVOICE SUB-TOTAL SOUS-TOTAL DE LA FACTURE	SHIPPING/HANDLING EXPÉDITION/MANUTENTION	INVOICE TOTAL TOTAL FACTURE
1				

U.S.A. - 33 EAST TUPPER STREET, BUFFALO, NEW YORK 14203
TEL. (716) 852-0342

340 NAGEL DRIVE, CHEEKTOWAGA, NY 14225
TEL (716) 683-4547

5T8

SOLD TO	VENDU À	PAGE

INDIVIDUALS
CASH WITH ORDER
PAYMENT RECEIVED

1

PLEASE QUOTE INVOICE NO. WHEN MAKING ENQUIRIES.
S'IL-VOUS-PLAÎT CITER CE NUMÉRO DE FACTURE POUR TOUTE DEMANDE DE RENSEIGNEMENTS ★ ★ ★ ★ ★

OUR REF. NO. NO DE RÉFÉRENCE	CUSTOMER CODE CODE DU CLIENT	AO	INVOICE DATE DATE DE FACTURE	INVOICE NO. NO DE FACTURE
94681	999993	28	14/08/87	4/63975

TRE	ISBN	CUSTOMER'S ORDER NO. NO. DE COMMANDE DU CLIENT	LIST PRICE PRIX LISTE	DISCOUNT ESCOMPTE	AMOUNT MONTANT
	8020-90236		.00	.0%	5.00
NS OF	8020-56792		35.00	.0%	35.00

RECEIVED
OUR RECEIPT
TORONTO PRESS

TOTAL BOOKS TOTAL DES LIVRES	B/O CANCEL DATE DATE DE CANC. DE COMM. À SUIVRE	INVOICE SUB-TOTAL SOUS-TOTAL DE LA FACTURE	SHIPPING/HANDLING EXPÉDITION/MANUTENTION	INVOICE TOTAL TOTAL FACTURE
1				US

recalls *Paradise Lost*) of Satan's role in the trial of Job. But we should not be surprised that Jesus, who while yet a boy could teach the doctors in the temple, can provide such a clear analysis of the motives and delusions of the evil one. Rather than posit, as some critics have done, that Jesus recollects his divine pre-existence and encounters with Satan in heaven, we should follow Lewalski in finding here 'an imaginative re-creation of the scene based upon traditional (Christian) exegesis of the Job story.' But if this is so, why do we need a 'special revelation' to account for his concluding words on prophecy? 'Christ,' writes Lewalski, 'cannot call at will upon the divine illumination but it is granted after he has withstood, in all human vulnerability, the test posed. He is in the process of winning back the understanding which he previously possessed by means of the teaching of the Father. ... '[16] Is it necessary to invoke this kind of restoration of more than human knowledge in order to account for the passage? Jesus' affirmation that he is himself God's 'living Oracle' can be based directly on the baptism itself, when the descending dove and the voice of the Father publicly confirmed his office as teacher of mankind. His faith in that pronouncement enables him to prophesy the cessation of Satan's false oracles, about which he has read or heard along with much else concerning classical and pagan civilization. In doing so, he is reaffirming and fulfilling the prophecy of Micah 5:12: 'and thou shalt have no more sooth sayers.' He knows that the prophecies concerning the Messiah are being fulfilled, as Isaiah 11:2: 'the spirit of the Lord shall rest upon him, the spirit of wisdom and understanding, the spirit of counsel and might, the spirit of knowledge and of the fear of the Lord' (a passage, it is worth noting, that *De Doctrina Christiana* maintains 'implies the light which was shed on Christ himself,' *Works*, XIV, 363).

Jesus' understanding of the 'inward' nature of the oracle derives partly from his own experience of the operation of the Spirit that has led him into the wilderness to meditate on things past and to come. In this sense the inward oracle might be 'that light of truth, whether ordinary or extraordinary, wherewith God enlightens and leads his people,' or even that 'divine impulse, or light, or voice, or word, transmitted from above either through Christ, who is the Word of God, or by some other channel.' In this latter sense, the passage refers to his prophetic office, for 'Christ alone ... is, properly speaking, and in a primary sense, the Word of God, and the Prophet of the Church' (*Works*, XIV, 361, 367, 369). But the inward oracle as 'Spirit of Truth' (1.462) also seems to anticipate the revelation of the person of the Holy Spirit and of its donation. The allusions to John 14:17 and 16:13 bring to mind the moment just before the betrayal by Judas when Jesus teaches his disciples concerning 'the Comforter, which is the Holy Ghost.' This is the inward oracle which will introduce Christian liberty by writing on the hearts of the regenerate the law of faith working through love (*Paradise Lost*, 12.487-90). It illuminates the heart which, like that of Mary, 'hath been a store-house long of things / And sayings laid up' (2.104-5). Jesus, knowing himself born to promote all truth, has faith that the virtue and power of the Father will enable him to 'make perswasion do the work of fear' (1.223).

In Jesus' words at the offer of a banquet Lewalski suggestively sees 'an anticipation of his priesthood.' The articulation of this second major theme she would also associate with 'another of those divine illuminations.'[17] Yet words and thought are consistent with Jesus' normal mode of discourse:

> Said'st thou not that to all things I had right?
> And who withholds my pow'r that right to use?
> Shall I receive by gift what of my own,
> When and where likes me best, I can command?
> I can at will, doubt not, as soon as thou,
> Command a Table in this Wilderness,
> And call swift flights of Angels ministrant
> Array'd in Glory on my cup to attend.   (2.379-86)

This falls short of an assertion of 'lordship over Nature due him as the Creator and Son of God.'[18] Jesus' opening words attack Satan's logic, pointing out that if, as Satan claimed, he has right to all created things, then it is foolish for Satan to offer him what is already his own. His claim to be able to command a table in the wilderness is an expression of faith, rather than a remembrance of former powers. The phrase 'as soon as thou' acknowledges that both act under providence, Satan temporarily possessing power to create his illusory shows (for 'thou are serviceable to Heaven's King,' 1.421) and Jesus acting with continual divine guidance and protection. The ministering angels that he could call to attend his cup, reminiscent as they are of Renaissance paintings of the last supper, are supported by prophecies like that in Psalm 91:11: 'For he shall give his angels charge over thee, to keep thee in all thy ways.' His whole answer is characterized by the narrator as temperate, which suggests the display of human virtue rather than divine power.

The temperance of the Son's carefully controlled argument stands out more clearly when compared with the speech by Satan to which he is replying:

> Hast thou not right to all Created things,
> Owe not all Creatures by just right to thee
> Duty and Service, nor to stay till bid,
> But tender all their power? (2.324-7)

These words recall the hierarchy established at the creation by which man rules over the rest of the creation (*Paradise Lost*, 7.515-16), and look forward to the time when the Son will be 'Head Supream' (ibid, 3.319). The drift of the passage, however, is to elicit from Jesus some large claim, perhaps that he is the creator and Lord of Nature: this he neither affirms nor denies.

According to Lewalski, the point at which a moment of illumination is given the Son about his office of kingship occurs after his rejection of Parthia and Rome, when he introduces the prophecies concerning his kingdom:

> Know therefore when my season comes to sit
> On *David*'s Throne, it shall be like a tree
> Spreading and over-shadowing all the Earth,
> Or as a stone that shall to pieces dash
> All Monarchies besides throughout the world,
> And of my Kingdom there shall be no end:
> Means there shall be to this, but what the means,
> Is not for thee to know, nor me to tell. (4.146-53)

Of this Lewalski writes: 'At length, after withstanding at the human level all those temptations regarding his kingship, Christ apparently receives another of those flashes of divine understanding, after which he can cite Daniel's metaphors of the tree and the stone evidently with full comprehension of their meaning for his kingdom. He can also lay claim to full knowledge of the means to his kingdom which we know that he did not have as he entered the desert. ... '[19] But Jesus did have some sense of the means as he entered the desert ('my way must lie / Through many a hard assay even to the death,' 1.263-4), and I see no reason to suppose that he has been given any supernatural illumination concerning the subject, although his encounter with Satan, and the Satanic review of the powers ranged against him, will have strengthened and made more specific his awareness of the source of his future suffering. His statement here asserts his faith in the means, rather than any new understanding of them. And Satan, if he had any sense, would be able to glimpse the means by now – indeed may have done so, but is prevented from moving to a firm grasp of the truth by his perversity: it is certainly not for Jesus to tell him.

Nor do I see any evidence that Jesus has through a flash of divine understanding achieved full comprehension of the prophetic metaphors of David. The metaphors speak for themselves concerning the flourishing of the Son's rule and the overthrow of his enemies, and his use of them is evidence of his faith in the word of God. His observation that his kingdom shall have no end is a forceful reply to Satan's threat that without his help there will be 'no sitting ... long / On *David*'s Throne' (4.107-8), a reply which emerges with a kind of inevitability out of the discussion of throne and kingdom, but it should be noted that in his first soliloquy Jesus recalls the prophecy that his kingdom shall have no end made at the annunciation (1.241; Luke 1:32-3), and that he has already made the same point before to Satan, basing it securely on scripture (through a reference to Isaiah 9:7): 'of my raign Prophetic Writ hath told, / That it shall never end ... ' (3.184-5). And is there anything in the style itself of Jesus' language at this critical point that lends his words more certainty than elsewhere? The same economy, force and lucid articulation are present in his response to the first temptation, a response which does not emerge from a preparatory dialectic of argument, but is delivered with surprising abruptness, like the temptation it counters:

> Why dost thou then suggest to me distrust,
> Knowing who I am, as I know who thou art?   (1.355-6)

The quiet irony, and the recognition of the polarity between first and second persons, are very similar to the close of the speech on the kingdoms:

> Means there shall be to this, but what the means,
> Is not for thee to know, nor me to tell.   (4.152-3)

The same problem of tone occurs in relation to the words which Jesus speaks from the pinnacle of the temple. Lewalski argues that they indicate how he has arrived through patient endurance at an understanding of his priestly office. He has had his nature as the image of the Father revealed to him, and 'is now permitted to exercise the divine power in standing.'[20] The question of the Son's understanding of his nature at this critical moment will concern us shortly. Here I wish to emphasize how difficult it is to ascertain the tone of the Son's words. If his simple statement on the tower 'rings with certainty and assurance beyond anything else in the poem,' it must achieve its effect through dramatic placing, for the words themselves are, of course, taken from Deuteronomy, which Jesus now cites at a critical moment for the third and final time. Our reading of the moment involves our imaginative response to the experience of Jesus through the poem as a whole.

A review of certain high points in the speeches of Jesus suggests that his divinity is not something which is suddenly manifested at climactic moments. There is a ring of authority in Jesus' words throughout the entire poem, and the glimpses of his Father's glory that shine in his face do so with a constant, not a fitful, radiance. The view that he suffers from a kind of amnesia which is gradually being dissipated by light from above, while it opens up possibilities for drama, fails to do credit to the strength and consistency of the human elements in his nature. Even when, as in Lewalski's persuasive and learned exposition, this view is modified so that the 'divine illumination' is something earned by trial on the human level, it involves assuming distinctions in the quality of the Son's responses which do not appear to exist. There are thematic high points, such as the passages on oracles, on the priesthood, and on the kingdom (and indeed, many others), but these do not correspond to the changes of style and tone indicative of the assertion of his divinity. There is no need to assume that the Son experiences the fitful return of his memory of the divine life that preceded his Incarnation. This is not what he is pointing to in his observation that 'what concerns my knowledge God reveals' (1.293). Rather he draws upon all his powers of rational insight, logic, and human memory in order to apprehend the revelation of scripture concerning the Messiah in terms of his experience on the human level. There is 'Light from above, from the fountain of light' (4.289), but it illuminates the man's mind, imagination, and judgment.

The two natures, then, are not represented as two modes of consciousness or two persons with distinct wills and intellects. The Jesus of *Paradise Regained* possesses a unity of being consistent with the Christology of *De Doctrina Christiana*. There is no suggestion that he is concealing his divinity or veiling it; rather the poem gives the impression that the whole being of the Son is engaged in the encounter with Satan in the wilderness. He does not appear to hold powers or attributes in reserve, although his faith in the Father gives him absolute confidence that whatever is truly needed will be supplied ('I can at will, doubt not, as soon as thou, / Command a Table in this Wilderness' (2. 383-4). He is absent from the councils of the Father in heaven, and clearly does not, like Calvin's Son, continue to exercise divine power in the government of the universe during the period of his Incarnation.

Divinity in Humanity: the God-man

In his words about himself, the Son does not make a distinction between one nature and the other, but speaks 'with reference to the whole of his character, and in his entire person' (*Works*, XIV, 229). The narrator, in his comments, also places the emphasis on unity. The biblical proof-texts associated with the Trinitarian controversy are absent or treated with restraint. It is in particular worth noting that the poem avoids the kinds of statements associated with the so-called *communicatio idiomatum*, the device of synecdoche by which attributes are communicated from one nature to the other. This Jesus, for example, does not lay claim to timeless personal existence. Instead of saying 'Before Abraham was, I am,' he sees his timeless relevance in terms of prophecy: 'of whom they spake / I am' (1.263-4). Nor is Jesus described as the son of man who came down from heaven: the poem contains few references to his departure from heaven at the Incarnation, and avoids paradoxical or startling substitutions of the divine and human terms for the Son. The Son's references to God are to the Father, and never appear to contain either explicit or hidden allusion to his participation in the Godhead or in the intelligence and will of the Father. When he says 'Who brought me hither / Will bring me hence, no other Guide I seek' (1.335-6), there is no suggestion that he is the guide as well as the one guided. Such passages do not hint at a divine nature lying behind the immediate identity of the speaker. Even when the Son refers to the word of the Father which produced all things, he speaks apparently as a reader of scripture rather than as a being who in another life acted as the Word.

One of the most interesting passages indicating the Son's view of his relation to the Father occurs during the discussion of glory:

Shall I seek glory then, as vain men seek
Oft not deserv'd? I seek not mine, but his

> Who sent me, and therby witness whence I am. (3.105-7)

For Milton, the person who speaks these words is not simply the mediator, but the Son in the fullest sense. To paraphrase what Milton says elsewhere, in attributing all glory to God the Father, Jesus does not wish to be thought essentially the same as God, for this would mean denying himself glory only to bestow it upon himself. Rather Jesus presents himself as the truthful messenger who seeks the glory of the one who sent him (as in John 7:17-18, see *Works*, XIV, 233).

The humanity of the Son thus appears intact and complete. The portrait is entirely consistent with Milton's insistence that the Son takes up manhood, not a conglomeration of human properties, so that his identity includes a human personality. Jesus' first soliloquy establishes from the outset that he increased in age and wisdom through a recognizable process of human growth, and repeatedly we are made aware of the limits of his knowledge and his dependence upon his spiritual guide. This is a Son of God who can ask, as he hungers in the desert, 'Where will this end?' (2.245) and who dreams of being fed like the prophets of old, but on waking finds 'all was but a dream' (2.283). He is also a Son who can allude to his delight in the poetry of scripture read in 'my private hours' (4.331).

For almost the entire poem, the divinity of the Son is connected not with his previous existence as the only-begotten in heaven, but with his generation by the Father from the seed of the woman. Indeed, what is remarkable about the Father's first speech in heaven (1.130-67), as well as the angel song which immediately follows it, is the absence of reference to the Son's pre-existence. This introduction might appeal to a Socinian who held that the Son of God first came into existence at the Nativity. Following the Gospels, the poem asserts that Jesus is 'call'd the Son of God' (1.136) because he has a divine, not a human, father. Throughout the Father's speech emphasis is placed on the perfect manhood of Jesus and his consummate virtue, so that he is also described as the Son of God by merit. The Father speaks as the initiator and director of the Son's career, observing that he produces him, exposes him, exercises him, chooses him, and sends him forth. The angels' comment that the Father 'knows' the Son does not appear to mean more than that he has complete confidence in him, for they add that he ventures the filial virtue even though it is 'untri'd' (1.176-7). This could not be said of the pre-existent Son, whose virtue was put to the test in such trials as the war in heaven, the creation, and the decision concerning man's redemption. There is no sense in which the pre-existent Son could be described as 'untri'd.' The word makes it clear that the incarnate Son represents a fresh start; he is a new being who, unlike Adam, will show perfect obedience to his maker. Yet as we have seen, the Father is not speaking of the human nature in distinction from the divine; there is no divine Son who continues to exercise government through the universe during the period of the Incarnation. The trial of the Son is a new encounter with evil because he has emptied himself of divine attributes and meets Satan in a new form. It is the Son of God himself and not simply the mediator who is sent, exercised, and tried. Continuity is established by the way the new identity is chosen by the pre-existent Son; discontinuity is introduced by the new terms and conditions of choice arising from the Incarnation.

The Son, then, will show his divinity through his perfect human nature. Milton does not have difficulty with this idea because for him the divine nature of the Son does not participate in the infinity of God the Father. The reduction of powers which occurs at the emptying does not remove anything essential to his divine identity. Precisely this point is made at the close of the poem in the single passage which authoritatively relates the Son's incarnate and pre-existent states. This occurs during the final chorus of the angel choir, who celebrate the Son as 'True Image' (4.596) of the Father whether he is throned in the bosom of bliss or, remote from heaven, wanders the wilderness in human form. Their point is emphatically that his nature as the image of God is not altered by these changes of state, since it consists in his perfect fulfilment of the will of the Father. His filial relation, his sonship, is expressed with godlike force in every place, habit, state, or motion. The point is amplified by their recital of past victories and the association of these with present and future triumphs. In Milton's ethical view, the act of choice is the final and absolute determinator of nature, and the Son can show his divinity by right choices on earth as in heaven. In this sense, then, there is remarkable continuity between his heavenly and earthly states. His assumption of humanity is simply the acceptance of new conditions of trial. Satan's complaint that the Son has not demonstrated himself to be more than 'meer man' (4.535) fails to recognize the expression of the divinity in the humanity. The divine and human nature are united in the Son through the act of choice, the man realizing in a human mode the will of the divine being. Both natures, so united, jointly act as mediator, demonstrating obedience to the Father. Whether in heaven, 'light of light / Conceiving' (4.597-8), or on earth, responding to 'Light from above, from the fountain of light' (4.289), the Son understands and expresses the will of the Father and acts as his perfect image.

The Development of the Son

The comments of the Father and angels provide some guidance in our effort to understand the Son. But the most important evidence arises from the way the poem presents the Son in dramatic terms. It is as a fully human individual that we see him, after the baptism, walking alone in the desert:

> Musing and much revolving in his brest,
> How best the mighty work he might begin
> Of Saviour to mankind. ...   (1.185-7)

The multitudinous thoughts swarm within him. As with other Miltonic heroes who are thinking creatively, he remembers the past. He recalls the stages that mark the gradual development of his understanding. His childhood was studious, for he thought himself 'born to promote all truth, / All righteous things,' mastering the law and drawing the admiration of the learned while yet young. But his spirit aspired to heroic deeds, for he wished to overthrow tyranny throughout the world and to free truth. However, he sensed that persuasion, which appeals to the rational in man, is a better instrument than the fear aroused by force. Thus he

> held it more humane, more heavenly first
> By winning words to conquer willing hearts,
> And make perswasion do the work of fear;
> At least to try, and teach the erring Soul
> Not wilfully mis-doing, but unware
> Misled; the stubborn only to subdue.   (1.221-6)

These words recall the speech by the Father during the council in heaven in book 3 of *Paradise Lost* in which he announces that his grace will save those who endeavour with 'sincere intent' (192); in both speeches there is the same pity for the misled soul, the same wish to restore liberty by leading and illuminating the conscience, and the same firm repudiation of the stubborn. And as in the council in heaven, a point has been reached that requires the recognition of the need for a redeemer. Having achieved an insight into liberty through his own exercise of reason, the Son now needs the assistance of revelation.

This comes to him in two forms. First is his mother's advice, in which she urges him to aspire 'above example high' (1.232), that is, to a new kind of heroism founded on the recognition that his father is the 'Eternal King, who rules / All Heaven and Earth' (236-7) and on the prophecy that he will sit on David's throne and that there will be no end to his Kingdom. As evidence, she tells of the annunciation, the Nativity, the song of the angel choir proclaiming the Messiah, the visit of the Magi, and the words of Simeon and Anna. Milton's characters treasure the prophecies that indicate their destinies, and demonstrate their freedom by employing them in timely fashion. The second source of revelation is of course scripture:

> This having heard, strait I again revolv'd
> The Law and Prophets, searching what was writ
> Concerning the Messiah, to our Scribes
> Known partly, and soon found of whom they spake
> I am; this chiefly, that my way must lie
> Through many a hard assay even to the death,
> E're I the promis'd Kingdom can attain,
> Or work Redemption for mankind, whose sins
> Full weight must be transferr'd upon my head.   (1.259-67)

Reading such prophets as Isaiah, he has already deduced the general nature of the act of ransom and satisfaction that he must make, and the process of justification that will result. He understands that teaching and heroic deeds will not in themselves earn the kingdom, but that it lies on the far side of death. Satan quite genuinely fails to understand this, his tendency, like that of the apostles, being to think of the Messiah's coming in terms of a worldly kingdom, and his final belated efforts to make something of adversity show his failure to comprehend its significance. Despite a moment of poignant regret, atonement lies outside his vision, and Jesus does not seek to enlighten him on this subject.

The soliloquy, then, shows Jesus using right reason and the revelation of scripture to arrive at self-understanding. The law has provided guidance in his earlier search for truth, justice, and righteousness, but revelation has enabled him to gain an insight into his role in introducing the new dispensation of the Gospel. His words indicate that his understanding of his Messianic role is tied very closely to his interpretation of scripture, rather than being based on some kind of private revelation. He trusts to time and the will of heaven to bring him further knowledge, his humility being clearly evident in his account of the baptism. His description shows his own limited, human awareness of the event. Of his own response to the descent of the Spirit and the voice from heaven he says little, although devices of emphasis, particularly repetition, testify to the extraordinary intensity of the moment:

> And last the sum of all, my Father's voice
> Audibly heard from Heav'n, pronounc'd me his,
> Me his beloved Son, in whom alone
> He was well pleas'd. ...   (1.283-6)

It is noteworthy that the event does not appear to be accompanied by a flash of memory recalling his previous experience in heaven. Instead, Jesus regards the statement not as an indication of his metaphysical status, but of his union of aim and will with the Father, and a sign also that the period of preparation is over and he is from now on to live more openly.

Providence remains his guide concerning times and seasons:

> And now by some strong motion I am led
> Into this Wilderness, to what intent
> I learn not yet, perhaps I need not know;
> For what concerns my knowledge God reveals.   (1.290-3)

The 'strong motion' of the Spirit that leads him into the desert might remind us of the 'rouzing motions' (*Samson Agonistes*, 1382) which lead Samson to the Philistine games. Both impulses are practical leadings of providence in the sense that they simply place the hero in a position where he may act or suffer to advantage. Each hero relies on providence and his judgment to make clear the nature of the occasion. There is about Jesus a kind of alert passivity as he waits for a clue, content to remain in ignorance but trusting to God to reveal anything necessary. It is a state of mind familiar to English Puritanism. But we may say with equal truth that Jesus' state of mind is characterized by a calm and unruffled activity as his thoughts swarm, ranging over 'things past and to come' (1.300) and seeking to comprehend more fully his Messianic office which will act as the hinge of time. These two conditions, the lively evolution of understanding and the quiet resting on the will of heaven, prepare for the time of action when the right occasion is catalyst for both understanding and will, making one the efforts of the individual and the guidance of grace.

The Spirit of Truth, as Jesus observes in John 14:26, 'shall teach you all things, and bring all things to your remembrance, whatsoever I have said unto you.' This passage was for Milton an important text concerning the operation of the Spirit in regenerate thought. The Son in *Paradise Regained* provides the model for such comprehension, interpreting the present in the light of the past, bringing prophecy into relation with experience, truth into relation with practice. What is restored to his memory is the core of the experience of the human race as this is expressed principally in the Bible, with its recognition of the need for a redeemer and all that this implies, but not without secondary reference to non-biblical history, of which the Son can say 'For I have also heard, perhaps have read' (4.116). What God reveals, then, is largely the significance of things already known, recalling to memory the fragments of individual and racial experience which define the role of Messiah, enabling him by light from above to comprehend the pattern that integrates past, present, and future. Sometimes this revelation takes the form of an objective, external event, as when the voice is heard from heaven. But more frequently it is present in the continuous leading of the Spirit, which brings occasions that elicit new recognitions. And it is continuously present in the operation of those human powers of love and right reason that are essential to the liberty which Jesus has come to restore to mankind.

As we have seen, Adam and Eve are given a wide range of feelings, including doubt and uncertainty, and they are permitted to experience conflict and yet retain their innocence. Jesus, however, acts in a strikingly different manner. For him there is no hesitation or anxiety, and his intelligence already appears to move with the alacrity and certainty which characterizes the intuitive reason mentioned by Raphael. To appreciate the drama of the Son's development, we must be able to respond to decisions which are neither instinctive nor mechanical, but which display without hesitation the power of reason to choose rightly. Adam and Eve, moreover, are required to exercise obedience within the context of a limited and simple revelation, while Jesus does so in a way that realizes and fulfills the Old Testament, partly through the types and prophecies, but also through the creative use of example. The whole scripture points to him, and the allusive and imaginative manner in which he communicates his awareness of this, linking part to part with a creative insight that suggests how all things have come to his memory, gives excitement and authority to the performance.[21]

The continuity in the Son's position is striking. It resists critical efforts to find in the hero's experience a conventional pattern of dramatic change and transformation. Many of the things which Jesus says to Satan towards the climax of the action are already present in a fairly explicit manner in his thought at an earlier point. His kingdom is spiritual, for to govern the inner man by saving doctrine is nobler than to rule by force (1.221-4, 2.443-76); it will be without end (2.442, 3.185); his own task will be not only to promote truth by persuasion, but to work redemption for mankind by bearing the full weight of sin and by giving a kingdom (2.481). His offices as prophet, priest, and king seem to be in large measure known to him at the outset. He foresees a life of active teaching led in humble state and concluded by passive obedience through suffering. All the important truths about his offices as saviour of mankind appear to be there from the beginning of the temptation, to be present, in fact, in the period of meditation following his mother's history of his birth, when he searched once again the law and the prophets concerning the Messiah, and 'soon found of whom they spake / I am' (1.262-3). The degree to which Satan's temptations cover ground already familiar to Jesus is made evident towards the conclusion of the second day's temptation. Observing that Jesus seems 'addicted more / To contemplation and profound dispute' (4.213-14) than to the king-doms of the world (the addiction, of course, is Satan's), and recalling how as a child Jesus slipped from his mother to dispute with the Rabbis in the temple, Satan proceeds to urge him to be famous by wisdom:

> The *Gentiles* also know, and write, and teach
> To admiration, led by Natures light;
> And with the *Gentiles* much thou must converse,
> Ruling them by perswasion as thou mean'st. ...   (4.227-30)

Here we are very clearly reminded of Jesus' soliloquy, of his reflection on the episode in the temple (an episode which Satan mistakenly and characteristically views as expressive of Jesus' mature teaching), and of his resolution to 'make perswasion do the work of fear' (1.223). In short, the preceding temptations have centred on issues which Jesus had already resolved before the meeting with Satan ('victorious deeds / Flam'd in my heart, heroic acts,' 1.215-16) and only now, at the end of the second day, does Satan approach (although misunderstanding it) the point arrived at by Jesus much earlier.

The change in the Son is thus not the result of the discovery of new doctrine, nor does it arise from a gradual awakening of more than human powers and insights. Rather it expresses his mastery of faith in experience, the wisdom that results when the meaning of doctrine is realized in the discipline of action and suffering.[22] His growth thus entails a new view of what he already knows. The development of Jesus in the desert builds on his past experience and the knowledge he has already reached. The first soliloquy shows the operation of this characteristic pattern in the past: a dialectical movement leads from the desire to promote all truth and righteousness by reading the law, through the aspiration to restore true liberty to earth by heroic deeds, to the recognition that persuasion may be more effective than fear, then on through the reinterpretation of all in the light of revelation to the concluding idea of a redeemer who must act heroically by suffering and persuade men to embrace life by his death. The dialectical movement is one that retains continuity and yet encourages shifts in awareness which introduce new aspects of the pattern. Nothing is rejected, but the previous level of awareness is placed in a new perspective at each new stage. The same human process of growth, I believe, is continuing in the temptation episodes. Jesus' beliefs and principles are being brought to the test of experience. Not that experience is the 'Best school,' as Satan claims (3.238), but that only through experience, as the Father recognizes, can his title be put to the proof. And the proof of faith, as Adam's failure makes pitifully clear, is not a mechanical display, but a living expression of the committed will and intelligence within varying situations. From experience the Son learns about the full context in which belief operates, a context made restless and urgent by feeling, imaginative pressures, the vividness of actualization:

> I never lik'd thy talk, thy offers less,
> Now both abhor, since thou hast dar'd to utter
> The abominable terms, impious condition. ...   (4.171-3)

In a sense, Jesus knew who Satan was from the start. But his anger and disgust reveal the fulness of his human reaction to the clear perception of the 'Evil one.'

Unlike Adam, of course, he remains a solid rock unshaken by the assault of the waves. His resistence displays not only his virtues, but also his mastery of scripture and the ways of providence. The drama of this mastery is sometimes underestimated. The temptation leads him to amplify, to extrapolate, to draw out the implications of his beliefs. He moves from theory to practice, from abstract understanding to the immediate experience of truth. While it is true that he appears already to know much about the Messianic role implied by scripture, his placing of the types, prophecies and examples, under the pressure of Satan's challenge, is not only an astonishing display of intellectual power and of the way the Spirit of his Father brings all things to memory at need, but also orders the scriptural themes in a coherent design so that the shape of his mission becomes clearly manifest. We are left with the strong impression that Jesus has passed through an initiatory experience which draws together his thoughts and gives him the insight necessary to begin his public work. The experience occurs within his human nature, although not without the assistance of grace and the Spirit.

The paradoxes of private and public action are here of some importance. In response to the public announcement made at the baptism, the Son retreats into the isolation of the desert in order to meditate on the best way to 'Publish his God-like office now mature.' Having conquered Satan there, he returns to society, ready to begin preaching that the kingdom is at hand, but the return is private. What he has learned, in his humanity, is the mature exercise of that individual liberty which is to be his gift to those who follow him. His ability to discriminate enables him to escape the snares employed by Satan. Christian liberty, Milton remarks, is the 'peculiar fruit' of adoption (*Works*, XVI, 153). The baptism is the event in the life of Jesus that in this sense corresponds to adoption in the life of the regenerate. Jesus was never in bondage to sin, of course, nor did he behave like one living entirely under the law as a servant or child. But his earlier plans concern heroic achievements, active in nature, military or intellectual. They contain the ingredients of his mission, but not the final shape. Satan's temptations urge him to accomplish his ends by performing works. Jesus responds by showing how the law of works gives place to the law of grace, so that as 'sons instead of servants, and perfect men instead of children, we may serve God in love through the guidance of the Spirit of truth' (*Works*, XVI, 153-5). Satan is baffled by Jesus' ability to respond by faith to appeals for works, and he is thus prevented from separating the divine and human natures. He hopes to catch his opponent in his dichotomies – the promised kingdom must be either external or internal, the time to act is now or never, the choice of life must be active or passive, truth exists either as fact or abstraction. To such attempts to force his hand, Jesus responds by affirming his faith and asserting his liberty. He draws from the Gentiles and yet repudiates their philosophy; he knows that the time to act has arrived, yet acknowledges that the occasion remains in God's hand; he chooses to act knowing that his kingdom is not of this world and that it will yet overcome the world, and also that his private life will bear public fruit. To the pure all things are pure; what is important is the quality of response. By the close Jesus has demonstrated his love of God, and he can proceed to the Sermon on the Mount, with its precepts of love (see *Works*, XVI, 145).

Satan's Protean Interpretations

The theme of the identity of the Son is given its richest statement in the temptation of the tower. In order to appreciate the Son's response to this final trial, it will be useful to pause to consider the motivation and strategy of Satan. Satan is, of course, the chief proponent of false views of the Son of God. It is sometimes maintained that Satan puts these views forward merely to deceive and mislead Jesus, and that he knows the real identity of his opponent from the start. Evidence for this interpretation is found in the words of the Son at the first temptation:

> Why dost thou then suggest to me distrust,
> Knowing who I am, as I know who thou art? (1.355-6)

But it is not necessary to conclude from this passage that the Son and Satan recall their previous encounter in heaven. The Son is a student of the Old Testament, and knows Satan as one of its more important *dramatis personae*. Shortly he will display his mastery of scripture, drawing upon the story of Job in order to characterize Satan. Moreover, he has a very clear and imaginative comprehension of the Satanic mind and predicament. There is nothing in the speeches that follow to suggest that he remembers ejecting Satan from heaven, however, or that he is reminding Satan of that event. Satan, on his part, knows who the Son is in the sense that he realizes that this is the promised seed of the woman and the Son of the heavenly Father. But what it means to be Son of God is beyond Satan, as is the nature of his kingdom. 'The Son of God I also am,' as he says much later, 'or was / And if I was, I am; relation stands' (4.518-19).

No doubt Satan's chief and overriding concern through the temptations is to gain power over the Son. But he also wishes to discover his full identity, not the least because knowledge is a form of power. Satan's misunderstandings of Christ's nature can thus be said to be partly strategic, for he is attempting to beguile his enemy into adopting a perverted view of his mission. But they are also an expression of his genuine bafflement, his inability to face and firmly grasp what he knows only in part, to comprehend what he suspects and fears. If he is to remain, as in the past, 'from despair / ... high uplifted beyond hope' (*Paradise Lost*, 2.6-7), these doubts must be carefully cultivated.

Satan is present at the baptism, sees the dove descend on 'th' exalted man' (1.36) and hears the Father's voice identify him as 'his beloved Son.' Flying to his place in mid-air, Satan summons a council and reveals that the circling hours have brought the time when they must 'bide the stroake of that long-threatn'd wound' (1.59). His words suggest that the devils have been aware since the Nativity of the birth of the promised seed, and that they have been anxiously monitoring the development of Jesus to 'youths full flowr' (1.67). This general impression is confirmed by the much later speech in which Satan admits to Jesus that from the time of the Nativity

> seldom have I ceas'd to eye
> Thy infancy, thy childhood, and thy youth,
> Thy manhood last, though yet in private bred. ...   (4.507-9)

Like Jesus, Satan takes direction from foreshadowings and prophecies, and he and his followers have read events with some accuracy. The baptism of Christ struck Satan as ominous indeed, a sign that the promised kingdom was about to be established, and it was this which galvanized him into action. The baptism also caused him anguish by its confirmation of the parentage of Christ:

> His Mother then is mortal, but his Sire,
> He who obtains the Monarchy of Heav'n,
> And what will he not do to advance his Son?
> His first-begot we know, and sore have felt,
> When his fierce thunder drove us to the deep;
> Who this is we must learn, for man he seems
> In all his lineaments, though in his face,
> The glimpses of his Fathers glory shine.   (1.86-93)

The linking of the exalted man with the first begot in this passage is highly suggestive, but Satan nonetheless remains in doubt concerning the identification. 'Who this is we must learn,' he says, hoping that it is not their fatal adversary. His doubt may be 'assiduously fostered,' as A.S.P. Woodhouse remarks,[23] but in this respect it is exactly like all the other 'hopes' of hell.

The doubt centres on the idea of appearance: 'for man he seems.' Here the language suggests the ancient heresy called Docetism in which Christ is a divine spirit who takes on the phantom appearance of manhood. This view is implicit in Satan's repeated invitations to Jesus to reveal his more than human power. Reformed apologetics consider this view to be evident in Apollinarianism and Eutychianism, the heresies which deny the full humanity of Christ. Satan grows increasingly frustrated by his inability to establish the presence of a divine spirit in the Son.

Another ancient and basic heterodoxy known as Ebionism is also of some relevance to *Paradise Regained*. This second-century Jewish movement denied the divinity of Jesus, viewing him as the predestined Messiah who would return to reign on earth. 'Ebion,' meaning poor, recalls the humble title by which the original Jewish-Christian community in Jerusalem liked to be known (Romans 15:26; Galatians 2:10).[24] The root idea that Jesus was a mere man, pre-eminently endowed, is found in the recurrent heresy of adoptionism, as in the teaching of Paul of Samosata in the third century, or, in a complex form, in that of Calvin's contemporary and *bête noire*, Servetus. It is such a view that is expressed in *Paradise Regained* at the beginning of book 2 by the 'Plain Fishermen'(27) who are distressed by Jesus' disappearance. Satan evokes a perverse version of such doctrine throughout the temptations of the kingdoms on the second day. He mocks Jesus for setting his heart on high designs while lacking means to put them into effect, being 'low of birth' (2.413) and 'Bred up in poverty and streights at home' (2.415). If Jesus really is what he appears to be, a mere man of lowly station, he will need Satan's help in order to fulfil the Messianic prophecies and establish his reign on Judah's throne. The Son replies by pointing to examples of men who have 'attain'd / In lowest poverty to highest deeds' (2.437-8). With ironic dexterity, he parries Satan's belittlement of his mere humanity by stressing its reality and completeness. This he does by speaking of the importance of the inner rule of the soul over lawless passions. Instead of responding to Satan's contempt by laying claim to divine power, the Son insists that he is no Apollinarian deity, no gnostic spirit in fleshly guise, but a whole man consisting of body and soul. It is precisely with language which suggests an adoptionist view that Jesus repeatedly baffles and frustrates Satan, as when he remarks that he may be tried by suffering before the beginning of his reign:

> best reign, who first
> Well hath obey'd; just tryal e're I merit
> My exaltation without change or end.   (3.195-7)

Satan, then, fears the Incarnation, with its union of divine and human elements in one person, for he recognizes that this would prove a bridgehead threatening his empire on earth. After the defeat of the first day, Satan's 'doubting' words to his consistory again link this man with the pre-existent Son, although indirectly:

> such an Enemy
> Is ris'n to invade us, who no less
> Threat'ns then our expulsion down to Hell. ...   (2.126-8)

There is 'far other labour to be undergon' in dealing with the Son (the words invite comparison with the Son's labour of redeeming man) than in the case of Adam, who was much inferior to this man:

> If he be Man by Mothers side at least,
> With more then humane gifts from Heaven adorn'd,
> Perfections absolute, Graces divine,
> And amplitude of mind to greatest Deeds.   (2.136-9)

Once again, he evinces his surprise and puzzlement that human nature can be raised to a condition in which it seems to have transcended itself.

Satan, of course, has failed to take the measure of his adversary; 'self deceiv'd / And rash,' he neglects to weigh 'The strength he was to cope with, or his own' (4.7-9). His reckless energy usually involves a defiance of logic, for a cool and dispassionate estimate of his position would lead to Belial's abject and melancholy sloth. With Eve, the lack of logic did not matter, and he was able to exploit doubts and contradictions which expressed his own pride and hunger for domination. With Jesus his lapses in reasoning are immediately exposed, for he is confronted with a mind which can without hesitation place the elements of the problem in correct order.

Satan's confusion throughout is centred on the meaning of the title 'Son of God.' In his temptations, he addresses the Son sometimes as man, sometimes as more than man, failing to acknowledge or to understand the unitive nature of the Son's being. Indeed, his temptations, and the whole drift of his thinking, are concerned to repudiate the Incarnation, with its union of God and man. Listening to Satan's attempts to probe the Son's nature, or elicit some revelation of his mission, one might conclude that he is one of those false theologians castigated in De Doctrina for their failure to see that Christ's words normally proceed from his entire person: 'they represent everything as ambiguous and uncertain, as true and false at the same time; it is not Christ that speaks, but some unknown substitute, sometimes one, and sometimes another ... ' (Works, XIV, 229). Satan shows this protean quality in his responses to the Son, although by the close we realize that through all his changes he has been firmly held by his opponent. Frequently Satan appeals in a flattering way to the 'more then humane' (2.137) side of Christ, fawningly eager to know and observe wisdom and Godlike deeds, urging him to publish his divine virtues, to imitate his great Father in seeking glory, to assert his lordship over nature. But such incitements to vainglory alternate with speeches stressing the Son's human vulnerability, his weakness and low station ('A Carpenter thy Father known,' 2.414), his lack of worldly experience, in this way pressing him to despair of succeeding without external help. For Satan, Jesus is now merely man, now divinity in disguise. His rhetorical strategy expresses his own deep-rooted doubts. This separation of the human and divine natures and persons corresponds to the Nestorian heresy as understood by the Reformers.

Alexander Sackton has argued that in the first and last encounters Satan seeks to make Christ reveal his divine nature, while in the second encounter he presents a whole series of temptations which appeal to Christ as a human being.[25] This is broadly true of the pattern, even though it ignores the individual fluctuations of Satan's protean strategy. Certainly as the middle temptation develops there are fewer appeals to the 'God-like' possibilities of the Son's nature and attention centres on the means to the fulfilment of his mission. The result is an increasing sophistication and worldly realism. The simple appeal to self-preservation represented by the stones-to-bread temptation, the more complex and sensuous appeal to various appetites in the banquet temptation, and the appeal to avarice in the offer of riches, all have a quality of magic or legerdemain about them, as if the divine aspect of the

Son required instant fulfilment. But the discussions of glory and zeal bring Satan to the realization that the Son wishes to earn his victory through effort and endurance, and consequently he emphasizes the need for practical means to bring about the achievement of the ideal within history. In this later stage of temptation, Satan assumes the great significance of the Messianic task and points to the limitations of those human powers on which the Son must rely to fulfil it. At the close of the second day, he berates the Son for lost opportunities, maintaining that he has given up his chance to realize his aims without serious difficulty. Jesus is too fastidious, too good for this world ('What dost thou in this World?' – 4.372), and his otherworldliness prevents the fulfilment of his task and renders ineffectual the kingdom foreshadowed by the stars.

The temptation of the kingdoms, then, offers Christ the means to worldly splendour and to the fulfilment of his Messianic task; Satan urges ways of fostering and developing the divine potential in the human condition of the Son. The first and third temptations, on the other hand, invite the Son to help himself by a miraculous assertion of divine powers to preserve his human state. The central attack treats the humanity of Christ as vulnerable and unable without help to realize his divine nature, but this is flanked by two appeals to his divinity to save his humanity. The effect is to underline Satan's inability to comprehend the unity, wholeness, and integrity of the nature of the Son.

As preparation for the last day of trial, Satan seeks to soften up his enemy by sending a storm and evil dreams, 'thinking,' as Jesus puts it, 'to terrifie / Mee to thy will' (4.496-7). His first words on the final morning are designed to provoke anxiety. Admitting that the Son will be what he is ordained to be, he casts doubt on the value of an achievement which is not accomplished at the proper moment. His argument produces a parody of the doctrine of kairos, the right time,[26] as he observes that the Son has missed the perfect season for action, and that 'each act is rightliest done, / Not when it must, but when it may be best' (4.475-6). The real point of this criticism is to arouse uneasiness mingled with fear of future suffering, the retribution for weakness. The Son replies by pointing to the self-seeking motives behind Satan's feigned concern, and dismisses him:

> desist, thou art discern'd
> And toil'st in vain, nor me in vain molest. (4.497-8)

The Son's words bring to an end the formal period of the temptation.

Satan's power, which will shortly expire, continues for the moment, but it is now exercised in direct defiance of the Son's command. His response to this prohibition is to swell with rage. His final speech of self-justification and analysis (4.500-40) is extraordinarily interesting, and we do Satan an injustice to think of it as a mere rhetorical strategy. Satan is meditating aloud, and the history of his preoccupation with Jesus displays a parallel with the soliloquy in which Jesus first meditates on his life. Like Jesus in that early speech, Satan retraces the past, and in doing so makes clear at last how closely and obsessively he has pursued the Son. From the prophets he learned of the Messiah. Warned by the annunciation, he was among the first to know of the birth. The angel choir that 'sung thee Saviour born' confirmed his suspicion that this infant would bear watching, and from that time he kept a careful eye on the development of Jesus through infancy, childhood, youth, and early manhood, until the voice from heaven proclaimed that this was indeed the Son of God. The phrase clearly exasperates Satan, since he finds it capable of a variety of meanings:

> All men are Sons of God; yet thee I thought
> In some respect far higher so declar'd.   (4.520-1)

Seeking in the desert to confirm this surmise, he has found by 'all best conjectures' that 'Thou art to be my fatal enemy,' that is, the seed of the woman that will bruise the serpent's head. The progressive nature of Satan's gathering awareness is significant, paralleling and contrasting as it does the Son's 'growing thoughts': the prophecies of the Messiah, the annunciation, the proclamation of the Saviour by the angel choir, the declaration from heaven at the baptism, and the confirmation by trial in the desert. Satan works from experience and from scripture – or rather his knowledge of the story set down subsequently in scripture. Yet his efforts to grasp the nature of the impending disaster have all been thwarted:

> Honours, Riches, Kingdoms, Glory
> Have been before contemn'd, and may agen:
> Therefore to know what more thou art then man,
> Worth naming Son of God by voice from Heav'n
> Another method I must now begin.   (4.536-40)

This is a surprising speech because Satan has again and again suggested that in the Son may be seen 'more then humane gifts' (2.137).

Is he bluffing, keeping hidden what he knows in order to drive Jesus back into his humanity, where he may best be threatened by death? That effect is certainly desired by Satan. Yet I think the speech also comes out of his immense bafflement concerning the Son's identity. All the clues are in his hand, yet he can not make sense of them. Graceless, he fails to understand that the mystery of the Incarnation is meaningful because it involves an act of accommodation, that the divinity of the man he has been tempting is expressed through his perfect humanity. This perfection in itself makes him 'worth naming Son of God.'

The Trial on the Pinnacle

The temptation on the pinnacle of the temple follows. The dilemma with which Satan confronts the Son on this last occasion is intended to drive a wedge between the two natures united in the person of the Son. As he places the Son on the 'uneasie station,' he scornfully adumbrates the possibilities:

> There stand, if thou wilt stand; to stand upright
> Will ask thee skill; I to thy Fathers house
> Have brought thee, and highest plac't, highest is best,
> Now shew thy Progeny; if not to stand,
> Cast thy self down; safely if Son of God:
> For it is written, He will give command
> Concerning thee to his Angels, in thir hands
> They shall up lift thee, lest at anytime
> Thou chance to dash thy foot against a stone.   (4.551-9)

The trial is an identity test, as well as an attempted murder. Satan does not expect the Son to stand upright for long. If he is merely human he will perhaps fall and be killed, or at the least make a desperate effort to save himself. Death, of course, is the desired outcome. But even if the Son commands the service of angels in order to save himself from a fall, the experiment will have been worth while. 'Now shew thy Progeny' returns to the issue that has been nagging him throughout: is this man or God? It is a question which has run like a musical figure through all Satan's commentary, a constant probing: 'His Mother then is mortal, but his Sire ... ' (1.86), 'If he be Man by Mothers side at least ... ' (2.136), 'A Carpenter thy Father known' (2.414), 'firm / To the utmost of meer man' (4.534-5). Satan has finally devised a situation by which he expects to show that the Son is either man or God. His astonishment and fall occur as Jesus demonstrates that his nature is a unity that enables him to elude Satan's dilemma.

The dramatic narrative through which Milton presents the temptation of the tower is remarkably successful and compelling. The narrative carries the reader by its effective dramatic form, arousing admiration, even amazement, at its deft economy. The moment of reversal is handled with astonishing ease and force, leading the reader through an experience which provides a mimesis of the experience of the two characters. It is worth recalling the shape of the episode before turning to the issues that arouse critical controversy.

Examining the narrative closely, we can see how the poet carries us along without leaving time for uncertainty. He exercises a sure control over the timing of the drama. The episode has a definite beginning, and there are no hesitations in its unfolding. It starts with Satan's abduction: 'So saying he caught him up, and without wing / Of *Hippogrif* bore through the Air sublime / Over the Wilderness ... ' (4.541-3). The impulse to imagine the flight is checked by 'without wing,' and this emphasizes the more than natural power which Satan continues to exercise over the Son. 'Caught up' serves to stress the violence of the event, and hints at the interior nature of the struggle (the apostles, missing Jesus, remember how Moses was 'caught up to God,' 2.14). In a moment we are over the holy city with its towers, and the imagery introduces a brief vision of suggestive beauty, reminding us both of the city of God and also of the garden of Eden (for readers of *Paradise Lost* there are strong echoes of the account of the garden). As E.M. Pope has shown, there was much contemporary interest in the pinnacle, with the majority of interpreters favouring the view that it was flat, having access by stairs and possibly a balustrade,[27] but there is no likelihood, I think, that a reader of Milton's poem would assume such a structure:

> the glorious Temple rear'd
> Her pile, far off appearing like a Mount
> Of Alabaster, top't with Golden Spires:
> There on the highest Pinacle he set
> The Son of God. ...   (4.546-50)

The implication is that the pinnacle is the highest of the spires; and spires, it seems clear, are pointed.

The exact time-sequence of the scene is in part controlled by the speeches. When the Son is 'set' on the highest pinnacle, Satan adds scornful words to the deed. The speech comprises nine lines. Our assumption as readers, I believe, is that during this brief time Satan will not allow the Son to fall. His taunting speech must first reach its climax. The implication is that the Son is still physically 'caught up' in the power of Satan, and that he is so held until Satan issues his riddling challenge. Ironically, the moment at which Satan expects his power to be fulfilled is the moment it expires. He lets go of the Son, and falls himself: 'To whom thus Jesus: also it is written, / Tempt not the Lord thy God, he said and stood. / But Satan smitten with amazement fell ... ' (4.560-2). Satan presumably hoped the Son would drop from the tower as soon as he finished speaking. During the very short time in which the true oracle cuts through the riddles of the false oracle, Satan has a chance to recognize that the Son is held by a power greater than his own. At the end of that time, he finds that his own power was but borrowed, and that he is no longer prince of the air.

Satan's fall is carried through two similes, but these indicate its moral, rather than its temporal and spatial, significance. As soon as they are over, we return to the sequence of events:

> So Satan fell and strait a fiery Globe
> Of Angels on full sail of wing flew nigh,
> Who on their plumy Vans receiv'd him soft
> From his uneasie station, and upbore
> As on a floating couch through the blithe Air,
> Then in a flowry valley set him down
> On a green bank. ...   (4.581-7)

'Strait' suggests that there is no lapse of time between the disappearance of Satan and the appearance of the angels, although the description does allow for a moment during which the angels swiftly approach. Like the standing of the Son on the tower, his rescue is miraculous in a low-keyed manner. In neither case does he say anything which would indicate that the miracles are of his working. The angels are not summoned, and unlike Satan they convey the Son in an imaginable manner. The Son displays no miraculous powers of levitation, but places his weight on the 'floating couch' until he can safely be set on the pastoral bank. The narrative has been careful to remark what we might call playing time from the time of the story teller, action from commentary, so that we are sharply aware that the Son stands without assistance from Satan on the point of the highest spire of the temple for a period of only a few seconds, after which he is gently returned to earth by the angels, the return presumably being unhurried but of short duration. On the spire he appears to stand neither by a feat of athletic prowess nor by floating without weight, but rather by the support of providence, which without a word from the Son sends the angels to rescue him and bring his trial to an end.

Does the description of the pinnacle as an 'uneasie station' undermine this later view? It has been taken to imply that the standing was not miraculous but a 'balancing feat,' and therefore seems to be 'decisively against the theory that any miracle occurs.'[28] But it is important to observe that it is the station which is characterized as 'uneasy,' not the stander. The adjective indicates the way the pinnacle appears to a human observer, not the character of the act by which the Son has maintained his position. The phrase 'he said, and stood,' does not convey the idea of maintaining a precarious position by virtue of strenuous physical effort, nor does Milton dwell on the physical character of the standing. It has also been suggested that the pinnacle offers a flat area of a size sufficient to enable a man to stand upright.[29] Standing for a brief moment on such a spot would require a cool head rather than exceptional physical skills. But the text offers nothing to aid us in further speculation concerning the fine line which distinguishes miraculous from either athletic or normal standing. The point, surely, is that such distinctions are of no importance. The Son's physical safety has been the responsibility of providence from the moment he entered the desert. The very plainness and simplicity of the account draws attention away from the circumstances of the physical act to its moral significance. As in parable, lapses of realism point to the importance of a spiritual reading. What is significant in the Son's act is the way it reveals his perfect trust in the Father. The pinnacle has been for the Son an 'uneasie station' not, as Satan argues, because standing there requires skill, but because the testing of the Son's faith has been strenuous. His standing is expression and symbol of perfect obedience.

Turning from the action to the question of the possible ambiguities of the Son's response, it is worth stressing that his oracular injunction is a direct reply to Satan's invitation to cast himself down from the pinnacle and thus show his progeny:

To whom thus Jesus: also it is written,
Tempt not the Lord thy God, he said and stood.   (4.560-1)

Jesus cites the command originally directed against those who ask for signs of God's beneficent providence, as the Jews did at Manassah, 'saying, is the Lord among us or not?' Ironically, it is not the wayward yet chosen people who now raise this question, but Satan himself, who wishes to tempt God by seeking to know of Christ 'what more thou art then man, / Worth naming Son of God' (4.538-9). He thus fulfils the typological implications of the temptations of God in the wilderness by the Israelites (see Psalm 95:7-9). In one sense, then, Jesus' response conveys his recognition that his identity is being investigated. While Satan clearly wants Jesus to fall to his death, he is on the alert for any sign that the Lord is in some special sense present in this Son of God.

Yet, as Newton saw, we should recognize that Satan is also pursuing his temptation of the Son.[30] It is for this cause that he will shortly be punished. Much better than a physical fall of the Son would be a moral fall. True, Satan has entered this final trial with 'no new device,' but rather 'to vent his rage, / And mad despight' (4.443-6). Yet as the situation develops, he provides it with a rationale. Not only will he try to discover whether the Son is something more than man, but by the same token he will tempt the Son to respond falsely.

Critics have sometimes argued that Milton does not understand this final trial as a real temptation, for the pinnacle does not seem to offer Jesus a choice. Here it is worth emphasizing two things. In the first place, moral decisions, while arising out of a long process of development, may be instantaneous, as Adam's moment of choice in book 9 of *Paradise Lost* makes clear. At the moment when Satan releases his victim, the Son must respond either by manifesting faith or displaying its lack. Temptation does not require that the tempted be allowed to deliberate at leisure, as Satan's own experience of sin must have taught him. Secondly, Milton thinks of distrust and presumption as closely related and as equally the opposites of faith. Presumption, it is true, was traditionally associated with the temptation of the tower by commentators, and in *De Doctrina Christiana* Milton cites Matthew 4:7, 'thou shalt not tempt the Lord thy God,' when treating of presumption as the opposite of faith. But when he considers distrust as the opposite of of faith, he cites a rather similar passage from Isaiah 7:12, 'I will not ask, neither will I tempt Jehovah,' which in itself suggests that the two conditions of faithlessness are closely related (*Works*, XVII, 55-7). Earlier in the poem the connection has already been demonstrated. The temptation to turn the stones into bread appeals to distrust, but if the Son had resorted to miracle to save himself, the act would have savoured also of presumption. All the temptations, in fact, combine these two aspects of faithlessness, urging both despair of the means and time appointed by providence and the need for the Son to take matters into his own hands. The twofold attack is directed at the human-divine nature, and seeks to arouse fear as a consequence of human weakness and to incite a perverse straining after the exercise of power through human or divine agency.[31]

While Satan expects the Son to slip and fall to his death as soon as he is released, he nonetheless considers the moment before the fall to be one of real temptation. 'Cast thy self down' (4.555), he says, in mockery of Jesus' abandonment by God, pressing his victim to despair and tempting him, as earlier, 'with terrors dire' (431). But he knows how presumption may arise out of despair, and he knows also how seriously the Son takes the prophecies concerning the Messiah (he himself, ambivalently, also takes them seriously). 'Cast thy self down' cuts the other way, also, acting as an incitement to perform miracles. In the instant in which he is exposed on the tower by Satan, the Son's faith is tested. He speaks in fact without knowing whether he will stand or fall. His 'Tempt not the Lord Thy God' expresses his firm faith in the sustaining presence of God, his conviction that God's will will be done and his refusal to tempt God by doubt or presumption.

The Son's citation of the deuteronomic command has thus a double reference; it comprehends both Satan's tempting of God by asking in mockery for a sign of his presence, and the Son's refusal to tempt God by seeking such a sign. Does it include a third level of significance in which the Son is in effect saying 'Tempt not me, the Lord thy God'? The answer must surely be in the negative. There is no evidence in the poem to support the conclusion that he has now departed from his earlier mode of speech and awareness in order to lay claim to Godhead. In this respect, his words are exactly parallel to his earlier response to the temptation of the kingdoms when he cited Deuteronomy 6:13: 'Thou shalt worship / The Lord Thy God, and only him shalt serve' (4.176-7), and there he clearly refers to the Father and not himself. In both cases the poem draws on the Gospels; in neither case does it suggest that the citations of Deuteronomy contain revelation of divine status. Nor is it likely that the Son would give Satan the answer that he seeks. When Christ was tempted by the Pharisees, Milton once wrote, he 'answer'd them in a certain forme of indignation usual among good authors; whereby the question, or the truth is not directly answer'd, but som thing which is fitter for them, who aske, to heare' (*Works*, IV, 168). As on the occasion of that later tempting, so here the Son wishes to demonstrate both 'the freedome of his spirit, and the sharpnesse of his discerning' (*Works*, IV, 143).

There is, then, no evidence to suggest that the Son is at this point recognizing his true identity in some way that has previously eluded him, or that he reveals here a new understanding of his divine nature. He has undergone the entire temptation in his 'character of God-man' (*Works*, XV, 303-5), and the unity of his person has been preserved throughout. Central to Milton's Christology is the principle that what the Son says about God the Father he does not say of himself. His divinity is not veiled by the Incarnation, but is expressed by his human nature, which remains the perfect image of his Father.[32] His achievement displays 'all the fulness of the Godhead bodily' in Milton's sense of that phrase from Colossians 2:9, which he understands 'not of the divine nature of Christ, but of the entire virtue of the Father, and the full completion of his promises (for so I would interpret the word, rather than "fulness"), dwelling in, not hypostatically united with, Christ's human nature ... really and substantially' (*Works*, XV, 261). The point is that his expression of the will of the Father does not make him hypostatically one with the Father: his divine nature does not consist in essential identity with the Godhead. The moral and spiritual perfection which enables him to fulfil God's will would be undercut if he were, in fact, the same being as God. Nonetheless it is that perfection which makes him divine in his own right and in his own being. Jesus' divine nature is thus located in the single will and mind and operation by which he displays that virtue which makes him the true image of God the Father. Satan, finding that human nature is capable of such virtue, falls in suicidal despair like that which overcame the sphinx at the solving of the riddle of man.

Up to this point in the poem, little attention has been given to the pre-existence of the Son. The adoptionist view of the Son as a man of pre-eminent virtue who becomes the chosen instrument of God has remained a possibility. The importance of this emphasis, as we have seen, lies in the way it strengthens the reality of the trial in the desert. Now, however, the angel choir connects the incarnate and the pre-existent states as it identifies the Son of God as 'True Image of the Father,' whether throned in 'the bosom of bliss' or 'remote from Heaven, enshrin'd / In fleshly Tabernacle' (4.596-9). As they celebrate his restoration of the paradise lost by the first Adam, they briefly review the great cycles of history – the overthrow of Satan in heaven by the Son, the fall of Adam, the reinstallation of man in a 'fairer Paradise,' the expulsion of the demonic from the world. Gathering angels and men into himself, the Son is 'heir of both worlds.'

The reader might be forgiven for wondering whether the Son literally and actually listens to the angel choir. We are not told that he does so, but only that the performance takes place while he is refreshed by the heavenly feast and then 'Brought on his way with joy.'[33] The doubt is beneficial at least in this, that it draws our attention to the way in which Jesus receives the song. The song is quite unlike the voice from heaven at the baptism, which was heard by many. Now Jesus is unobserved, private, and the song also seems to be a private, spiritual experience, a fitting close to his inward meditations. The song confirms and rounds out in apocalyptic language those things which the Son has already discovered about himself and his mission by reading scripture under the guidance of the Spirit. The song thus does not serve as a gloss upon some flash of illumination by which Jesus has realized his identity with the pre-existent Son. Rather it is confirmation and restatement in apocalyptic language of the understanding he has reached through meditation on scripture, including the recognition of his previous existence and future triumphs. The important yet muted or elliptical place which the angels give the Crucifixion, as well as their recognition that the next step consists of works of faith, reflects precisely the degree of understanding reached by the Son. While they add a prophecy to their celebration (629-30), even that is according to the method of typology, for the casting out of the devils and their flight in the herd of swine looks back to the initial defeat of Satan and forward to his final overthrow, as well as paralleling the present fall of Satan from the tower of temptation. The typological continuities of the divine plan, by which the casting out of Satan occurs many times but in varying dispensations, have enabled the Son to grow in his understanding of himself and his mission. In so far as the angel's song has reference to the Son's understanding, then, it does so by expressing the process by which the Spirit brings all things to memory and illuminates the mind of the regenerate.

Ransom for Sin

The primary focus of *Paradise Regained* is thus on the inward aspects of salvation. Jesus lays down the 'rudiments' of the warfare against Satan, undergoing trial in exemplary fashion, displaying the faith, obedience, and liberty that characterize the spiritual life. The 'external' aspect of the atonement – the payment of Christ's blood as ransom for man's sin, and the consequent satisfaction of divine wrath and justification of believers, is given only limited attention of a formal and explicit sort. Yet we know how important this side of the atonement is to Milton the theologian: 'It is in vain that the evidence of these texts is endeavored to be evaded by those who maintain that Christ died, not in our stead, and for our redemption, but merely for our advantage in the abstract, and as an example to mankind' (Works, XV, 317-19). It is not surprising, then, that the theme is frequently evoked by implication and suggestion.

Anticipations and foreshadowings of the passion and death of Christ are woven throughout the poem and are significant in its final effect. Some of these are fairly direct, and others oblique. The theme is inescapable:

> I send him forth
> To conquer Sin and Death the two grand foes,
> By humiliation and strong Sufference.   (1.158-60)

The Son in his opening soliloquy shows that he understands this from reading scripture, and sees his way

> must lie
> Through many a hard assay even to the death,
> E're I the promis'd Kingdom can attain,
> Or work Redemption for mankind, whose sins
> Full weight must be transferr'd upon my head.   (1.263-7)

This is a comprehensive statement of the doctrine of atonement. The ideas of suffering and death are thus present from the start in Jesus' thoughts, and his encounter with Satan simply gives them body and context. While Adam does not figure directly in the conversations of Satan and Jesus, the visions of the fallen world raised by Satan are a sufficient reminder of those sins which must be paid for by the Son. Satan reveals the world of sin – of lust, violence, and oppression – from which man can only be released by the Son's act of redemptive love. As the darkness of that world becomes more and more oppressive, the Son's willingness to confront it grows increasingly evident, and receives clearer and stronger expressions. Critics who speak of the Son as cold and withdrawn are looking in the wrong direction – he still breathes immortal love for mortal man.

Satan is unable to grasp the idea of atonement, even though the Son gives him clues and becomes increasingly explicit in his handling of the subject:

> What if he hath decreed that I shall first
> Be try'd in humble state, and things adverse,
> By tribulations, injuries, insults,
> Contempts, and scorns, and snares, and violence,
> Suffering, abstaining, quietly expecting
> Without distrust or doubt, that he may know
> What I can suffer, how obey?   (3.188-94)

'Quietly expecting' – this is one of the dominant themes of the whole poem. We have met it before in the 'But let us wait' (2.49) of the disciples, and in Mary's 'But I to wait with patience am inur'd' (2.102). Jesus' words describe what he has been doing in the desert, but they also indicate his understanding of the prophecies concerning the Messiah and of the manner in which he will bear man's sin. The interrogative mood of the passage is appropriate because Satan does not deserve a straightforward answer, but it also implies the movement of Jesus' thoughts as he presses toward a fuller realization of his mission.

There is irony when Satan makes a last minute effort to pre-empt the prophecies concerning suffering in order to frighten Jesus (4.380-93). What he pretends to read as a necessity written in the stars – the fatal error that will make Jesus a figure of tragedy – is the experience of violence already foreseen by Jesus through his reading of such prophecies as that of the man of sorrows in Isaiah 53:3-4: 'he is despised and rejected of men; a man of sorrows ... stricken, smitten of God, and afflicted. ... ' Arguing that the prophecies concerning Jesus would be best fulfilled if he accepted the kingdoms of the world, Satan failed to acknowledge that suffering is predicted for the Messiah: now his account of suffering as punishment ignores its positive function, so strongly emphasized by the prophet: 'But he was wounded for our transgressions, he was bruised for our iniquities: the chastisement of our peace was upon him; and with his stripes we are healed. ... he bare the sin of many, and made intercession for the transgressors' (Isaiah 53:5, 12). Satan cannot understand that this is how he will receive his fatal bruise, and continues to dream of their fight as of a duel; and, as always, he uses his own doubts as the basis for the temptation of others.

The night of terrors that precedes the third day and the temptation of the tower itself have frequently been seen as prefigurations of the passion and Crucifixion. The picture of the Son of God 'unappall'd in calm and sinless peace' (4.425) under the onslaught of the wild elements and the fiends appears to allude to the passion and death of Christ. Memories of the upheavals of nature which occurred at Christ's death (the darkness, the earthquake, the splitting of rocks and opening of graves) should not be from our minds.[34] Yet as so often, the foreshadowing involves difference, as well as similarity. 'Sinless peace' is not Christ's condition during the Crucifixion, when he feels, as Milton insists, the wrath of God in both his natures, and cries 'my God, my God, why hast thou forsaken me.' It is Satan, after all, who wishes to find in the 'ominous night' a 'sure fore-going sign' of 'many a hard assay' which must be undergone by Jesus before he takes up the sceptre of rule (4.478-83). Moreover, the phrase 'many a hard assay' was first used by Jesus (1.264), and this should alert us to the way Satan is trying to capitalize on what he has learned. Having finally understood that the Son intends to accept hard assays, he is making a last minute effort to suggest the futility and horror of suffering. It is worth stressing that Jesus does not see the storm as a sign of anything but Satan's anger: 'false portents, not sent from God, but thee' (4.491).

With the temptation of the tower, however, menace gives way to a direct assault on the Son. Most critics agree in finding in the episode a foreshadowing of the Crucifixion. It is suggested both by Jesus' physical position on the pinnacle and by his moral stance of patience and fortitude. Recalling that Jesus will see 'Satan fall like Lightning down from Heav'n' (*Paradise Lost*, 10.184) at the time of his resurrection, Lewalski proceeds to note how 'in *Paradise Regained* Satan's falling awestruck as Christ stands unmoved suggests that other "fall" at Christ's death; Christ's escape from death foreshadows his resurrection; and the angelic banquet and hymn honoring Christ as "Son of the most High, heir of both worlds" (IV.633) foreshadows his enthronement at the right hand of the Father.'[35] Such an interpretation of the tower temptation, as Lewalski has shown, is quite traditional. Bearing this in mind, it is worth noticing the restraint and economy with which Milton handles this motif. No direct linking of the tower and the cross is made by the narrator, nor are we given to understand that Jesus experiences the spiritual death which is so anguishing at the Crucifixion, that 'dreadful consciousness of the pouring out of the divine wrath upon his head' (*Works*, XV, 305-7).

The muted handling of the motif is clearly important to the effect of the close, and allows the angel choir to celebrate the founding of 'A Fairer Paradise' while yet looking forward in anticipation to Satan's future 'fall from Heav'n' and the saving of mankind. Satan has been given one wound; soon he will receive another, his 'last and deadliest.' This muted foreshadowing of the passion and death of the Son is perfectly accommodated to the point reached in the Son's growth. What he is realizing in terms of human will and intellect is the decision made originally in his divine being. This final act – the end towards which all moves – is thus taken into the rhythm of Jesus' experience of calling and becomes a goal chosen by him in his unified nature as God-man, not something added to his career by a decision made elsewhere. His encounter with Satan reveals to him the rightness and significance of his decision to fulfil the prophecies respecting the trial 'even to the death' (1.264) which is to be endured by the Messiah.

Redemption, Milton tells us, is 'that act whereby Christ, being sent in the fulness of time, redeemed all believers at the price of his own blood, by his voluntary act, conformably to the eternal counsel and grace of God the Father' (*Works*, XV, 253). That act was in one sense performed in heaven before the Incarnation, but in another it will not occur until after the events presented in *Paradise Regained*. Since the act of redemption is both in time and timeless, the poem can both assume it and foreshadow it. The anticipations of the Crucifixion we have noted point to the external cause of regeneration (*Works*, XV, 377), the act by which the regenerate are absolved from sin and death through the satisfaction made by the Son (*Works*, XVI, 25). This external cause, the act of redemption, is the climax of Christ's ministry, during which he submits himself to divine justice in death, as well as life (*Works*, XV, 303). But the poem centres on one of the episodes that Milton cites as belonging to the first phase of the humiliation of Christ, his submission to divine justice in life. Touching on the act of redemption allusively and by anticipation, the poem concentrates on the internal condition, the condition that is the goal of that process of regeneration by which the inward man is 'regenerated by God after his own image, in all the faculties of his mind, insomuch that he becomes as it were a new creature.' (*Works*, XV, 367).[36] Although sinless himself, Jesus demonstrates what is involved in the destruction of the old man, and in the inward expression of the divine image. The poem, in Whichcote's language, is most obviously about Christ 'as a principle of divine life within us' rather than 'as a saviour without us,' about Christ the pattern of regeneration rather than about Christ the ransom for sin, although it does not neglect to make clear the way in which the first function is based on the second. At the close, then, it must be affirmed that the two aspects are closely integrated and finally unified, each being an expression of love. Only such love can save the world, the Son as the true mediator setting an example which is persuasive to both God and man.

The narrative of *Paradise Regained*, like that of the longer epic, reaches towards an event which lies outside the poem. In each epic the ending produces the sense that a successful beginning has been made, that the period to follow will be one of exertion and trial. The Son does not leave the impression that he is oriented towards death. He has demonstrated an awareness of the unity of his office, of the way his whole career, including his death, will establish his kingdom. The final emphasis is on his readiness to proceed with his work of teaching and illumination as he *begins* 'to save mankind' (4.635).

Notes

Index

Notes

Unless otherwise indicated, all citations of the poetry and prose of John Milton are from *The Works of John Milton*, gen ed Frank Allen Patterson (New York: Columbia University Press 1931-8), XVIII vols in 21. After prose citations the Columbia edition is signified by the abbreviation *Works*. I have cited the Columbia edition when referring to *De Doctrina Christiana* because it provides the Latin text opposite the translation, but I am throughout indebted to the translation and annotation in *The Complete Prose Works of John Milton*, vol VI, ed Maurice Kelley, trans John Carey (New Haven 1973). I have not reproduced the capitalization by which Milton and his editors draw attention to passages of definition in *De Doctrina Christiana*.

CHAPTER ONE

1 David Cairns, *The Image of God in Man* (London 1953, rev ed 1973), p 48
2 Ira Clark, 'Milton and the Image of God,' *JEGP* 68(1969), 431; for a seminal study of the idea of the image in *Paradise Lost*, see Cleanth Brooks, 'Eve's Awakening,' *Essays in Honour of Walter Clyde Curry* (Nashville 1965), pp 281-98; rpt *Milton*, ed Alan Rudrum (London 1968), pp 173-88.
3 A.S.P. Woodhouse, *The Heavenly Muse: A Preface to Milton*, ed Hugh MacCallum (Toronto 1972), pp 109-10
4 Milton is not given to name-dropping, but most of the authors to whom he refers in *De Doctrina* are men noted for careful and distinguished scholarship. Thus when dealing with a potentially radical topic, the abrogation of the law, he draws on the witness of Heironymus Zanchius, a pillar of Reformed thought (*Works*, XVI, 147).
5 Christopher Hill, *Milton and the English Revolution* (New York 1977), pp 462, 465
6 Ibid, p 85

7 Mary Ann Radzinowicz, *Toward 'Samson Agonistes': The Growth of Milton's Mind* (Princeton 1978), p 314

8 Hugh MacLean, 'Milton's *Fair Infant,*' *ELH* 24 (1957); rpt *Milton: Modern Essays in Criticism,* ed Arthur E. Barker (Oxford 1965), pp 27-8. See also Jackson I. Cope, 'Fortunate Falls as Form in Milton's "Fair Infant,"' *JEGP* 63 (1964), 660-74.

9 J.G. Broadbent, 'The Nativity Ode,' in *The Living Milton,* ed Frank Kermode (London 1960), p 23

10 J.H. Hanford, 'The Youth of Milton,' in *Studies in Shakespeare, Milton and Donne, by Members of the Department of English of the University of Michigan* (New York 1925), p 124

11 F.T. Prince in *The Italian Element in Milton's Verse* (Oxford 1954), p 63, notes that Milton's Petrarchan model for his verse form is a poem of 137 lines, but concludes that the brevity of Milton's effort may mean only that his talent did not function easily within the restrictions of such a stanza form.

12 On the use of Revelation in *At a Solemn Music,* see Ernest Sirluck, 'Milton's Idle Right Hand,' in *Milton Studies in Honor of Harris Francis Fletcher* (Urbana 1961), pp 153ff.

13 Northrop Frye, *Anatomy of Criticism: Four Essays* (Princeton 1957), pp 121-2. See also W.G. Madsen, 'The Voice of Michael in *Lycidas,*' *SEL* 3 (1963): 'we can see what the uncouth swain cannot see, that the fragmentary symbols of rebirth and immortality scattered throughout the pastoral landscape are gathered up into the perfect image of Christ and given significance only because He really did rise from the dead' (p 6).

14 Mother M. Christopher Pecheux, in the most suggestive study of the 'dread voice' to date, concludes that the speaker is 'a composite figure, an ideal shepherd and bishop, approximated most closely in the Old Testament by Moses and by Peter in the New – both, however, serving only as delegates of the supreme bishop, Christ, who embodies the mighty power of God.' 'The Dread Voice in *Lycidas,*' *Milton Studies* 9 (1976), 232. For the argument that the dread voice is that of Christ, not Peter, see Ralph Hone, ' "The Pilot of the Galilean Lake," ' *SP* 56 (1959), 55-61, and David Berkley, *'Inwrought with Figures Dim'* (The Hague 1974), pp 75ff. I consider it more suitable to the structure of the poem, as well as the symbolism of the passage, to view the speaker as a representative of Christ. He expresses the Son's powers of judgment and retribution, as Phoebus expresses the Son's powers of creation and divine life. Only with the pattern of death and resurrection in the third movement does the poem approach Christ the mediator.

15 The transformation of the swain has been observed by Donald M. Friedman in *'Lycidas:* The Swain's Paideia,' *Milton Studies* 3 (1971), 18.

16 Lynn Veach Sadler, in 'Regeneration and Typology: *Samson Agonistes* and Its Relation to *De Doctrina Christiana, Paradise Lost* and *Paradise*

Regained,' SEL 12 (1972), 141-56, discusses Samson as 'a type of regenerative religious experience responsive to God's ways as put to pattern in Christ' (p 156). Sadler argues that Samson makes his way to individual or prophetic liberty which is perceived by the Christian reader to be related to the liberty enjoyed under the Gospel.

17 See the discussion of the date of composition in Radzinowicz, *Toward 'Samson Agonistes,'* pp 387-407.

18 Tertullian, for example, who is mocked in *Of Prelaticall Episcopacy* (1641) for attempting 'to prove an imparity betweene *God* the Father, and *God* the Sonne. ... The Father is the whole substance, but the Son a derivation, and portion of the whole, as he himselfe professes because the Father is greater than me' (*Works*, III.i.97; see also *Of Reformation, Works*, III.i.10, 23, 25).

CHAPTER TWO

1 In *Toward 'Samson Agonistes'* (Princeton 1978), Mary Ann Radzinowicz has written with rare perception and accuracy of the way in which 'Milton's theology is progressive theology, a radical universal theology,' and his heresies are 'signs of augmented free religious speculation' (p 314). Agreeing with her assertion that Milton's heresies remain the clearest index by which to measure his theological independence, I find myself dissenting only when she argues that it is futile and unliterary to try to discover whether Milton's doctrine of the Son 'resembled the Christology of this or that group of earlier theologians.' Milton's heterodox ideas, *and* his more orthodox ones, can only be recognized for what they are in terms of the intellectual history of the age. To understand his doctrines, we must see them as he did, that is, in comparison with the ideas of the regenerate and developing audience for which he wrote.

2 'Quod si odit anima mea vocem homoousion, it nolim ea uti, non ero haereticus. Quis enim me coget uti, modo rem teneam, quae in Concilio per scripturas definita est?' Martin Luther, *Rationis Latomianae Confutatio*, in *Werke*, VIII (Weimar 1889), 117-18

3 Ian D. Kingston Siggins, *Martin Luther's Doctrine of Christ* (New Haven 1970), p 223

4 Ibid, pp 54ff

5 Ibid, pp 230ff

6 John M. Headley, *Luther's View of Church History* (New Haven 1963), p 185

7 See John T. McNeill, *The History and Character of Calvinism* (Oxford 1954, rpt 1977), pp 141ff; Philip Schaff, *History of the Christian Church*, VIII (New York, 1903), 351-2.

8 E.D. Willis, *Calvin's Catholic Christology* (Leiden 1966), p 122

9 McNeill, *Calvinism*, pp 176, 183

10 See J.I. Packer, 'Calvin the Theologian,' in *John Calvin*, ed G.E. Duffield (Grand Rapids, Michigan 1966), p 169.
11 John Calvin, *Institutes of the Christian Religion*, I, xiii. 1.21
12 Calvin, *Institutes*, I, xiii, 3, ed John T. McNeill, trans Ford Lewis Battles (Philadelphia 1960), p 124
13 Ibid, xiii, 2-6
14 Ibid, xiii, 7-15
15 Ibid, xiii, 18, ed McNeill, p 143
16 Ibid, xiii, 19, ed McNeill, p 144
17 Ibid, xiii, 25
18 Ibid, xiii, 23, ed McNeill, p 150
19 See Calvin's remarks on John 1:49 in *Calvin's Commentaries ... The Gospel According to St. John*, eds D.W. Torrence and Thomas F. Torrence, trans T.H.L. Parker, 2 vols (Grand Rapids, Michigan 1959), I, 43.
20 Siggins, *Luther's Doctrine of Christ*, p 48
21 Calvin, *Institutes*, II, xii, 1
22 Ibid, II, xii, 1, ed McNeill, p 464
23 Ibid, II, xiii, 4, p 481; see Willis, *Calvin's Catholic Christology*, pp 76-8
24 Calvin, *Institutes*, II, xiv, 1-3. See below, p 222.
25 See, for example, Calvin, *Institutes*, II, xvi, 12.
26 Ibid, II, xiv, 5, 7
27 Ibid, II, xiv-xvi
28 Ibid, II, xv, 5, ed McNeill, p 501
29 Ibid, II, xiv, 3
30 See Maurice Kelley, Introduction, *Christian Doctrine*, in *The Complete Prose Works of John Milton*, VI (New Haven 1973), 117-10. For an important reservation concerning the completion of *De Doctrina Christiana*, see Gordon Campbell, '*De Doctrina Christiana*: Its Structural Principles and Its Unfinished State,' *Milton Studies* 9 (1976), 243-60. His carefully reasoned argument concludes that the treatise as it now stands is 'almost complete: All that remained was the working out of an arrangement for the final chapters of Book I and a final revision to eliminate the theological discrepancies inevitably present in a work written "from time to time" over the course of many years' (p 253).
31 Calvin, *Institutes*, I, xiii, 24
32 Ibid, II, xii, 1-2
33 Ibid, I, xiii, 6
34 Ibid, II, xvi, 12, ed McNeill, p 520
35 Ibid, II, xvii, 6, ed McNeill, p 534
36 Heinrich Heppe, *Reformed Dogmatics Set Out and Illustrated from the Sources*, ed Ernst Bizer, trans G.T. Thomson (Great Britain 1950, rpt Grand Rapids, Michigan 1978), p 494; see Marvin P. Hoogland, *Calvin's Perspective on the Exaltation of Christ in Comparison with the Post-Reformation Doctrine of the Two States* (Kampen 1966), pp 61-8; 89-92.

37 Henry Bullinger, *The Decades*, trans H.I., ed Thomas Hardy (Cambridge 1951), III, 158-9; see also 243.
38 John Wollebius, *Compendium Theologiae Christianae*, in *Reformed Dogmatics*, ed and trans John W. Beardslee III (Oxford 1965; rpt Grand Rapids 1977), pp 41, 91, 113-4.
39 W.B. Hunter, 'Milton's Arianism Reconsidered,' *HTR* 52 (1959); rpt *Bright Essence*, ed W.B. Hunter, C.A. Patrides, J.H. Adamson (Salt Lake City 1971), pp 50-1
40 See Maurice Kelley, 'Milton's Arianism Again Considered,' *HTR* 53 (1960), 195ff, and *Complete Prose*, VI, 278-9, n 190.
41 Barbara Lewalski, *Milton's Brief Epic: The Genre, Meaning and Art of 'Paradise Regained'* (Providence, Rhode Island 1966), p 144
42 Bullinger, *Decades*, p 160
43 Woodhouse, *The Heavenly Muse* (Toronto 1972), p 169; Lewalski, *Brief Epic*, p 145
44 Lewalski, *Milton's Brief Epic*, p 145
45 Ibid, pp 145, 147
46 Kelley, *Complete Prose*, VI, 50.
47 No doubt Milton's doctrine of the Son will continue to be spoken of as displaying Arian tendencies in this general way. The question of whether his position approximates Arianism in a more particular sense of the term is still being explored. C.A. Patrides, firmly convinced that it does not do so, would abandon the term altogether. He lists eight areas of disagreement between Milton and the Arians, and concludes that the 'source' of Milton's subordinationism is not the Arian heresy but the Patristic writers prior to Nicea. 'Milton and Arianism,' *JHI* 25 (1964); rpt *Bright Essence*, pp 63-70. Yet some of these points of comparison and contrast in themselves raise issues of considerable difficulty about which Milton's views need interpretation, and one is left wondering whether the clear differences are sufficient to preclude Arian influences and affinities. A Platonist or a Marxist need not conform in all respects to his patron. Lewalski finds many striking similarities between Milton's theology of the Son and Arianism: the avoidance of the traditional metaphors of ray from light and stream from fountain; explicit denial of the eternity of the Son; explicit rejection of the emanationist theory; insistence that it consisted with the perfection of the Father's essence not to beget the Son; emphasis on the deliberate gift of divine attributes by the Father to the Son; the assumption that the Son is mutable and subject to change; emphasis on self-existence as an indispensable characteristic of deity and rejection of the idea that the Godhead can communicate its own essence; denial of the Son's omniscience. Of special significance is the fact that many of the views Milton shares with Arius serve to distinguish his position from that of the early Fathers. Thus his emphatic rejection of the emanation theory, which he sees as marked by the same kind of empty paradoxes that

characterize Trinitarian thought in general, and his insistence upon will and response in his description of the Son's subordinate relation to the Father, run counter to the tendency in the thought of the early Fathers to see the relation as inevitable. See Lewalski, *Milton's Brief Epic*, pp 146-7. Arian thus seems a term of real if limited use in the discussions of Milton's thought. There is no evidence that Milton would have called himself an Arian (such classification he repudiated by his insistence on the primacy of scripture in any case), but he would surely have recognized the Arian elements in his doctrine of the Son.

48 Kelley, *Complete Prose*, VI, 66

49 Henry Bullinger provides a useful contrast, for at point after point Milton reverses his arguments: 'For yet again he sayeth more plainly: "I and the Father are one": one, I say, not in concord or agreement, but in self sameness and being'; 'if he be the image of the invisible God, he must needs be fellow (or co-equal) with God'; 'he is called "the first-born" because he is Prince and Lord, not because he is reckoned among the creatures'; 'to be in the form (or shape) of God is nothing else than in all respects to be fellow (or equal) of God'; 'the Son is not Lord of the Holy Ghost; but the Lordship is common to the three Persons, which are only one Lord' (*Decades*, III, 244; 245; 245; 245; 304).

50 C.A. Patrides, 'An Open Letter on the Yale Edition of *De Doctrina Christiana*,' *Milton Q* 7 (1973), 74

51 See also *Works*, XIV, 275: '"To be in the form of God," therefore, seems to be synonymous with being in the image of God; which is often predicated of Christ, even as man is also said, though in a much lower sense, to be the image of God, and to be in the image of God, that is by creation.' The difference appears to be one of degree.

52 Patrides, 'Open Letter,' p 74

53 Milton's view of Christ has been seen as Nestorian by W.B. Hunter, 'Milton on the Incarnation: Some More Heresies,' *JHI* 21 (1960); rpt *Bright Essence*, pp 131-48. See chapter 6 below.

54 John Owen, *Of Communion with God: The Father, Sonne, and Holy Ghost, Each Person Distinctly, In Love, Grace and Consolation* (Oxford 1657), pp 257, 259

55 Calvin, *Institutes*, I, xiii, 14

56 Ibid, III, i, 1

57 Ibid, III, 1, 2

58 *The Racovian Catechism*, ed and trans Thomas Rees (London 1818), p 285; this chapter summary appears first in the Amsterdam edition of 1680; Milton, *De Doctrina Christiana*, *Works*, XIV, 365.

59 *The Racovian Catechism*, p 287ff; Milton, *Works*, XIV, 365; *Catechesis Ecclesiarum*, p 162ff

60 John Biddle, *A Confession of Faith Touching the Holy Trinity* (London 1648), p 51, in *The Apostolical and True Opinion concerning the Holy Trinity*

61 Ibid, p 23. Cf Milton, *De Doctrina Christiana, Works*, XIV, 377.

62 See Hunter, 'Milton's Arianism Reconsidered,' p 51.

63 Ralph Cudworth, *The True Intellectual System of the Universe* (London 1678), pp 547-8; see also Hunter, 'Milton's Arianism Reconsidered,' pp 44-5. The view that the heathen learned of the Trinity and other mysteries from the Jews was widespread. See, eg, William Pemble, *Vindiciae Fidei* (Oxford 1625), pp 69-70; Charles Leslie, *Theological Works* (London 1721), I, 244.

64 Cudworth, *The True Intellectual System*, p 606ff, and Henry More, *An Explanation of the grand Mystery of Godliness* (London 1660), p 456

65 More, *Mystery of Godliness*, p 454

66 More asks of his opponents (*Mystery of Godliness*, p 454), 'By what Faculty can they demonstrate, that the Divine Oracles should mention nothing to us but what is the adequate Object of our Understandings?' Milton might well have answered in the words of the Son in *Paradise Regained* (1.460-4): 'God hath now sent his living Oracle / Into the World, to teach his final will, / ... an inward Oracle / To all truth requisite for men to know.'

67 More, *Mystery of Godliness*, p 453

68 Ibid, p 454

69 John Biddle, *The Testimonies of Irenaeus, Justin Martyr, Tertullian, Novatianus, Theophilus, Origen, ... Arnobius, Lactantius, Eusebius, Hilary and Brightman; Concerning That One God, and the Persons of the Holy Trinity* (London), pp 84-6, in *The Apostolical and True Opinion concerning the Holy Trinity, revived and asserted; Partly by Twelve Arguments Levyed against the Traditional and False Opinion about the Godhead of the Holy Spirit: Partly by A Confession of Faith Touching the three Persons. Both which, having been formerly set forth in those years which the respective Titles bear, are now so altered, so augmented, what with explications of the Scripture, what with Reasons, what finally with Testimonies of the Fathers, and of others, together with Observations thereupon, that they may justly seem new* (London 1653).

70 John Biddle, *A Twofold Catechism ...* (London 1654), Preface

71 Ibid

72 Hunter, 'Milton's Arianism Reconsidered,' p 33

73 See, for example, M.A. Larsen, 'Milton and Servetus: A Study of Sources of His Theology,' *PMLA* 41 (1926), 891-934; Louis A. Wood, *The Form and Origin of Milton's Antitrinitarian Conception* (London, Ontario 1911).

74 Milton, *Defensio Secunda, Works*, VIII, 123

75 On the history of the *Racovian Catechism*, see H. John McLachlan, *Socinianism in Seventeenth-Century England* (Oxford 1951), and L.M. Oliver, 'An Early Socinian Publication in England,' *Harvard Library Bulletin* 7 (1953), 119-21. For Milton's mysterious but significant connection with the work, see J.M. French, *Life Records of John Milton*, under the following

dates: 10 Aug 1650; 27 Jan 1652; 5 Mar 1652; 2 April 1652; and the addition in V, 421.

76 The extent of Milton's familiarity with Socinianism is suggested by his use of a work by Josue De La Place (Placaeus of Saumur), a French theologian who was an opponent of the Socinian movement. In a treatise called *Disputationes de Testimoniis et Argumentis e Veteri Testament Petitis ...* (Saumur 1651), La Place draws upon contemporary debates and attempts to demonstrate that the doctrine of the Trinity is supported by passages in the Old Testament. Milton, in his discussion of those who 'revert from the gospel to the times of the law' in order to maintain the coessentiality of Father and Son, attacks several of the arguments put forward by La Place. He names his opponent three times and quotes directly from his work (*De Doctrina Christiana, Works*, XIV, 277ff). We thus find Milton consciously aligning himself with the Socinians in his attack on Trinitarian dogma.

77 See *The Racovian Catechism*, p 45; *Catechesis Ecclesiarum* (London 1651), p 35.

78 *The Racovian Catechism*, section IV, chapter 1; *Catechesis Ecclesiarum*, pp 38-100

79 See C.A. Patrides, 'Milton and the Protestant Theory of the Atonement,' *PMLA* 74 (1959), 7-13, and L.W. Grensted, *A Short History of the Doctrine of Atonement* (Manchester 1920)

80 '... that the Lord Jesus was the first of the things made in the old creation, even our opponents cannot admit, unless they would become Arians. They must therefore grant that he is one, and indeed the first, among the productions of the new creation.' *The Racovian Catechism*, pp 136-7; *Catechesis Ecclesiarum*, p 85

81 Milton's rejection of the Socinian doctrine extends to details of argument. When he explains that the Greek expressions for 'ranson' employed in the New Testament 'clearly denote the substitution of one person in place of another,' he is deliberately ruling out the Socinian view that 'ransom' is a highly metaphoric and rather vague term, and when he remarks that Christ's death pays the required price 'for, that is to say, instead of,' all mankind, he undoubtedly has in mind the Socinian claim that Christ dies, not instead of, but on account of, mankind. *Works*, XV, 317; see *The Racovian Catechism*, pp 315-16, 311; *Catechesis Ecclesiarum*, pp 183-4, 186.

82 It is in his preoccupation with reform and his exegetical methods that he most resembles the Socinians, and the citation of *Civil Power in Ecclesiastical Causes* in *[Panharmonia]* or the *Agreement of the People Revised*, a tract published in 1659 by a group of Gloucestershire Socinians, is witness to this relation (noted by A.S.P. Woodhouse, *The Heavenly Muse*, p 167). But Milton differs in certain crucial matters of doctrine from the Socinians, such as in his view of the pre-existence of the Son. And while he

shares positions with such figures as Episcopius of Amsterdam or Stanley Knowles in England, he is clearly working out his own position, rather than adopting the views of others. See W.B. Hunter, 'The Theological Context of Milton's *Christian Doctrine,*' in *Achievements of the Left Hand,* ed Michael Lieb and John T. Shawcross (Amherst 1974), p 282; see also Woodhouse, *The Heavenly Muse,* p 126. An element of subordinationism is of course not infrequent in the Puritan treatments of the relations between Father and Son. Boyd M. Berry remarks that the popular sermon fare of Milton's age 'offered plenty of examples of a loose, casual tendency to disregard the equality of Father and Son. That orthodox Puritan habit of mind was not, therefore, idiosyncratic to Milton nor did he have to dig back in dusty tomes to find models of what he thought.' *Process of Speech: Puritan Religious Writing and 'Paradise Lost'* (Baltimore 1976), p 224. But 'loose' and 'casual' do not describe Milton's clearly formulated position.

83 Packer, 'Calvin the Theologian,' p 161
84 Calvin, *Institutes,* III, ii, 24, ed McNeill, pp 570-1; see also III, xi, 10
85 Benjamin Whichcote, *Moral and religious aphorisms ... To which are added, Eight Letters: which passed between Dr. Whichcote ... and Dr. Tuckney,* ed Samuel Salter (London 1753), p 4
86 Whichcote, *Moral and religious aphorisms,* p 15
87 On the importance of this idea in Milton's theology, see Arthur Barker, *Milton and the Puritan Dilemma* (Toronto 1942), chapter 17.
88 Whichcote, *Moral and religious aphorisms,* pp124-5

CHAPTER THREE

1 Thus such a stalwart defender of reformed doctrine as John Owen can assert: 'Men may be really saved, by that Grace which Doctrinally they do deny; and they may be justified by the *Imputation of that Righteousness* which in opinion they deny to be imputed.' *The Doctrine of Justification by Faith Through the Imputation of the Righteousness of Christ* (London 1677), pp 228-9
2 John Toland, *Life,* in *Milton: The Critical Heritage,* ed John T. Shawcross (London 1970), p 120
3 William Warburton, letter iv to Thomas Birch, in *Milton 1732-1801: The Critical Heritage,* ed John T. Shawcross (London 1972), p 89
4 Charles Leslie, *The History of Sin and Heresy,* in *Theological Works,* I, 777-8; see *Milton:The Critical Heritage,* ed Shawcross, pp 117-18
5 John Dennis, 'The Grounds of Criticism in Poetry,' in *Milton: The Critical Heritage,* p 130
6 Daniel Defoe, *The Political History of the Devil,* in *The Novels and Miscellaneous Works of Daniel Defoe,* X (Oxford 1840), 68; see B. Eugene McCarthy, 'Defoe, Milton and Heresy,' *Milton N* 3 (1969), 71-3

7 Jonathan Richardson, *Explanatory Notes and Remarks on Milton's 'Paradise Lost,'* in *Milton 1732-1801*, ed Shawcross, p 84
8 'Philo-Spec,' in *Milton 1732-1801*, ed Shawcross, pp 93, 97
9 Thomas Newton, 'The Life of Milton,' in *Paradise Lost*, ed Newton (London 1749), I, lii-liii
10 Samuel Johnson, *Lives of the English Poets*, ed G.B. Hill, I, 155
11 *Milton 1732-1801*, ed Shawcross, p 25
12 Balachandra Rajan, *'Paradise Lost' and the Seventeenth-Century Reader* (London 1947), p 33
13 Ibid, p 25
14 Rajan, *'Paradise Lost' and the Seventeenth-Century Reader*, p 25; Allan Gilbert, 'Form and Matter in *Paradise Lost*, Book III,' in *Milton Studies in Honor of H.F. Fletcher* (Urbana 1961), p 53
15 David W.D. Dickson, 'Milton's "Son of God": A Study in Imagery and Orthodoxy,' *Papers of the Michigan Academy of Science, Arts and Letters* 36 (1950), 281
16 Rajan, *'Paradise Lost' and the Seventeenth-Century Reader*, p 25
17 Nat V. Daniel, Jr, 'The Theology of *Paradise Lost*, III, 183-4 Re-examined,' *Renaissance Papers 1963* (1964), p 29. Daniel finds a more rewarding path of exploration in his argument that Milton's handling of scripture displays his recognition that our knowledge of God is extremely limited. Daniel takes the lines on election in *Paradise Lost* 3.183-4 as an example of the poem's method:

> Some I have chosen of peculiar grace
> Elect above the rest; so is my will. ...

Milton, he argues, has purposely phrased the passage in which these lines occur in such a manner that its argument partakes of the complexities and ambiguities, as well as the phraseology, of its biblical parallels. Compressing everything the Bible says about election into the Father's speech, Milton refrains from providing a definitive interpretation, and thus 'he was able to capture the essential nature of the Bible in the words of his epic.' The poem asks the reader to think and to respond, but it does not always lead him to a particular conclusion. Biblical citation preserves the richness of the Bible itself, and places the burden of judgment on the reader.

But while Daniel's view catches the challenging nature of the poetry, it does not do justice to the quality of its beliefs. The Father's words on election, cited by Daniel, may be capable of a variety of interpretations, ranging from Arminian through moderate Calvinist to Calvinist, but there is one that is more persuasive than the others, more consistent with the evolving argument of the poem, as Daniel himself appears on the verge of recognizing, and that is the interpretation which sees that Milton's theory of the operation of grace includes the 'special calling' of the saints (p 27). This view is consistent with the treatment of grace and free

will throughout the poem and also in the theological treatise. 'Those
who receive it are called not only to salvation, but more important, to the
performance of some duty or office. Among those who have received it
are Abraham, Moses, Joshua, the twelve apostles, and St. Paul. In terms of
lines 183-4, those who receive God's special call are "elect above the
rest" because he has arbitrarily chosen them; and they have "peculiar
grace" because the call is so strong that they can scarcely fail to answer
it' (p 28). This is offered by Daniel as one *possible* interpretation, but it
agrees with what Milton says clearly in *De Doctrina, Works*, XIV, 147-
79; 'That an equal portion of grace should not be extended to all, is attributable to the supreme will of God alone; that there are none to whom he
does not vouchsafe grace sufficient for their salvation, is attributable to his
justice.' See Gary D. Hamilton, 'Milton's Defensive God,' *SP* 69 (1972),
97-8. See Also A. Barker, '*Paradise Lost*: The Relevance of Regeneration,'
in '*Paradise Lost': A Tercentenary Tribute*, ed B. Rajan (Toronto 1969), p
75.

18 Woodhouse, *The Heavenly Muse*, p 125. See also Mary Ann Radzinowicz,
Toward 'Samson Agonistes': The Growth of Milton's Mind (Princeton,
1978), p 284: 'The treatise gives a biblical theology of sifted and reconsti-
tuted scriptural doctrines; the poems give a biblical theology through the
God-man relationship dramatized in the scriptural narratives of both the
Old and New Testaments.'

19 John Owen, *Meditations and Discourses on the Glory of Christ in His
Person, Office and Grace* (London 1684), p 5

20 See Earl M. Wilbur, *A History of Unitarianism* (Cambridge 1952), p 251;
McLachlan, *Socinianism in Seventeenth-Century England*, chapters 16-
17. The author of 'An Impartial Account of the Word Mystery' in *The Faith
of One God* (London 1691) states the position forcibly: 'Divine Truth is
not hid in a Well, as *Democritus* saith: it is like a City standing upon a Hill,
which may be seen by all Men. Christ has brought all things to light, and
as the woman of *Samaria* speaks, *He has taught us all things*. He is called a
Word, not a *Silence*, his Gospel is a Revelation, not a Mystery' (p 13).

21 Allen Apsley, a royalist who prospered in the court of Charles II, provides a
good example of the topos as he embarks on his version of the creation
story in *Order and Disorder: or the World Made and Undone* (London
1679), p 4:

> Yet all the three, are but one God most High,
> One uncompounded, pure Divinity,
> Wherein subsist so, the Mysterious three,
> That they in Power and Glory equal be;
> Each doth himself, and all the rest possess
> In undisturbed joy and blessedness.
> There's no Inferior, nor no Later there,
> All Coeternal, all Coequal, are.

> And yet this Parity Order admits.
> The Father first, eternally begets,
> Within himself, his Son, substantial Word
> And Wisdom, as his second, and their third
> The ever blessed spirit is, which doth
> Alike eternally proceed from both.
> These three, distinctly thus, in one Divine,
> Pure, Perfect, Self-supplying Essence shine. ...

22 Donne, *Holy Sonnet XVI* (Gardner 12) 1.3

23 *Psyche: or Loves Mysterie in XX Cantos* (Cambridge 1702), XV, stanzas 311-12, p 242. Beaumont, in a manner similar to Milton's, speaks of the Son as 'enthron'd' by the Father ('Thron'd in highest bliss,' *Paradise Lost*, 3.305). Some few lines earlier, in stanza 305, the Father embraces the Son and greets him as follows:

> Come, come, said He, no more to part from hence;
> My highest *Will* thou hast completely done,
> And by perfection of *Obedience*
> Approv'd thy worthy Self *my only Son.* (p 242)

This sounds like the Father's description of the Son as 'By Merit more then Birthright Son of God' (3.309). Beaumont's poem was first published in 1648, and could have been known to Milton. Beaumont holds a traditional conception of the Trinity, yet dramatizes the return of the Son in a manner that suggests an earned Godhead. Such an emphasis is natural when a son returns in triumph to a father. However, it fits less well with Beaumont's Trinitarian views than with Milton's subordinationism.

24 Gilbert, 'Form and Matter in *Paradise Lost*, Book III,' p 54

25 Edward Benlowes, *Theophila*, VII, stanzas 64-5, in *Minor Poets of the Caroline Period*, ed George Saintsbury (Oxford 1905), I, 386. The three, however, are paradoxically on one throne. Benlowes revels in the paradoxes of the Trinity through canto VII. The language occasionally echoes Milton, and one is reminded of the *Nativity*, and of Milton's early Trinitarianism, by the following:

> There God in Essence, one in
> Persons Three!
> Here Nature's two in One agree!
> > Thou, sitting in the midst of Trinal-Unity
> > At Heav'ns high council-table. ... (p 386)

On the influence of Milton on Benlowes, see W.R. Parker, *Milton: A Biography* (Oxford 1968), I, 411; II, 1008.

26 Beaumont, *Psyche*, stanza 107, p 95. In stanzas 90-1 Beaumont compares the action of the Holy Spirit at the creation of the world to its action at the conception of Jesus.

27 Kelley, *This Great Argument* (Princeton 1941), p 109

28 See Williams, *The Common Expositor* (Chapel Hill, North Carolina 1948), pp 67-8. Augustine states the view firmly, finding in Genesis 1:26 evidence

that 'the image of the Trinity was made in man, that in this way men should be the image of the one true God ...' *On the Trinity,* in *The Works of Aurelius Augustine,* ed M. Dods (Edinburgh, 1873), VII, 289. Calvin rejects Augustine's speculations concerning the image of the Trinity as too refined, but affirms that Christians properly contend from the testimony of the passage that there is a plurality of persons in the Godhead. *Commentary upon the Book of Genesis,* trans John King (Edinburgh 1847), I, 91-3.

29 Francelia Butler has shown how odours accompany the acts of divinity in *Paradise Lost;* Milton's use of this symbolism invites comparison with the practice of such contemporaries as George Herbert and Henry Vaughan. She concludes that Milton found odours 'an ideal metaphor to explain the presence or absence of God, as manifest in his fragrant and creative breath, the Holy Spirit.' 'The Holy Spirit and Odors in *Paradise Lost,'* *Milton N* 3 (1969), 68. This is a useful conclusion, but we should understand by the Holy Spirit not the third person of the Trinity but simply the power and virtue of the Father operating through the Son or some other channel. Her examples are in keeping with this interpretation – the fragrances of Eden or of heaven, the odour of the oil used to anoint the Son, the fragrance of prayer. While possessing a particular intimacy, odour is of course only one of the modes by which the divine presence is expressed. Such presence is often associated with vision or voice, as in the appeal to the Muse in the invocation to book 3, or in the celebrations in heaven following the creation (7.599). Odour does not seem to be the particular emblem of the action of the Spirit; light and sound are of primary importance, and fragrance generally provides supporting imagery, along with references to sweetness and warmth. This is in keeping with the language of the chapter on the Holy Spirit in *De Doctrina Christiana,* where the image of Spirit as creative breath is touched upon (*Works,* XIV, 359), but not that of odour, and where the important manifestations of Spirit take the forms of light and sound. It is worth observing also that while fragrance plays some part in the imagery of Michael's history of the world – as in the opening scene in which Abel's sacrifice 'with Incense strew'd' is consumed in 'grateful steame' by fire from heaven (11.439-42) – nonetheless the transition from flesh to spirit leads to a recognition of the inward nature of the divine presence. In book 12 the person of the Holy Spirit, the Comforter, is introduced with little sensuous imagery and none of fragrance, although it is with the assistance of the Spirit that the regenerate will achieve the paradise within.

30 Two passages from book 8 also suggest Milton's anti-trinitarianism, and both, as Kelley has shown (*Complete Prose,* VI, 110), are of particular interest because of their close relation to passages in *De Doctrina.* One occurs when Adam reports to Raphael how God described himself as

alone
From all Eternitie, for none I know
Second to me or like, equal much less. (8.405-7)

The second passage occurs in Adam's reply to the divine presence, when he observes that the Almighty needs no companion because he is perfect in himself:

> No need that thou
> Shouldst propagat, already infinite;
> And through all numbers absolute, though One. ... (8.419-21)

The first passage is very close to Milton's argument in *De Doctrina Christiana* concerning the first and greatest commandment, that God is *one* (*Works*, XIV, 49-51). Milton's discussion of this attribute in book 1, chapter 2, prepares the way, as he points out, for his treatment of the Son as subordinate in chapter 5. The second passage echoes the argument against the eternal generation of the Son in *De Doctrina Christiana*, an important argument in which Milton decides that the generation of the Son occurred within the limits of time and at the will of the Father (*Works*, XIV, 187-9). The two passages establish an undeniable connection with the prose treatise. There is some difficulty in ascertaining their implications for the treatment of God in the poem, however, since the divine presence with whom Adam converses is not identified explicitly as the Father, and both verse passages can be interpreted as having reference to the creation of the world, rather than of the Son.

31 Dennis, *The Grounds of Criticism in Poetry*, in *Critical Works*, ed E.N. Hooker (Baltimore 1939), pp 144-5

32 See John Calvin, *Institutes of the Christian Religion*, II, xii, 7, ed John T. McNeill, trans Ford Lewis Battles (Philadelphia 1960), p 472: 'in so far as he is God's eternal Word he is "the first-born of all creation" [Col.1:15]. This is not because he was created or ought to be numbered among the creatures, but because the world ... had no other origin but him.'

33 Patrides, 'Open Letter,' *Milton Q* 9 (1973), 74

34 Woodhouse, review of *A Study of Milton's 'Christian Doctrine'* by A. Sewell, *MLR* 34 (1939), 595; see Kelley, *Complete Prose*, VI, 110.

35 See *Eclectic Review* ns 25 (1826), 17, cited Kelley, *Complete Prose*, VI, 112, n 58.

36 As Fowler remarks in his note on *Paradise Lost* 6.679 in *The Poems of John Milton*, ed John Carey and Alastair Fowler (London 1968).

37 Marvin P. Hoogland, *Calvin's Perspective on the Exaltation of Christ in Comparison with the Post-Reformation Doctrine of the Two States* (Kampen 1966), p 190

38 Calvin, *Institutes*, II, xvi, 15, ed McNeill, p 524; see also II, xiv, 15, and xv, 5.

39 Ibid, II, xiv, 3

40 Ibid, II, xiii, 4, ed McNeill, p 481

41 Dickson, 'Milton's "Son of God," ' p 276; J.H. Adamson, 'Milton's Arianism,' *HTR* 52 (1959); rpt *Bright Essence*, p 54

42 'The generating flame is coeval with the light which it generates: the gen-

erating flame does not precede in time the generated light; but from the moment the flame begins, from that moment the light begins. Show me flame without light, and I will show thee God the Father without Son.' *On the Gospel of St. John*, in *Works*, ed Marcus Dods, X (Edinburgh 1873), 291; cited Dickson, 'Milton's "Son of God," ' p 279; see also the passage from Origen cited as providing a parallel to Milton's invocation to light by Adamson, 'Milton's Arianism,' p 54: "[the Son] is as eternal and everlasting as the brilliancy which is produced from the sun.'

43 John Tombes, *Emmanuel; Or, God-Man* (London 1669), p 105. For a modern interpretation of Milton's symbolism, see William Kerrigan, *The Sacred Complex* (Cambridge, Massachusetts 1983), p 186: 'Milton's Son is somehow his Father's Eve, receiver and reflector of his phallus of light ... this is one of the radical fantasies varied in *Paradise Lost*: the father inseminating the son; the son as mother, materializer.'

44 Kelley, *This Great Argument*, pp 29-30

45 Stella Purce Revard, 'The Dramatic Function of the Son in *Paradise Lost*: A Commentary on Milton's Trinitarianism,' *JEGP* 66 (1967), 46; John A. Clair, 'A Note on Milton's Arianism,' in *Essays and Studies in Language and Literature*, ed Herbert H. Petit (Pittsburgh 1964), p 45. Robert J. Wickenheiser, in 'Milton's "Pattern of a Christian Hero": The Son in *Paradise Lost*,' *Milton Quarterly* 12 (1978), 1-9, argues that 'the Son grows by responding properly to situations seemingly almost staged by his Father, and with each situation must be seen to be moving one step nearer to becoming "divine love" fulfilled and consequently to acting, as he finally does, in his own right and with full cognizance of who he is' (p 3).

46 Milton does not appear to be directly indebted to anyone for this scene, for no exact parallel has been found. See Stella Purce Revard, *The War in Heaven* (Ithaca 1980), p 78. Charles Leslie, that staunch opponent of deism and Socinianism, felt the scene to be a strained and wayward invention, and suggested that the most likely cause of the angels' rebellion is to be found in their envy of the Incarnation: 'they cou'd not believe the incarnation cou'd be meant literally by God, as being unworthy his greatness and so vast a diminution of his majesty, to empty himself into the basest of the order of Spirits, and mingle infinite with Flesh and Blood: and therefore argued against it; not knowing that true power and sovereignity are in the conquests of love, which delights to condescend itself, and advance others.' *Theological Works*, I, 781. Yet as Arnold Williams has demonstrated, Milton's interpretation of the fall of Satan is closer to the view of Leslie than to the more commonly accepted interpretation in which Satan falls from pride rather than envy. The view that Satan fell from envy of man or of the Incarnation stems from the medieval *Vita Adamae et Evae*, and enjoyed some popularity among literary men in the seventeenth century. See Williams, 'The Motivation of Satan's Rebellion in *Paradise Lost*,' *SP* 42 (1945); rpt *Milton*, ed Alan Rudrum (London 1968), pp 137, 146.

In Valmarana's poem *Demonomachiae* (1623), the serious use made of
the motive of envy is emphasized by the subtitle, *The Battle of the Angels
over the Incarnation,* as Grant McColley has pointed out in *'Paradise
Lost': An Account of Its Growth and Major Origins,* (Chicago 1940), p 33.
Closer to home, Thomas Heywood in *Hierarchie of the blessed Angells,*
reflecting on the way in which the Incarnation is founded on God's eternal
decree, writes that

This Grace showne
Unto Mankinde, was to the Angels knowne;
That such a thing should be they all expected,
Not knowing how or when't would be effected.

It is this knowledge which in Heywood's treatment provides the motive for
the rebellion of Lucifer:

Ambitiously his Hate encreasing still,
Dares to oppose the great Creators Will:
As holding it against his Justice done,
That th'Almighties sole begotten Sonne,
Mans nature to assume purpos'd and meant.
And not the Angels, much more excellent.

The Hierarchie of the blessed Angells, their Names, orders, and Offices,
(London 1635), p 339. Other writers employing this view who are identi-
fied by Williams include Zanchius, Andreini, Joseph Beaumont, and Joost
Von Vondel.

47 Leslie, *Theological Works,* I, 777-8; see *Milton: The Critical Heritage,* ed
Shawcross, pp 117-18.

48 See John Wollebius, *The Abridgment of Christian Divinitie,* trans and
enlarged by Alexander Ross (London 1650): 'Christ is the Mediator of
Angels and men, but not after the same manner; for he is Mediator to those
in respect of their gracious union with God, but of these in respect of
reconciliation and redemption' (p 104). On the importance of the similarities between the begetting and the incarnation of the Son, see Albert C.
Labriola, '"Thy Humiliation Shall Exalt": The Christology of *Paradise
Lost,' Milton Studies* 15 (1981), 29-42. Stevie Davies, in *Images of Kingship in 'Paradise Lost'* (Columbia 1983), pp 172-84, notes that Satan's rejection of the Father figure is evident in the way the language of sonship
and family love appears in his conversation only as parody.

49 Sir Herbert Grierson, *Milton and Wordsworth: Poets and Prophets* (Cambridge 1937), p 99. Some such distinction is frequently made by those
commenting on Psalm 2:7 and its citation in the New Testament. The
notion that the generation of the Son was made manifest by an outward
act on a particular occasion was adopted by such commentators as John
Calvin, John Owen, and Henry Hammond. It is frequently assumed by
translators of the Psalms, as can be seen in the treatment of Psalm 2 by
Sternhold and Hopkins, which identifies the Son as Christ and implies

that his begetting is his assertion of kingship. Stevie Davies, in *Images of Kingship*, pp 142-3, stresses that the proclamation is a ceremony of kingly anointing, and draws attention to the way Milton emphasized kingly exaltation in his translation of Psalm 2, the royal Psalm used in Hebrew coronation ritual.

50 Revard, *The War in Heaven*, pp 75-8
51 Calvin, *Commentary on the Psalms*, 2: 6-7, trans James Anderson (Grand Rapids, Michigan 1949) I, 17-18
52 William Perkins, *An Exposition of the Symbole or Creed of the Apostles* (Cambridge 1595), p 137. See also H. Hammond, *A Paraphrase and Annotations Upon the Books of the Psalms* (London 1659), p 16.
53 John Owen, *An Exposition of the Two First Chapters of the Epistle of Paul the Apostle, unto the Hebrews*, in *Excercitations on the Epistle to the Hebrews* (London 1668), p 80. Stella Revard notes that for John Owen there is a variety of acceptable opinion concerning the occasion being commemorated in Psalm 2:6-7, and that Calvin views the begetting as having to do with Christ's relationship to us, as an outward begetting serving as a metaphor signifying that Christ is the Father's agent and his head ambassador. 'Satan's Envy of the Kingship of the Son of God: A Reconsideration of *Paradise Lost*, Book 5, and Its Theological Background,' *MP* 70 (1973), 193-4. Owen in *Exercitations on the Epistle to the Hebrews ... the Two First Chapters* (London 1668) is willing to refer the begetting of Psalm 2:7 to the Son's Incarnation, baptism, resurrection, or ascension (p 80). While he does not specify a scene like that in *Paradise Lost* 5.600, he does view Hebrews 1:5 as asserting the Son's 'Exaltation and Preheminence above Angels.' Owen was a strong opponent of Socinian views, and insists that the Son was generated from eternity, even though in Acts 13:33 that generation is taken 'only declaratively ... in his Resurrection and Exaltation' (p 80). When combating heresy directly, Owen uses Psalm 2:7 to emphasize the unique character of the Son of God, who unlike the angels or men is the natural Son of God by eternal generation. *Vindiciae Evangelicae* (Oxford 1655), p 238. He was deeply suspicious of Grotius, whose *Annotations* fed the Socinian heresy by taking Psalm 2 to be about David rather than the Son. Like many Reformation commentators, he wished to place the modern interpretation by which the verse refers to the Son's exaltation within a context that recognizes his eternal generation (see, for example, the annotations of Henry Ainsworth, 1627, and Henry Hammond, 1659). Milton adopted the idea of successive exaltations without believing in the eternal generation of the Son.
54 Kelley, *This Great Argument*, p 105
55 Calvin, *Institutes*, II, xii, 1, ed McNeill, p 465. The idea that Christ was from the beginning of the creation a mediator because he held primacy over the angels is developed by Calvin in his *Responsum ad Fratres Polonos* (1560).

56 The idea that the Son was always a mediator was a commonplace: 'It is demaunded,' notes Zacharias Ursinus in *The Summe of Christian Religion*, trans Henry Parry (Oxford 1601), '*Whether Adam had need of a Mediator before his fall?* Answere is to be made by distinguishing of the divers meanings and significations of a Mediator. If a Mediator be ment to be such a one, *through whose mediation, or by whome God doth bestow his benefits, and communicate himselfe unto us*, Adam verely even before his fall had neede of a Mediator, because Christ ever was that person, by whome God the Father createth and quickeneth al things ...' (p 212).

57 Austin C. Dobbins rejects Kelley's suggestion that Milton indulged in 'theological fiction' and argues that 'to Milton, the view that Christ was exalted literally in heaven, before the beginning of time, was a serious statement of theological truth.' *Milton and the Book of Revelation* (Alabama 1975), p 5. This strikes me as true, but when Dobbins proceeds to argue that the exaltation of the Son before the creation of the world is not metaphorical but literal (p 14), I think he confuses the distinction Milton is concerned to draw. The evidence suggests that the scene of begetting at 5.600ff is not the literal or real generation of the Son, but that the word 'begot' (*gignere* rather than *generare*) is used figuratively to denote the calling into being of a new relationship, just as by a similar figure of speech, but in a much lower sense, the saints are said to be begotten of God (*Works*, XIV, 185). At the begetting the Son is anointed as Messiah and King. Embosomed first in the dazzling glory of the Father, the Word is now manifested to the angels in his filial and regal nature, sitting at the Father's right hand. Certainly this is a real event, and in this sense literal, but the begetting is of a metaphorical kind. The literal begetting of the Son (*generare*) occurred before the opening of Milton's story.

58 It is also necessary to emphasize that in the poetry these occasions of exaltation are distinct from each other. W.B. Hunter, who brings out in brilliant fashion the similarity of such occasions, tends to neglect their distinctiveness. Hunter's resolution of the dilemma raised by the placing of the exaltation is to say that the Son was first begotten metaphorically in eternity, then actually in time. The whole account of the begetting of the Son in *Paradise Lost* is thus an enormous metaphor. 'The War in Heaven: The Exaltation of the Son,' *ELH*, 36 (1969); rpt *Bright Essence*, p 124. The difficulty with this view is that unless some qualification is introduced it prevents us from distinguishing among the various moments of divine history. The begetting of the Son merges with his victory over the rebels in book 6 and his acceptance of the role of mediator in book 3. This is to deny to the Son a gradually unfolding 'career,' and it is precisely such a progress which is implied by the history of his triumphs. Each triumph is discriminated from the next, although they are also complementary and cumulative. While there is a close relation

between the begetting of the Son as Messiah of the angels in book 5, and the celebration of his anticipated exaltation as the Messiah of mankind in 3, the two events occur in remarkably different contexts, the one before the creation of the world, the other as a response to the foreknowledge of man's fall. At the time of the Son's elevation over the angels, the problem resolved by his later acceptance of the mediatorial office has not yet arisen. While all time may be as one moment in the vision of God, there *is* time and real history in heaven, as Raphael points out to Adam (5.580-3). This is not to deny the typological and anticipatory elements in the narrative, more examples of which are well presented by Gerald J. Schiffhorst, 'Patience and the Humbly Exalted Heroism of Milton's Messiah: Typological and Iconographic Background,' *Milton Studies* 16 (1982), 97-113.

59 The poem repeatedly reminds us that the begetting occurs at a particular time – 'This day' (5.603). This conforms to the argument of *De Doctrina*, where it is said that the begetting takes place 'within the limits of time' (*Works*, XIV, 189). The engaging suggestion has been made by J. Douglas Canfield that when the Father says 'This day I have begot whom I declare / My onely Son,' we are intended to realize that 'This day' is the anniversary of the literal begetting, a day when the Son's coming of age is to be celebrated by something like a coronation. In this way the Father's phrase can 'refer to both the metaphoric and the literal generation Milton delineates in *De Doctrina Christiana*,' *ELN* 13 (1975), 114. This interpretation assumes that when Raphael speaks of 'such day / As Heavn's great Year brings forth' he means that the day marks the end of an era – 'such a day as is brought forth by the completion of heaven's great year.' It is more probable, I think, that the passage means simply that the day is representative of the days of eternity – 'such a day as is characteristic of time in eternity' (as in 'Tears such as Angels weep,' 1.620). This interpretation is strengthened, I believe, by the fact that the text at line 582 reads 'such day,' and not 'such a day.' The passage is one of the first in which the angel, likening spiritual to corporeal forms, shows Adam that earth is but the shadow of heaven. This interpretation also suits the behaviour of the angels, who do not appear to have expected a birthday party and need to be summoned, and of Satan, who is surprised and outraged. Milton emphasizes *this day* because he wants the scene to be a manifestation of the absolute freedom of the Father, whose will is not conditioned by any predetermined pattern and who acts at his own pleasure.

60 For the identification of the biblical passages employed by Milton in the two scenes, I am indebted to James H. Sims, *The Bible in Milton's Epics* (Gainsville, Florida 1962) pp 262, 264.

61 For another view of the separation of the two events, see Edmund Creeth, 'The "Begetting" and the Exaltation of the Son,' *MLN* 76 (1961), 696-700.

62 William Empson, *Milton's God* (London 1965), p 97

63 For a valuable account of the 'transfusions' of power from Father to Son and the Puritanic modes of expression see Boyd M. Berry, *Process of Speech*, chapter 15. Berry considers that the Son is 'cast in the mold of a Puritan hero, even though he is, quite clearly, not an earthly hero' (p 224).

64 Leland Ryken, *The Apocalyptic Vision in 'Paradise Lost'* (Ithaca, New York 1970), p 171; also see Ryken's article 'Milton's Dramatization of the Godhead in *Paradise Lost*,' *Milton Q* 9 (1975), 1-6.

65 An illuminating parallel to this pattern of divine action can be found in the prose of *De Doctrina Christiana*, not in chapter vii on the creation, but rather in chapter v on the Son, where Milton is dealing with biblical passages which may be applied to both Father and Son, although on different grounds: 'There is still greater doubt respecting the reading in I Tim. iii.16. "God was manifest in the flesh". ... The whole passage must be understood of God the Father in conjunction with the Son. ... Why ... should God the Father not be in Christ through the medium of all those offices of reconciliation which the apostle enumerates in this passage of Timothy? "God was manifest in the flesh"; namely, in the Son, his own image; in any other way he is invisible: nor did Christ come to manifest himself, but his Father. ... he who was in the Son from the beginning, after reconciliation had been made, returned with the Son into glory, or was received into that supreme glory which he had obtained in the Son.' *Works*, XIV, 265-7. In a similar manner, the Father acts through the Son at the creation, as is clear from the angels' hymn as well as the whole preceding narrative.

66 Revard, 'The Dramatic Function of the Son in *Paradise Lost*,' p 46

67 Northrop Frye, *The Return to Eden* (Toronto 1965), pp 113, 112, 111

68 John E. Parish, 'Milton and an Anthropomorphic God,' *SP* 56 (1959), 619-25. Milton's use and transformation in the council of the patriarchal examples of intercession has also been studied by M. Lieb, '*Paradise Lost*, Book III: The Dialogue in Heaven Reconsidered,' *Ren P* 1974 (1975), 39-50.

69 See Randel Helms, ' "His Dearest Mediation": The Dialogue in Heaven in Book III of *Paradise Lost*,' *Milton Q* 5 (1971), 52-7. Kitty Cohen has also noted Hebraic elements in the council, and particularly in the picture of God as the powerful Creator and God of Justice who is certain of victory over his enemies but who displays paternal care for his devoted believers, such as Abraham and Moses. The Son, too, can be viewed through the patriarchal prototype in whom 'love of justice and mercy are fused with a boundless devotion to God.' Cohen, 'Milton's God in Council and War,' *Milton Studies* 3 (1971), 165

70 M.Y. Hughes, 'The Filiations of Milton's Celestial Dialogue,' in *Ten Perspectives on Milton* (New Haven 1965), p 116

71 John Evans, *'Paradise Lost' and the Genesis Tradition* (Oxford 1968), pp 235-6

72 The style of the heavenly dialogue has been much discussed. The speeches
of the Father are generally admitted to be more direct, logical and dispassionate than the poetry of the preceding books. The Father develops his
argument through assertions couched in language suggestive of the Bible.
This relatively plain style has its own authority, an authority which is
enhanced by contrast with the corrupt rhetoric of Satan: Milton's God,
as Anthony Low observes, avoids enslaving his hearers to persuasive rhetoric because 'as he so often states, he wants to be loved and served freely.'
Anthony Low, 'Milton's God: Authority in *Paradise Lost,' Milton Studies*
4 (1972), 26. See also Jackson Cope, *The Metaphoric Structure of 'Paradise Lost'* (Baltimore 1962), p 170; Gilbert, 'Form and Matter in *Paradise
Lost*, Book III,' p 50; Stanley Fish, *Surprised by Sin: The Reader in
'Paradise Lost'* (Berkeley 1967), p 75; G.E. Miller, 'Stylistic Rhetoric and
the Language of God in *Paradise Lost*, Book III,' *Lang and S* 8 (1975),
111-26; Peter Berek, ' "Plain" and "Ornate" Styles in the Structure of *Paradise Lost,' PMLA* 85 (1970), 237-46.

73 See Arthur Barker, 'Structural and Doctrinal Pattern in Milton's Later
Poems,' in *Essays in English Literature*, ed Millar Maclure and F.W.
Watt (Toronto 1964), p 185.

74 Irene Samuel, '*Paradise Lost*: The Dialogue in Heaven,' *PMLA* 72 (1957);
rpt *Milton: Modern Essays in Criticism*, ed Arthur Barker (New York
1965), p 235

75 Ibid, pp 235-6

76 Gary Hamilton, 'Milton's Defensive God,' *SP* 69 (1972), 97. See also Christopher Hill, *Milton and the English Revolution* (New York 1977), pp
275-6

77 See Ernest Sirluck, '*Paradise Lost*': A Deliberate Epic* (Cambridge 1967),
p 21

78 Owen, *The Glory of Christ*, p 83

79 Joan Webber, 'Milton's God,' *ELH* 40 (1973), 526. As St Augustine remarked, in a passage used by Calvin, God 'knew how, at the same time,
to hate in each one of use what we had made, and to love what he had
made.' Cited from *In Joannis evangelium tractatus*, CX, 6, by Calvin in
Institutes, II, xvi, 4, ed McNeil, p 507

80 Barker, '*Paradise Lost*: The Relevance of Regeneration,' pp 68, 69

81 Owen, *The Glory of Christ*, p 123

82 The Son knows that he 'shall not long / Lie vanquisht' by death (3.242-3),
but imagines himself returning 'long absent' with the 'multitude of my
redeemd' (260-1). The Father agrees that this apocalyptic moment of renewal will be after the 'tribulations long' of the Saints (336), but to the
Son speaks only of 'loosing thee awhile.' It is the Father who points to the
Resurrection as a separate event from the final renewal of all things
(296ff), and explains the subsequent role of the Son by reference to the
exaltation of his manhood to 'this Throne' (314). The Son's view of

history is general and condensed; it is the Father who points to the difference between the Resurrection and the second coming.

83 John Owen, meditating on the doctrine of the gathering of all things into the Son, speaks of it with fervour: 'Who can express the Divine beauty, order and harmony of all things that are in this their *Recapitulation* in Christ? ... One view by Faith of him in the place of God as the supreme head of the whole Creation, moving, acting, guiding and disposing of it, will bring in spiritual refreshment unto a believing Soul.' It is just such a glimpse that the Father provides, and the effect is exhilarating. Owen, *Glory of Christ*, p 167. According to Owen, the two families of angels and men will be gathered 'into one, and that under a new head, in whom the one part should be preserved from sinning, and the other delivered from sin committed' (p 163).

84 Desmond M. Hamlet urges that there is fundamentally no validity to the conclusion that justice belongs to the Father and mercy to the Son: 'in *Paradise Lost*, both what is generally regarded as God's justice and also what is usually thought to be His mercy belong *both* to the Father and to the Son. Moreover, what is generally regarded as God's justice (that is, His anger, His wrath, and His punishment of evil) is as much a part of the person and function of the Son as is God's mercy or love. For, in the last analysis, the Son of God in *Paradise Lost* is the justice (or righteousness) of God ...' *One Greater Man: Justice and Damnation in 'Paradise Lost'* (Lewisburg 1976), p 136. Hamlet demonstrates that God's justice should not be seen strictly and exclusively as an instrument of his wrath, and provides a useful context in which to understand Milton's identification of justice with righteousness (and even, according to Hamlet, love). While God's justice has a restorative and liberating aspect, however, the process by which it is fulfilled involves the recognition that it may also be contrasted with mercy so that its retributive and distributive aspects are made plain. Justice as a principle or order prepares the way for the comprehension of justice by love, as the law prepares for the Gospel.

85 See W.B. Hunter, 'The Obedience of Christ in *Paradise Regained*,' in *Calm of Mind* (Cleveland 1971), p 71 and 'The War in Heaven: The Exaltation of the Son,' *Bright Essence*, p 122; see also Dennis Berthold, 'The Concept of Merit in *Paradise Lost*,' *SEL* 15 (1975), 163.

86 Helms, in ' "His dearest Mediation": The Dialogue in Heaven,' p 52, remarks that here God reveals his plans 'through a righteous intercessor's rise to greatness before the Mercy Seat.'

87 As Arthur Barker has emphasized, this is a state which is 'the equivalent for the Son, of Christian liberty, as the process is the equivalent of the renovating process that will follow upon willing response to calling.' 'Structural and Doctrinal Pattern in Milton's Later Poems,' *Essays in English Literature*, p 186

88 John Owen, *Vindiciae Evengelicae; or The Mystery of the Gospel Vindicat-*

ed and Socinianisme Examined (Oxford 1655), p 568. McLachlan notes that Owen undertook this work at the request of the Council of State in reply to John Biddle's *Scripture Catechism. Socinianism in Seventeenth-Century England*, p 129
89 Richard Baxter, *The Divine Life: in Three Treatises* (London 1664), pp 91-2

CHAPTER FOUR

1 Calvin, *Institutes*, I, i, 1-3, ed John T. McNeill, trans Ford Lewis Battles (Philadelphia 1960), 35-9
2 C.S. Lewis, *A Preface to 'Paradise Lost'* (London 1942; rpt 1954), p 112; A.J.A. Waldock, *'Paradise Lost' and Its Critics* (Cambridge 1947; rpt 1966), pp 22-3; E.M.W. Tillyard, 'The Crisis in *Paradise Lost*,' in *Studies in Milton* (London 1951), pp 8-13; Millicent Bell, 'The Fallacy of the Fall in *Paradise Lost*,' *PMLA* 68 (1953), 863-83; for a different view of potential evil in Milton's picture of the state of innocence, see A. Bartlett Giamatti, *The Earthly Paradise and the Renaissance Epic* (Princeton 1966), chapter 6.
3 Augustine, *The City of God*, in *The Works of Aurelius Augustine*, ed Marcus Dods, II (Edinburgh 1872), 21. Augustine recognized that there was a secret and private declension of man's will before the public act of eating the fruit. His usual emphasis, however, is on the equanimity of unfallen happiness (XIV, xxvi). See John Evans, *'Paradise Lost' and the Genesis Tradition* (Oxford 1968), pp 93-4. Luther's *Lectures on Genesis* offer a closer parallel to Milton's views in their emphasis on the vigour and growth of Adam before the Fall: 'Paul ... teaches [1 Corinthians 15:45], that even if Adam had not sinned, he would still have lived a physical life in need of food, drink, rest. He would have grown, procreated, etc., until he would have been translated by God to the spiritual life in which he would have lived without any animal qualities ...' *Luther's Works*, ed Jaroslav Pelikan, I (Saint Louis 1958), 86. On Milton and Luther, see A.G. George, *Milton and the Nature of Man* (Bombay 1974), pp 43ff.
4 A.S.P. Woodhouse, *The Heavenly Muse*, ed Hugh MacCallum (Toronto, 1972), pp. 241, 258-60; Arthur Barker, 'Milton's Later Poems,' in *Essays in English Literature from the Renaissance to the Victorian Age*, ed M. MacLure and F.W. Watt (Toronto 1964), p 189. See also Barbara Lewalski, 'Innocence and Experience in Milton's Eden,' in *New Essays on 'Paradise Lost'*, ed Thomas Kranidas (Berkeley 1969), p 116; Evans, *'Paradise Lost' and the Genesis Tradition*, pp 245-6, 271; Thomas H. Blackburn, '"Uncloister'd Virtue": Adam and Eve in Milton's Paradise,' *Milton Studies* 3 (1971), 119-35. The defence of Milton's presentation of the state of innocence as a condition of trial has drawn a cloud of witnesses. For an early statement of the controversy, see the correspondence between Millicent Bell and Wayne Schumaker in 'The Fallacy of the Fall in *Paradise Lost*,' *PMLA*, 70 (1955), 1185-1203. A firm answer to the Tillyard-Bell

view was provided by H.V.S. Ogden in 'The Crisis of *Paradise Lost* Reconsidered,' *PQ* 36 (1957), 1-19. Ogden argues that the original state of rectitude included the liability to sin, and that man was created *perfect* in the sense that he was 'sufficient to have stood.' See also Peter Amadeus Fiore, 'Freedom, Liability, and the State of Perfection in *Paradise Lost,*' *Milton Q* 5 (1971), 47-51; Dan S. Collins, 'The Buoyant Mind in Milton's Eden,' *Milton Studies* 5 (1973), 229-48; J. Max Patrick, 'A Reconsideration of the Fall of Eve,' *Etudes Anglaises* 28 (1975), 15-21. Diane Kelsey McColley in 'Free Will and Obedience in the Separation Scene of *Paradise Lost,*' *SEL* 12 (1972), 103-20, argues persuasively that before the Fall Adam and Eve are engaged in the process of growing by making responsible choices in a world of limitless potentiality. Authority fosters growth, for hierarchy in *Paradise Lost* is 'a means of teaching and learning which promotes that sensitively balanced awareness of the whole harmony of creation and of one's own position in it which is the basis of creative liberty' (p 108). This view is elaborated and developed further in her study *Milton's Eve* (Urbana 1983).

5 George Eliot, *The Mill on the Floss* (Boston 1908), II, 224

6 Tillyard, *Milton* (London 1956); 'The Crisis in *Paradise Lost*'

7 J.M. Evans, *'Paradise Lost' and the Genesis Tradition*, chapter 8: 'Adam and Eve's physical relationship to the garden is in fact an image of their psychological relationship both to their own passions and to each other' (p 250).

8 See Laurence Stapleton, 'Perspectives of Time in *Paradise Lost,*' *PQ* 45 (1966), 734-48.

9 Thomas Aquinas, *Summa Theologica*, Pt I, Q. 93, Art 2, trans by the Fathers of the English Dominican Province, American edition in three volumes (New York 1947), I, 470. John Weemse, *The Pourtraiture of the Image of God in Man* (London 1627), p 73

10 Calvin, *Institutes of the Christian Religion*, I, xv, 3, ed McNeill, p 188

11 Calvin, *Commentary upon the Book of Genesis*, trans John King (Edinburgh 1847), I, 96 (on 1:26). See the similar handling of this theme by Thomas Aquinas, *Summa Theologica*, Pt I. Q. 93, Art 4, and John Salkeld, *A Treatise of Paradise* (London 1617), p 104.

12 See Arnold Williams, *The Common Expositor* (Chapel Hill, North Carolina 1948), p 81. Diane McColley, in *Milton's Eve*, stresses that Eve is clearly the bearer of the divine image, and suggests that Milton delicately evokes a parallel between her subordination to Adam and the subordination of the Son to the Father (pp 40-57). While the analogy is present in the poem, we should also recall its limits.

13 See *Tetrachordon*, in *Works*, IV, 77. On Milton's affirmation of Eve as image, see Dorothy Durkee Miller, 'Eve,' in *JEGP* 61 (1962), 542-7.

14 Calvin, *Commentary upon Genesis*, I, 94 (on 1:26); *Institutes*, I, xv, 3, ed McNeill, p 186. Calvin appears to be echoing a traditional distinction,

made forcefully by Thomas Aquinas, who writes that the creation of man in the image of God 'is not to be understood as though the image of God were in man's body; but in the sense that the very shape of the human body represents the image of God in the soul by way of a trace' (Pt I, Q. 93, Art 6, ibid, p 474).

15 Calvin, *Commentary upon Genesis*, I, 94-5 (on 1:21)
16 On the dramatic interpretation of the Fall, see Mary Ellen Nyquist, 'The Temptation against the Word in Reformation Theology and in Milton's "Paradise Lost" and "Paradise Regained,"' diss University of Toronto 1978.
17 An interesting example of the view that the whole man comprises the image is found in Hieronymus Zanchius, *De Operibus Dei* in *Operum Theolgicorum* (Geneva 1613), III, col 681; see Williams, *The Common Expositor*, pp 74-5.
18 See Williams, *The Common Expositor*, p 72, and Heinrich Heppe, *Reformed Dogmatics*, ed E. Bizer, trans G.T. Thomson (London 1950; rpt Grand Rapids, Michigan 1978), pp 233-4.
19 Luther, *Commentary on Genesis*, ed Pelikan, p 65
20 Calvin, *Institutes*, I, xv, 3, ed McNeill, p 187
21 N.P. Williams, *The Ideas of the Fall and of Original Sin*, Bampton Lectures, 1924 (London 1927), pp 400-2; 421
22 Ibid, p 363
23 Calvin, *Institutes*, II, ii, 12, ed McNeill, pp 270-1
24 Wollebius, *Compendium Theologiae Christianae*, in *Reformed Dogmatics*, ed and trans John W. Beardslee III (Oxford 1965; rpt Grand Rapids, Michigan 1977), p 65
25 In Heppe, *Reformed Dogmatics*, p 239; for discussion of the issue, see pp 236-40.
26 Weemse, *Pourtraiture*, pp 295-7
27 John Davenant, *Determinationes Quaestionum Quarundam Theologicarum* (Cambridge 1634), p 75; see also Nathaniel Culverwell, *An Elegant and Learned Discourse of the Light of Nature*, ed R.A. Greene and Hugh MacCallum (Toronto 1971), p 106.
28 Sister M.I. Corcoran, *Milton's Paradise with Reference to the Hexaemeral Background* (Chicago 1945), pp 98-106
29 See Dennis R. Danielson, *Milton's Good God: A Study in Literary Theodicy* (Cambridge 1982), chapter 4.
30 Corcoran, *Milton's Paradise*, pp 101-2; Weemse, *Pourtraiture*, p 295
31 Corcoran, *Milton's Paradise*, p 106. Whether 'habitual,' with its weight of scholastic and Aristotelian definition, is the right term here is a question. Reformed writers sought new ways of defining grace in terms of the Word. Gerhard Ebeling writes that for Luther 'grace does not alter something within man, but alters his standing in the sight of God, the way he is regarded from God's point of view. Whereas the concept of grace as a *habitus* directs attention within man, Luther ... considered grace only and

wholly as an event which affects man in ... his being in the sight of God.'
Luther: An Introduction to His Thought, trans R.A. Wilson (London 1970),
p 156. See also Georgia B. Christopher, *Milton and the Science of the
Saints* (Princeton 1982), p 118.

32 In *Tetrachordon (Works*, IV, 92), Milton remarks that Adam had the wisdom given him 'to know all creatures, and to name them according to
their properties,' and that he no doubt had the gift to discern that which
concerned him more nearly, that is 'to apprehend at first sight the true
fitnes of that consort which God provided him.' While suggesting the possibility of scientific knowledge, this passage emphasizes a recognition of
the differences between man and the animals.

33 Weemse, *Pourtraiture*, p 107. As Christopher observes, reformation grace
is 'dramatic' rather than 'organic,' for 'it does not manifest itself in the
rational unfolding of the potentialities of a seed, as it were, but in sudden
and extreme shifts in rapport between two "persons" − a shift experienced by man as a changed perception of God.' *Milton and the Science of
the Saints*, p 118

34 Evans, *Milton and the Genesis Tradition*, pp 11-14

35 Williams, *Ideas of the Fall*, p 300; Evans, *Milton and the Genesis Tradition*, p 86 and elsewhere

36 Evans, *Milton and the Genesis Tradition*, p 94

37 Ibid, p 270

38 Calvin, *Commentary upon Genesis*, I, 117 (on 2:9)

39 Wollebius, *Compendium Theologiae Christianae*, p 64; Heppe, *Reformed
Dogmatics*, pp 281-300, see especially selections from Johannes Coc-
ceius, *Summa Doctrina de Foedere et Testamento Dei*, 1648. A useful
discussion is found in John Steadman, 'The "Tree of Life" Symbolism in
Paradise Regained,' *RES* ns 11 (1960), 384-91.

40 See *The Westminster Confession of Faith*, VII, 2, in *The Creeds of Christendom*, ed Philip Schaff, 3 vols (New York 1877; rpt 1919), III, 616-17:
'The first covenant made with man was a covenant of works, wherein life
was promised to Adam, and in him to his posterity, upon condition of
perfect and personal obedience.' Michael Lieb, in *Poetics of the Holy*
(Chapel Hill 1981), finds some inconsistency in Milton's treatment of
the prohibition: 'if Milton dismisses the covenant of works in his consideration of the first prohibition, he also imposes upon that prohibition a
dispensational framework, one that has affinities with none other than that
ceremonial dimension that he would presume to reject in his consideration of the first prohibition. If he rejects it doctrinally, he accepts it in
terms that must be called "cultic" ...' (p 118). Lieb's point is that the tree
of prohibition is associated with the magical and demonic, that it inhabits
the world of myth. Here and elsewhere his perspective enriches our
reading of the poem by drawing on both modern and ancient anthropology.
Yet Milton's position is not self-contradictory, nor is there a real parallel

between the state of innocence and the condition of those existing under the ceremonial law in the time of Moses. Living freely by the law within, Adam can give moral and rational assent to a decree proclaimed by a loving God. Only after the Fall does the darkened mind of man view such injunctions as taboos. The poem's drama asks us to distinguish between the creative and the compulsive implications and uses of myth.

41 Augustine, *On the Trinity*, XII, vi, in *The Basic Writings of St. Augustine*, ed Whitney J. Oates (New York 1948), II, 811

42 Calvin, *Institutes*, I, xv, 3, ed McNeill, p 187; *Calvin's Commentaries*, ed David W. Torrance and Thomas F. Torrance, *The Epistles of Paul ... to the ... Colossians*, trans T.H.L. Parker (Grand Rapids, Michigan 1965), p 350

43 Heppe, *Reformed Dogmatics*, p 552

44 Weemse, *Pourtraiture*, p 72

45 Calvin, *Institutes*, II, xiv, 5; III, vi, 3; III, xviii, 1; IV, xvii, 3; ed McNeill, pp 488, 686, 822, 1362

46 Williams, *The Common Expositor*, p 73

47 Augustine, *The City of God*, in *The Works*, ed Marcus Dods, I, 468

48 John Donne, *The Sermons*, ed Evelyn Simpson and George R. Potter (Berkeley 1958), IX, 83-5

49 Calvin, *Commentary on Genesis*, I, 94; see also *Institutes*, I, xv, 4, ed McNeill, p 190

50 See Louis L. Martz, '*Paradise Lost*: Princes in Exile,' *ELH*, 36 (1969), 240

51 For a suggestive account of Adam's growth into self-consciousness, see Charles Monroe Coffin, 'Creation and the Self in *Paradise Lost*,' ed C.A. Patrides, *ELH* 39 (1962), 1-18: 'these quickly emerging questions signify Adam's sense of the mystery of his being, wherein the moment of the awakening of the self is crossed by a feeling of its limitation. Here is the Self's complex awareness that being implies the Other than itself as a condition of existence and that its complete identity somehow requires at least the acknowledgment of the fact' (p 7). As D.C. Allen points out in 'The *Scala Religionis* in *Paradise Lost*,' *MLN* 71 (1956), 404-5, the natural theologians of Milton's age elaborated the idea of the double stair, the *extra* and the *intra nos*, as proof for the existence of God. A passage by St Bonaventure, as translated into English in the mid-seventeenth century, provides a statement of the traditional view: 'I will return from the external to the internal, and from the internall I will ascend to the supernall, that I may know from whence I came, and whither I go; from whence I am, or what I am: and so by the knowledge of myself I may ascend to the knowledge of God.' In the manner of Raphael or Michael, he adds that it is much more commendable 'if thou knowest thyself, then if (thy self being neglected) thou knowest the course of the stars, the virtues of Hearbs, the complexions of Men, the natures of living creatures, hadst the knowledge of all heavenly and earthly things.' *The Soliloquies of St*

Bonaventure (London 1655), pp 3-5. See also Martha Lifson, 'Creation and the Self in *Paradise Lost* and the *Confessions*,' *Cent R* 19 (1975), 187-97, and Robert L. Entzminger, 'Epistemology and the Tutelary Word in *Paradise Lost*,' *Milton Studies*, 10 (1977), 93-109.

52 Isabel G. MacCaffrey, 'The Theme of *Paradise Lost*, Book III,' *New Essays on Paradise Lost*, p 58-85

53 Edward Reynolds, *A Treatise of the Passions and Faculties of the Soul of Man* (London 1640), p 458

54 Nathaniel Culverwell, *Discourse of the Light of Nature*, p 85; see also p 65, and the association of Milton, Culverwell, and Alexander Gill by the editors, p xlv, n 14.

55 John Weemse, *Exercitations Divine* (London 1637), III, item 3 (separately dated 1634), 34

56 Dennis H. Burden, *The Logical Epic* (London 1967), p 85

57 On the Platonic suggestiveness of the picture of Eve looking at her image in the pool, see Lee A. Jacobus, 'Self-knowledge in *Paradise Lost*: Conscience and Contemplation,' *Milton Studies* 3 (1971), 116. For a convincing and imaginative interpretation of Eve's speech as a creative act of memory and a poem for her husband, see McColley, *Milton's Eve*, pp 74-85.

58 Manfred Weidhorn, in 'The Anxiety Dream in Literature from Homer to Milton,' *SP* 64 (1967), 65-82, classifies the dream with precision: 'This anxiety dream, though of the old-fashioned diabolic objective kind, at one and the same time reflects Eve's restlessness under the prohibition and provides her with a vicarious experience of the horror of sin' (p 82). One can accept this illuminating account without agreeing that the dream shows Eve 'already fallen.' Causes for such a diabolic dream are examined by W.B. Hunter, 'Eve's Demonic Dream,' *ELH* 13 (1946), 255-65. Much has been written about the dream, but of particular relevance to the present argument is Irene Samuel's essay, '*Purgatorio* and the Dream of Eve,' *JEGP* 63 (1964), 441-9, in which she argues that the dream provides an occasion for Eve to turn from self-love and for Adam to turn to his responsibility for Eve (pp 448-9). This observation should be seen in relation to her view that unfallen life in *Paradise Lost* 'is no blank innocence ... but the best possibilities of the life we know, spared no awareness of evil, rather protected by growing awareness.' '*Paradise Lost*,' in *Critical Approaches to Six Major English Works*, ed R. Lumiansky and Hershel Baker (Philadelphia 1968), p 238. McColley, in *Milton's Eve*, argues that the dream 'allows a growth in moral understanding and the proper use of fancy that might have proceeded in innocence; and their response to it prepares for the first steps in their regeneration ...' (p 103).

59 H.V.S. Ogden, in 'The Crisis of *Paradise Lost* Reconsidered,' argues that such experience as Eve's dream and Adam's discussion concerning love with Raphael 'could have ... strengthened innocence and confirmed rectitude as readily as in the event it destroyed them' (p 3).

60 Balachandra Rajan, *The Lofty Rhyme* (London 1970), p 71
61 Jonathan Richardson, as cited by Newton, *Paradise Lost* (London 1749), I, 354. Among modern critics, Albert Fields emphasizes that Adam's first knowledge is theoretical, not experiential, in 'Milton and Self-Knowledge,' *PMLA* 83 (1968), 392-9, although Field's notion of the darker side of the self tends to link self-discovery and sin.
62 Salkeld, *A Treatise of Paradise*, p 197
63 Calvin, *Institutes*, I, xv, 3, ed McNeill, p 187
64 Murray W. Bundy, in 'Milton's Prelapsarian Adam,' *Research Studies of the State College of Washington* 13:3 (1945); rpt *Milton*, ed Alan Rudrum (London 1968), pp 151-72, provides a cogent analysis of the varied aspects of Adam's unfallen experience in book 8, but places such stress on the psychological dualism of the nature of Adam that his liability to fall somewhat obscures his potential for good and freedom to stand. Bundy makes use of Sumner's translation of a passage of *De Doctrina Christiana* which argues that sin originated first in the instigation of the devil, 'secondly, in the liability to fall with which man was created' (*Works*, XV, 181). The difficulty with the translation is in the ambiguity of *liability*. To be *liable* can mean either to be likely to suffer from or undergo something prejudicial (or a change of any kind), or simply to be subject to the possibility of doing or undergoing something undesirable (*OED*, 3a, b). Milton does not use the term in *Paradise Lost* in relation to Adam and Eve, but Samson employs it in the first sense when describing how in the past he was 'Proudly secure, yet liable to fall ...' (55). Adam and Eve were not created liable to fall in this sense, and Milton's usage suggests that we should avoid employing the word in connection with man's freedom to disobey. The Latin passage causing the difficulty is *deinde a natura ipsa hominis non immutabili profectum*, and John Carey's translation seems less open to misconstruction: 'secondly it [sin] was instigated by man's own inconstant nature.' *Prose Works*, VI, ed Maurice Kelley (New Haven 1973), 383
65 Pascal, *Pensées*, ed L. Lafuma (Paris 1951), p 142. Adam's question finds interesting parallels in Pascal's meditation on the disproportion of man, *Pensées*, pp 134-42.
66 Lewalski, 'Innocence and Experience in Milton's Eden,' p 108
67 Edward Reynolds, *A Treatise of the Passions and Faculties of the Soule of Man*, p 24
68 Lewalski, 'Innocence and Experience in Milton's Eden,' p 112
69 Pascal, *Pensées*, p 138
70 Lewalski, 'Innocence and Experience in Milton's Eden,' p 110
71 Arnold Stein, *Answerable Style* (Minneapolis 1953), p 102
72 The cryptic account of the Fall in Genesis implies that Eve's conversation with the serpent and her eating of the fruit took place when Adam was inattentive or absent, and that she subsequently persuaded him to join her

in sin. Painters, who can telescope time, found no difficulty in presenting this event. In many Renaissance treatments, Eve reaches for the apple,
or proffers it, while the serpent watches hopefully from the branches,
and Adam, frequently drawn back in a half-crouch that suggests fear or
amazement, is held fascinated by her gesture or her eyes (see, for example, the treatments of the Fall by Lucas Cranach the Elder, Raphael, Titian,
Tintoretto, and Rembrandt). Poets, however, need to be more explicit
about time, place, and motive. The kind of difficulty they faced in explaining the absence of Adam at the critical moment can be illustrated by
Thomas Peyton's unconvincing narrative in *The Glasse of Time* (London
1620). Satan, in serpent form, spies on Adam and Eve, until the occasion
for his temptation is offered

> when *Adam* stept aside,
> Even but a little from his lovely Bride,
> To pluck perhaps a Nut upon the Trees,
> Or get a combe amongst the hony Bees;
> Or some such thing to give his welcome Spouse. ... (p 32)

The implication, a dangerous one for the justification of God's ways to
man, is that Adam's absence at the crucial moment was a piece of bad
luck. Allen Apsley, in *Order and Disorder; or the World Made and Undone* (London 1679), was similarly impressed by ill chance, but hints at
something else too as he describes how Satan

> within a bright scal'd serpent lies,
> Folded about the fair forbidden tree,
> Watching a wish'd for opportunitie,
> Which *Eve* soon gave him, coming there alone
> So to be first and easier overthrown;
> On whose weak side, th'assault had not been made
> Had she not from her firm protection stray'd. (p 50)

This is closer to the Eve of *Paradise Lost*, binding up the flowers but 'from
her best prop so farr' (9.433). In Milton's account it is, appropriately,
Satan who associates the event with fortune:

> let me not pass
> Occasion which now smiles, behold alone
> The Woman, opportune to all attempts. ... (9.479-81)

But we see around the occasion in a way that Satan cannot, for we know
that Eve's isolation has come about by choice, not chance. Milton thus
dexterously allays the suspicion that circumstance played a malignant role
in the Fall; at the crucial moment, Adam and Eve find themselves in
positions expressive of character and moral stance.

73 Anthony Low, 'The Parting in the Garden in *Paradise Lost*,' *PQ* 47 (1968),
35
74 Obedience to God is never at issue here. The subject of their dispute is one
that required to be dealt with sooner or later in any case, for it concerns

their freedom in relation to each other. 'To see the scene solely as evidence of self-love perversely symbolized,' remarks Diane Kelsey McColley, 'is to overlook its concern with their growing awareness of their place in the order of creation and their responsibility to it.' 'Freewill and Obedience in the Separation Scene of *Paradise Lost*,' p 114. On this topic Raphael has already given Adam some advice:

> weigh with her thy self;
> Then value: Oft times nothing profits more
> Then self esteem, grounded on just and right
> Well manag'd; of that skill the more thou know'st,
> The more she will acknowledge thee her Head,
> And to realities yield all her shows. ... (8.570-5)

This is a difficult doctrine, for it makes clear that Adam's authority over Eve depends directly on his control of himself. At the same time, it is not a counsel of perfection, for it leaves room for growth and gradual evolution. Adam must earn his position as head of Eve by merit, and this means that they must work out their relationship through trial.

75 *Spectator* no 351, 12 April, 1712, in *Addison's Criticisms on 'Paradise Lost,'* ed Albert S. Cook (Boston 1892), p 121

76 J.S. Diekhoff, 'Eve, the Devil, and *Aeropagitica*,' *MLQ* 5 (1944), 430-2. As Diana Benet has argued, however, Eve's heroic terms counter Adam's superficial perspective on trial as she draws on what she learned from Abdiel: 'The Abdiel episode proves that in itself temptation is neither sin nor dishonor.' See 'Abdiel and the Son in the Separation Scene,' *Milton Studies* 17 (1983), 136.

77 As Anthony Low has made clear, 'to command someone to do something is not the same as to force him, and is not necessarily a violation of freedom.' 'The Parting in the Garden in *Paradise Lost*,' p 34. See also the treatment of this subject in Danielson, *Milton's Good God*, pp 126, 198ff.

CHAPTER FIVE

1 A fellow of Emmanuel during Milton's early years at Cambridge, Tuckney left England to serve as a pastor in Boston in 1629, returned in 1643 to participate in the Westminster Assembly, and probably took up residence again at Cambridge in 1649, now as Master of Emmanuel College. Having laboured to rectify doctrine through the confession and catechisms of the Assembly, Tuckney must have found it peculiarly galling to discover on his return to Cambridge that the university once considered the fount of Reformed thought in England had been infected by rationalism and deistic tendencies, and he threw himself vigorously into an effort to purge the institution of Arminianism, Socinianism, and deism. He found himself especially opposed to the rationalism of his former student, Benjamin

Whichcote, and of such younger colleagues as Nathaniel Culverwell, whom he associated with the teachings of Whichcote. Controversy between Tuckney and Whichcote consisted in an exchange of letters and a series of sermons, and it ranged over such topics as the light of nature, the operation of grace, and the significance of the mediation of Christ.

2 *The Confession of Faith and Catechisms, Agreed upon by the Assembly of Divines at Westminster* (London 1649), chapter 10, section 4, p 25; see also A.A. Hodge, *A Commentary on the Confession of Faith* ... (Philadelphia 1869), p 241.

3 Anthony Tuckney, *None But Christ, or a Sermon Upon Acts 4:12. Preached at St Maries in Cambridge ... July 4, 1652. To which is annexed, an Enquiry ...* (London 1654), p 50

4 Ibid, pp 134, 63, 68-78, 137, 140; for a discussion of Tuckney's citation of Culverwell, and of his role at Cambridge, see Nathaniel Culverwell, *Discourse of the Light of Nature*, ed R.A. Greene and Hugh MacCallum (Toronto 1971), pp xxxv-xlviii.

5 Calvin, *Institutes*, II, vi, 4; x, 1; ed McNeill, pp 346-8; 429-30. See also III, ii, 1, ed McNeill, pp 542-4.

6 Tuckney, *None But Christ*, p 43

7 Interpreters agree that Adam received special knowledge, but most maintain that he was not able to communicate it adequately to his descendants. In *None But Christ*, Anthony Tuckney is confident that Adam instructed his offspring concerning the promise, but concludes that they soon forgot it and fell off from God: 'as the greatest sound faileth by little and little, and at last comes to nothing, so here at last they came quite to lose the sight of the Lord, and the light of that evening growing lesse and lesse at last closed up in a dark night of Ignorance, Idolatry, or Atheism' (p 64). William Perkins observes in *An Exposition of the ... Creed* (Cambridge 1595) that the covenant or promise was known to the first fathers, who 'offered sacrifices, and observed externall rites of the Church, but afterwards fell away from the syncere worship of the true God to idolatrie,' endeavouring to bury and extinguish 'the memorie of that which they hated' (p 120). William Pemble, in *Vindiciae Fidei* (Oxford 1625), argues that while Adam instructed his children, and they theirs for some generations, in the mystery of redemption, 'yet wickednesse increasing in men as fast as men multiplied in the earth, and by reason of the darksome obscurity of this mysterie in the first times of the world, it came to passe that this knowledge quickly decreased ...' (p 64). Milton gave Adam a clear rather than an obscure knowledge of the redeemer, but he did not suggest that this revelation was fully communicated by Adam to his sons. Unlike Tuckney, Perkins, and Pemble, Milton held that salvation may be achieved even by those who do not know Christ, and therefore he was not drawn into speculation concerning the extent to which the promise was communicated to the Jews and beyond them to the Gentiles in Old Testament times.

8 Mary Ann Radzinowicz makes some acute observations about the knowledge of the patriarchs in *Toward 'Samson Agonistes': The Growth of Milton's Mind* (Princeton, New Jersey 1978), pp 299-300: 'Their experiences are relevant to deducing God's nature because they derived a faith in God from their experiences, without an anachronistic sense of the coming of the Son being prefigured in those experiences.'

9 Georgia B. Christopher, 'Adam's "Literary Experience" in Book X of *Paradise Lost*,' pp 69-74

10 As Radzinowicz observes, the scriptural context for Samson's experience is drawn particularly from the Psalms. *Toward 'Samson Agonistes*,' pp 208-26

11 *Moral and Religious Aphorisms ... To which are added, Eight Letters which passed between Dr. Whichcote ... and Dr. Tuckney*, Samuel Salter (London 1743), p 126

12 A significant element in Milton's treatment of the function of the Son in *De Doctrina Christiana* is his systematic analysis of the way in which both the Father and the Son take part in the process of 'internal' renovation, as well as in the 'external' process of ransoming man from sin. Milton is careful to discriminate effects that pertain to the Father from those that pertain to the Son, or to both together. Regeneration itself, the renewal of the 'inward man,' is ultimately attributed to God the Father, 'for no one generates, except the Father' (*Works*, XV, 367). Milton stresses that the Father is often called 'our Saviour,' since it is 'by his eternal counsel and grace alone that we are saved' (*Words*, XV, 255). The 'external cause' of regeneration or sanctification is, as we have seen, the death and resurrection of the Son (*Works*, XV, 377). The first internal effects of regeneration, namely repentance and saving faith, are both spoken of as gifts of God, that is, 'of the Father through the Son' (*Works*, XV, 379). Next follows 'ingrafting in Christ,' which occurs when believers are 'planted' in Christ by the Father, that is, 'are made partakers of Christ, and meet for becoming one with him.' Now the understanding is 'restored in great part to its primitive clearness, and the will to its primitive liberty, by the new spiritual life in Christ' (*Works*, XVI, 3-5). In the increase of the regenerate, the next two stages have particular reference to the Father. The first, Justification, concerns absolution from sin and death through the satisfaction of Christ, and this has to do principally with the process by which man is 'clothed' (*Works*, XVI, 29) with the righteousness of Christ, although human response becomes important in the discussion of the faith and 'works of faith' that are made possible by justification. Those who are so justified are said to be adopted by God, and this next stage of regeneration also has particular reference to the Father. The fruit of adoption is liberty, found in the old dispensation as well as the new, but belonging in a special manner to the Gospel (*Works*, XVI, 55).
At this point the parallel contributions of Father and Son to the process

of salvation appear to merge. Christ writes the inward law of God by his Spirit in the hearts of believers, and leads them as willing followers (*Works*, XVI, 151) so that the Father can adopt them as sons who express his image. The increase of the regenerate man can now be spoken of in terms of union and fellowship with Christ in the church mystical, which 'has reference to Father and Son conjointly' (*Works*, XVI, 57). In the body of Christ believers are mystically one with God and each other, enjoying a communion of saints which is not confined to place or time, but 'composed of individuals of widely separated countries, and of all ages from the foundation of the world' (*Works*, XVI, 63). Glorification, the final stage of spiritual increase, has now commenced, imperfect in this life, but ultimately assuming the form of eternal life and the perfect happiness arising from the divine vision (*Works*, XVI, 375), when even the Son will deliver up his Kingdom to God the Father, that 'God may be all in all' (*Works*, XVI, 367). An obvious parallelism integrates the process, the Son providing a mediatorial version of each act of the Father: as the Father regenerates the inward man and 'plants' the believer in Christ, so the Son seeks to arouse in his followers a new spiritual life; as the Father justifies believers, so the Son clothes them in his righteousness; as the Father adopts the faithful, so the Son writes the law of God in their hearts. In these transformations, the Father initiates, the Son responds and implements. The Father's acts are expressed in terms of authority (he justifies, adopts, ingrafts), the Son's in terms of guidance and service (he leads, clothes, intercedes). The pattern is elaborated with elegant precision and consistency.

13 Gary Hamilton, 'Milton's Defensive God: A Reappraisal,' *SP* 69 (1972), 96. From the point of view of Calvinism, Milton's position was distinctly radical, as Richard Baxter's experience makes clear. While Baxter rejected the Arminian doctrine of grace, he maintained a view of universal redemption parallel in some respects to Milton's. In *Universal Redemption of Mankind, by the Lord Jesus Christ* (London 1694), Baxter held that those who hear not the Gospel may be justified without that faith which 'to us' is necessary, and that God 'can if he please pardon and save men for the sake of Christ's satisfaction, without letting them know that Christ satisfied for them' (p 477). These ideas were developed in the fifties, but when first made public created such controversy and drew such fierce replies that Baxter delayed publication of his full treatment of the issue until the end of his life.

14 On the tradition behind Milton's treatment of the revelation of Christ to Adam, see John E. Parish, 'Milton and the Pre-Miltonic Representations of Adam as a Christian,' *Rice Institute Pamphlet* 40 (1953), 1-24; John M. Steadman, '"Taught by His Example": Adam and the Prophesied Redeemer,' *Milton's Epic Characters* (Chapel Hill 1959), pp 72-81

15 Whichcote, *Moral and Religious Aphorisms ... To which are added, Eight Letters*, pp 123-6
16 Ibid, aphorism no 742
17 See Glenn Loney, 'Milton and Natural Law,' diss University of Toronto 1981.
18 See Theodore L. Huguelet, 'The Rule of Charity in Milton's Divorce Tracts,' *Milton Studies* 6 (1975), 199-214.
19 On this subject see C.A. Patrides, 'The "Protevangelium" in Renaissance Theology and *Paradise Lost*,' *SEL* 3 (1963), 19-30
20 Joseph Summers, *The Muse's Method: An Introduction to 'Paradise Lost'* (London 1962), p 177
21 See Jun Harada, 'The Mechanism of Human Reconciliation in *Paradise Lost*,' *PQ* 50 (1971), 547. Georgia B. Christopher dissents from Summer's view of Eve's speech, urging that her words seem 'as much an expression of her own needs as of gratuitous love.' 'Adam's "Literary Experience" in Book X of *Paradise Lost*,' *PMLA* 90 (1975), 74. This is not only the first speech of human love after the Fall, however, but the first speech of fallen human love, and we can expect it to be marred by self-regarding concerns. Style is part of the issue here. Peter Berek finds in the style of Eve's speech a return to a world where there is no discontinuity between action and language; where the way something is said is 'an accurate and inevitable reflection of its real nature.' ' "Plain" and "Ornate" Styles and the Structure of "Paradise Lost," ' *PMLA* 83 (1970), 243
22 Christopher, 'Adam's "Literary Experience" in Book X of *Paradise Lost*,' pp 75-6. Christopher argues that 10.1026-37 presents 'the *instant de passage* from despair to faith' for here 'Adam recalls Christ's words and perceives the promise in them' (p 75). Her stimulating essay finds this the 'grand moment' in *Paradise Lost*, and argues that to the eyes of Reformation faith the miracle of book 10 is 'the sudden opening of the promise' (p 76). Agreeing with her about the significance of the action of God's 'motions' upon memory, I find the moment important but not climactic. While it belongs to the turning point in the response of Adam and Eve, it is only a beginning. Adam has much to learn both about Christ and the meaning of the promise. Useful comment on Adam's state at this point is found in George W. Muldrow's *Milton and the Drama of the Soul* (The Hague 1970), p 74. See also Christopher's *Milton and the Science of the Saints* (Princeton 1982), pp 166-71.
23 See Calvin, *Institutes*, III, iii, 1, ed McNeill, p 593: 'There are some, however, who suppose that repentance precedes faith, rather than flows from it, or is produced by it as fruit from a tree. Such persons have never known the power of repentance, and are moved to feel this way by an unduly slight arugment.' Calvin seems to be thinking partly of the Anabaptists, who 'exult in being considered spiritual,' and he proceeds to define re-

pentance as regeneration. Milton's departure from Calvin is appropriate to his Arminian view of grace.

24 This is a standard view in Reformed theology. Forcefully rejecting the doctrine of implicit faith, Calvin nonetheless admits 'that so long as we dwell as strangers in the world there is such a thing as implicit faith; not only because many things are yet hidden from us, but because surrounded by many clouds of errors we do not comprehend everything.' He gives particular attention to those who are beginners in faith: 'we may also call that faith implicit which is still strictly nothing but the preparation of faith.' *Institutes*, III, ii, 4-5, ed McNeill, pp 546-7'

25 Mary Ann Radzinowicz, ' "Man as a Probationer of Immortality": *Paradise Lost* XI-XII,' in *Approaches to Paradise Lost*, ed C.A. Patrides (Toronto 1968), pp 37-8. Arnold Stein, in *The Art of Presence* (Berkeley 1977), p 161, takes this as a critical moment in the development of the narrator also, who now gives up 'the privilege of his position.'

26 Radzinowicz, ' "Man as a Probationer," ' p 40

27 Lawrence A. Sasek notes that Adam's fallen nature is not only 'an abstract theological concept; it is portrayed in his behaviour. In spite of his repentance, evident in his manner while he repents is the fact that his heart is "variable and vain"; his repentance is caused by grace won for him by the son.' 'The Drama of *Paradise Lost*, Books XI and XII,' in *Studies in English Renaissance Literature*, ed W.F. McNeir (Louisiana 1962); rpt A. Barker, Milton: *Modern Essays in Criticism*, p 347

28 Jackson C. Boswell, 'Milton and Prevenient Grace,' *SEL* 7 (1967), 86

29 Such grace may clearly be distinguished from those subsequent manifestations of divine favour which characterize the climactic event in the career of the Miltonic hero, as most obviously in *Paradise Regained* and *Samson Agonistes*. For a discussion of this aspect of grace, see Dick Taylor Jr, 'Grace as a Means of Poetry: Milton's Pattern for Salvation,' *TSE* 4 (1954), 90

30 Calvin, *Institutes*, III, ii, 4. On the idea that for Milton the imagination provides the ground or evidence of faith, see Paul Stevens, 'Milton and the Icastic Imagination,' *Milton Studies* 20 (1984), 43-73.

31 Interesting discussion of pattern and revelation in the final books include E.N.S. Thompson, 'For *Paradise Lost*, XI-XII,' *PQ* 22 (1943), 376-82; F.T. Prince, 'On the Last Two Books of *Paradise Lost*,' *E&S* ns 11 (1958), 38-52; G.W. Whiting, *Milton and This Pendant World* (Austin 1958), chapter 6, 'The Pattern of Time and Eternity,' pp 169-200; Barbara Lewalski, 'Structure and the Symbolism of Vision in Michael's Prophecy, *Paradise Lost*, Books XI-XII,' *PQ* 42 (1963), 25-35; George Williamson, 'The Education of Adam,' *MP* 61 (1963); rpt *Milton: Modern Essays in Criticism*, ed Arthur E. Barker, pp 284-307; V.R. Mollenkott, 'The Cycle of Sins in *Paradise Lost* XI,' *MLQ* 27 (1966), 33-40; Alastair Fowler, in *The Poems of John Milton* (London 1965), p 1049, note to 12.466-7; Jon S. Lawry, *The Shadow*

of Heaven (Ithaca, New York 1968), pp 267-88; Balachandra Rajan, *The Lofty Rhyme* (London 1970), pp 79-99; Jason P. Rosenblatt, 'Adam's Pisgah Vision: *Paradise Lost*, Books XI and XII,' *ELH* 39 (1972), 66-86; Raymond Waddington, 'The Death of Adam: Vision and Voice in Books XI and XII of *Paradise Lost*,' *MP* 70 (1972), 9-21; Louis L. Martz, *Poet of Exile* (New Haven 1980), pp 175-84; see also my 'Milton and Sacred History: Books XI and XII of *Paradise Lost*,' in *Essays in English Literature from the Renaissance to the Victorian Age*, pp 149-68.

32 Waddington, 'The Death of Adam,' pp 18-19
33 Adam's reaction, as Lawrence A. Sasek observes, 'shows a developing conscience, a growing knowledge of moral right, as he denounces the usurpation of power by one man over another (XII, 63-78). But Michael must point out to Adam the reasons for tyranny, which is a consequence of Adam's sin, and the justice of God in permitting evil to exist.' 'The Drama of *Paradise Lost*, Books XI and XII,' p 353.
34 See Robert Crosman, *Reading 'Paradise Lost'* (Bloomington, Indiana 1980), p 233.
35 See Muldrow, *Milton and the Drama of the Soul*: 'the episode emphasizes man's responsibility in his salvation in a way which is not possible during Michael's account of the life of Christ. There man's moral responsibility is subordinate to Christ's actions, those great manifestations of divine love. In this second episode, the important feature is man's responsibility, his need to follow the guidance of the Holy Spirit ...' (p 104).
36 See, for example, Milton's discussion in *Tetrachordon* of the '*trope* of indignation' (*Works*, IV, 169), of proverbs (IV, 136), of contradiction (IV, 136ff), and in *The Doctrine and Discipline of Divorce* his comments on brevity (III.ii.449ff).

CHAPTER SIX

1 Eg, E.M.W. Tillyard, *Milton* (London 1956), p 305. E.L. Marilla argues that Milton's belief in the Crucifixion is more than perfunctory in 'Milton on the Crucifixion,' *EA* 22 (1969), 7-10. Georgia B. Christopher, in *Milton and the Science of the Saints* (Princeton 1982), pp 128-33, shows that Milton writes in the Reformed tradition concerning the crucifixion which stressed the promissory import of the event. The emphasis shifts from the moment of the crucifixion to its ever-ongoing results.
2 J.N.D. Kelly, *Early Christian Doctrines* (London 1958; 3rd ed 1965), p 317; G.L. Prestige, *Fathers and Heretics* (London 1968), p 143
3 Kelly, *Early Christian Doctrines*, p 331
4 H.A. Wolfson, *The Philosophy of the Church Fathers* (Cambridge, Mass 1956; 3rd ed 1970), I, 372
5 Prestige, *Fathers and Heretics*, p 145
6 Ibid, pp 167-8

7 Calvin, *Institutes of the Christian Religion*, II, xiv, 1, ed John T. McNeill, trans Ford Lewis Battles (Philadelphia 1960), p 482

8 Ibid, II, xiv, 6, ed McNeill, p 490

9 Ibid, II, xiv, 8, ed McNeill, p 493

10 See Zanchius in *Reformed Dogmatics*, ed Heinrich Heppe (London 1950; rpt Ann Arbor 1978), p 418.

11 *Reformed Dogmatics*, ed Heppe, ch xvii; John Wollebius, *Compendium Theologie Christianae*, in *Reformed Dogmatics*, ed and trans John W. Beardslee III (Oxford 1965; rpt Grand Rapids, Michigan 1977), p 91

12 W.B. Hunter, 'Milton on the Incarnation: Some More Heresies,' *JHI* 21 (1960); rpt in *Bright Essence* (Salt Lake City 1971), pp 133ff

13 For a discussion of this topic, see Hugh F. McManus, 'The Pre-existent Humanity of Christ in *Paradise Lost*,' *SP* 77 (1980) 271-82.

14 G.L. Prestige, *God in Patristic Thought* (London 1964), chapter 8. Milton's position is that a nature in this context must be an essence, and a perfect essence existing *per se* is a hypostasis. But hypostasis, in its turn, may be translated person as well as subsistence or substance. Person, 'a metaphorical word, transferred from the stage to the schools of theology,' means 'any one individual being,' any 'intelligent ens, numerically one, whether God, or angel, or man' (*Works*, XV, 269). The three major terms thus appear concentric, *nature* being the most general, *person* the most specific, and the middle term, *hypostasis*, mediating between the other two since it may be defined as essence as well as person.

15 Milton could have made his point seem less heterodox by using a term such as *subsistence* rather than the loaded term *person*. His definition of *person* avoids the notion of personality or character, and views its meaning in terms of the separate subsistence of an intelligent being.

16 Richard Hooker, *Of the Laws of Ecclesiasticall Politie, the fift Booke* (London 1597; rpt Menston, England 1969), section 52, p 109

17 Wollebius, *Compendium Theologiae Christianae*, p 91

18 For examples of more intricate and hair-splitting attempts at the definition of the Son's human nature, see the selection of commentary in *Reformed Dogmatics*, ed Heppe, pp 416-19.

19 Wolfson, *Philosophy of the Church Fathers*, I, 372; *Reformed Dogmatics*, ed Heppe, p 414

20 Wolfson, *Philosophy of the Church Fathers*, I, 455; Kelly, *Early Christian Doctrines*, pp 312-16

21 See Prestige, *Fathers and Heretics*, p 169.

22 Wollebius, *Compendium Theologiae Christianae*, p 93

23 See ibid, p 91; Riissen's comments in *Reformed Dogmatics*, ed Heppe, p 432

24 Barbara Lewalski, *Milton's Brief Epic* (Providence, Rhode Island 1966), pp 155-6

25 See Prestige, *Fathers and Heretics*, pp 144-5.

26 See Wolfson, *Philosophy of the Church Fathers*, I, 469-70. Parallels to

Milton's position are found in the Christology that preceded Chalcedon, when theologians such as Cyril stressed the unity of the incarnate Son. St Athanasius himself speaks of the unity in terms that would appeal to Milton. But Milton does not seem to be following the lead of any single writer of the past; rather he is reinterpreting scripture in the context of Reformation discussion.

27 Calvin, *Institutes*, II, xiii, 1, ed McNeill, pp 483-4
28 *Calvin's Commentaries. ... A Harmony of the Gospels; Matthew, Mark and Luke*, eds D.W. Torrance and Thomas F. Torrance, trans A.W. Morrison, 3 vols (Grand Rapids, Michigan 1972), I, 106-7 (on Luke 2:40); III, 99 (on Matthew 24:36)
29 Calvin, *Institutes*, II, xii, 1, ed McNeill, p 465
30 Ibid, II, xvi, 12, ed McNeill, p 520
31 *Calvin's Commentaries. ... The Gospel According to St John*, eds D.W. Torrance and Thomas F. Torrance, trans T.H.L. Parker, 2 vols (Grand Rapids, Michigan 1959), I, 21 (on John 1:14)
32 *Calvin's Commentaries ... The Epistles of Paul ... to the ... Philippians ...* , ed D.W. Torrance and Thomas F. Torrance, trans T.H.L. Parker (Grand Rapids, Michigan 1965), p 248 (on Philippians 2:7)
33 *Calvin's Commentaries ... A Harmony of the Gospels*, II, 198 (on Matthew 17:2); I, 280-1 (on Matthew 8: 27, 25)
34 Ibid, I, 131 (on Matthew 3:16)
35 The Second Helvetic Confession, XI, 10, in *The Creeds of Christendom*, ed Philip Schaff, 3 vols (New York 1877), III, 256
36 Calvin, *Institutes*, II, xiv, 2, ed McNeill, pp 483-4
37 Servetus, *On the Errors of the Trinity*, in *The Two Treatises of Servetus on the Trinity*, ed Earl Morse Wilbur (Oxford 1932; rpt New York 1969), pp 18, 118
38 Wolfson, *Philosophy of the Church Fathers*, pp 418-28
39 *Reformed Dogmatics*, ed Heppe, pp 440-1

CHAPTER SEVEN

1 Ira Clark, '*Paradise Regained* and the Gospel According to John,' *MP* 71 (1973), 1
2 The soliloquy that follows (196-293) points to subjects which were in Jesus' thoughts during this period, and which were to some degree communicated to the disciples, as we see by 2.1-57. On the way the apostles' choric meditation parallels the soliloquy of Christ, although with thematic variation and change of emphasis, see John Spencer Hill, *John Milton: Poet, Priest, and Prophet* (London 1979), pp 182-3.
3 Pertinent here is Ira Clark's emphasis on the importance Milton attributes to the guidance of the Spirit in the interpretation of scripture and especially in coping with manuscript corruptions. Milton, Clark observes, recounts the temptation in the Johannine spirit 'almost as if he were

supplying a manuscript loss.' '*Paradise Regained* and the Gospel according
to John,' p 6. Recent criticism has explored the manner in which such a
recreation of the past is liturgical or ritual. As A.B. Chambers observes,
liturgy demands that the special moments in the life of Christ be 'constantly reviewed and renewed ... in order to base the activity and thoughts
of one's own life on the exemplary history recorded in the Gospels.' 'The
Double Time Scheme in *Paradise Regained*,' *Milton Studies* 7 (1974), 191.
Chambers finds in the repetitions of *Paradise Regained* evidence of the
liturgical view of time, and suggests that the argument of the poem is
consistent with the Collect and Epistle for the first Sunday in Lent, the
day on which the Gospel lesson concerns the encounter between Christ
and Satan in the wilderness as described in Matthew 4. Yet one does not
find in the epic the same awareness of the calendar of the church year that
marks Milton's early poems on the Son; there is no emphasis on 'this
day' as the present moment in which the past is recalled. Instead there is a
Protestant-Puritan sense of the importance of the 'opening' of scripture,
the emphasis which turns the Bible itself into a kind of sacrament. If we
approach the poem as ritual, its aim becomes celebration rather than
discovery. Richard Jordan denies that *Paradise Regained* is 'a realistic drama of psychologically complex characters,' but having emphasized that
it is 'a biblical drama, a ritual drama,' and that the reader is expected to be
totally familiar with its story, he perceptively adds that Milton has
changed the story so that 'we are constantly being dramatically surprised.'
'*Paradise Regained* and the Second Adam,' *Milton Studies* 9 (1976), 273;
see also Jackson I. Cope, '*Paradise Regained*: Inner Ritual,' *Milton Studies*
1 (1969), 51-65. This suggests to me that the dichotomy of psychological
and ritual drama is too sharp, and that the poem is not to be contained by
the latter category. Chambers is right, I believe, to stress not only the
liturgical time scheme but also the poem's dramatization of the unique
moment in which Christ matures to the point where he can undertake
his mission (p 202). Useful here is Gordon Teskey's more broadly based
concept of ritual trial, developed by an exploration of the parallelism
between the story of Christ and the Indian myth of Prince Gautama.
'Balanced in Time: *Paradise Regained* and the Centre of the Miltonic
Vision,' *UTQ* 50 (1981), 277.
4 Northrop Frye, *The Return of Eden: Five Essays on Milton's Epics* (Toronto
1965), 'Revolt in the Desert,' pp 118-43; Barbara Lewalski, *Milton's Brief
Epic: the Genre, Meaning and Art of 'Paradise Regained'* (Providence,
Rhode Island 1966), pp 164-82 and passim
5 E.M. Pope, *'Paradise Regained': The Tradition and the Poem* (New York
1962), chapter 5, 'The Triple Equation'; Patrick Cullen, *Infernal Triad:
The Flesh, the World, the Devil in Spenser and Milton* (Princeton 1974),
chapter 4, 'The Structure of *Paradise Regained*'
6 See Pope, *'Paradise Regained': The Tradition and the Poem*, p 5.

7 Calvin, *Commentary on a Harmony of the Evangelists*, trans W. Pringle (Edinburgh 1845), p 259

8 A.H. Gilbert, 'The Temptation in *Paradise Regained*,' *JEGP* 15 (1916), 607-8

9 Pope, *'Paradise Regained': The Tradition and the Poem*, chapter 7.

10 Lewalski, *Milton's Brief Epic*, pp 315, 317, 316

11 Thomas Langford, 'The Temptations in *Paradise Regained*,' *TSLL* 9 (1967), 43

12 Irene Samuel, 'The Regaining of Paradise,' in *The Prison and the Pinnacle*, ed Balachandra Rajan (Toronto 1973), pp 126; 120, n 8; 123

13 Don Cameron Allen, *The Harmonious Vision* (Baltimore 1954), p 118

14 Lewalski, *Milton's Brief Epic*, p 159

15 Ibid, p 213

16 Ibid, pp 212, 213-14

17 Ibid, p 221

18 Ibid

19 Ibid, p 260

20 Ibid, p 317

21 The importance of the mind of Jesus, the placing of the centre of the drama within his consciousness, is reinforced by what has been called the 'staggered' arrangement of books and temptations. See Woodhouse, *The Heavenly Muse: A Preface to Milton*, ed Hugh MacCallum (Toronto 1972), p 367. To make the climax of each temptation coincide with the end of a book would not only create a heavy and mechanical symmetry, but would give to Satan a prominence which is not really his. The spiritual state of self-control and understanding displayed by Jesus is more important than the ritual of his repudiation of Satan. The dismissal of Satan's offers is not as crucial as the context of reflection and argument built around them. Thus the first book introduces abruptly the temptation to distrust, and ends with discussion of prophecy; the second book, concerned with temperance and with wealth, begins with the vision of the banquet table in the wilderness and ends with the discussion of money and kingdoms; the third opens in prolonged argument concerning glory and zeal, and comes to a climax with the vision of Parthian might; the fourth moves through a series of climactic moments, the offer of the magnificence of Rome, then of the wisdom of Athens, and concludes with the temptation of the tower. Vision, discussion, and decision are mingled; the result has some affinity with the method of *Samson Agonistes* in spite of the differing heroes, for each work conveys a sense of the primacy of the mental processes of its central figure.

22 Gary Hamilton has very perceptively pointed to the analogy between Jesus' development and the development by which Adam and Eve before the Fall are to be raised 'by degrees of merit' (*Paradise Lost*, 7.157) and open for themselves a way to heaven: 'What we see in *Paradise Regained* is a

human Christ in the process of raising himself up. ... [The] flares into "divine certainty" which Christ experiences need not be explained as occasional rewards given out by God but as evidence that the process whereby Earth becomes "chang'd to Heav'n" is taking place.' 'Creating the Garden Anew: The Dynamics of *Paradise Regained*,' *PQ* 50 (1971), 571. This places the right stress on continuity, although as I have already indicated I find the suggestion that there are flares of certainty misleading. For Stanley Fish, in 'Things and Actions Indifferent: The Temptation of Plot in *Paradise Regained*,' *Milton Studies* 17 (1983), 163-85, to adopt the view that there are in the narrative beginnings, middles, and endings and other distinctions and progressions is to succumb to the 'temptation of plot,' and thus as a critic to do the Devil's work: 'Satan's rhetoric continually suggests that he is ascending a scale of progressive lures, Christ's responses have the effect of levelling that scale by refusing to recognize it.' One cannot say that this or that moment is crucial, because all are crucial. Fish's penetrating and challenging analysis shows how the reader discovers that the quelling of Satan requires a discipline which refuses to locate value in things indifferent but insists that the struggle of good and evil belongs rather to the inner world of spiritual choice. Yet readers will undoubtedly continue to look for the poem's form, and in this effort the organization of themes and topics, as in Lewalski's discussion, continues to be one of the most useful guides. Fish's expert analysis of indifferency perhaps requires as complement a discussion of the form of the inner action which is being realized by the Son. That process is ultimately the love which fulfils the law, and which can best be understood with reference to Milton's antinomianism (pp 167, 176, 181 and passim).

23 Woodhouse, *The Heavenly Muse*, p 328. See Edward Le Comte, 'Satan's Heresies in *Paradise Regained*,' *Milton Studies* 12 (1978), 256: 'Actually this demon does not know what to think. ... The fallen angel no longer has the mental equipment to grasp celestial mysteries.' Mary Ann Radzinowicz, in '*Paradise Regained* as Hermeneutic Combat,' *UHSL* 15 (1984), 99-107, argues persuasively that Satan develops a carnal interpretation of the Psalms in order to define sonship so broadly as to include himself or so narrowly as to exclude Jesus, and that Jesus rebuts this with a spiritual hermeneutic drawn from Hebrews which expounds the ideal of sonship found in the Psalms (especially 2:7 and 82:6) and exalts the priestly office fulfilled by the obedience and suffering of the Son (Hebrews 5:8-9).

24 See J.N.D. Kelly, *Early Christian Doctrines* (Edinburgh 1958; 3rd ed 1965), pp 139ff, and Le Comte, 'Satan's Heresies,' p 259.

25 Alexander Sackton, 'Architectonic Structure in *Paradise Regained*,' *UTSE* 33 (1954), 37

26 On the idea of *kairos*, see Laurie Zwicky, 'Kairos in *Paradise Regained*: The Divine Plan,' *ELH* 31 (1964), 271-7, and Edward W. Tayler, *Milton's Poetry: Its Development in Time* (Pittsburgh 1979), pp 166, 170, and passim.

27 Pope, *'Paradise Regained': The Tradition and the Poem*, pp 82-5
28 Alastair Fowler, *The Poems of Milton* (London 1968), p 1163, note to 4.560-6
29 See W.A. McClung, 'The Pinnacle of the Temple,' *Milton Quarterly* 25:1 (March 1981), 13-15. McClung suggests that Milton had in mind the kind of spiky battlement exemplified by the pinnacles of King's College Chapel in Cambridge, which would afford a place for Christ's feet while placing him in danger of falling. Yet I think that if Milton had wanted the reader to imagine the scene in such a circumstantial manner, he would have provided more clues.
30 Thomas Newton, ed, *Paradise Regained* (London 1752), p 182, note to 4.561
31 The other opposites of faith, carnal reliance, and idolatry (*Works*, XVII, 57), are more directly involved in the temptations of the second day, while the first and last day's temptations appeal to a presumptive reliance upon divine identity. In a sense, however, even the first and last day's temptations involve a carnal understanding of spiritual power, and turn the Son himself into an idol.
32 See Irene Samuel, 'The Regaining of Paradise,' in *The Prison and the Pinnacle*, p 123. The spire has proved an uneasy station for criticism, partly because this crux appears to require the interpreter to achieve an overview of the poem as a whole. A.S.P. Woodhouse, with his usual cogency, argued that while the primary theme of *Paradise Regained* is Christ as the second Adam, the secondary theme concerns the identity of Christ, and that on the pinnacle the two themes are finally and securely united: '"Tempt not the Lord thy God" carries a double meaning, for, in addition to its immediate application, it is Christ's first claim to participate in the Godhead. In an instant, and by the same event, Satan receives his answer and Christ achieves full knowledge of himself.' 'Theme and Pattern in *Paradise Regained*,' *UTQ* 25 (1955-6), 181. Louis L. Martz finds a trinity of meanings in the passage, of which the third concerns identity; 'he understands now what he has not known earlier, or has known by glimpses only; that he is himself divine.' *Poet of Exile* (New Haven 1980), p 254. Lewalski, as cited above (p 230), and Northrop Frye in *The Return of Eden* (Toronto 1965), p 140, appear to be in agreement. Edward W. Tayler, in *Milton's Poetry: Its Development in Time*, p 172, carefully distinguishes between Godhead and sonship by arguing that Jesus' words and actions show 'not that He is God the Father but that He is "indeed divine," that He is "first begot" as well as "perfect man." ' But much recent criticism has tended to reject such possibilities for anagnorisis and theophany. Jon S. Lawry, in *The Shadow of Heaven* (Ithaca, New York 1968), suggests that the annunciation at Jordan has already supplied as much revelation as is necessary concerning the divine identity of the Son and that 'the Son has intimated the part of his nature that is divine throughout,

and Satan has recognized it insofar as his mind can receive intimations of spirituality' (p 334). A limiting position is traced by J.B. Weber's contention that Milton's hero changes 'only in fortune.' *Wings and Wedges* (Carbondale 1975), p 91. More common, however, is some version of the position adopted by Irene Samuel which has already been cited. An early statement of a similar view was made by Arnold Stein in his disagreement with Woodhouse: 'What has happened? Surely not that Christ is directly replying to Satan's challenge by finally declaring himself, by saying: thou shalt not tempt *me*, the Lord thy God! That would be to violate the whole discipline, so perfectly sustained, of Christ's moral and intellectual example. ...' *Heroic Knowledge* (Minneapolis 1957), p 128: see also pp 224-5. Critics who are concerned to exclude the possibility that Christ formally lays claim to the Godhead normally agree with Stein that the hero displays 'a positive process of self-definition' and thus acts out 'the perfection of the image of God in man' (pp 130-1). Thus Mary Ann Radzinowicz argues that 'the uniqueness of the Son's priesthood lies in his sufficient obedience to the utmost of human humiliation and suffering.' '*Paradise Regained* as Hermeneutic Combat,' *UHSL* 15 (1984), 106. Yet critics who stress the universal import in the depiction of the Son's humanity are often concerned to find in the moment an act of communion with God. Stanley Fish puts the matter subtly but effectively in terms of the paradoxes of service to God: 'the assertion that the figure on the pinnacle is the Lord God is anything but prideful, for Christ's "claim" to that identity rests on his demonstrated willingness to lose his own.' 'Inaction and Silence: The Reader in *Paradise Regained*,' in *Calm of Mind*, ed J.A. Wittreich, Jr (Cleveland 1971), p 43. Georgia B. Christopher, finding in the words on the tower 'the last and most impressive self-denial,' stresses the way the Son is the 'unique bearer of the Spirit,' which he possesses in no measurable degree but which is also available to the ordinary Christian. *Milton and the Science of the Saints* (Princeton 1982), pp 203, 210, 224. Mary Nyquist stresses the ambiguity of the Son's words of self-revelation on the pinnacle, 'where he both takes the place of the Father and yet appears as if dependent on his Father's Word and aid.' 'The Father's Word/Satan's Wrath,' *PMLA* 100 (1985), 200. Three observations must serve to indicate my own position. First, I do not think the view that Jesus here lays claim to identity with God is tenable, for it runs against the distinction of Son from Father which is crucial to Milton's subordinationism. Secondly, as the perfect image of the Father, the Son is exemplar not only of selfless obedience to the spirit but of reason and choice (notice how human intelligence and wit gleams in the phrase 'Also it is written'). Milton gives the filial being authority and independence, and his acceptance of the will of his Father is simultaneously a realization of his own powers. Finally, while the Son remains perfectly obedient throughout his trial, we should not conclude that the moment on the tower marks the fulfilment or climax of this process. It is, rather, a threshold, standing to the new movement (in which he *begins* to save mankind) as the soliloquy after the baptism stands to the temptation. Although it is prefigurative, looking forward to the resurrection and the apocalypse, the episode marks the end of initiation and the beginning of the Son's active and public life. While it makes a superb climax to the epic, this last encounter with Satan does not represent the completion of the Son's development.

William Kerrigan, in *The Sacred Complex* (Cambridge, Mass 1983), finds here the moment when Christ achieves the paternal identification which 'resolves the oedipus complex and organizes his autonomy' (p 108). Kerrigan's vigorous exploration of the implications of the allusion to the sphinx in the simile describing Satan's fall opens up new interpretations and ties in with his original and often penetrating view of Milton's life. Kerrigan's evidence that Christ has assimilated his mother is persuasive (p 107), but the assumption of an oedipal struggle now resolved does not appear well supported by a text which shows the Son hungering to do his Father's will from the start.

33 While part of the song is directly addressed to him ('him long of old / Thou didst debel ...'), part is also directly addressed to Satan ('But thou, Infernal Serpent'), and clearly this is not heard in Hell. Moreover, it contains an explicit prophecy of the future concerning the casting out of the devils recorded in Matthew 8:28-32, and one might wonder whether Milton would feel free to make such an addition to the Gospel. Yet after such objections have been expressed, it is sensible to assume that the angels' song contributes to the joy and refreshment of the banquet.

34 See Lewalski, *Milton's Brief Epic*, pp 311-12.

35 Ibid, pp 313-14

36 For further comment on the distinction between the internal and external roles of Christ in *Paradise Regained*, see George M. Muldrow, *Milton and the Drama of the Soul* (The Hague 1970), pp 108-14.

Index